ALVIN YORK

AMERICAN WARRIORS

Throughout the nation's history, numerous men and women
of all ranks and branches of the U.S. military have served their
country with honor and distinction. During times of war and
peace, there are individuals whose exemplary achievements
embody the highest standards of the U.S. armed forces. The aim
of the American Warriors series is to examine the unique historical
contributions of these individuals, whose legacies serve as
enduring examples for soldiers and citizens alike. The series will
promote a deeper and more comprehensive understanding of the
U.S. armed forces.

SERIES EDITOR: Roger Cirillo

An AUSA Book

ALVIN YORK

A NEW BIOGRAPHY
OF THE
HERO OF THE ARGONNE

DOUGLAS V. MASTRIANO

UNIVERSITY PRESS OF KENTUCKY

Scholarly publisher for the Commonwealth,
serving Bellarmine University, Berea College, Centre College of Kentucky,
Eastern Kentucky University, The Filson Historical Society, Georgetown
College, Kentucky Historical Society, Kentucky State University,
Morehead State University, Murray State University, Northern Kentucky
University, Transylvania University, University of Kentucky, University of
Louisville, and Western Kentucky University.
All rights reserved.

Editorial and Sales Offices: The University Press of Kentucky
663 South Limestone Street, Lexington, Kentucky 40508-4008
www.kentuckypress.com

The views of the writer are not those of the Department of Defense or its
components.

Library of Congress Cataloging-in-Publication Data

Mastriano, Douglas V.
  Alvin York : a new biography of the hero of the Argonne / Douglas V.
Mastriano.
     pages cm. — (American warriors)
  Includes bibliographical references and index.
  ISBN 978-0-8131-4519-8 (hardcover : alk. paper) —
  ISBN 978-0-8131-4521-1 (pdf) — ISBN 978-0-8131-4522-8 (epub)
  1. York, Alvin Cullum, 1887-1964. 2. Soldiers—United States—
Biography. 3. Argonne, Battle of the, France, 1918. 4. World War, 1914-
1918—Campaigns—France. 5. United States. Army—Biography. I. Title.
  D570.9.Y7M37 2014
  940.4′1273092—dc23
  [B]   2013045082

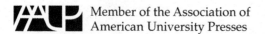 Member of the Association of
American University Presses

To the two most important people in my life—

my wife, Rebbie,

and son, Josiah

Alvin York's account of his conversation with his brigade commander, General Lindsey, in February 1919, when they toured the site where York captured 132 Germans:

"York, how did you do it?"

"Sir, it is not man power. A higher power than man power guided and watched over me and told me what to do."

The general bowed his head and put his hand on my shoulder and solemnly said: "York, you are right."

There can be no doubt in the world of the fact of the divine power being in that. No other power under heaven could bring a man out of a place like that. Men were killed on both sides of me; and I was the biggest and the most exposed of all. . . . When you have God behind you, you can come out on top every time.

Contents

Illustrations

Maps

Photographs

1

A Life Well Lived

Many good Americans have died fighting for this country
and there was one guy in my outfit who was a conscientious
objector—but once he was in the thick of battle, he fought like
a true American and almost captured the whole d—nmed
German Army single-handed. His name was Alvin York and
he was a hero.

—Otis Merrithew (aka William B. Cutting),
21 October 1965

The life and legacy of Alvin C. York continues to have an influence
on the American psyche. This fixation has as much to do with his
battlefield heroism as it does with his lifelong legacy of trying to
make a lasting contribution to improve the lives of his people. It is
this that perhaps makes him stand out among so many other worthy heroes of the Great War. Clearly, it was the 8 October 1918 battle
in the Argonne that brought Alvin notoriety, but it was what he did
with the fame that so impressed his nation. It was York's endeavor
to use his name and fame to build schools, to help the poor and
needy in Tennessee's Cumberland Valley, that served as evidence to
the public at large that this man was "the real thing."

Considering this, it seems that there were two major turning
points in the life of Alvin York. The first was his conversion to Christianity on 1 January 1915. It was this which brought a moral and personal transformation that set the conditions for Alvin's subsequent
life. It also led him to initially object to military service and then,
once that matter was resolved, gave him the spiritual assurance that
no matter what happened, he would come out alive. It also gave
him the humility to use his fame to help others. Without his conversion, York would have faded into history as so many had, and
certainly would not have performed as he did on the field of battle.
This is because his new faith was the basis of his confidence and re-

solve, and laid the foundation from which he went on to accomplish what he did. The second turning point was the 8 October 1918 Argonne battle, which brought him renown and forever changed his life. Both of these dates are inseparably and firmly linked. For York, one could not have transpired without the other.

Of course, throughout his life, and even to this day, there has been a string of detractors who question whether the York saga is genuine, or the result of propaganda. Usually the detractors suggest that his feat of 8 October 1918 was contrived, or exaggerated for some nefarious reason. Another tactic employed by his detractors is to belittle him by portraying his religion in a negative light. Both of these approaches require attention.

The subtle approach of assailing York's fundamentalist type of Christianity seems more informed by a postmodern negative view of faith in general than by fact. Earlier biographers and writers on York from the interwar period never questioned his faith. Writing at a time when church attendance was still the norm and faith was more widely accepted, authors such as Thomas Skeyhill and Sam Cowan treated York's beliefs respectfully. Modern writers, however, use harsh words or phrases when addressing Alvin's deep faith, calling it a volatile mixture of faith and violence. They assume, reflecting the cynicism of our age, that faith is naive, irrational, and misguided.

In fact, York's faith seems more in line with New Testament practices of grace, mercy, and kindness than modern-day detractors would have one otherwise believe. For instance, when York was thrown in with his rowdy, partying platoonmates, there is no record that he condemned, judged, or otherwise told them that he disapproved of their drinking and womanizing. Instead, York and his friend Murray Savage sought to live out their faith in honesty and integrity in the army without casting aspersions on those who lived differently. York looked to his own house and did not sit in judgmental condemnation over those who did not share his faith. It was this that impressed his officers. Despite his moral dilemma, York tried not to cause trouble in his unit, and whatever work he was given, he did it to the best of his ability. This may in part explain why Major G. Edward Buxton and Captain E. C. B. Danforth tried so hard to convince him to fight for his nation as a Christian. This is also borne out by the fact that there is no derogatory information in his service record. Furthermore, his church proved that it was not so strict and legalistic as to excommunicate him for fighting in the war.

Finally, what of York's detractors, those who assailed his integrity and character? York answered the critics without harsh censure. The only time he defended his war record was in May 1919, when a *New York Times* reporter made a fabricated claim that there were those in his unit who questioned his Medal of Honor. York remarked, "Sure 'nough? Well the [soldiers] made affidavits . . . that I had done all the things claimed."[1] Years later, when Merrithew (aka Cutting) attacked York's war record, York refused to be baited to discuss the matter. Such is the measure of a man walking in grace and freedom, and not under the self-righteous patterns of a stern and "volatile mixture of faith and violence."

The most common approach to undercut York is to question the accuracy of the 8 October 1918 Argonne action. Although it is true that newsmen and other York boosters added hyperbole and exaggeration to what transpired, neither York nor the army ever claimed that he single-handedly mastered the Germans that day. As this study demonstrates, based upon the archival record, battlefield archeology, ballistic forensic evidence, and analysis done by the nation's leaders in these fields, what was claimed by York and the army about the action did happen. However, we now know that York did have good help in that battle, which the army investigation of 1919 alludes to, with the ballistic evidence specifically pointing to Private Percy Beardsley. Beardsley had the opportunity during the division's investigation in 1919 to "blow his own horn," but instead he took the honorable road. York was not aware of how important Beardsley's support was that day, being focused on the charging enemy. Despite this, York continuously mentioned the other men who were with him in that fight and *never* claimed or alluded to being a "one-man army."

Another increasingly popular approach to undermine what York accomplished on 8 October 1918 is to dismissively suggest that those Germans were eager to quit the war. However, such an assertion is not supported by historic fact. If the Germans were in such a poor condition, why did they fight so hard? When York's sister battalion (1st Battalion) attacked through Châtel Chéhéry on 7 October 1918 to seize Hill 223, they suffered their highest single-day casualty rate of their service in the Great War. It seems doubtful that they were facing a broken force of old and battle-weary Germans.

Likewise, when York's unit attacked into the Argonne the next day, they too suffered their highest one-day casualty rate in World War I. Historically stated, the Germans fighting in the Argonne were not eager to quit, but rather did their best to make the Americans pay for every foot of ground.

Even the lead detachment of the 210th Prussians, who were caught eating breakfast that 8 October morning, redeemed themselves thereafter. When York's unit clashed with them a week later near the Kriemhilde Stellung, they fought tenaciously. So it was all along the line. Although these were not the same fresh troops of 1914, they knew how to fight and did so until the Armistice went into effect, causing nearly eleven thousand Allied casualties in the last hours of the war, more than the American losses in Normandy over a twenty-four-hour period on 6 June 1944. (It will be remembered that the Great War ended at 11:00 A.M.).

Another popular theme among York's detractors is to avoid talking about the history and instead suggest that there was some great conspiracy to elevate York because "America needed a hero." The premise is that since York was Caucasian, Protestant, and Anglo, he fit the mold of an American hero. This weak hypothesis goes on to suggest that because of this ethnic-religious blend, York was given special treatment and elevated above all other heroes of that time. Yet nothing could be further from reality.[2]

First, York would have been more palatable had he been from a mainline denomination, and not from a fundamentalist, "back to the Bible" branch of Christianity. Furthermore, there was no clamoring for a hero in 1918, as scores of them were being written about and introduced to the public. Even the *Ladies' Home Journal* touted heroes for some years after the war had ended. Frankly, modern writers making these statements that "America needed a hero" betray their ignorance of the period.[3] Indeed, there were heroes aplenty, as one would expect from 1.2 million men fighting in the Meuse-Argonne Offensive. In addition, there were scores of national heroes available from the other campaigns fought by the AEF on the Marne, in Belleau Woods, Cantigny, etc. America had plenty of heroes. It was not looking for another one, especially not York, at least not yet.

York's rise as an icon had more to do with the personal initiative of the war artist Joseph Chase in contacting reporter George Pattullo than with some sort of government orchestration. It was Pattullo's article in the *Saturday Evening Post* that gave York notoriety, and then the initiative of the Tennessee Society, which wanted its native son to have a celebration in New York City. This denotes the acts of private citizens and not some national conspiracy to elevate a hero. Understandably, both Chase and Pattullo were intrigued by York's unique story. They both correctly noted something unusual in York's going from objector to fighter.

This begs the question then, why does York continue to stand out as an American icon while hundreds of other Great War heroes have been virtually forgotten? It appears that York stood out for a number of reasons, not least of which being what he did with his fame. Had he been a typical person, he would have accepted the offers of fame, made his fortune, and then perhaps faded from the collective memory. Yet Alvin York was different. He not only refused offers to become rich, but as soon as he could, he returned to Tennessee to go back to his life as a farmer.

Adding to this curious case, after Alvin returned to Pall Mall he realized that he could not let life go on in the Cumberland Valley in blissful ignorance. With that awareness, he used his fame to build schools and make other improvements to life in the region. He did this not to enrich himself, but to help others. Adding to his unique personality, York typically refused to talk about his war experience. When his heroism was mentioned, he dispelled ideas that he acted alone and continually pointed to the fact that there were other men with him. When Cowan and later Skeyhill came forward to write a book on York's experience, he agreed to their doing so only so that he could use the money to build and maintain his schools. That he died a pauper is testimony to the fact that the money he raised went to the schools, and not his bank account. York's continual touring of the nation to solicit donations for his school projects also had the effect of keeping his heroism alive in the memories of the general public.

Some writers suggest that Alvin was a confused isolationist, wanting to withdraw the nation behind the oceans, as it had been before the Great War. This is a misrepresentation of the facts. Like most people even today, York preferred that the nation fight only defensive wars. However, as the threat of Japan and Germany became clear, he was one of the very few public voices calling the nation to arms. To be sure, the 1930s were a turbulent era for the United States. It was reeling from the Great Depression, with the preponderance of the public and politicians demanding some form of isolationism. This was endorsed by America's most popular citizen, Charles Lindbergh, and bolstered by the America First Committee under the political leadership of U.S. senators Gerald P. Nye and Burton Wheeler.[4] It was at this point that the United States needed a hero, someone of credible public influence to withstand the political clout of the anti-interventionalists. That hero would be York. York's credentials were already established, and the attempts of earlier detractors to damage his reputation had largely failed.

In 1936, at the height of the isolationist grip on power, York called the nation to stop Japanese aggression in China. In 1938 he was calling the nation to "knock Hitler off of the block." York, on his own initiative, and at the risk of being condemned as a warmonger (the approach of Senator Nye), took the unpopular position of calling the nation to military intervention. This could have hurt him both personally and publicly, in that by taking such a stand his endeavors to raise money for his Bible school would suffer. At this point, he was virtually a solitary voice taking on the influential Lindbergh and the powerful anti-interventionalist senators in Washington, making his cause a rather brave position to take up at that time.

York's prediction about another war with Germany and his public view on Hitler and Nazism proved correct. With this in mind, Jesse Lasky came forth with the proposal in 1940 for making the *Sergeant York* movie and successfully appealed to Alvin's patriotism to convince him to do it. It was this movie that would forever burn the York saga into the collective memory of the American identity. Interestingly, the movie would propel York to such renown that he is even used as a comparison for other nations in propelling their own heroes, with Canada claiming their own Sergeant York in Normandy in 1944 and the Red Chinese in their 1949 civil war.[5]

There seems to be much that appealed to the American public in the movie at that time. In one sense, York served as a bridge between America's colonial past and the World War II generation. He looked like a modern Davy Crockett or Daniel Boone to many, and personified the minuteman ideals of the farmer-soldier of the American Revolution putting down his plow to take up his rifle and fight off the Redcoats, or in this case the Germans. But there is more to the saga. The *Sergeant York* movie not only presented the past; it also represented the present.

When *Sergeant York* came out in 1941 the nation was literally preparing for war. Never before was a movie so well timed to reflect what the average American family was going through in real life. The scene of York registering for the draft in 1917 was really happening to millions of young Americans in 1941. The portrayal of York saying good-bye to his tearful mother and crying girlfriend was being played out around the nation. Americans saw themselves reflected in York, if not as him, then as the girl being left behind, the mother, brother, sister, or others seeing a loved one off to war. The young man, registering for the draft, saw himself in watching York deal with the moral dilemma of killing in the name of his country, and then, the struggle to fit in with strange and different recruits from around the nation.

Such serendipitous timing served to engrave the ideals of Alvin York on an entire generation, who would then keep his name alive for generations to come. In this way, York represented not only the First World War generation but also the Second World War generation. He seems to personify how and what Americans thought of themselves, and the value of seeking the greater good of the nation.

Alvin C. York proved to be a hero throughout his life. He took politically unsafe positions in the 1930s to call the nation to arms, he nearly went broke to build schools, and he gave more back to his community and nation than his community and nation gave to him. Throughout it all he never compromised his faith. The decision he made in 1915 to become a Christian was the single most important point in his life and was the hinge on which everything else he put his hands to swung. It was this that made him the hero in the end, as he actually lived up to the lofty ideals that Americans believed about themselves. In York many saw a connection with America's past, perhaps a glimpse into the nation's founding fathers, or the pioneers of old. This unassuming, modest man appealed to the very soul of America, even those struggling with the ideas of isolationism and war, Christianity and peace, and the rise of America as a global power. Only when pressed and all other options had been exhausted did York take the call to arms. This seemed a shadow of the nation's own struggle with going to war.

Despite being repeatedly tempted to compromise his faith, he consistently chose the right over the expedient. Whether being surrounded by French wine and women in 1918, the enemy in the Argonne, or hostile board members in Jamestown in 1934, York endeavored to do the right thing. Had he watered down his beliefs to appeal to the public at large, or given in to the temptations that come with fame and money, York's name would have become a byword for our cynical postmodern generation. It was, however, his faith in daily choosing to walk his talk that continues to intrigue people.

For some, his personal testimony is too much to bear, and they seek a way to cast aspersions on him to avoid the conviction that one must face when looking into the life of a genuine hero. Yet, with York we find a man who was faithful in both the small and big things, in his private and public life. Meanwhile, for others, Alvin York serves as an example of what one can accomplish in choosing this day to serve the Lord. York remains an interesting subject of discourse not only because of what he did, but also for what he believed. Either way, it is evident that in the case of Alvin York, he lived life well and left behind a legacy worthy of emulation.

2

Without Prospect

The Hard Life in the Upper Cumberland Valley

I am a-telling you I kept going from bad to worse, drinking
more and more, and gambling whenever I had the chance
or the money, and fighting a whole heap. I was never once
whipped or knocked off my feet. I jes kinder thought I could
whip the world and more than oncet I set out to do it. I was in
a couple of shooting frays too.

—Alvin York

For Alvin York, growing up in the Cumberland Valley of Tennessee
was little different from what the pioneers of the early 1700s experienced. It was a foreign place to most Americans, a land that time
seemed to have forgotten. In many ways, York's world was little
changed from when Daniel Boone and Davy Crockett lived there.
Legend reflected the Cumberland's time-locked nature with its tales
of Indian fighters and Civil War bushwhackers.[1] Despite the inno-
cent yarns spun about life in Appalachia, there was a dark side to it
as well. In the shadows of the rough valleys, bootleggers, gun runners, and other men of ill repute made the region dangerous for the
uninitiated. Adding to this was the fact that swathes of the region
were largely outside the control of federal and state law. Alvin York
would soon find himself lured into this dark world.

The third of eleven children, Alvin York was born on 13 December 1887 and grew up in a loving and hard-working home. His father, William York, and mother, Mary Brooks York, owned a small
farm in Fentress County, near Pall Mall. This county was rural; the
largest town of any consequence was the county seat of Jamestown,
ten miles south of the York farm. York's parents had a heavy burden
with so many children. The entire York family worked to provide for

9

one another. Life in the valley was hard. Living in a one-room cabin, Alvin was required to contribute to the family just as his siblings did. He helped his mother around the house as soon as he was old enough to do so, and was in the fields working the family's seventy-five acres with his father before he was six years old.[2] York wrote: "I begun to work almost as soon as I could walk. At first I would help Mother around the house, carrying water, getting a little stove wood, and carrying and nursing the other children to keep them from yelling around after Mother while she was trying to get a bite of dinner for us all. I would go out to the field with Father before I was six years old. I would have to chop the weeds out of the corn."[3]

The rocky soil made growing corn difficult.[4] Despite this, Alvin learned to raise crops, take care of farm animals, and work in the family blacksmith shop in the cave next to the cabin. Here he learned how to shod horses and mules.[5] Yet, the most thrilling thing he learned from his father was hunting. Before he was old enough to join them, Alvin recalled being "red-eyed, by the gate of his home [as he] watched his father and the hounds go off to the hunt."[6] When that day finally arrived for him to join his father hunting, he displayed an unusual skill that caught his father's attention.

It was during the long hunting trips in the mountains and fields around Pall Mall that Alvin was able to spend quality time with his father. The hunting was a way for the York family to put meat on the table and to make money on pelts. In such a large family, Alvin became a typical middle son, both quiet and resolute. It was difficult for him to stand out in the shadow of his two older brothers, Henry and Joe, or to distinguish himself from the half dozen younger siblings who needed their parents' attention. During these hunting outings Alvin was able to observe his father's Christian character and learn hunting skills.[7] "But I most loved getting out with Father to help him shoot. We would hunt the red and gray foxes in the daytime and skunks, possums, and coons after dark. Often we would hunt all day and do the blacksmithing at night."[8]

Alvin's passion and talent for hunting created a personal bond between him and his father.[9] In Alvin his father found a willing apprentice. At his father's side, Alvin learned how to track animals, to read the weather, to train coon dogs, and to move unseen in the deep Tennessee woods.[10] Shooting remained his passion, and he took every opportunity to perfect his skills with both handguns and rifles. Before long, Alvin matched his father's skill in hunting raccoons, foxes, turkeys, wild hogs, and squirrels and had begun winning community turkey shoots.[11] Alvin described the importance that this passion played in his relationship, saying, "It was sorter easy for me to talk [to his father] about guns and hounds and horses and all those things he loved and taught me to love."[12]

York's father was renowned across the region as a hunter and marksman. His expertise as a shooter was so great that often, in "beeve" (beef) shooting matches, when the best five shooters would divide a cow betwixt them, William York would win all five matches and bring the animal back alive and "on the hoof."[13] It was not just in beef shoots that William excelled, but in turkey shoots as well. In these matches, shooters would pay for each shot to kill a captured turkey. A live turkey was tied behind a log, with the shooters trying to hit the bird in the head from a distance of sixty yards. Such a crack shot was Alvin's father that he was often placed at the bottom of the firing order. This gave the hosts a chance to raise more money by allowing other shooters a chance before William York hit the bird. Alvin admired his father's skills and would take up his father's rifle in a like manner.[14] Little did he know that it was this love of his father's shooting and hunting that was to prepare him for a dark day in France only a few years later.

The weapon of choice for the York family was the muzzle-loaded rifle. These long and unwieldy rifles were difficult to use, but when handled by a proficient rifleman were deadly accurate.[15] Alvin also became an expert shot with a pistol. Finding his inspiration from tales of the bank robber Jesse James, Alvin recalled, "I used to practise and practise to shoot like them James boys. I used to get on my mule and gallop around and shoot from either hand and pump bullet after bullet in the same hole. I used to even throw the pistol from hand to hand and shoot jes as accurate. I could take that old pistol and knock off a lizard's or a squirrel's head from that far off that you could scarcely see it."[16]

Religion, too, played a central role in eastern Tennessee and in shaping Alvin York's character. Yet, this was not the Christianity of liturgy and tradition, but one of which the German Reformer Martin Luther advocated in 1517: "Sola Scriptura," which is using only the Bible and not church doctrine as a guide for living.[17] Although the region was largely influenced by Methodist theology, they welcomed itinerant Baptist and Church of Christ in Christian Union (CCCU) preachers due to the lack of ministers.[18] Called "saddlebaggers" because of the large bags of Bibles, evangelical tracts, and hymnbooks they traveled with on their horses, these circuit preachers brought the Gospel to the mountain folk through revival meetings. The local population honored the Sabbath, and usually the only book any family owned and read was the Bible, so the preachers found a willing group to minister to. Daily family devotions with prayer and Bible reading were conducted by most folks in the region. Saying grace to give thanks to God for each meal was the norm as well, so that faith was expressed throughout the average day.[19]

Church services were important social events that every family in the area endeavored to attend, dressed in their "Sunday finest."[20] The church meetings included singing and a basic sermon on the need of an individual to confess and repent of his sins and turn his life over to the Lord and Savior Jesus Christ.[21] These church events could last all day and included people bringing food to share in a sort of potluck fellowship. These were appropriately named "basket meetings."[22]

The church in Pall Mall was unremarkable, having been built of wood planks by Methodists in the late 1800s. It was pleasantly situated in the valley near town. The interior was unpainted and lined with rough benches. The women sat to the right side of the church during services and the men to the left. The pulpit was slightly raised at the front of the church, with an altar, or "mourners' bench," just below it.[23] As with most churches in the region, the one in Pall Mall was barren of symbols, icons, and illustrations. All that mattered was the Bible.

Public education, although available, was not practicable to the hard-working folks of Pall Mall and the Valley of the Three Forks of the Wolf River. Due to the time constraints imposed by a busy farming schedule, school was limited to the summer months, and often interrupted by the potato harvest, tomato harvest, etc.[24] For Alvin, it was a good summer if he was able to squeeze in a month of school. By the time he entered adulthood, he had the equivalent of a third-grade education.[25] As a result, the greatest influence on Alvin York was his parents: "Both my father and mother were honest, God-fearing people, and they did their best to bring us up that way. They didn't drink, or swear, or smoke themselves, and they didn't believe in us doing those things. They didn't have no use nohow for people who told lies or broke promises. They believed in being straight out and aboveboard. I'm a-telling you they honoured the truth so much

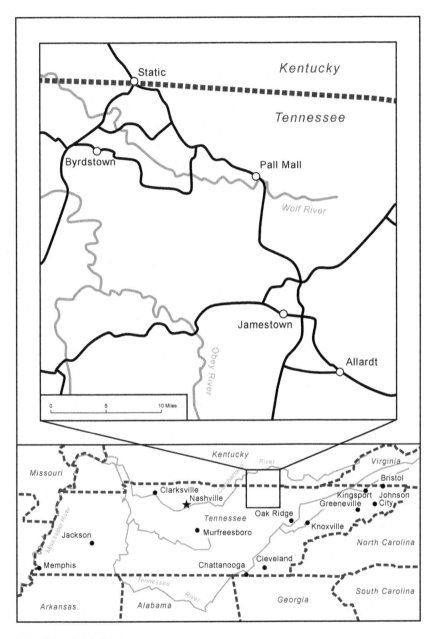

Map 1. Pall Mall, Tennessee.

that they wouldn't hide it nohow for nobody even if they was to suffer an awful lot."[26]

Alvin grew up in a house filled with stability and acceptance. Behind it all, his father stood out as a man of integrity. William York was not just a Sunday Christian, but one who endeavored to live out his faith transparently, in humility and honesty. Whatever he put his hand to, he sought to "do it as unto God." This applied to his work ethic and to his private life: "He was so fair and just in all relations with his neighbors that the people of the valley called him 'Judge' York; and his honesty was so rugged and impartial that not infrequently he was left as sole arbiter even when his own interests were involved."[27]

The year 1911 was a turning point in the York household. By then, Alvin's two older brothers, Henry and Joe, had their own farms and families, leaving York as the oldest son still living at home. William York was renowned throughout the region for his skill at shoeing horses and mules. One day in 1911 he was severely kicked by a mule, which triggered an illness from which he subsequently died.[28]

Almost overnight, Alvin went from being the overlooked middle child to the head of the household.[29] This required him to run the seventy-five-acre farm and blacksmith shop and provide for his widowed mother and younger siblings.[30] It seemed as if the weight of the world had fallen on him; indeed, it was a burden he was not ready for.[31]

Unfortunately for Alvin, temptation and escape from the stress of life were just a few miles north of Pall Mall, Tennessee, on the Kentucky state line, where plenty of moonshine was to be had.[32] To avoid liquor laws, drinking establishments called "Blind Tigers" were built on the state border. Inside these "bars" the state line literally was painted across the floor.[33] Whenever law enforcement officers turned up, the patrons and the booze moved to the Kentucky side of the saloon to avoid arrest.[34]

It should be no surprise that moonshine was the preferred liquor at the Blind Tigers, since Kentucky was the leading producer of it in the United States. The proximity of Kentucky to so many markets, in addition to plentiful grain and corn, made it a natural source for illegal booze. As the industry was not regulated, there was a danger of the whiskey being watered down or contaminated with lye, radiator fluid, or lead.[35] Corn whiskey, which was locally called "John Barleycorn" or "Mountain Dew," was a particularly potent drink.[36] Some of the brew was 80–90 percent in alcohol content.[37] One of the popular drinks was a corn-based sugar brew that resembles ethanol.[38]

The Blind Tigers drew a rough crowd and were places where one could gamble, meet women, fight, and most of all drink. Alvin wrote, "I am a-telling you Sodom and Gomorrah might have been bigger places, but they weren't any worse. Killings were a-plenty. They used to say that they used to shoot fellows jes to see them kick. Knife fights and shooting were common, gambling and drinking were commoner, and lots of careless girls jes used to sorter drift in. It shore was tough."[39] One of the local establishments along the Kentucky-Tennessee border was operated by the Huddleson family. Twenty-five people were killed there in bar fights. The Huddlesons, York said, were "an ornery and right smart bad, tough lot of men. They wouldn't do nothin' downright dishonest, but they'd kill you at the drop of a hat."[40] Because of the violence at the Huddleson's Blind Tiger and the poor nature of the moonshine that they served, York preferred another border dive called "Marter's Place."[41]

The trouble was that when York drank, he would get into fights. On occasions, he avoided fights by showing off his shooting skills. Once Alvin was with his usual group of friends and brothers and had a winning string of poker games. The losers were infuriated and pulled out their guns to settle the matter. To avoid a shootout, Alvin quickly pulled out a pistol and shot off the head of a lizard on a distant tree, saying, "If there's going to be any shooting here I will do it." That ended the argument.[42]

As with most men his age, Alvin's path to self-destruction was slow. Particularly responsible for his moral decline was that Alvin was surrounded with companions who encouraged and enabled his downward slide. Describing his slip into perdition, Alvin wrote:

> At the beginning we used to have a few drinks of a weekend and sit up nights, gambling our money away; and of course, like most of the others, I was always smoking and cussing. I don't think I was mean and bad; I was jes kinder careless. But the habits grew stronger on me. Sorter like the water that runs down a hill at first it makes the ravine, and then the ravine takes control of the water that's the way it was with me. I jes played with these things at first, and then they got a-hold of me and began to play with my life. I went

from bad to worse. I began really to like liquor and gambling, and I was 'most always spoiling for a fight.[43]

Before Alvin knew it, his occasional drinks turned into weekend binges during which he would lose most of his money gambling "at poker, dice or some other game of chance."[44]

Joining Alvin on his weekend jaunts to the Blind Tigers in the border settlements of Bald Rock and Static were his brothers Henry and Albert, and friends Marion Lephew, Everett Delk, and Marion Delk.[45] "We were a wild crowd," Alvin said, "wilder than wild bees when they're swarming. On a week-end we would go across the Kentucky line and get drunk and look for trouble, and we shore enough found it."[46] Once armed with booze, Alvin and his companions would go on long drinking binges with hard Tennessee or Kentucky moonshine. In addition to shooting under each other's mules, getting into fights, and gambling, the group found other ways to mix drunkenness with competition. One of Alvin's favorite games was "last man standing."[47] The six men would drink as much as they could to see who would be the last not to pass out. Often the last two to stand were Alvin and Everett Delk, with Delk usually lasting the longest. The winner would take away all of the unconsumed liquor.[48] On some weekends the group would purchase its whiskey at the Blind Tigers and then go to Jim Crabtree's farm to consume it. Farmer Crabtree would join Alvin and his companions in a drink, and then his wife would feed them a large meal. After this, they would drink until they passed out.[49]

As expected, this behavior put York in trouble with the law. It started when he delivered a weapon for a friend and was subsequently arrested. York was called before a judge on charges of selling weapons across county lines, but he had the case dismissed after proving that it was not his rifle. Alvin's next confrontation with the law occurred shortly after this, when he was returning from a weekend drinking binge in Kentucky. While riding on his mule intoxicated, Alvin spotted a flock of turkeys sitting on a fence. Alvin sluggishly pulled out his revolver and killed all six. But the birds belonged to a neighbor, and York was charged with a crime. Only by paying restitution was Alvin set free.[50]

On another occasion, in the same state of intoxication, Alvin and Everett spotted something white in the darkness. Everett thought that it was a "white pillow." Not wanting to miss a chance to use his weapon at a distant target, Alvin fired. Upon closer inspection they were appalled to see that he had shot a neighbor's pet goose. The guilty party fled the scene to avoid a court hearing.[51] Alvin would often go into hiding after committing a crime, "until the excitement died down," so as to avoid jail time.[52]

This pattern of behavior troubled his mother. Although Alvin was twenty-seven years old, his mother made a habit of waiting for him during his extended drinking binges. With violence being so common at the Blind Tigers, she was right to be concerned.[53] Mrs. York, nevertheless, never assailed Alvin for his behavior, but tried to lovingly lead him back to the Lord's way. As Alvin said: "Often she would remind me of my father, of how he never drunk, or gambled, or played around with bad company, and of how he would not like it nohow if he knowed what I was doing; and she used to meet me at the door and put her arms around me and tell me that I was not only wasting this life, but I was spoiling all my chances for the next. She used to say that she jes couldn't bear to think of where I would go if I died or was killed while I was leading this wild life."[54]

How far from his father's counsel his life had drifted troubled Alvin, as he held his father in high esteem. Yet this was not enough to draw him to the straight and narrow. Mrs. York prayed for him and, with tears of despair, shared hope from the Bible with him.[55] A passage that left an impression on Alvin was the parable of the Good Shepherd, which described a shepherd who left his flock of ninety-nine to find the one who strayed. Alvin knew that he was that lost sheep and was interested to hear the Savior's desire to bring him back to the fold despite being stained with sin. This notwithstanding, the draw of alcohol was difficult to break, and he found himself in a moral conflict.[56]

> All of this was making me feel kinder bad. I jes knowed I was wrong. I jes knowed there was no excuse for me. . . . When you get used to a thing, no matter how bad it is for you, it is most awful hard to give it up. It was a most awful struggle to me. I did a lot of walking through the mountains and thinking. I was fighting the thing inside of me and it was the worstest fight I ever had. I thought of my father and what a good man he was and how he expected me to grow up like him, and I sorter turned over in my mind all the sacrifices Mother had made for me.[57]

As Alvin York struggled with deciding what path in life he would follow, a lady caught his attention. The girl, Gracie Loretta Williams, lived near the York farm, just across a little stream called Butterfly Branch.[58] Gracie's quiet nature as well as her good looks appealed to Alvin. Alvin would often take the long way to the woods to hunt squirrels near her family's farm, in the hopes of meeting with Gracie, who was often tending to the family's cows nearby. Here they would have long conversations. Both looked forward to these "chance meetings." But Gracie's father, Francis "Frank" Asbury Williams, refused to allow the two to associate.[59] As far as F. A. Williams was concerned, Alvin was too old for her and an unbeliever.[60] Mr. Williams, a devoted Christian, felt Alvin was a drunkard and a gambler and unfit for any man's daughter.[61]

F. A. Williams sought to live out his faith, and as such was a highly respected member of the community. His reputation for honesty was so impeccable that he served as a circuit judge. Williams believed that men were not born Christians, but had to choose to become so, just as Joshua proclaimed: "And if it seem evil unto you to serve the LORD, choose you this day whom ye will serve; whether the gods which your fathers served that were on the other side of the flood, or the gods of the Amorites, in whose land ye dwell: but as for me and my house, we will serve the LORD."[62] The most important concern for Mr. Williams was his family of thirteen children. To raise them in the understanding of the Lord, he led them in daily devotions, and endeavored to walk in God's ways before them in word and deed. Of the decision to prohibit Gracie from seeing Alvin, Williams referred to 2 Corinthians 6:14: "Be ye not unequally yoked together with unbelievers: for what fellowship hath righteousness with unrighteousness? What communion hath light with darkness?"[63]

This prohibition did not pertain to chance meetings along the lane or in the pasture. But despite these work-arounds, there was no way York could romantically pursue Gracie.[64] There had to be a way, as Alvin had found in Gracie something unusual. She was not naive, but virtuous in her Christian faith. Although she was shy around strangers, there was an inward strength that made her stand out.[65] These were the traits that Alvin sought in a wife, as she was in every manner opposite to the girls he met at the Blind Tigers.[66] Alvin could only publicly see Gracie at church. With this incentive, he became more interested in attending, for the sake of speaking to her and walking home with her family after service.[67] As Alvin was a "backslider," these were often awkward encounters. The bottom line was that as long as he was not a practicing Christian, she would never concede to marrying.[68]

Alvin was torn between the choices before him. For now, the easiest thing was to continue along the path of least resistance—that is, feeding his earthly desires. The weekend forays to the Bald Rock and Static Blind Tigers continued, as did his efforts to avoid arrest for various infractions of the law.[69] But Alvin began to struggle in prayer and doubt. His daylong hunting excursions gave him time to wrestle with the direction of his life. There was a deep emptiness from the choices he had made. Alvin knew that he would end up dead soon if things did not change. A nagging guilt haunted him about the path that his parents had laid out for him, and there was Gracie, who was only interested in a Christian man.[70]

During the period leading up to New Year's Day 1915, the Pall Mall church hosted a weeklong revival service led by Reverend Melvin Herbert Russell of Indiana.[71] Reverend Russell was a saddlebag preacher bringing the Gospel across Indiana, Ohio, Kentucky, and Tennessee. His years of experience preaching the Gospel in the region, and years of studying the Bible, made him well suited to reach the locals.[72] Alvin was invited to attend and did not need much urging, as he wanted to see Gracie.[73]

Alvin attended most of the revival meetings that week, with the meeting house being packed full. Russell's preaching was straight from the Bible, and he did not mince words. Alvin described the preacher as being like one of the Apostles of old, speaking God's words with an urgency borne of the conviction that "now is the time of salvation," for we are all sinners doomed to hell unless we repent and call upon the Savior.[74]

Alvin watched scores of his neighbors and friends go forward to the "mourners' bench" to repent of their sins and accept Jesus as Lord and Savior at the end of each service. Although the sermons moved him, and what Reverend Russell preached made sense, it was not enough to cause Alvin to join the penitent. Nonetheless, he felt a power behind what Russell preached.[75] If he was to follow the Lord, he knew he would have to do it for himself, not for his mother, or for his father's sake, or even Gracie's. During that week he experienced soul-felt conviction, causing him to contemplate life: "Sometimes I used to walk out on the mountainside and do a heap of thinking and praying before the meetings. Then I would go and listen and pray and ask God to forgive me for my sins and help me to see the light. And He did."[76]

Alvin's life-changing decision occurred on New Year's Day 1915. During the last night of the revival service, he listened to Reverend Russell preach that "the wages of sin is death; but the gift of God is eternal life through Jesus Christ our Lord."[77] At that moment it all made perfect sense to him. York would later say that the Gospel message was so clear to him at that moment that "it was as if lightning struck my soul."[78] He saw the sin in his life for what it was, a death sentence, and also understood his need for the Savior. When the invitation was given by Reverend Russell, a neighbor, Sam Williams, saw York getting ready to go forward to accept the Lord. Sam Williams had hired Alvin to work around his farm for several years and was concerned about the path the young man was on. Sam too stood up, put his arm around Alvin, and walked with him to the mourners' bench at the front of the church.[79] Reverend Russell led the penitent in a prayer of repentance and then welcomed Alvin heartily into the family of God. Alvin stood up a changed man.[80]

3

At War with the Army

Life's tol'ably queer. You think you've got a grip on it, then
you open your hands and you find there's nothing in them.
It doesn't go in straight lines like bees to their hives or quail
from the covey.

—Alvin York

Alvin York's life completely changed after he "got religion," and
he left church on 1 January 1915 a different man. York's family,
and above all his mother, was elated at his decision to become a
Christian.

I found out the truth of what the Bible says: "There is more
rejoicing over one sinner that repenteth than over ninety-
nine just persons that need no repentance." I truly felt as
though I had been borned again. I felt that great power
which the Bible talks about and which all sinners feel when
they have found salvation, I felt in my soul like the stormy
waters must have felt when the Master said, "Peace, be
still." I used to walk out in the night under the stars and
kinder linger on the hillside, and I sorter wanted to put my
arms around them-there hills. They were at peace and so
was the world and so was I.[1]

Of the neighbors, Pastor Rosier C. Pile was perhaps the hap-
piest. He had watched Alvin's fall into sinful living and felt help-
less to get him on the straight and narrow. But once Alvin made
his decision to serve the Lord, Pastor Pile took the responsibility to
mentor and disciple him in the ways of the faith.[2] To help him grow
as a Christian, Pastor Pile involved Alvin in the church fellowship,
helped him to study the Bible, and encouraged him to pray for victory over his personal sins. This trinity of prayer, Bible study, and

fellowship under the mentorship of Pastor Pile was central to Alvin's newfound faith. He embraced the idea that it was not enough to "get saved," but that it also was necessary to demonstrate his faith with works that furthered the Gospel. In just a few months Alvin was transformed from a drunkard, brawler, and malcontent to a leader in the church, a Sunday school teacher, a choir leader, and a respected man in the community.

Yet Alvin found old habits difficult to break. He had developed a taste for alcohol and smoking, and he missed the thrill of fighting, cussing, and gambling. When the weekends came, the temptation to go back to his old ways was intense. "Sometimes Everett or Marion or some of the other boys would drop around and tell me they were putting on another party and invite me to join them. Then it was that I was most sorely tempted. I prayed most awful hard and got a good hold on myself and didn't go." Alvin did not give into temptation and found that "each time I refused, it was so much easier next time; and every day it became easier. In a few months I got them there bad things out of my mind."[3]

This time of struggle with personal sins was arguably the most significant point of his life. Standing against peer pressure and choosing to do the right thing built moral courage in Alvin's life.[4] Looking back, he summed up the struggle: "And that is the greatest victory I ever won. It's much harder to whip yourself than to whip the other fellow, I'm a-telling you, and I ought to know because I done both. It was much harder for me to win the great victory over myself than to win it over those German machine guns in the Argonne Forest. And I was able to do it because . . . God . . . showed me the light, and I done followed it."[5]

It was commonplace in York's day to think of character as a moral muscle that became stronger with exercise.[6] In this view, every time Alvin chose to do what was right, he developed additional character and moral courage. Using this line of reasoning, the courageous pattern in his private life allowed him to accomplish unimaginable feats in the heat of battle as an outward manifestation of his inward courage.[7]

About a year into his new faith, Alvin was concerned by the hypocrisy he saw in the church. The problem was his former weekend partymates. York's unrepentant friends attended Sunday worship services, but then did not hesitate to get drunk on moonshine after church. York was not interested in bringing judgment upon them, but rather in finding a church where the congregation took seriously what the Bible said about Christian living. About this time Pastor Pile hosted a revival service led by circuit preachers from the Church of Christ in Christian Union (CCCU).

The CCCU was a Protestant denomination formed during the American Civil War and based in Ohio and Indiana. The founders sought to lead Christians away from divisive social and religious disputes and back to the Bible. Their concern was that the politicization of the pulpit over slavery as well as the heated and often counterproductive theological Arminian-Calvinist debate of free will versus election had no place in the church and that instead members ought to live their lives in goodwill toward their fellow man. To join this denomination, people had to make a public confession of Jesus Christ and accept the Bible as the inerrant Word of God. The key tenet of the CCCU that would have a cascading effect upon Alvin was its lack of formal church doctrine. The denomination upheld a literal interpretation and application of the Bible. Therefore, when the Bible said, "Thou shalt not kill," that was it as far as the CCCU believed—a Christian could not kill for any reason.[8]

The simple nature of the CCCU and its "Sola Scriptura" Bible basics appealed to Pastor Pile. At the end of the revival, a CCCU congregation was established in Pall Mall, with Rosier Pile being elected to serve as its leader. In 1916, Pile oversaw the construction of a church facility on the north side of Pall Mall.[9] Alvin followed Pastor Pile's lead and also joined this new CCCU congregation, becoming the "second elder," the assistant pastor of the church. What appealed to Alvin about the CCCU was that it required its members to pursue clean living and therefore would not tolerate open hypocrisy among its members. In York's words: "A man can't [gamble, drink, or swear] and belong to our church. He just can't be a Christian on Sundays. He's got to live up to it all the time."[10] As the church's second elder, Alvin "worked harder than ever . . . read the Bible. . . . led the singing in the church, and . . . helped in the Sunday school."[11] To reach the area's youth, Alvin led Sunday afternoon singing lessons. After singing, the young people would head off for an afternoon swim in the Wolf River or a game of marbles.[12] So strong did Alvin grow in his faith that he was called upon to preach sermons when Pastor Pile was absent.[13] To Alvin's delight, the Williams family also joined the CCCU, which gave him opportunities to see Gracie.[14]

Alvin was falling in love with Gracie Williams. His frequent work in the church brought them together often. "I am a-tellin you there was somethin' grand about her, the way she talked in that quiet voice of hers that sometimes got shaky, she was that shy, and the way she looked at you with those big blue eyes as though she was jes trying to see inside of you and help you be good. I jes wanted to be near her and talk to her."[15] She enjoyed practicing singing with Alvin after church on Sunday afternoons.[16]

Now that he was a practicing Christian, Alvin hoped that Mr. Williams would not prevent him from courting Gracie.[17] Virgil Pile, one of York's neighbors, observed, "Frank Williams looked on the young buckaroo's wildness askance and was inclined to doubt the parlance of his later religious convictions."[18] Mr. Williams's opposition was rooted in several concerns. First, he wanted to see if Alvin's newfound faith was enduring. Second, he had doubts that Alvin would be able to provide for a wife. As a hillside "patch" farmer, working the rocky soil, Alvin was barely able care for his mother and siblings. The only way they could overcome this was to augment the income with hunting, blacksmithing, and hiring out for other work. But even this often was not enough to pay the bills. With these concerns Mr. Williams would not allow Alvin to openly court Gracie.[19]

> Her parents were agin me. I couldn't blame them nohow. But I wasn't in love with them at that time, I was in love with Gracie, and we managed to steal meetings, and nobody but us knowed much about them nohow. There was a long winding lane between our homes. It was lined with big shady trees. And there was wild honeysuckle there. And, best of all, it sorter dipped out of sight between the two hills. It was sorter made for us to meet in. So of an evening Gracie would come along this way to get the cows for milking, and I most awful sudden found out there were a heap of squirrels along that old lane. So I would tote the old muzzle-loader and go hunting down that way. I don't recollect getting many squirrels. But I kinder used to always go back there every evening.

Alvin's friend Marion Lephew was courting Gracie's older sister Maudie, and while at the Williams's house he would pass messages from Alvin to Gracie.[20] Gracie and Alvin would also leave notes for each other in an old fence post where she tended the cows.[21] Their relationship grew steadily until June 1917, when Gracie accepted his marriage proposal. Alvin nervously sought her father's consent and found Mr. Williams in the fields hoeing potatoes. He slowly approached him and said, "[Gracie and me] . . . decided to get married." Mr. Williams paused, then answered, "Well, she don't need to marry nobody, but if she's going to marry, I'd as soon she marry you as anybody."[22] Everything seemed to be going his way, even finding a job paying $1.65 for ten hours of work a day helping to build a road to Pall Mall.[23] (The road that he helped build would later be named the Sergeant York Highway.)

Alvin's world would soon be turned upside down when in April 1917 the United States declared war on Imperial Germany. Events in Europe over the past three years were so distant and unrelated to Alvin.[24] The death and destruction along the Western Front was something that the locals knew very little about. But, comparing it to a dark cloud that gradually became impossible to ignore, York sensed that things were changing not only for his nation, but for his valley as well once news of President Wilson's declaration of war reached them. Alvin tried to ignore the gathering storm in 1917 by focusing on his work and courting Gracie, but this changed when he received a red card in the mail from the federal government directing him to register for the draft.

The draft registration card filled Alvin with confusion on how to reconcile the demands of his government with those of the Bible. The dilemma was deeper than a religious conflict for him. His ancestors were patriotic people, even fighting on the side of the Union during the American Civil War, an unpopular move in a state that ended up throwing its lot in with the Confederacy. They had paid a high price for this at the hands of Confederate renegades and bandits during that war, with several of Alvin's ancestors being killed. There was no question of Alvin serving his nation. The issue was how to reconcile the Bible's commandment of "Thou shalt not kill" with "Render therefore unto Caesar the things which are Caesar's." To find an answer, Alvin spent hours in prayer and poured himself into the Bible seeking an answer to the dilemma. Of this, Alvin wrote:

> I wanted to follow both. But I couldn't. They were opposite.
> And I couldn't reconcile them nohow in my soul. I wanted

to do what was right. I wanted to be a good Christian and a good American too. I had always figured that the two were sort of connected. And now I was beginning to find out that they were kinder opposed to each other. If I went away to war and fought and killed, according to my reading of the Bible, I weren't a good Christian, And if I didn't go to war and do these things, according to Uncle Sam, I weren't a good American.[25]

Alvin turned to his spiritual mentor, Pastor Pile, for guidance. Ironically, it was Pile who delivered York his draft notice, while he was working with a crew on building the new highway.[26] As the proprietor of the local store, Pile also operated the town's post office. In this capacity, the federal government directed him to serve as the draft registrar for Pall Mall. Pile was the right man for Alvin to confer with for advice. Pastor Pile encouraged him to register for the draft as the government ordered, but to request exemption as a conscientious objector for religious reasons. With that, York filed his draft registration card in June 1917. At the bottom of it, on line 12, which states, "Do you claim exemption from draft (specify grounds)?" Alvin wrote, "Yes, Don't Want to Fight."[27]

As Alvin's words for exemption on his draft card were inadequate, the Fentress County Draft Board refused his first request for exemption and summoned him to Jamestown for a physical exam on 28 August 1917 to see if he were fit for duty. Weighing 165 pounds and just above six feet tall, Alvin York was certified as physically qualified for military service by a family friend, Dr. W. E. Mullinix (D.D.S.), and Dr. J. N. Chism (M.D.).[28]

While being administratively approved physically for military service, York seized the opportunity to formalize his request for exemption.[29] Assisted by Pastor Pile, Alvin filed U.S. Form 153 with the Fentress County Draft Board. York wrote, "I hereby respectfully claim discharge from selective draft on the following ground, that I am a member of a well recognized sect or organization, organized and existing May 18, 1917, whose then existing creed or principles forbade its members to participate in war in any form and whose religious principles are against war or participation therein in accordance with the creed or principles of said well recognized religious sect or organization."[30]

The draft board's reply to his request was, "Denied, because we do not think The Church of Christ in Christian Union is a well-recognized religious sect, etc. Also, we understand it has no especial creed except the Bible, which its members more or less interpret for themselves, and some do not dis-believe in war at least there is nothing forbidding them to participate."[31] One of the draft board members, Dr. Mullinix, commented on York during this process, saying, "He didn't object to going to war, but he did object on account of his religion. . . . He just filed his objection with the board. I think Rosier Pile fixed that up. [But] he didn't discuss his objections before the board."[32]

Alvin thought that the board would decide in his favor, but when it did not, his world spun out of control. "I was bothered more than ever. I done done what I thought was right. I followed God, so I thought, even against the judgment of my country. . . . I couldn't accept the written word of man against the written command of God. So I appealed against their decision."[33] The appeal went to the State of Tennessee Draft Board. Alvin included two notarized affidavits, one from him and one from Pastor Pile, affirming his religious objection to war. Nevertheless, this appeal was also refused. In the end, Alvin submitted four appeals for exemption, all of which were refused by the draft boards.[34] Yet, there appears to be considerable inconsistency in what is written in relation to York's explanation of these requests and subsequent appeals for exemption from military service as a conscientious objector.

The problem started with the 26 April 1919 George Pattullo article in the *Saturday Evening Post*. In this, Pattullo states, "York is the Second Elder in the Church of Christ in Christian Union . . . they are conscientious objectors. But York refused to ask exemption."[35] Additionally, the first book written on York, in 1922, says that York "had to make the plea for exemption, no one could make it for him. Alvin never made it."[36] However, the fact is that there are four requests from York on record for exemption. The confusion is that while York submitted no further written appeals for exemption once he entered service, additional requests were submitted in April 1918 without his consent. It seems that York considered his requests for exemption when he was a civilian separate from his time in the army. Pattullo and Cowan therefore created a false impression that York simply swallowed his pacifism and went off to fight for his country. The truth is more complex, and this remained an issue that he wrestled with even on the morning of his great combat heroism on 8 October 1918.

With his exemption denied, the only recourse remaining was to hope and pray that he would not be called up for the draft. This waiting was a time of mental and spiritual anguish for York. He prayed for God's intervention to change the hearts of the draft board and had faith that God's Word would prevail over men. Alvin wrote of this: "I wuz sorter mussed up inside worser'n ever. I thought that the word of God would prevail against all of the laws of man and of nations."[37] Things came to a head on 10 November when he received his draft notice to report to Jamestown, Tennessee, for duty. He was filled with confusion and wondered if his prayers had gone unheeded. Only two options remained, either report for duty or flee to the mountains, where he would be hunted as a fugitive.

Pastor Pile encouraged Alvin to put his faith in God, saying, "For my thoughts are not your thoughts, neither are your ways my ways, saith the LORD. For as the heavens are higher than the earth, so are my ways higher than your ways, and my thoughts than your thoughts."[38] With this, Pile assured Alvin that everything would turn out alright as long as he remained faithful to God's word. With no options remaining, York packed a bag and reported to Jamestown for military service on 14 November 1917.[39] Before leaving he had a private meeting with Gracie, where they promised devotion and reaffirmed their marriage plans upon his return from the army.[40]

York waited in Jamestown for several days until the required number of men arrived. After this, the men were transported to Oneida, Tennessee, and then by train to Camp Gordon, Georgia. He would remain at Camp Gordon for five months before shipping off to France. These five months of army training would prove woefully inadequate, but the men would ship off to war nonetheless when the time came.

After completing the mundane administrative tasks of being integrated into the army at Camp Gordon, York was assigned to the 157th Depot Brigade, issued uniforms and military equipment, and began basic training.[41] Many soldiers with Alvin knew that this was going to be the experience of a lifetime. With this in mind, York purchased a small, red, pocket-sized book in which to record his thoughts during the adventure.[42] Naming it "A history of places where I have been," this booklet would serve as the basis for the diary that he published ten years later.

The first morning as a soldier for Private York was a sign of how alien this new world was. As generations of soldiers have done since, his platoon was lined up between the barracks and ordered to police dropped cigarette butts. As most nonsmokers still assert, York commented, "I thought that was pretty hard as I didn't smoke. But I did it just the same."[43] The flat pinewoods of Camp Gordon, Georgia, were far different from the land that he was accustomed to. Additionally, he was working with a strange mixture of people and ethnic groups from across the United States that included immigrants from virtually every corner of Europe, many of whom could not speak a word of English. Until things made sense to him, Alvin determined that it would be best to keep a low profile. This would not be too difficult, as the training schedule provided little free time. Additionally, he shared little in common with his fellow draftees, especially on their views of war. This made things awkward, and with this in mind, Alvin wrote:

> I jes went to that old camp and said nothing. I did everything I was told to do. I never once disobeyed an order. I never once raised my voice in complaint, but I was sick at heart jes the same, heard the boys around me talking about what fun it would be to go overseas and fight in the trenches. I heard them telling of how many Germans they were going to kill if ever they got a chance. I heard all sorts of things about the glory of war. But I couldn't see it like they seed it no-how. I prayed and prayed that God would show me His blessed will.[44]

Ironically, York's willingness to quickly and without protest accomplish the tasks given him did make him stand out to his leaders. But through it all, his struggle to reconcile military service with his beliefs remained a burden. The concern was that he was being trained to be an infantryman, where bayonet practice and rifle skills were all focused on how best to kill another human being. Had he been assigned to a clerical position, or logistics, he could have reconciled his conflict between faith and fighting, but being trained to kill kept this quandary ever before him.

Alvin remained in this training unit for three months, enduring daily inspections, learning how to march, salute, construct trenches, and perform an array of other diverse tasks.[45] Even so, the hardest part to inculcate to the new recruits was military bearing and discipline.[46] York's training records show that he had a solid camp record, both on and off duty. As for character, his commander wrote that it was "Very Good." This was a good start for him, particularly when he finished basic training and was assigned to the 328th Infantry Regiment, 82nd Division, on 9 February 1918.[47]

The 82nd Division was also located at Camp Gordon, which made his move from the depot brigade easy. The division had experienced considerable organizational challenges since its creation in August 1917.[48] It was to be a southern division, composed of men from Tennessee, Georgia, and Alabama. In spite of this, the War Department could not keep up with expanding requirements and ordered that the preponderance of the 82nd's soldier's fill under-strength southern National Guard units so that these could be more quickly shipped to France.[49] Thus, the 82nd found itself a shell of a unit in late 1917 until sufficient draftees arrived to make it a viable organization. A large number of these replacements were from New England and the Middle Atlantic states, and they soon outnumbered the remaining southerners.[50] After a survey was done of the soldiers enrolled in the 82nd, it was discovered that nearly every state in the Union, forty-six of the forty-eight, was represented in the division, thus giving it the moniker the "All-American Division."[51]

The early days of the 82nd Division were daunting to say the least. After losing its initial allotment of soldiers to other units, it had to start training again with a variety of recruits from diverse regional and ethnic backgrounds. Many of these soldiers were recent immigrants from Italy and Eastern Europe, and "approximately twenty per cent, of these men were of foreign birth and several hundred were not citizens of the United States. Training was seriously handicapped by a substantial percentage of men who were unable to read, write and in some cases even speak English. These were those who could neither speak nor understand the common tongue."[52] This was what the entire army faced. Although American draftees came from some forty-six nationalities, the preponderance of the foreigners entering the U.S. Army were Italians, Slavs, Russian Jews, Greeks, and Armenians.[53] In this strange and foreign world of the 82nd "All-American" Division, York would serve for the next fifteen months.[54]

Such was the situation for the fledgling American Expeditionary Forces, of which the commander, General John J. Pershing, commented, "Although the thirty-four National Guard and National Army divisions that eventually came to France were, with two exceptions, organized in August and September 1917, they did not receive training as complete units from that time on. They were filled gradually and by piecemeal, weeks and even months usually elapsing before they reached full strength."[55] What Pershing did not grasp was that even had the units trained as he wished prior to arriving in France, they still would not have been ready for war. Regardless of what transpired, these Americans would not enter combat fully ready.

The training tempo for the 82nd Division was ambitious and difficult to sustain. Due to America's lack of preparation, there was a shortage of everything, especially weapons and implements of war. While waiting for their rifles to arrive, the soldiers used wooden guns, which the men mockingly referred to as the "Camp Gordon 1917 Model Rifle."[56] As one of the battalion's officers wrote, "Up till now the men thought that we were going to beat the Boche with sticks and rocks, while the officers had a hazy idea that we were going to shoot a few with some kind of rifle."[57] Compounding this was that the equipment arrived piecemeal and sporadically, thereby throwing any training plan off-kilter on a recurring basis.[58]

To overcome the challenges of building soldiers from civilians and lacking sufficient equipment, the division conducted training day and night. The training week included instruction and drills Monday through Thursday, forced marches on Friday, and daylong inspections on Saturday. The average day began at 5:30 A.M. with the "agonizing strains of Reveille, blown by one of our new buglers," and ended at 7 P.M.[59] This helped to make up for the time lost teaching the non-English-speaking immigrants the common tongue and enabled the rest of the unit to learn skills that ranged from the use of the bayonet to wearing a gas mask.[60] Additionally, Camp Gordon bristled with all sorts of special training schools, of which, one soldier wrote, "We had schools galore; schools for non-coms, schools for officers, primary schools, and schools for general information, at which the Captain, supported by an all-star cast of company officers, talked himself hoarse, and the company asleep on any subject that came into his mind, from Army Regulations to the care of the feet."[61]

York's regimental commander, Colonel Julian Lindsey, preferred training composed of hours of marching in formation. Called the "Lindsey Special," the recruits learned close-order drills and the manual of arms in addition to moving as a well-trained formation

York's regimental commander was Colonel Julian R. Lindsey. Lindsey was a professional soldier who poured his soul into the unit to make it the best it could be. Like York, Lindsey was a devout Christian. He was also an 1892 graduate of West Point, with service in Cuba, China, and the Philippines. With a wealth of military experience, Lindsey expected results and would not tolerate incompetence in his subordinate leaders. (AHEC)

that would be the envy at any parade.[62] The 82nd Division was also ordered by its commander, Major General William P. Burnham, to be a "singing division." Believing that this helped to improve morale and build esprit de corps, Burnham had copies of the *Official Camp Gordon Songbook* issued to the troops and demanded that they sing on the march, in the barracks, and anywhere else appropriate. The songbook featured a selection of Christian hymns, patriotic choruses, and a few contemporary hits, including "Pack Up Your Troubles," "Dixie," "Battle Hymn of the Republic," and the "Star-Spangled Banner."[63] The men did not throw themselves into singing, but, as a soldier recalled, whenever a senior officer appeared, they would burst into an enthusiastic chorus until they were well out of hearing range.[64]

Soldiers in the regiment complained that the training schedule

York's division spent hours on often useless tasks that would do little to prepare them for combat. One of these tasks was singing. The division commander, Major General William Burnham, declared the 82nd a singing division and issued each soldier a book of patriotic songs and Christian hymns to sing. Here, soldiers are seen at Camp Gordon singing with gusto from their division song book. (NARA)

was too arduous, claiming that, "Colonel Lindsay lay awake devising cute little schemes at midnight . . . inspections and the like to keep us from idleness during the hours from 10:00 P.M. till 5:50 A.M. Goodness, how we wanted to get to France and forget these inspections and reviews."[65] Some of York's officers echoed this sentiment, saying that they overtrained on nonessential skills, but, being almost totally new to the army, and not understanding modern warfare, the leaders honestly did not know what they would face in France.[66] In fact, few of the 2 million American soldiers who arrived in France were adequately trained for the realities of the Western Front.[67] This training deficit was exacerbated by contradictory messages that the soldiers were given by "expert" French and British instruction. One soldier in York's regiment wrote, "Foreign instructors arrived on the scene, each to show us the only way to win the war. The French swore by the hand-grenade and the Chauchat [a light machine gun], the British swore by the bayonet, and we swore by . . . well, anyway, we swore and worked a little harder."[68]

York was assigned to G Company, 328th Infantry Regiment. The leadership was a mix of diverse personalities and leadership styles. The regimental commander was Colonel Julian R. Lindsey. Lindsey was a professional soldier who poured his soul into the unit to make it the best it could be. A devout Baptist and an 1892 graduate of West Point, he had served in Cuba, China, and the Philippines. As a cavalryman, Lindsey gained fame in 1914 as one of the U.S. Army's best polo players.[69] With a wealth of military experience, Lindsey was the force behind the almost impossible training schedule, but like a bull elephant on the African savannah, he would not take no for an answer. He expected results and was unmerciful to weak leaders.

York's battalion commander was Major G. Edward Buxton, from Rhode Island, a Harvard graduate with a sharp, intellectual mind and fatherly approach to his men. Buxton was the first New Englander York met, and he was pleased to hear that Buxton was a Christian.[70] But, hearing Buxton speak of Christianity, York was confused as to how the major could reconcile his faith with military service and war: "He was a very good man, but at that time I was most troubled for his soul. I disliked to think that such a good man as he appeared to be would be willing to go to war and lead other men to fight, I couldn't understand how he could sorter square war and killing with his professed religious beliefs."[71] Knowing that Major Buxton was a Christian gave Alvin a glimmer of hope that he might find a sympathetic ear in regard to his religious views against war.

The company commander, Captain E.C.B. Danforth, was also a Harvard graduate. York thought him as tall and fit as a hickory pole.[72] Danforth had the hometown advantage, as he was not just from Georgia, but also from Augusta, just outside the gates of Camp Gordon.[73] York's platoon leader was Lieutenant Kirby Pelot Stewart, an energetic and spirited young officer from Lake City, Florida. The platoon sergeant was Harry M. Parsons, who hailed from Brooklyn. Parsons was a big man with dark hair, blue eyes, and a heavy New York City accent, which was referred to as "a distinct Bowery brogue."[74] Despite his upbeat and outgoing personality, he was fierce when antagonized and someone the soldiers learned not to cross. He mixed well with the soldiers and enjoyed joking and singing with them to keep up their spirits both in the barracks and during the long forced marches. In civilian life Parsons was a vaudeville actor, and he made good use of this skill to earn the respect of the men. Parsons would prove to be a positive force for York and a stalwart combat leader.[75]

York's platoon "was made up of Greeks, Slavs, Swedes, Jews, Irish, Germans, and Italians."[76] Describing this diverse group of ethnicities, Alvin wrote:

> So there they put me by some Greeks and Italians to sleep. Well, I couldn't understand them and they couldn't understand me . . . I had never had nothing to do no-how with foreigners before. When I first heard them talk I kinder thought they were angry with each other; they seemed to talk so fast and loud. I couldn't pronounce their names nohow. There was a great big Pole whose name was Private Feodor Sok. That was easy. We jes called him Sok. There was another, Private Maryan E. Dymowski. I never could get the straight of that nohow. And then there was Private Joe Konotski [Kornacki]. I couldn't do much with that either. And there was Private Mario Muzzi and Michael Saccina. These are only a few of the foreigners we done had in my platoon. But they kinder give some idea of what a mixed-up gang we had in the All-American Division.[77]

In the platoon, the men tended to gravitate into regional and ethnic groupings, especially in the cases of the Italians, Poles, and Irish. This tribalization compounded Alvin's alienation. It was hard enough for him to fit in, as he was an odd addition to the unit, being a Tennessee mountain man, the tallest of the bunch, who had no experience in mixing with other ethnic groupings.[78] Combining this with his Christian faith and antiwar views as a conscientious objector would be a recipe for disaster. Fortunately for him, his platoon had not yet heard of his antiwar views. Once word got out, he knew that life would only become worse for him, as men with such beliefs were considered cowards and shirkers.[79]

Alvin felt the urge to fall back into his old sins. He was under pressure from his platoonmates to fit in, and the lure to join the men in heading to downtown Augusta to party and chase women was intense. The temptation was particularly acute in that he was far from home and away from the accountability of his church, mother, and

Pictured here are seven of the soldiers who served with York in the army. (*Niagara Falls Gazette*, 11 November 1929)

pastor. This was perhaps the lowest ebb in Alvin's military career, as he felt alienated and homesick in this environment and sought peace by studying the Bible and in prayer.[80] His faith enabled him to pass this test of his values, and no doubt his life experiences had prepared him for this moment as well. Although he was not well traveled by 1917, he knew the ways of the world, as his experiences in the Blind Tigers helped him to face pressure and not be intimidated by those around him. York had seen much of the world between his humble home in Pall Mall and the wild bars on the Kentucky border. Although wrestling with temptation, he vowed to maintain a professional outlook and to obey every order given him without a complaint. This trait earned Alvin praise from Captain Danforth, who said that "he made a good soldier, being willing and quick to pick up work and obeying all orders."[81] Nevertheless, in early 1918 Alvin decided to express to his leaders his concerns about fighting in war as a Christian.[82]

As Alvin settled into camp routine, he found that there were opportunities to meet other believers. He discovered that there were numerous Bible studies conducted at Camp Gordon, and eagerly participated in many.[83] The most encouraging event for him, however, was befriending Private Murray Savage in his platoon. From

East Bloomfield, New York, Savage, although not a conscientious objector, shared York's Christian faith. Being like-minded, the two were inseparable.[84]

While waiting for an opportunity to see if his leaders would be sympathetic to his objection to fighting, Alvin, along with his regiment, finally was issued the M1917 U.S. Enfield "Eddystone" rifle in March 1918.[85] These rifles, covered in grease, arrived in large boxes. Alvin was horrified to see this, understanding how critical it was to always keep one's rifle clean. After cleaning the weapons, they marched to the division's rifle range at Norcross, Georgia.[86] Having soldiers proficient in shooting their rifles is always imperative in a modern army, but it was the premier soldier skill for the commander of all American forces in Europe, General John "Blackjack" Pershing. Pershing's idea was that as soon as large numbers of American riflemen were put into the lines, they would, with élan and audacity, break the stalemate of the Western Front trench warfare.[87] Because of this emphasis on marksmanship, the judgment cast upon a soldier was often rooted in how good a shot he was. Here, Alvin would find his redemption.[88]

Since the division's rifle range was in an isolated location, each battalion would do nothing but shoot for an entire week.[89] When his unit had its first go at the rifle range, York watched in horror and amusement, as "them-there Greeks and Italians and Poles and New York Jews and some of the boys from the big cities hadn't been used to handling guns. Some of them didn't even know how to load them, and when they fired they not only missed the targets, they missed the backgrounds on which the targets were fixed. They missed everything but the sky." When York's turn to shoot came, his routine of wetting his front site with his thumb before shooting— "to reduce halation and glare"—caused some laughter, but this was forgiven when he proved to be the best shot in the battalion.[90] This caught the attention of his officers, who asked him to train his platoon on how to shoot.[91]

Being introduced to the rifle that he would carry to France to kill Germans brought York's dilemma back to life. He at long last nervously approached his company commander, Captain Danforth. York told him that although he endeavored to be a good soldier, he had reservations about killing his fellow man. He added that he had "prayed and prayed" but could not come to a resolution on the matter. Interestingly, York said that he would remain a soldier if he was ordered, but explained that his denomination was opposed to war and that killing would be a transgression for him.[92]

Danforth listened patiently to York's concerns and told him that there were other conscientious objectors at Camp Gordon, but that most of these were fakes trying to get out of military service. Unlike these, Danforth knew, York was sincere in his opposition to war. He promised to discuss the matter with Major Buxton, and promised York a "square deal." Alvin's measured and thoughtful approach, without resort to threats and ultimatums, gained Danforth's empathy. This was helped by the fact that York had a reputation for being a hardworking and reliable soldier.[93]

Later that week, Danforth escorted York to Major Buxton's sparse quarters. Alvin carried his Bible along so that he could go to the source of his faith in the discourse. Although Major Buxton had a friendly demeanor, and was an outspoken Christian, York was not sure what to expect. He knew that the army had an institutional bias against conscientious objectors, and his cause was certainly not helped by those who were using religion as a pretense to escape the war. Furthermore, with such a rigorous training schedule, York could not expect either Buxton or Danforth to invest time in him, as there was none to spare.

Much to York's relief, Buxton immediately put him at ease by welcoming him to discuss the matter informally as fellow Christians. York recollected: "The major was very friendly-like; he always was with us boys. He told us to sit down. He said he didn't want to discuss this question as a battalion commander discussing it with an officer and a private. He wanted us to discuss it as three American citizens interested in a common cause. He said he respected any honest religious conviction and would be glad to discuss things as man to man."[94]

Displaying an incredible grasp of the Bible, both Danforth and Buxton walked through the scriptures to discuss verses that favored war, while York answered with verses that opposed war. The discourse lasted hours, and Buxton later recalled that it remained civil and respectful.[95] York may have felt it providential to have been assigned officers with well-informed Christian views who were willing to openly discuss their faith with him.[96] The pattern of the debate was like a page out of Saint Augustine's writings, with a discussion of prowar and antiwar verses. When Buxton read Luke 22:36, "he that hath no sword, let him sell his garment, and buy one," York replied with Matthew 5:39, "But I say unto you, That ye resist not evil: but whosoever shall smite thee on thy right cheek, turn to him the other also." When Major Buxton reminded him that Jesus chased the money changers out of the temple, York answered with John 18:36, "Jesus answered, My kingdom is not of this world: if my kingdom were of this world, then would my servants fight, . . . but now is my kingdom not from hence."[97]

York was impressed by the character of the meeting: "We didn't get annoyed or angry or even raise our voice. We jes examined the old Bible and whenever I would bring up a passage opposed to war, Major Buxton would bring up another which sorter favoured war. I believed the Lord was in that room. I seemed somehow to feel His presence there."[98] As the discussion progressed, Buxton explained that Jesus Christ delegated duties to the Christian in regard to earthly governments when he said, "Render therefore unto Caesar the things which are Caesar's; and unto God the things that are God's," in addition to Saint Paul's admonition from Romans chapter 13, "Let every soul be subject unto the higher powers. For there is no power but of God: the powers that be are ordained of God. Whosoever therefore resisteth the power resisteth the ordinance of God: and they that resist shall receive to themselves damnation."[99] These were important scriptures for York to ponder.

From this, Buxton transitioned to lay out Augustine's Just War arguments and then drew parallels between the German aggression, its atrocities against Belgium, and the obligations of government to protect the liberties and freedoms of people. York was not convinced by the allegations of German abuses in Belgium, yet he understood that there were obligations for a Christian to "render unto Caesar" and, in so doing, defend the defenseless. At that moment, Captain Danforth delivered the coup de grace by reading Ezekiel chapter 33,

Again the word of the LORD came unto me, saying, Son of man, speak to the children of thy people, and say unto them, When I bring the sword upon a land, if the people of the land take a man of their coasts, and set him for their watchman: If when he seeth the sword come upon the land, he blow the trumpet, and warn the people; Then whosoever heareth the sound of the trumpet, and taketh not warning; if the sword come, and take him away, his blood shall be upon his own head. He heard the sound of the trumpet, and took not warning; his blood shall be upon him. But he that taketh warning shall deliver his soul. But if the watchman see the sword come, and blow not the trumpet, and the people be not warned; if the sword come, and take any person from among them, he is taken away in his iniquity; but his blood will I require at the watchman's hand. So thou, O son of man, I have set thee a watchman unto the house of Israel; therefore thou shalt hear the word at my mouth, and warn them from me. When I say unto the wicked, O wicked man, thou shalt surely die; if thou dost not speak to warn the wicked from his way, that wicked man shall die in his iniquity; but his blood will I require at thine hand. Nevertheless, if thou warn the wicked of his way to turn from it; if he do not turn from his way, he shall die in his iniquity; but thou hast delivered thy soul.[100]

This scripture, with Buxton's logical presentation of the scriptures and the Just War concept, impacted York. York parted that evening saying that he would like time to think over all that was said. Major Buxton told him to take all the time that he needed, and implied that if he could not come to terms with fighting, then there was a possibility to transfer him into a noncombat function or to dismiss him entirely from the army.[101] With that, York returned to his duties. Yet, due to the training schedule, York was unable to reconcile the clash of ideas of whether to fight or not to fight. He just did not have time to think. Additionally, word had gotten out about his objection to military service, pitting some of his platoonmates against him. The two who were most troubled by York's religious views were Bernard "Bernie" Early and William Cutting. (Cutting enlisted under an alias; his real name was Otis B. Merrithew).[102]

Early was a naturalized citizen hailing from Ireland who worked as a bartender before entering the army in New Haven, Connecticut. He liked to drink, curse, fight, and go absent without leave (AWOL). Cutting was Early's particular friend, and he shared the same interests. As part of his fictional persona that he created to match his assumed name, Cutting told the men that he was an iceman in Boston. The truth was that he was a farmhand.[103] Early and Cutting were like what Alvin was before his discovery of Christ on 1 January 1915. Neither Cutting nor Early knew of Alvin's checkered past or that he once fought and drank like the best of them. As far as they were concerned, York was a coward, and they wanted him to know it.[104]

As York anticipated, his objection to war led to heated arguments in the barracks. According to Cutting, during one of these verbal spats "York and . . . Early had fought over the subject of killing. . . . York had continued on about the foolishness of war until Bernie threatened to blow his brains out and that had ended the argument."[105] A dark cloud settled over the platoon.

The consequence of Early's and Cutting's hostility, combined with the intense training schedule, was that York could not get off alone to pray and contemplate his dilemma. As a final recourse, he applied for and received ten days' leave (21–31 March 1918) to return to Pall Mall to prayerfully consider his decision in the quiet of the Cumberland Mountains.[106] Upon arriving home, York was thrilled to see his family, to attend his church, and, of course, to speak with Gracie. He even helped lead a revival service in Pall Mall where several people came forward to accept the Lord. Despite this, a burden was upon him: what to do about the army.[107]

Alvin sought counsel from Pastor Pile, but his advice merely added to Alvin's confusion, as the antiwar arguments did not reconcile Buxton's convincing arguments about obeying governments. With that, Alvin headed up the lonely mountain with his hunting dogs to make his decision. After thirty-six hours of fasting and praying, calm settled upon his tortured soul. Alvin said that he was visited by the presence of God, who filled him with a "peace . . . , which passeth all understanding."[108] Gone was the doubt, and he came down that mountain full of assurance, saying to his mother, "I am going to war with the sword of the Lord and of Gideon. . . . I have received my assurance. I have received it from God himself—that it's right for me to go to war, and that as long as I believe in Him, not one hair of my head will be harmed."[109] With this confidence, York returned to Camp Gordon a new man and ready spiritually for what lay ahead.[110]

4

Marching as to War

It was a quiet sector where they put new troops into training
before sending them out to No Man's Land. The Greeks and
Italians and all of the other boys done fairly well. They shore
were turning out to be the bestest soldiers. I was often out on
No Man's Land.

—Alvin York

Alvin returned on 31 March 1918 to Camp Gordon just as his unit
received orders to deploy to France. The division had a farewell
parade on 4 April that was reviewed by Georgia governor Hugh
M. Dorsey and the widow of the celebrated Confederate Civil War
general for whom the camp was named, John Brown Gordon. Thus
the odyssey of moving York's unit to France began. The next weeks
were dedicated to frantic deployment activities that included pack-
ing, issuing equipment, organizing movement routes, preparing rail
and ship manifests, developing load plans, and having soldiers fill
out stacks of predeployment documents that ranged from wills to
financial allotments.[1] Adding to the confusion was an order from
the War Department to "comb out alien enemies [Germans, Austri-
ans, Turks, or Bulgarians] and men unfit for service."[2] This created
gaps in the regiment that were later filled by raw recruits.

The movement of the 82nd Division from Camp Gordon to
France began when elements of the division departed on 10 April.
York's regiment left Camp Gordon on the 19th. The men marched
in complete gear, with packs and rifles, to the nearby rail station
at Chamblee, Georgia, where local soldiers in the regiment were
given a tearful farewell by family and friends.[3] The regiment spent
two days on the train, arriving at Camp Upton, New York, on 21
April. Although the conditions on the train were cramped, York
was taking in the new experiences, being sustained by his faith,
praying:

York's 328th Regiment marches in the 4 April 1918 divisional parade that marked the end of its time at Camp Gordon, Georgia. After this, the men boarded trains for New York, to board ships destined for Europe and war. (AHEC)

O God, in hope that sends the shining ray,
Far down the future's broadening way;
In peace that only Thou canst give;
With Thee, O Master, let me live.[4]

The soldiers were cheered by American citizens whenever the train made a stop, with the largest welcome in New York City, where there was "shouting, blowing whistles and tooting horns."[5] The soldiers stayed at Camp Upton for nine days, until the ships that would send them to France were ready. While at Camp Upton, York and the men were put through endless inspections, marching, drills, and issued more seemingly useless equipment and clothing "to ensure that the cause of Democracy was satisfied."[6] The leaders foolishly went so far as to say that no time would be given off even for a large number of the men from New York City, which was less than an hour away. This was too much to bear for the Mid-Atlantic and New England soldiers, who were close to home and had not seen their families for some six months. In response, large groups went AWOL.[7]

As most of the 328th's officers were southerners, and were close enough to their families at Camp Gordon to see them often, they did not anticipate that their northern men would desire the same courtesy of seeing their families before going overseas. To stem the flow of AWOLs, the regiment eventually caught on and offered furloughs, but this was too little, too late. Most of the men returned, but several hundred arrived at Camp Upton after the regiment had shipped out. These men were reprimanded and boarded later ships to catch up with the 328th in France. For many, it would be the last time that they would see their loved ones.[8]

York's regiment commenced rail movement to the Port of Boston late on 30 April and boarded two Canadian ships of the Montreal, Canada Allan Line during the early morning hours of 2:00–4:00 A.M. on 1 May 1918. The ships that the 328th boarded were the SS *Scandinavian*, which transported the 2nd Battalion (York's unit) and 3rd Battalion, and the SS *Grampian*, which transported the "1st Battalion, Regimental Headquarters, Machine Gun and Supply Companies."[9] The weather during the men's early morning departure was a cold light rain. Combined with the darkness, it matched many of the men's mood of "feeling gloomy and . . . dismal" on going off to war.[10]

As soon as boarding was completed, the *Scandinavian* and *Grampian* sailed to New York, where they remained until a convoy of sixteen ships was ready. The convoy began its journey across the Atlantic on 3 May 1918 and was escorted on the first leg of the journey by the armored cruiser USS *San Diego*, a veteran of the acclaimed Great White Fleet.[11] Veterans of the regiment commented on the sadness they felt as the Statue of Liberty faded into the horizon. Nonetheless, the men had troubles of their own. In addition to getting used to the sea, the conditions were so tight that some in the regiment commented that "there wasn't enough room left in the ship for an extra shoe lace."[12]

This was the first time that Alvin had seen the ocean or sailed on a ship. The cramped quarters, combined with seasickness, made the trip difficult for him. "It was too much water for me. Like me, Mark Twain, whose parents come from Jimtown, was borned inland. And he never seed the open ocean until he growed up. And when he stood on the beach and seed it for the first time, his friends asked him what he thought of it, and he said, 'It was a success.' But when Mark said that he weren't on the ocean. He were on the shore. And when our old boat got away out and begun to pitch and toss I jes knowed Mark was wrong."[13]

The trip improved Alvin's opinion of his foreign troopmates, many of whom had only a few years before crossed the Atlantic to immigrate to the United States. "The Greeks, Italians, and Poles, and New York Jews stood the trip right smart. That kinder impressed me. It sorter made up for their bad shooting. I sorter got to like them more."[14] During the voyage, York's regimental commander, Colonel Lindsey, was promoted to brigadier general and given command of the 164th Infantry Brigade, which included both York's 328th Infantry Regiment and the 327th. Major Frank Jewett was given temporary command of the 328th until Colonel Hunter B. Nelson arrived on 26 June 1917.[15]

The men had a busy schedule of training and lectures throughout the journey. As there was little room to spare on the ships, a training schedule was published when particular units would go to the deck to conduct boat drills, perform physical exercise, or participate in a lecture on some topic of military importance.[16] During the long voyage the men experienced convoy zigzag operations whenever a suspected U-boat was spotted, and had to sleep in their clothes with their lifebelts on from time to time. The interaction of the Doughboys with the ship's crew was interesting. A soldier in York's unit wrote that the ship was operated by the "cockiest gang of Britishers. . . . They didn't get us and we couldn't 'compree' them. They compared us to the Canadians, of whom they had transported . . . and said that they came over singing and praying, but the bloody bloomin Americans didn't seem to care a darn and they came over gambling and cussing."[17] Other than spotting a few whales in the open sea, the trip across the Atlantic was uneventful. The highlight for Alvin was studying the Bible with Murray Savage, his best friend in the army.[18]

When the convoy entered the "danger zone" near Ireland, where the risk of being attacked by a German U-boat was the most likely, an escort of six fast-moving British antisubmarine destroyers joined them. York said that they reminded him of "a bunch of well-trained bird dogs trying to get wind of birds."[19] Finally, on 16 May, after a twelve-day journey, the ships arrived at Liverpool, England.

The soldiers spent the greater part of the day unloading the ships before marching to the Knotty Ash Rest Camp.[20] There, Alvin and his fellow soldiers learned that the army's idea of a rest camp belied its title. "We learned that we were to march a 'little way' to a 'rest camp.' Reader: take the 'little' out of way and the 'rest' out of camp and put the two together and you have the result. . . . Oh Boy! Something doing every minute! The magic phrase 'Rest Camp' never fooled us again."[21] These camps had been active throughout the war, witnessing tens of thousands of men passing through, with the ultimate destination being the Western Front. York was now in the midst of the machines of war, and those machines were quickly moving him forward to face off with Germany.

The Knotty Ash Rest Camp was in eastern Liverpool, five miles from the ships. To add insult to injury, this was no parade, and the soldiers all carried added burdens.[22] In addition to their own excessive equipment and their rifles, they also carried the equipment and rifles of the soldiers who did not return in time to board the ships, plus an assortment of field desks, extra boxes of rations, and the like. Soldiers in York's regiment wrote that although the residents of Liverpool were elated to see the Yanks, they were perplexed by the vast quantities of equipment that the Americans hauled. When asked by an Englishman why some of the soldiers carried two rifles, one of the Americans answered, "We shot so fast that our rifles got too hot to handle and hence it was necessary to carry some extra pieces."[23]

The next day, 18 May, York's unit boarded a train for a 236-mile ride across England to another rest camp near the channel port of Southampton to prepare the men for the final leg of the journey to France. For soldiers recently completing two weeks at sea, they found the scenic countryside awe-inspiring.[24] What Alvin saw of England impressed him: "The English countryside was . . . beautiful. It was sort of rolling-like and the parks and fields were so neat and tidy that it 'most looked as though they had special gardeners to look after every few acres of them."[25]

The men were disgusted to learn that the Southampton Rest Camp was also nowhere near the railhead, and thus they began another long road march. The soldiers experienced the same revulsion to the Southampton Rest Camp as they had to the Liverpool Knotty Ash Rest Camp. One soldier said, "The bird that named that 'Rest Camp' would call hell an ice box. . . . We got up very early the next morning and started doing a great many unnecessary things that we had no chance of finishing—just something to keep us busy."[26] While awaiting transport to France at Southampton, the unit was officially welcomed by a British officer, who gave every soldier in York's unit a letter from King George V that read, "Soldiers of the United States, the people of the British Isles welcome you on your way to take your stand beside the Armies of many Nations now fighting in the Old World the great battle for human freedom. The Allies will gain new heart & spirit in your company. I wish that I could shake the hand of each one of you & bid you God speed on your mission. Signed, George R. I."[27]

Despite the warm welcome by England and its monarch, the soldiers were eager to get into the fight: "We wanted to get into it and get it over." Their wish was not far from being fulfilled. Late on 20 May 1918, they moved to the Southampton port and boarded the channel transport *Viper*, arriving at Le Havre, France, early on the 21st. During the trip across the English Channel, Alvin was again seasick, saying that it was like being on something "more like a bucking mule than a boat."[28]

After arriving in France, and wearing their M1911 Montana campaign hats, the 328th Regiment marched through Le Havre to the excited cheers and waves of the French and toward their final phase of training.[29] The pre-battle bravado of these green troops was dulled as a train full of battlefield casualties pulled up. The injured men were loaded aboard ships for medical evacuation to England, giving the 328th a glimpse of the grim reality of war.[30]

The regiment remained in Le Havre briefly. The first order of business was to shed the unnecessary equipment issued at Camp Upton to lighten the load. The men were also finally issued gas masks and helmets. Training was given by British soldiers in the use of the gas mask. They informed the Americans that this little device would be their "best friend" and save their lives if used properly. Six-second drills were conducted over and over again until the men were able to get the masks on in that time, with the training culminating in a trip through the gas chamber.[31] Alvin wrote, "That brought the war a whole heap closer."[32] After this, the men deployed behind the British Fifth Army in the Amiens area of France, to both serve as a reserve and to receive more combat training. Soon there would be ten American divisions near the Fifth British Army.[33]

The idea of stationing ten American divisions behind the British

Fifth Army was a compromise in supporting the British and French armies. The German high command knew that the American Expeditionary Forces would ultimately give the Allies a decisive quantitative advantage in soldiers and thereby end any chance of a German victory along the Western Front.[34] It was regarding this that Ludendorff said, "with the American entry into the war, the relative strengths would be more in [German] favor in the spring than in late summer . . . unless we had by then gained a great victory. . . . Only a far reaching military success which would make it appear to the Entente powers that, even with the help of America, the continuation of the war offered no further prospects of success, would provide the possibility of rendering our embittered opponents really ready to make peace. This was the political aim of the Supreme Command in 1918."[35]

Time was of the essence for the Germans. After having secured victory against Russia in late 1917, they hurriedly transferred nearly 1 million men from the Eastern Front to France. Berlin hoped to deal the Allies a knockout blow before the Americans could stem the tide. The resulting German attack, Operation Michael, was launched on 21 March 1918 and nearly destroyed the British Fifth Army. Two months later, putting the Americans with the Fifth Army bolstered their line should another German offensive transpire in this sector. To compound the crisis of 1918, the French Army was close to collapse. This was in part due to the massive casualties it suffered during the 1916 Battle of Verdun, and its failed Chemin des Dames Offensive in 1917, which triggered widespread mutinies across the front, with soldiers refusing to attack any longer. It was in this dire situation, of weakened French and British armies desperately trying to hold back the tenacious assaults of Germany, that the Americans arrived.

In the midst of the 1918 crisis, the French and British worked out an ambitious shipping schedule to move the Americans to Europe faster than planned.[36] In the end, the German spring-summer offensives of 1918 failed, with the Americans playing an important part in holding them at bay.[37] General Pershing's concept of operations was to regain control over all American forces in Europe once the crisis was over. Thanks to the Allies' help, the independent American Expeditionary Forces (AEF) would be ready for operations by September.

In his memoirs, General Pershing went to great lengths to

General John J. Pershing was the overall commander of the American Expeditionary Forces. He successfully resisted pressure from his British and French counterparts to amalgamate the newly arrived Americans into their respective forces. Instead, Pershing formed an independent American army. Pershing would endorse York's being awarded the Medal of Honor in the spring of 1919. (NARA)

describe the strategic and operational challenges that he faced in getting an independent American army into the field during this turbulent period of the war. This was no small matter, in that the British and French demanded that they be allowed to use the Americans as replacements (via amalgamation) within their depleted forces, while Pershing intended to create an independent American army. Through amalgamation, the British and French vehemently argued, the Americans would be in the fight faster. Indeed, their appeals for amalgamation made sense during the crisis of the German spring offensives, as there was a real chance for German victory in the West.[38]

Still, Pershing and President Wilson remained committed to the idea of fielding an independent American army in France so as to keep the soldiers under American command. This organizational structure would also increase Washington's influence in the conduct of the war.[39] The United States' commitment to establishing an American army was perhaps the single most important decision shaping the American "soldier" experience in the Great War. In fact, it would shape the identity and collective memory of the "Doughboy."[40]

The British unit that trained York's regiment was the 66th (2nd East Lancashire) Division. While with the British, the Americans turned in their M1917 Eddystone Rifles for the British .303 Lee-Enfield. The reason for this was that the British did not use or supply the American standard .30-06 ammunition required for the M1917 Enfield. Therefore, the Americans used the British .303 Lee-Enfield while in the line with the Brits. Upon completion of this phase of the training, "the Lee-Enfield rifles . . . [would be] turned back to the British and the U.S. M1917 Rifle (Eddystone) [would be] reissued."

The 328th Regiment moved out of Le Havre on 22 May, "packed as tight as sardines in a box" in French troop trains labeled "40 hommes 8 Chevalier."[41] This caused much joking for the soldiers, of which York remarked, "One of our boys who was detailed to load the cars went to the Captain and said: 'Captain, I loaded the forty men all right, but if you put the eight horses in too they will shore trample the boys to death.'"[42] The regiment moved one hundred miles east, to the French town of Eu, located in the Somme River Valley. From there, the regiment marched twelve miles south across the countryside to billet in area villages. The 328th Regiment's headquarters was centered at the village of Horcelaines, with its units set up in battalion groups, under the supervision of British trainers.[43]

York's battalion was based out of the village of Floraville, where it trained hard, conducted frequent road marches, and prepared to rotate through the British trenches. General Burnham directed that his divisions march to a different village every day so as to get reconditioned for combat after the sedentary weeks on ships.[44] During marching, the men were ordered to sing songs like "Dixie" and "Over There." These were sung with gusto and were a source of national pride, to the interest of the nearby Brits, or admiring French girls.[45] During this period most of the soldiers were billeted in barns, where they were introduced to the menace of lice (cooties). In this strange old world, the Americans shared a comical view of their French hosts, as the regimental history noted:

> All the "easy methods to learn French" that had been bought in the States were brought out, and everyone started to try out his particular brand of "Parlez vouz," with surprisingly unsatisfactory results. We got on pretty good terms with "Vin Rouge" and "Vin Blanc." All the towns the Regiment had been billeted in were about the same, several centuries old and badly out of repair. The village "Vamp" ran the "Vin Rouge" stand, the mayor was the oldest and most disreputable looking citizen in the town and a man's wealth was judged by the size of his manure pile.[46]

York had respect for the British veterans, but generally did not like their "scant" rations. One of the officers wrote: "with British NCOs, British equipment and British rations, we were in a fair way to become regular John Bulls. For the first two we had some respect, but as for the rations—well, give us gold fish and corn willie every time."[47] Nonetheless, the regiment benefitted from the schools that the British Expeditionary Force had established in the Saint-Valery-sur-Somme training area that were designed to prepare the Americans for combat. Under the guidance of the British 66th Division commander, Major General H. K. Bethell, the Americans learned how to operate the Lewis Gun, fight with the bayonet, fire the Vickers machine gun, use hand grenades, navigate through wire entanglements, properly react to incoming artillery, use mortars, and prevent death and injury from gas attacks. The enthusiasm with which

After arriving in La Havre in June 1918, York's unit marched across large swathes of France. Here, French children watch as American Doughboys pass by. (NARA)

the British soldiers threw themselves into the training was infectious to the Americans, who were to mimic their unique training methods, with one of York's officers later commenting, "The flash and pep they put into their drilling and games were refreshing."[48]

The American officers and senior NCOs also rotated through the British frontline trenches, where the division suffered its first combat fatalities. Despite the losses, the men were gradually becoming ready for action. Alvin's opinion of his fellow platoonmates was improving as well. After seeing them weather the Atlantic crossing, they improved too in their shooting (thanks to British instruction). York wrote, "The Greeks and Italians and Jews and Poles were improving. They had stayed continuously on the rifle range for a month or two, and got so they could do shooting. They were fairly good pals, too."[49]

This period of training brought in a series of senior officers eager to inspect the readiness of these Americans. The first to visit was the British Expeditionary Force (BEF) commander, Field Marshal

Douglas Haig. His visit was to see how well the 66th British Division was doing as trainers and to take a look at the American soldiers that he wanted to keep in his command. Haig hoped that the Americans would undo the German gains of March and April and "redeem the lost battlefields of Picardy."[50] With this in mind, Haig knew how to win the hearts of the Doughboys. While inspecting American field kitchens, he inquired of the cooks if everything was in order, to which York recounts what a fellow Tennessean said to the field marshal: "No, everything is all wrong, most awfully all wrong there is no salt. The Field Marshal turned to the Quartermaster General, who was with him, and asked for an explanation. The Quartermaster said the two last salt ships were torpedoed and there was a shortage. The Field Marshal then instructed him to immediately send some salt to the American kitchen. That kinder tickled our boys."[51]

Haig's visit was followed two days later by Pershing's. This caused quite a bit of excitement in York's battalion. "We were anxious to make a right-smart impression on him, because we knowed if we did we would get up to the front-line trenches so much quicker, and our boys were jes rarin to go."[52] Pershing gave the unit good marks and made plans to move it into the lines. Although York and his platoon were raring for getting into the war, he was philosophical about it. "Anyone who thinks that soldiering is jes goin' back in again and fightin, is jes plumb foolin' himself. Weeks passed and we never even seen a trench except the training ones. We never once heard the sound of guns. All we did was hike, and hike, and hike and then hike again. They shore kept us a-going hiking. It seemed as though they had sent us to France to kinder test out the strength of them-there American military shoes."[53]

After a month of being out of contact with their loved ones, the first of the mail caught up with the 82nd in June, while training with the British. York longed to hear how things were back on the farm and with Gracie. During the time in France, many of the soldiers received "Dear John" letters from their girlfriends breaking off the relationship. Alvin would have none of that, and frequently wrote to Gracie, "I'm so glad to know that you have promised to be true to me until I come back . . . so please promise me that you will not go with one while I am in France . . . I am trusting to you to do what you said."[54]

The division received marching orders to move out beginning 16 June for the French XXXII Corps sector east of Verdun, where an American sector would be created.[55] The soldiers turned in their

British rifles and gear, while retaining the British Tommy helmet and gas mask. Again carrying their American M1917 Eddystone rifles, the men climbed into the now legendary "40 hommes 8 Chevalier" train cars and began a two-day ride to the Lorraine region of France. Keeping an ever positive view of the month of rigorous training, York reflected: "We shore were a different outfit to the rambunshus crowd of half-wild men that first got together in Camp Gordon, in Georgia."[56] Most of his mates had a more circumspect view, with the regimental history recording a widely held view of the British:

> We never became very enthusiastic over staying with the British for there was that "British Army Ration." We heard a lot about the "blooming bloody offan"; being "fed up" and learned to know what "carry on" meant, but never could understand when and how to use the expression "cherry-oh," or just what it signified; nor could we ever feel comfortable or know just how to act in the presence of the all powerful British "Sergeant Major." We rather liked the four o'clock tea, which nothing must be allowed to interfere with, but on the whole, were indeed glad to get back to an American outfit.[57]

York and all of the 82nd Division, save for its artillery brigade (which was still training with the French), arrived at Toul, France, on 18 June and billeted in the surrounding villages. York's battalion was assigned to the village of Lucey. In addition to their American rifles and side arms, the men were issued several French weapons with which they would enter combat. This included the notoriously unreliable Chauchat light machine gun, as well as the 8 mm Hotchkiss machine gun, all of which required extra training to learn how to operate and maintain. Thus was the cost of America's lack of preparedness, forcing it to rely on British and French war stocks.

Time was given for the men to blow off steam before going into the trenches, although York usually steered clear of the cafes and bars, where the temptations of wine and women were available. While in Lucey, although refraining from drinking himself, York watched his comrades partake of a bit too much wine and cognac, and "being soldiers, they was right smart when it come to finding them-there pretty French girls. Some of them shore knowed more about hunting and finding them, too, than I did about trailing coon and fox back there on the mountains at home." Although the training had improved the unit, it still struggled with the tendency of the men to fall into ethnic or regional groups. Combined with the mixture of wine and women, there was certain to be trouble. At the Lucey cafe, York saw this explosive mix come to a head. "There was a heap of Irish and Poles in our platoon, and one night in one of the cafes one of the Irish boys said he didn't believe the Poles could fight nohow. Ho! Ho! That shore started it! They went at it with fists and belts. They turned that cafe into a No Man's Land, only worse, and we had to turn out the guard to stop it."

Alvin stood by his convictions and continued to sharpen his moral courage by steering clear of such temptations. He was helped by the encouragement of Corporal Murray Savage, who studied the Bible with Alvin. York described this difficult time:

> I didn't go into the towns much. I had put all of the drinkin' and fist-fightin' away behind me. I left it back home on the Kentucky line. I didn't have a drink all the time I was in France. I didn't have a fist fight or an argument. I didn't swear or smoke either. I wasn't any better'n any of the other boys. It was jes my way of livin', that was all. They did what they wanted to do. So did I. Our ways were different. We left it at that. I did a heap of reading from the Bible. I read it through several times over there.[58]

Despite Alvin's generous recollection of simply going separate ways from the men when it came to partying, this is far from a complete view of the situation. In addition to the clash between ethnic groups, there were some in his platoon who still resented his beliefs and morals, with William Cutting being the chief protagonist. Cutting said that he was sure that York would be a coward in combat, and therefore could not be trusted. Bernard Early shared this view of York.[59] Simply put, Alvin did not fit in, and his faith exacerbated this. Cutting and Early's view that Alvin lacked what it took to be a soldier was ostensibly confirmed when York again expressed misgivings about killing during bayonet training in late June, just before entering the trenches.[60] With this friction in the platoon, whether ethnic (Irish versus Pole), regional, or religious, they all were soon to get their baptism of fire that would ultimately demonstrate if such suspicions were warranted.

5

Into the Trenches!

> We were going in at last. We could hear the guns away in
> the distance now, jes like the thunder in the hills at home.
> We seed a right-smart lot of deserted trenches with wire
> entanglements, all snarled and mussed up. We seed gun
> emplacements half full of water. We passed an awful lot of
> graves, with little wooden crosses at their heads. I'm a-tellin'
> you that brought it home to us.
>
> —Alvin York

Orders were issued to the 82nd Division to move to Rambucourt
and man the front lines on 26 June. This "quiet sector" east of Verdun
was known as the Woevre Front, Lagny Sector. The last heavy fighting here had occurred in 1915 during a French attempt to reduce this
salient. However, the Germans managed to hold the bulge, which
protruded south to the village of St. Mihiel, as well as retaining the
important hill of Montsec, which dominated the area. This bulge jut-
ted into France like a giant "V," with the western base of it anchored
near Haudiomont and in the east on the Moselle River and Pont-à-
Mousson. After the nine-month battle of Verdun concluded in late
1916 the area had been relatively quiet—a good place to introduce
the Americans to combat.[1]

The 82nd was not the first American division to serve in this
area of the Western Front. Before them was the New England
National Guard's 26th "Yankee" Division, who had been in the line
here for several months. The challenge though was squeezing an
American division into a French division sector, as the European
divisions were half the size of the twenty-eight-thousand-strong
American divisions. As the 82nd Division moved into the line, the
French Army ensured that these inexperienced soldiers were well
looked after with experienced support. The 82nd was backed by the
French 154th Division, had French artillery support, and had French

officers working in the trenches with them. The American regiments each occupied a portion of the front, putting one battalion in the line, a second in support (about two miles back), and a third in general reserve (about six miles back).[2] The battalions would rotate roughly every week over the next forty-five days.

The support and reserve would either train or dig new trench lines. Ironically, the time in the front was more relaxing, except of course during the brief periods of horror they encountered while in combat.[3] York's battalion of the 328th Regiment, still under the command of Lieutenant Colonel Buxton, was the first in its regiment to occupy the forward trenches.[4]

The idea that this was a quiet sector is only accurate in comparison to the casualties along the more active areas of the line. Here, in April and May, the Germans had launched attacks consisting of some four hundred specially trained trench raiders into the American line. During this encounter, the Yankee Division had performed commendably but suffered hundreds of casualties. Additionally, artillery barrages, gas attacks, enemy air strafing, snipers, and the like were daily experiences at this part of the front.

The men of York's battalion were naturally nervous as they moved into the forward trenches, with nothing more than "no-man's-land" standing between them and the Germans. All movement occurred during hours of darkness, as anything detected by the Hun would bring artillery and gas attacks. This was the first time that these soldiers had actually served on the front, and they were shocked by the reality of war. The most striking impression was the smell of death and decay. The men were also appalled by the condition of the trenches, which often were knee deep in water and difficult to live in.[5] Finally, the destroyed moonlike landscape, combined with the ruins of the villages of Xivray-et-Marvoisin in the midst of the line, added a "spooky" dimension. Here, especially at night, the men saw that "shattered walls made a fine hiding place for the Boche—both real and imaginary."[6]

The endless hours of watch, daily gas warning alarms (usually false), patrolling no-man's-land, and having all the men on guard during "stand-to" (the period before dawn when most attacks occurred) wore the men out physically and mentally. Some patrols and relief columns had the misfortune of getting lost in no-man's-land at night and spending a day ducking from German rifle fire while waiting for the cover of darkness before being able to move back to the relative safety of the trenches.[7] Although German artillery was the greatest danger, so too were overly nervous American sentries. On several occasions these inexperienced soldiers, either because of bad nerves, inability to pronounce the French passwords, or poor English skills, opened fire on a friendly relief column, killing or wounding scores of men.[8]

During these trying times York found comfort in his faith. He spent most of the hours of his free time in the trenches studying his pocket New Testament and praying. Despite the ribbing and mocking by his platoonmates, York was noted by his officers as steady under fire and as having a "can-do" attitude. These attributes earned him a promotion to corporal during this time in the Lagny Sector.[9]

As a corporal, York was given command of an automatic weapons squad. His men were armed with a French Chauchat light machine gun, and he led them on several forays deep into no-man's-land. Despite the danger, York was unmoved and confident. As German bullets buzzed over his trench "like angry hornets," he reflected, "I did a heap of thinking and praying at this time. And more'n ever I jes knowed I was going to get back all right. I believed in God and in His promises."[10]

For the next two months, York's division rotated in and out of the Lagny Sector trenches, slowly gaining experience.[11] He was encouraged by the plethora of Christian aid volunteers who tried to ameliorate the soldiers' hardships. Volunteers from the Salvation Army, the Young Men's Christian Association, and the Christian Commission set up tents close to the lines to provide hot chocolate, coffee, lemonade, donuts, and cake to the soldiers while sharing the Gospel with them.[12] This was usually a highlight for the men just coming into and going out of the trench lines and a great witness for the faith as far as York was concerned.[13]

Despite the occasional artillery barrages, gas attacks, and isolated trench raids, the preponderance of the soldiers in York's regiment wanted to get into the fight. This itch grew when the division came back empty handed after a series of trench raids to capture a German. These trench raids usually ended with the Americans being thrown back by enemy artillery and concealed machine guns operated by seemingly invisible foes. Seldom seeing a live "Hun" led to a belief that the sector was held only by "a one-legged Boche who operated a dozen machine guns and a battery of 77s by use of a keyboard."[14]

The relief of York's division from this sector was completed on 10 August. They had suffered 374 casualties during their time at the front, most by poisonous gas.[15] The 82nd planned on conducting maneuver training exercises, in compliance with General Pershing's orders that the Americans be ready for open warfare when the German trenches were overrun. But orders directed them to reinforce the Marne Sector. That order was soon rescinded with the proviso to instead move twenty-five miles northeast to occupy the Marbache Sector in the town of Pont-à-Mousson. This put the division on the eastern edge of the St. Mihiel salient, where it would support the first American army offensive on the Western Front, scheduled for 12 September.

The 82nd Division took its position with satisfaction, as Pont-à-Mousson was a vibrant locale on the Moselle River, with its thirty thousand residents carrying on normal life despite being only about a half-mile from the front. Apparently the Germans and French had an unwritten agreement to keep this sector quiet, and the town had very little physical damage because of this "live and let live" understanding.[16] The men completed relief of the 2nd U.S. Infantry Division there on 17 August. York's 328th Infantry Regiment replaced the 16th Marine Regiment, which had covered itself with glory in its defense of Château Thierry only two months before.[17] Upon entering Pont-à-Mousson, York wrote that it "was a kinder earthly paradise. . . . The trees and vines were loaded with grapes and apples and everything. The gardens were all kept up nice, with everything kinder ripe and ready, and there was plenty of green grass and shade and cool, clean water. It was most hard for us to imagine that we were still in the war."[18]

General Pershing's St. Mihiel Offensive was intended not only to exercise the American army for the first time, but to set the conditions for a strategic blow against the Germans by taking the fortress city of Metz. As Pershing took command of the St. Mihiel salient on 30 August, he met with the overall Allied commander, France's Marshal Ferdinand Foch, who suggested canceling the operation to support a broader attack. After a series of discussions, Pershing convinced Foch to allow the St. Mihiel operation to proceed, albeit with the limited objective of reducing the salient. Pershing then would rapidly move his forces about sixty miles northwest, to launch the Meuse-Argonne Offensive a week later. This was no easy endeavor, even for a seasoned army, but Pershing viewed the St.

Mihiel Offensive as being important both for a morale boost for the AEF and for the preparation of his staff for the next big operation.[19]

As forces arrived for the attack, the Americans began rotating in and out of the trenches like they had in the Lagny Sector. At first these trenches were quiet, but in early September the worst-kept secret in France was that the Americans were poised to launch an offensive to reduce the German salient around St. Mihiel. One of York's officers even heard open talk in Paris while there attending gas training.[20] The days leading up to the attack encompassed the evacuation of citizens from Pont-à-Mousson, an increase of artillery exchanges, and more aggressive patrolling between the belligerents.[21]

Meanwhile, the German High Command contemplated a withdrawal from the St. Mihiel salient. Yet, if it came to fighting, they had three lines of fortified positions from which to defend it. Although the Germans saw the buildup of American forces around the salient, they were slow to react. There were existing plans by the German staff to withdraw from the pocket should a viable threat appear. This would involve more than just having the troops depart; it would also entail the removal of war materiel, the destruction of defensive positions, and a scorched-earth policy to deprive the Americans of any advantage. This would require eight days to complete.[22]

The Germans belatedly issued orders on 9 September to evacuate the salient. As noted by the senior German military leaders, Erich Ludendorff and Paul von Hindenburg, this was too late. The Americans began their assault on 12 September.[23] The reluctance of the Germans to order a withdrawal from the St. Mihiel salient is understandable in that it served as a buffer to protect the important city of Metz, which gave them strategic depth in defending the crucial east/west rail networks and safeguarding the iron basin at Briey-Longwy.[24]

As the Germans displaced their artillery, began removing war materials, and started destroying defensive positions, the American attack began.[25] The attack included fourteen U.S. divisions (each twice the strength of a European division) and four French divisions, facing eleven German divisions. The force ratio was 3 to 1 in favor of the Allies and was supported by concentrated French and American artillery fires from nearly three thousand guns that swept deep into the German lines. This was followed by an impressive combined arms operation that included more than four hundred tanks (manned by both French and American crews)[26] and fifteen hundred Allied aircraft, which gained air superiority thanks to the superb planning of Colonel Billy Mitchell, of the U.S. Army.[27] Commenting on the beginning of the battle, York wrote, "It done opened with a most awful barrage from our big guns. It was the awfulest thing you ever heard. It made the air tremble and the ground shake. At times you couldn't hear your own voice nohow. The air was full of airplanes, and most of them American planes. There must have been hundreds of them. They were diving and circling around all over the place like a swarm of birds. We seed several right-smart fights away up there above us."

York's 82nd Division played a supporting role in St. Mihiel by holding the right shoulder, the hinge on which the attack would swing.[28] They were to "keep in contact with the enemy at all times."[29] This meant that the men would conduct aggressive reconnaissance so as to keep the German division in front of them from being able to reposition or withdraw. As the attack was under way, York's battalion launched two attacks, with Lieutenant Bertrand Cox of F Company leading men valiantly in overcoming the German strongpoint at Maison Gauthier, on the west bank of the Moselle River. Such local successes, combined with the rapid advance of the American attack, resulted in the 82nd also being ordered to advance.[30]

York's battalion "went over the top" on the second day of the St. Mihiel Offensive (13 September) and captured Norroy, the first of many towns that the 82nd Division would liberate in 1918. When the Americans attacked, the scene was just like any other along the Western Front, with the men climbing out of their trenches and holes and then charging across an expanse of wire and craters. The men were greeted with intense fire from German rifles, machine guns, and artillery. But the unit had good leaders, with young Lieutenant Kirby Stewart leading his men by example and getting them through the most difficult zones. Advancing with the battalion was Lieutenant Colonel Buxton and his adjutant, Lieutenant Joseph Woods, who made it a point to always advance with their men.[31] York, as a corporal and squad leader, planned on leading his men by being out front as well, but once the whistle was blown to signal the attack he could hardly keep up with his men, much less stay ahead of them:

> So I led the squad. I kinder think they almost led me. I mean
> I was supposed to be in the front and they were supposed

to follow. But no matter how fast I went they wanted to go faster, so that they could get at the Germans. The Greeks and Italians, the Poles and the Jews and the other city boys were still firing pretty wild. They were still mostly hitting the ground or the sky. They burned up a most awful lot of Uncle Sam's ammunition. But they kept on a-going jes the same. They were that full of fight that wild cats shore would have backed away from them. . . . They wanted to push right on and not stop until they got to Berlin. They cussed the Germans out for not standing and they kept yelling at them to wait and fight it out.[32]

The battle for Norroy was a bit of an anticlimax for York's men. Although they encountered heavy artillery fire, small arms fire, and machine guns, the Germans did not stay and fight. As the Americans swept down the heights into the village, the Germans withdrew to a better position north of the town. York observed: "But fast as we went forward the Germans kept on moving backwards, faster. They jes wouldn't stand and fight it out. Our battalion was right in the thick of it, and some of the other companies got mussed up right smart, but ours never lost a man."[33]

After capturing the town, York's men went from house to house, taking a German sniper prisoner. The captured German told the Americans that his unit was ordered to pull back and occupy the high ground 1.25 miles north of Norroy, near Vandieres.[34] The men also discovered that most of the French civilians were forcefully evacuated by the Germans before the attack, to reduce casualties. Unbeknownst to the Germans, 17 of the 330 residents hid in their cellars. They were elated to see the Americans.[35] While in town, York and his squad cautiously approached a house that looked like a fortified headquarters. They quickly broke down the door, expecting to find a group of die-hard Germans holding out inside. Instead, they were greeted by thousands of Belgium Hares, who jumped at the chance for freedom and scattered into the town instead of being served up for lunch. The men also liberated several barrels of German beer and French wine: "They knocked the bungs out of them and drinked a whole mess of it."[36]

Captain Danforth tried to organize his men for an anticipated German counterattack. As he yelled orders to his men to abandon their booty of German beer and French wine, he saw a soldier walking a goat on a leash. Danforth asked the solider what he was doing. The soldier replied, "Sir, I am jes going back to put a little cream in my coffee."[37] Danforth could only shake his head at such remarks, but he did get his men organized and dug in along the high, defendable ground north and northwest of Norroy. This placed the unit 1.25 miles in advance of its starting position, a location exposed to German enfilade fires from the east bank of the Moselle.

The anticipated German counterattack did not materialize. In spite of that, the Germans fired a heavy concentration of gas-laced artillery rounds into Norroy to stop any further American advance.[38] The attack began with a type of sneezing gas, to prevent the men from keeping their masks on. This was followed at noon with poisonous mustard gas. Fortunately, the unit's gas officer, Lieutenant Frank Holden, saw to it that every man kept his mask donned. Being in the valley, the gas settled over Norroy. The command set up their headquarters in the old town hall, but moved it outside of town to get away from the gas, just as German artillery destroyed the building.[39]

This German gas and artillery barrage was an attempt to block the Moselle River Road, which passed through Norroy, and prevent reinforcement of York's battalion, now deployed north of the town. What this German gas-laced barrage actually succeeded in doing was to prevent food from being brought to the men and force them to wear their gas masks throughout the day.

Late on 13 September the men saw a vineyard rich with grapes forward of their positions, near the German lines. Not having had food all day, the men attempted to liberate the grapes from the vines. But this placed them under the watch of a large, sausage-shaped German observation balloon. Whenever an American was in the vineyard, the Germans fired an artillery barrage. Orders were eventually issued forbidding the men from getting any more grapes. Later that night, York could not resist the temptation and quietly crawled into the vineyard because "we were very hungry, and them-there grapes jes natcherly made our mouths water."[40] As Alvin filled his belly with the French grapes, German artillery exploded around him. He quickly ran for cover, crashing into another American. It was Captain Danforth, who also could not resist the Norroy grapes. Both scurried back to their positions for a good laugh.[41]

As the Americans completed their reduction of the St. Mihiel salient, the 82nd advanced 1.25 miles north to seize Vandieres, so as to support the advance of the American 90th Division to their left. They took this area against heavy German resistance on 16 September. With this the offensive ended, having achieved all of its objectives with astonishing speed. As to the outcome of the St. Mihiel Offensive, the Americans performed superbly, having inflicted seven thousand German casualties, captured sixteen thousand men, seized 450 enemy artillery pieces, and liberated two hundred square miles of French territory.[42] The plan could not have occurred at a better time, catching the Germans in the midst of their retrograde operations out of the salient. General Pershing watched with satisfaction, as it was due to him that "after seventeen months . . . an American army was fighting under its own flag."[43] The attack cost the Americans seven thousand casualties, with the 82nd suffering 816. The All-Americans, although having a supporting role, achieved remarkable success in their advance up the Moselle River Valley.[44]

The St. Mihiel Operation resulted in changes to the unit's leadership. York's regimental commander, Colonel Nelson, was replaced by Lieutenant Colonel Richard Wetherill. York's battalion commander, Buxton, was moved to the division staff to serve as the inspector general. (Buxton had been directed to move to the division staff before St. Mihiel, but had asked for a postponement so that he could lead his battalion in combat.) The loss of Buxton was a tough blow to the battalion, for the men respected his humility and no-nonsense leadership style. This change also had implications for York. It was only due to Buxton's empathetic leadership style and Christian faith that Alvin had stayed in the army. Replacing Buxton was Captain James Tillman, the senior company commander in the battalion, who would lead the men in the Meuse-Argonne battle yet to come.[45]

With no time to rest, the 82nd All-American Division was replaced by the 69th French Infantry Division on 21 September.[46] After this was completed, the 82nd began a rushed sixty-two-mile westward journey by truck to support the Meuse-Argonne Offensive that was to begin on 26 September. The Meuse-Argonne Offensive would encompass some 1.2 million men and remains America's largest ever offensive. Reflecting on the week at St. Mihiel, York said: "It was a great success. The feeling of the majority of the boys was one hundred per cent, for General Pershing. As a whole the Army was back of him, believed in him, and would follow him anywhere. . . . But I never did hear of that-there goat any more. I don't know whether the boy got the cream for his coffee or not."[47]

6

Prelude to Battle

The Military Situation Before York's Battle

[The American soldiers looked like] Tommies in heaven. I
pressed forward . . . to watch the United States physically
entering the War, so god-like, so magnificent, and so
splendidly unimpaired in comparison with the tired, nerve-
racked men of the British army.
                    —English nurse Vera Brittain, on seeing
            the Americans arrive in France in April 1918

On 26 September 1918, the American Expeditionary Forces (AEF)
launched the Meuse-Argonne Offensive. The AEF initially had the
support of one hundred thousand French soldiers, encompassing six
of their divisions. These men reverted to French control after additional American units arrived from St. Mihiel. The Meuse-Argonne
Offensive was the first of four Allied attacks that spanned some two
hundred miles of the Western Front. This broad attack was designed
by Field Marshal Foch, the Allied generalissimo, to bring the war to
an end in 1918. This offensive, and the events that followed, would
elevate Alvin York to fame.

Foch's grand strategy looked much like American Confederate
general Robert E. Lee's "en echelon attack" that he used on 2 July
1863 at the Battle of Gettysburg.[1] The point of an en echelon attack is
to launch a series of assaults across a front to not only fix enemy units,
but also to draw away reserves, so that by the time the later attacks
occur, the enemy has little to no reserves remaining to bolster the
newly threatened sectors. The key to success in an en echelon attack
is forcing the enemy to weaken portions of his front, creating a vulnerability that the attacker can then exploit. With this in mind, Foch
ordered the AEF to spearhead the offensive on 26 September 1918.

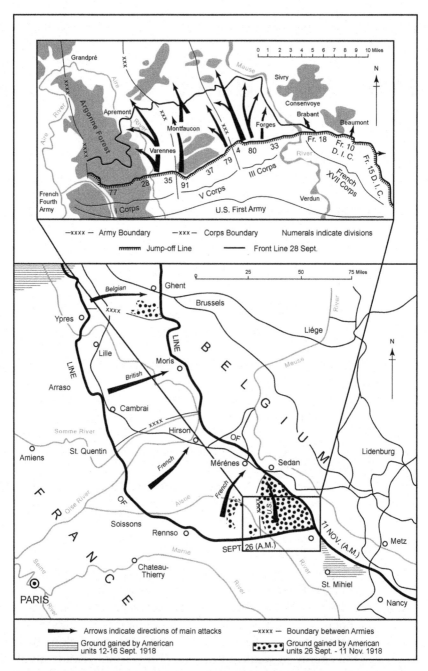

Map 2. The Western Front and the Meuse-Argonne Offensive, September 26, 1918.

The design of Foch's grand plan was that on 27 September—the day after the American assault—the First and Third British Armies were to strike, led by the Canadian Corps, against Canal du Nord, west of Cambrai. After this, King Albert's Belgians would advance north of Ypres on 28 September. The last attack would occur on 29 September, a Franco-British assault near St. Quentin. These four Allied hammer blows were to be sustained attacks that would over-whelm the German lines.[2] Being the first to attack, the AEF would receive the most attention from Germany's Field Marshal Hindenburg, who later said:

In the following days [after the German spring offensives failed], we essentially held the front against the enemy attacks. However, the situation changed with the expansion of the enemy offensive against Champagne on 26 September [the day that the American Meuse-Argonne Offensive commenced], which expanded the threat from the coasts to the Argonne. There, [in the Argonne region] the Americans penetrated our lines between the Argonne and Meuse River. Here, the . . . American power made itself manifest on the battlefield in the form of an independent army for the first time and validated itself there decisively.[3]

Thanks to the arrival of more than 1 million Americans, and the loss of nearly 1 million German soldiers during the spring offensive, the Allies now had a 37 percent advantage in men, giving them the flexibility to launch this new broad front offensive.[4] After only six weeks of action, Foch's grand strategy worked. The sustained pressure of these four massive attacks across a large portion of the Western Front was too much for the German Army.

General Pershing endorsed Foch's grand strategic plan, although in his view the American Expeditionary Forces had the most difficult task. The AEF had to fight against some of Germany's best divisions, across impossible terrain that threatened the heart of their vital Western Front command and control network: the Sedan-Mezieres rail line. According to Hunter Liggett, the commander of the American First Army, without this rail network the German Army in France and Belgium would wither on the vine.[5]

What complicated the American task was that the depth of German defenses across the Western Front varied greatly in late 1918, the most narrow point being in the Argonne region. This influenced how the German command responded to the American offensive. Below is the depth of German defenses across the Western Front:

Argonne	11.2 miles
Cambrai	18.6 miles
Laon	37.3 miles[6]

With the shallow sector in the Argonne, the Germans had little space to give up in the defense and were compelled to defend every line tenaciously. This is why the German command used the preponderance of their strategic reserves to stem the American attack, unlike at the BEF sector, where they could afford to trade land for time.

Called the "Meuse-Argonne Offensive," the American attack commenced on 26 September and continued until the Armistice on 11 November 1918. To accomplish this mission, the Americans poured more than 1.2 million men into the front, making the Meuse-Argonne Offensive the largest American military operation *ever.* By the time the guns fell silent, the Americans had deployed twenty-two divisions here, the equivalent of fifty-five French or British divisions.[7] To stop the Americans, Germany deployed forty-seven of its divisions and the last of its strategic reserves to the Meuse-Argonne area.[8]

In his desire to use the Americans to siphon off Germany's strategic reserves, Field Marshal Haig asked that his attack not occur until forty-eight hours after the Americans'. He wanted the Germans to send their reserves south, so that they would not be available to oppose his offensive. In his own words, Haig said to Foch, "I therefore do not propose to attack until the American-French attack has gone in [the Meuse-Argonne region]. This latter attack might draw off some of the enemy's reserves from our front. I therefore would like to attack two or three days after the main American-French attack. If we could arrange this, there is a chance of the enemy's reserves being unavailable."[9] The day that the Meuse-Argonne Offensive began, the German leadership committed most of its operational reserve divisions to guard its vulnerable flank, thus giving Haig's attack less German opposition than he otherwise would have confronted.

The severe terrain, combined with expert German defense,

made fighting in the Meuse-Argonne intense, and the lack of training made the offensive a costly episode for the United States. As the fighting droned on, the Germans grew increasingly concerned about the continual audacious attacks and pulled twenty-one of their divisions from the French and British sectors to stem the American offensive.

Although facing 25 percent of Germany's strength on the Western Front, the AEF broke the German lines on 1 November and penetrated the Kriemhilde (Siegfried) Stellung. In forty-seven days of combat in the Meuse-Argonne, the AEF inflicted 100,000 casualties, took 26,000 prisoners, and captured 847 cannons and some 3,000 machine guns. When the Armistice went into effect at 11:00 A.M. on 11 November, the Americans had more men on the front (more than 2 million) and controlled more of the line (21 percent of the Western Front, for a total of eighty-three miles)[10] than all other Allied nations except France.[11] Suffering some twenty thousand casualties a week, Pershing was certain that the AEF played a central role in ending the war in 1918.[12]

Due to the pressure that the Americans put on the enemy, the German military leadership lost flexibility as it gave up land in the north and flung most of its strategic reserves to the south. If the Americans broke through, it would be a catastrophe, as they would outflank the German Army. That was the crux of the matter. The Germans could only give up land in the north, where they conducted a lateral line of battle as part of a slow fighting withdrawal. Yet, victory in 1918 would not have been achieved without the combined effects of Foch's brilliant four-prong Belgian, French, British, and American offensive that overwhelmed the Germans. None of these armies had an easy time fighting the Germans in the last days of the war. For instance, the Canadian Corps, which spearheaded the BEF attack in the north of France, suffered 60 percent of its casualties in the last one hundred days. Such was the nature of the determined adversary that the Allies faced at the close of the war.

The Germans could not trade space for time in the Meuse-Argonne, as the Americans were close to severing the vital command network at Sedan. This was the challenge that General Max von Gallwitz faced as the German commander of the area—how to stop the Americans. Although a breakthrough came much later and at an incredibly higher cost in lives than Pershing had hoped, it did occur on 1 November.

The Meuse-Argonne campaign was not a smooth operation, as many American units lacked training in modern warfare and went into the war with a flawed, perhaps even outdated, military doctrine. This was compounded by Pershing's refusal to adopt the lessons that the British and French had acquired over the past three years of combat, out of fear that it would drive the offensive spirit from the Americans. Pershing's "cult of the rifle"—the flawed belief that the rifleman alone could break the stalemate of trench warfare—would cost many Americans their lives.[13] The idea was that élan and the bayonet would carry the day. Yet, when faced with machine guns this idea was proven wrong.[14] Pershing "tried to overcome this by increasing its forces in the front line; but this only intensified these difficulties and resulted in complete blocking of its rear and bottling up of its communications."[15] The tactic of throwing men into the line was so flawed that it caused Pershing to order a tactical pause of six hours during the *first day* of the attack to reset his divisions. Although the pause was necessary, it gave the Germans what they needed: time for reserves to bolster the line.

By October the American attack was hopelessly bogged down. From the western edge of the Argonne Forest and across the wide Meuse Valley, the combination of German ingenuity and American inexperience worked to frustrate Pershing's concept of the operation. The situation had to be altered. Pershing's staff, under the leadership of Colonel George C. Marshall, attempted to find a way to break the German lines.

Despite the staff planning, success in this phase of the Meuse-Argonne would turn upon the actions of three individuals.[16] These stretched across the front. Along the western edge of the Argonne Forest was the 77th "Liberty" Division, whose joint attack with the French seemingly failed on 2 October. However, a mixed command of 590 Americans found the seam between the German 76th Reserve Division and 2nd Württemberg Division and penetrated a mile behind the German lines. These Americans were called the "Lost Battalion" by the Allies and the "Amerikaner Nest" by the Germans. Despite incessant German attacks, the Americans held on for five days under the incredible leadership of Major Charles Whittlesey, ultimately resulting in the collapse of the German defense in the western Argonne.[17] However, the Germans would make the Lost Battalion pay heavily before the five days ended.

Farther to the east, in the midst of the Meuse Valley, the Germans here too thwarted American attempts to break out. During one of these attacks, an American company led by Lieutenant Sam Woodfill encountered sharp opposition around the village of Cunel. Despite the risks, Woodfill took action, fearlessly charging three successive groups of German defenders, even resorting to hand-to-hand combat in overcoming them.[18]

The third and final action that Pershing says played a central role in the AEF regaining the initiative was by Corporal Alvin York and sixteen other men from the 328th Infantry Regiment. That story will be told in the next chapter.[19]

Although the Meuse-Argonne Offensive was not as efficient as it should have been in its execution, it was indeed effective in supporting the overall Allied offensive by drawing off the preponderance of the German strategic reserves. This enabled the British-led forces farther to the north to exploit gaps in the German lines and thereby bring the war to a conclusion in November 1918. Yet, the question remains whether this could have been accomplished with less loss of life had the Americans been prepared for war instead of cobbling together an army at the last moment.

The sixty-two-mile move from Pont-à-Mousson to the Argonne was quite an adventure for Alvin. After riding part of the way in a small train and marching a fair distance, the regiment boarded a massive convoy of buses operated by colonial soldiers from French Indochina. The Americans called them Chinamen, and they gave York a harrowing fourteen-hour ride to the Argonne. York was intrigued by these foreign people: "I done never seen Chinaman before, and I jes couldn't keep my eyes off them. . . . Them Chinamen were the awfulest drivers you ever seed. They must have sorter had the idea they had to get us there before they even started. The way they done tore and bumped those old French buses over those old French roads was enough to make your hair stand up straight."[20]

The convoy took a break in Bar le Duc, where the soldiers purchased grapes and other fresh fruit from stands set up by French farmers. The men were heartened to be welcomed by their division commander, General William P. Burnham, who would be replaced by Major General George Duncan on 4 October. Burnham had been with the division since its creation at Camp Gordon and had a close affiliation with it. Pershing's order for Duncan to replace Burnham was based on an inspector general report in August 1918 that said Burnham lacked forcefulness and aggressiveness. One note in

31850

Buses operated by French Indochinese colonial soldiers. These bus drivers moved the Americans the one hundred miles from St. Mihiel to the
Argonne, giving York a harrowing fourteen-hour ride in the process. York
was intrigued by meeting these foreign people.

Pershing's file says that he was not "pushy" enough with his subor-
dinates. Although he performed well in the St. Mihiel Offensive in
September, Pershing had already decided that he would oust him
once he identified a suitable replacement.

On 3 October 1918, Pershing ordered Duncan, a personal friend,
to replace Burnham. Duncan was a proven leader, having already
commanded the 77th Division, and Pershing viewed him as the type
of aggressive—even ruthless—leader needed to carry the division
forward into the merciless battlegrounds of the Argonne. Duncan
was in Paris when the order arrived assigning him as the commanding general of the 82nd. He hurriedly packed his belongings and
set off for the Argonne region to find the division. (He had no idea
where it was.)[21] Meanwhile, Burnham was shipped off to Greece to
become the American military attaché.[22]

York's unit arrived at its debarkation point near Auzeville,
just east of Clermont-en-Argonne, where the buses stopped and

Major General George Duncan became the division commander of the 82nd on 4 October 1918, replacing Major General William Burnham, who was viewed as not aggressive enough by the overall American commander, John Pershing. Duncan was a true war fighter and would later order an investigation into the actions surrounding York's battle to see if it merited the awarding of the Medal of Honor. (AHEC)

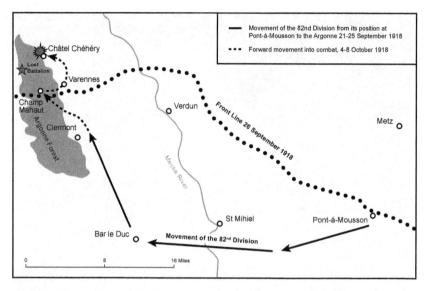

Map 3. Movement of York's unit from St. Mihiel to the Argonne Forest 21–25 September 1918.

the drivers announced, "Fini!" With that, the regiment off-loaded and moved to a bivouac south of the Argonne in a small wood. Some men were quartered in buildings, but most had to sleep on the muddy ground in their shelter halves. As the tired men settled in, they were startled awake by the opening barrage of the Meuse-Argonne Offensive, which shook the ground and lit up the sky as twenty-seven hundred artillery pieces fired a barrage against the German lines during the predawn hours. The men knew that it would be just a matter of time before they would be called forward to fight in the titanic struggle before them.[23]

York's division was placed in reserve. Meanwhile, the preponderance of the AEF was in the bloodiest fighting that they were to experience. During this time the AEF comprised forty-four divisions, twenty-nine of which saw combat. The AEF had by then more men on the front (1.3 million) and controlled more of the line (23 percent, or 101 miles) than every Allied nation except France.[24] Facing the Americans were forty German divisions.

The wait to go into the lines was no time of rest. The soldiers were on two-hour deployment orders: ready to go into the line at any moment. The rainy weather was punctuated with occasional sunshine, at which point the regimental band performed for the men. The records state that the men were in rather high morale, sensing that this could be the last great push, although "most of the men of the Division had now been in continuous bivouac in rain and cold weather since September 16. As a result of this exposure, many . . . were suffering from diarrhea, and hard colds."[25]

While waiting to be called into the battle, the men trained and received warm clothing, "which were mighty welcome because of the sudden drop of temperatures."[26] They also received several false alarms to deploy into the Argonne. York reflected on waiting to go into combat: "The war brings out the worst in you. It turns you into a mad, fightin' animal, but it also brings out something else, something I jes don't know how to describe, a sort of tenderness and love for the fellows fightin' with you. . . . I kinder did a lot of thinking and praying about these things as we moved out into the Argonne. Somehow, I seemed to jes know that we were going to get into it right, in them-there woods." York was correct. The Americans suffered some twenty thousand casualties a week during the Meuse-Argonne Offensive, and the 82nd All-American Division would soon pay its share.

York and the other Americans could not help but feel confident as they prepared to go into the lines. There were signs that Germany was weakening politically. On 29 September 1918, Kaiser Wilhelm was compelled to accept a less than obliging parliamentary government composed of Social Democrats who demanded an end to the war. Bulgaria also quit the war that same day, while the Ottoman Turks were close to capitulation as well, leaving only the weak Austro-Hungarian Empire as an ally. However, the Austro-Hungarians were ready to quit the war and had already made a peace overture. Among the many rumors that circulated was that the division would not enter the line because there were too many foreign-born soldiers in the ranks.[27]

Despite the various rumors, the 82nd was ordered into the Argonne. From 4 to 6 October, the division gradually made its way into the southern portion of the Argonne Forest, west of Varennes-en-Argonne. The route was roughly where the American 77th Division and the 28th U.S. Division had attacked on 26 September.[28] As the 82nd moved forward, the men were shocked by the carnage and devastation left behind from four years of war by the French and Germans that had left some 150,000 dead here between 1914 and

1918. The contrast was profound as the men walked through the lush virgin Argonne, being much as it had been since Noah's Flood, and then into an ugly landscape unlike anything they had traversed before. Devoid of vegetation, the ground was churned from the thousands of artillery rounds that had exploded upon it. Huge, gaping craters from the subterranean mine also scarred the land. It was a three-mile-wide swath of death.[29] York said, "The woods were all mussed up and looked as if a terrible cyclone done swept through them. But God would never be cruel enough to create a cyclone as terrible as that Argonne battle. Only man would ever think of doing an awful thing like that. It looked like the 'Abomination of Desolation' must have been."[30]

The men were happy not to bivouac in the graveyard of devastation from the war and continued their march a few miles farther north, into an "untouched" portion of the forest. York's regiment spent time near the extensive German bunker complex at Champ Mahaut.[31] Champ Mahaut is a large series of reinforced concrete bunkers built for the German Fifth Army headquarters that was commanded by Crown Prince Wilhelm. He used this complex to command the German assault against the west bank of the Meuse River during the Battle of Verdun in 1916. After this, on 5 October 1918, the 82nd Division deployed near the ancient French town of Varennes, where King Louis XVI and Queen Marie Antoinette were captured in 1791 while trying to flee the Paris revolutionaries. Ironically, the unit was stationed next to a large and well-kept German war cemetery.[32]

The morning of 6 October was deceptively calm for the 82nd. There was a slight breeze and a bright sun shining that day on the hillside where York and the rest of the 2nd Battalion, 328th Regiment, 82nd Division, were waiting for orders. As it was the Lord's Day, York's battalion chaplain, Daniel S. Smart from Cambridge, New York, gathered the men to preach his last sermon before being killed in action. It was an odd place for a church service, among the ruins of Varennes, with the rumble of artillery nearby and the ever-present German aircraft buzzing overhead.[33] At 10:00 A.M., Chaplain Smart pulled out his pocket Bible and read a selection from the New Testament to the hundreds of Doughboys who gathered to hear God's Word:

> I charge thee therefore before God, and the Lord Jesus Christ, who shall judge the quick and the dead at his appearing and

his kingdom; Preach the word; be instant in season, out of season; reprove, rebuke, exhort with all long suffering and doctrine. For the time will come when they will not endure sound doctrine; but after their own lusts shall they heap to themselves teachers, having itching ears; And they shall turn away their ears from the truth, and shall be turned unto fables. But watch thou in all things, endure afflictions, do the work of an evangelist, make full proof of thy ministry. For I am now ready to be offered, and the time of my departure is at hand. I have fought a good fight, I have finished my course, I have kept the faith: Henceforth there is laid up for me a crown of righteousness, which the Lord, the righteous judge, shall give me at that day: and not to me only, but unto all them also that love his appearing.[34]

Chaplain Smart's sermon and scripture were remembered by the men who survived the carnage that lay ahead.[35]

As many of the men heard their last sermon, the unit leadership was ordered forward to reconnoiter the terrain they would follow on the way to entering the battle.[36] At 8:00 P.M., the order finally arrived. The entire regiment would conduct an eight-mile night movement along the congested roads leading north out of Varennes, up the Meuse-Argonne Valley. Just a few miles west of this route was the formidable Argonne Forest, whose heights the Germans still possessed.

As this land was under German occupation for four years, the Huns knew where every choke point and intersection was located, and were sure to keep these areas under frequent barrage and gas attack to make night movement difficult. As long as the men moved in the darkness, and did not use lights, their chances of being bombarded by the Germans were reduced.[37] But even without German harassing fires movement would be difficult. The roads were packed with traffic—men, equipment, ambulances, horses, tanks, and supplies going forward to the battle, or back from it. In the darkness and chaos, the men were directed by yelling military police, who would order, "Hold up there! Move to the right of the road; Make room for an ambulance to pass!"[38]

The movement was stop and go, living up to the army maxim of hurry up and wait. After barely making it through Varennes, the regiment waited three hours on the sides of the road in a downpour to allow the 157th Artillery Brigade to pass. It had gotten bogged down in the old no-man's-land and had finally caught up with the division, disrupting its movement. This delay meant that the attacking units would go directly from the march into action.[39]

While waiting for the order to continue moving, the soldiers entertained themselves with boisterous singing (it was a singing division, after all) and storytelling. Trained entertainers, such as the vaudeville player Sergeant Parsons, rose to the occasion.[40] Despite the diversion, most of the soldiers had trouble masking their fear. Although disturbed by the death and devastation, Alvin found that his soul was at peace. Relying heavily on his personal faith, he prayed:

> O Jesus, the great rock of foundation
> Where on my feet were set with sovereign grace;
> Through Shells or Death with all their agitation
> Thou wilt protect me if I will only trust in thy Grace
> Bless thy holy name.[41]

Later that night the men were ordered to continue the march. The darkness was punctuated by German flares and star shells, which not only deprived the men of their night vision, but brought with them artillery and gas attacks. The heavy rain combined with the constant movement of men and materiel made the roads a terrible mess.[42]

The order given to the 82nd Division instructed it to "seize the eastern slopes of the Argonne Forest. . . . The . . . 82d Division will attack October 7."[43] The plan was in part to support an effort to relieve the Lost Battalion. With this in mind, the 82nd Division was to attack into the Argonne to rescue the Lost Battalion by outflanking the Germans. The idea was that a strike into the German flank would cause them to lift their siege of the 590 Americans. This attack would also clear the Germans from the eastern Argonne and thereby stop the fire that they had been pouring into the flank of the stalled American attack up the Meuse Valley.[44] But Major General Duncan was concerned about the lack of coordination and preparation that had gone into the plan being directed from higher headquarters, saying, "I was just handed the problem of making the attack. . . . There were no intelligence reports of the enemy."[45] Furthermore, no coordination had been conducted with the neighboring units (the

Map 4. American plan of action to move into the east flank of the Argonne Forest so as to outflank German forces besieging the Lost Battalion.

1st and 28th Infantry Divisions), upon whom Duncan would rely to secure his flanks. To compound the situation, Duncan would have to advance his division up one heavily congested road in hours of darkness, meaning that there was no way that the men would be in position on time. The bottom line was that York's unit would attack alone and blind deep into enemy territory, something that would cost them dearly in casualties. While considering the dilemma before him, Duncan wrote, "We were all rather depressed," and worried that simply throwing "a large body of troops to an assault without thorough orientation . . . presented very grave difficulties."[46]

York's 328th Regiment was to be in place on 7 October by 5:00 A.M. along the meandering Aire River. They needed to be in position before the Germans could detect their location, or else the enemy artillery would make them pay a heavy price. York's sister unit, the 1st Battalion, was ordered to attack through the village of Châtel Chéhéry and clear Hill 223 behind the town, referred to by the Germans as Schlossberg (Castle Hill). After sweeping past what intelligence predicted would be "token German resistance," the 1st Battalion would continue the attack into the Argonne Forest to sever the German supply road and rail network that was about 1.25 miles west of Châtel Chéhéry.[47] The Germans called this supply network the North–South Road. It was a wide road that also had a small-scale train network parallel to it (the Decauville Railroad).[48] If 1st Battalion could not seize the German supply road in the Argonne, the burden of doing so would fall to York's battalion. The idea was that if this road and rail line were severed, it would force the Germans out of the Argonne once and for all by depriving them of the only supply network in the forest.[49]

The movement to the staging areas was difficult, but most made it there before light. York's unit was set up in muddy craters along the military road. The 321st Machine Gun Battalion had to give way during their movement to allow an artillery unit to pass, which meant that when they took their positions they would be observed by the ever-watching Huns. Thankfully, a heavy fog delayed any German fires for the time being.[50] While York's 328th Regiment aligned itself for battle, its sister regiment, the 327th, stormed Hill 180, the bald hill north-northeast of Châtel, sweeping the Germans off of it in a well-orchestrated attack. The 327th came away with eighty-one German prisoners and captured four machine guns.[51] But the Germans proceeded to lay waste to Hill 180 with an artillery barrage and suppressive fire from nearby machine guns. Despite this, the men hung on. Thus far, the 82nd Division was giving a good showing of itself.[52]

As the fog slowly burned away, the 1st Battalion of the 328th Regiment moved across the Aire River in battle formation and attacked into Châtel Chéhéry to clear Hill 223 of Germans. Although the Americans were briefed by their intelligence section that the unit they were facing was not a highly rated force, the Germans here were the same ones that held off the 28th U.S. Division for more than a week along the Apremont Heights to the south, and were part of the force attacking the American Lost Battalion. This so-called second-rate division, the German 2nd Württemberg Landwehr

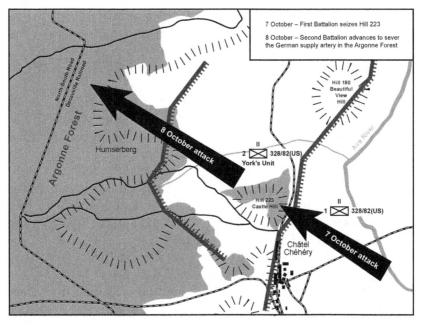

Map 5. Planned U.S. 82nd Division attack into the Argonne, 7–8 October 1918.

Division, was good enough not only to stop the American advance in the Argonne Forest, but also to play the key role in blunting the entire American offensive.[53] This German division took pride in that it only lost ground when the high command ordered it to do so. In fact, when the American 28th U.S. "Keystone" Division had moved into Châtel Chéhéry the previous day, it had been forced back by the Württembergers from the 2nd Landwehr Division.[54] The American intelligence picture of the enemy situation was so clouded that day that they even reported to the 82nd not to expect resistance on Hill 223 as it was "already in American hands." In fact, Hill 223 was firmly German. They would not give up easily, and would bleed the 1st Battalion, 328th Regiment, so badly that the Americans would not even come close to achieving their objective.[55]

The German 2nd Württemberg Landwehr Division commander, General Anton Franke, knew that the Americans would attack Schlossberg (Hill 223), and he fortified it under the command of Hauptmann (Captain) Müller and assigned him the mission of holding the hill.[56] The rough Argonne terrain favored the defense, with its steep hills, rugged valleys, and thick forests. Adding to this barbwire, machine guns, and rifle pits, it seemed impregnable.[57] The importance of Castle Hill/Hill 223 was that whoever controlled it controlled access to the Argonne. Because of that, it had strategic value.[58]

York and the men watched as their brother soldiers moved across some 1.25 miles of open, up-sloping terrain to attack into Châtel Chéhéry. Thankfully, the regimental commander, Colonel Wetherill, secured a good look at Hill 223 and realized that, contrary to intelligence reports, it was firmly held by a German battalion. There was no way his men could take it without a heavy artillery preparation. Because of this, Wetherill delayed the attack for two hours, until the barrage could precede his men up the hill. Once the barrage commenced, the men advanced.[59]

As the Americans advanced, a heavy German artillery barrage erupted on the battalion as it crossed the Aire River. This was witnessed by York and the men of 2nd Battalion, watching from their support position. The German barrage was supported by heavy machine gun fires from the hill that the 1st Battalion was about to storm.[60] In spite of this, the Americans of 1st Battalion, 328th Regiment, pushed on, successfully taking Hill 223 around 1:00 P.M. after a heavy American barrage racked the hill. This barrage fatally wounded the German commander, Hauptmann Müller, who was captured by the Americans where he fell, with his regimental surgeon, Doctor Kögel, remaining by his side. It seemed that just perhaps the Americans had captured the hill.[61]

Despite the good news, the capture of Hill 223 was only the beginning. The German 2nd Württemberg Landwehr Division commander planned on throwing the Americans off of this vital key terrain feature and launched a series of counterattacks that would last through the night. To do this, he moved up a battery of 77 mm field guns from his divisional artillery regiment to provide direct fire that he hoped would blast the Americans off of the hill. Additionally, the Pahl Kompanie of the top-rated 5th Prussian Guards Division was to support the attack.[62] The Germans nearly prevailed in winning back the hill, with the Americans resorting to their .45 Colt pistols and their backs literally at the edge of the eastern cliff overlooking Châtel Chéhéry. It was such a close-run battle that a regimental runner reported that the hill was lost.[63]

The cost for the Germans was incredible. From the 125th

German Württembergers on the attack. The overall German commander of the region looked upon his Württemberg soldiers as the most reliable fighters he had. Von Gallwitz had planned a devastating counterattack against York's regiment for 10:30 A.M. on 8 October 1918. York's action foiled this plan. (Mastriano Collection)

Württemberg Landwehr Regiment, two company commanders, Leutnant Gugeler and Leutnant Butz, were seriously injured in the attack, while another officer was missing in action and presumed dead. Hauptmann Bast charged up the hill, leading his company, but died in the attempt with many of his men. Perishing with him was the Württemberg 3rd Machine Gun Company commander, Leutnant Pfizer.[64] Despite their losses, the Germans attacked through the night and into the early morning of 8 October.

As the battle raged, York and the men of 2nd Battalion could only hope and pray that their brothers in 1st Battalion could hold Hill 223. However, the Germans did all they could to make life miserable for York and his men as well. To prevent the battalion from moving up in support, the Germans barraged it with artillery and strafed it with German aircraft, and German forward observers directed artillery fire against the 82nd's machine gun unit, wounding and killing scores. This was only a few feet from where York and his men were deployed, and they helped recover the dead and mangled bodies.[65]

Other units from the regiment suffered scores of casualties from these German barrages as well. The Germans fired primarily a mix of 77s and Austrian 88 mm field guns. The difference was that the men usually heard the 77s incoming, while the 88s were not heard until the explosion. This made the Meuse Valley a terrible place to seek refuge, with disfigured horses, dead Americans, dead Germans, destroyed tanks, and hundreds of wounded everywhere—and the ever-present artillery constantly adding to the casualty toll.[66] Meanwhile, York's unit took cover in muddy craters to avoid the shrapnel of bursting artillery. This was a view of the war that these men hitherto had not witnessed. York wrote: "And oh, my! we had to pass the wounded. And some of them were on stretchers going back to the dressing stations and some of them were lying around moaning and twitching. And the dead were all along the road and their mouths were open and their eyes, too, but they couldn't see nothing no more nohow. And it was wet and cold and damp. And it all made me think of the Bible and the story of the anti-Christ and Armageddon."[67]

Due to the stubborn defense of the German Württembergers, the American 1st Battalion failed to get anywhere near the Decauville Railroad; barely holding onto a narrow piece of Hill 223 was the best it could do. The burden now fell to York's 2nd Battalion. Field Order number 2 reached the men at 11:00 P.M. on 7 October, directing the 2nd Battalion, 328th Regiment, to pass through the remnants of the

1st Battalion at 5:00 A.M. and resume the attack into the Argonne to seize the German supply network.[68]

As York's officers feverishly planned the attack, the Germans launched night attacks to dislodge the fractured survivors of the American 1st Battalion. When the attacks ended, the Germans retained control of the western half of Hill 223, with the Americans barely holding the eastern edge.[69] York and his men would face these stalwart Germans the next day. This so-called second-rate German unit would make 8 October 1918 the single bloodiest day in the 2nd Battalion's history.[70] Yet, if the Americans managed to puncture the line here, it could result in the encirclement of several German regiments. To prevent this, the German command ordered their units to pull back from the Lost Battalion siege, thus ending the five-day ordeal for the Americans four miles to the west.[71]

As York's 2nd Battalion prepared to attack into the Argonne, the Germans were busy with their own preparations. The German command had its hands full on 7–8 October 1918. Since the start of their campaign, the Americans had cut an eleven-mile thrust up the Meuse Valley deep into German lines. To counter this, the Germans used the rugged nature of the Argonne Forest to stem the American push. As a result, the Germans had a deep salient that overlooked the western half of the American flank. By 7 October 1918 there were three significant threats facing General von Gallwitz in the Meuse-Argonne region.

German General Max von Gallwitz commanded the forces fighting the Americans in the Meuse-Argonne Offensive. Von Gallwitz proved an adept and perceptive foe. (Mastriano Collection)

The first problem for the German command was the "Ameri-kaner Nest," the Lost Battalion of the 77th U.S. Infantry Division along the western edge of the Argonne Forest already discussed. The second issue for the Germans was the American attacks against the eastern flank of the Argonne Forest by the 82nd and 28th Infantry Divisions. This was sound tactical doctrine, and von Gallwitz knew that the Americans intended to liberate the Lost Battalion "Ameri-kaner Nest" by hitting his flank. The third issue for the Germans was that they had to stop the main U.S. attack up the Meuse River Valley. This American push threatened to cut the main German rail network and supply artery in Sedan, thirty miles to the north. This was the most dangerous of the three tactical situations facing the 5th German Army. The 2nd Württemberg Landwehr Division chroni-cled the predicament:

> The General HQ was concerned about these occurrences and committed elements of the 1st Guard Infantry Divi-sion, a portion of the 52nd Reserve Division, the 210th and 212th Regiments of the 45th Reserve Division, the Machine Gun Sharpshooters 47 and 58. However, fighting east of the Aire River, in the woods around Sommerance and Romagne fighting suddenly became intense, so that one could not support both locations. We had to stop the enemy's main attack, which was now east of the Aire [in the Meuse River Valley]. So our artillery around Hohenbornhöhe was used to provide fires against his flank.[72]

Before York's unit attacked into the Argonne, the German 2nd Württemberg Landwehr Division, which included the 120th, 122nd, and 125th Regiments, was digging defensive positions along the eastern edge of the forest. They had been making preparations here since 2 October.[73] A few miles off to the west, portions of the 122nd Landwehr Regiment were helping to fight the Lost Battalion, the "Amerikaner Nest."[74] Meanwhile, the German 1st Battalion, 120th Regiment, under the command of Leutnant Paul Vollmer, was the last of the division to pull back from Apremont Woods to the valley behind Châtel Chéhéry to serve as a reserve.[75] This was a welcome reprieve for Vollmer's men, who had been in the thick of the fight-ing since the Americans launched the Meuse-Argonne Offensive on 26 September.[76]

Leutnant Paul Jürgen Vollmer, or "Kuno" as his friends called him, was a highly decorated soldier. He would play *the* central role in the action against York on 8 October. Vollmer was from the German kingdom of Württemberg and a member of the 2nd Württemberg Landwehr Division, which was similar to an American National Guard division. Vollmer had participated in Western Front campaigns going back to 1914.[77] The Argonne was like a second home to both him and his division, for they had served and fought in this area for nearly four years. Vollmer had assumed command of the 120th Regiment's 1st Battalion after its commander was wounded fighting off an American attack on 29 September. The majority of the soldiers in the 120th were from his hometown of Ulm, where he worked as the assistant postmaster. Vollmer actually started off the war in the sister regiment, the 125th, but transferred back to the 120th in 1916 to command a company.[78]

The six-mile move for Vollmer's men on 7 October to a position west-northwest of Châtel Chéhéry proved difficult. Harassed on the way by American artillery, the battalion took a greater part of the day before it finally arrived at its assigned location.[79] Vollmer described his move to Châtel Chéhéry as difficult: "While marching back to the reserve line, 7 October, and again while returning to the firing line the same day, we passed a great number of artillery positions that had been shot to bits and were in a state of chaos. Part of my own company, the 5th Company 120th Landwehr, was lying on the North South Road; some dead and others wounded, these men were the victims of one single shell."[80]

While Vollmer's men were on the march, the 2nd Württemberg Landwehr Division saw that the Americans were preparing to attack into the Argonne Forest. Initial elements of the 28th U.S. Division approached Châtel Chéhéry, but they were easily repulsed. After this, troops from the U.S. 82nd Division moved into the town and prepared to attack Castle Hill and a smaller hill a little over a half-mile to the north that the Germans called Beautiful View Hill (Hill 180). Both were key pieces of terrain that dominated Châtel Chéhéry and provided an excellent view of the Meuse Valley, perfect for calling artillery strikes against the American main attack down in the valley.

With the Americans in control of Hill 180 and the eastern slope of Hill 223, the last of the reserves available in the area were called to deploy in support of the 2nd Württemberg Division. This included two regiments (the 210th and 212th) of the 45th Prussian Reserve Division that would launch counterattacks at 10:30 A.M. on 8 October.[81] The 212th Prussian Reserve Infantry Regiment was directed to help the 125th Landwehr retake Beautiful View Hill (Hill 180), and the 210th Prussian Reserve Infantry Regiment was to assist the 120th in recapturing Castle Hill (Hill 223) and thereby push the Americans out of the Argonne.[82]

As another rainy and muddy autumn day ended, Vollmer's battalion finally arrived at its position west of Châtel Chéhéry in the Argonne late on 7 October. The battalion was supposed to deploy 0.9 miles northwest of Castle Hill. Yet, like the rest of what Vollmer was supposed to accomplish that day, this was too difficult to execute. As Vollmer's men occupied the area, American artillery began falling on them. Vollmer saw the valley and meadow below him, about a half-mile closer to the front, and decided to position his unit there. The meadow below "Humserberg," the center hill in the valley behind Châtel Chéhéry, commanded everything in this part of the Argonne. The 2nd Landwehr's operations officer, Major Spang, noted that the division was "lacking sufficient men to form a solid line, [so] we put up strong points and machine gun nests at vantage points in the terrain." This was a good plan and enough to gain the time needed for the 212th and 210th Regiments to arrive for the counterattack the next morning.[83]

Late on 7 October, the 125th and 120th Regiments prepared for battle. The 120th's 2nd Machine Gun Company set up positions along Hill 2, just forward and south of Vollmer's battalion. Later that night, Vollmer's 4th Company commander, Leutnant Fritz Endriss, identified gaps in the regiment's line between his position and the 2nd Machine Gun Company. One of Endriss's platoon leaders, Leutnant Karl Kübler, was so anxious to fill the gap that Endriss allowed him to personally ask Vollmer for permission to move his platoon between the battalion and the machine gun company. He told Vollmer, "I regard our situation as very dangerous, for the Americans could easily pass through the gaps in the sector of the 2nd Machine Gun Company and gain our rear."[84]

Vollmer directed Kübler to establish liaison with the 2nd Machine Gun Company, which meant that the gap in the line was larger than anticipated. To remedy this, Kübler insisted that Endriss send a note to Vollmer that stated, "I will, on my own responsibility, occupy Hill 2 with part of 4th Company."[85] Vollmer appreciated his initiative but wrote back to him that Major Spang's orders to establish strongpoints stood. Besides, reinforcements were due to arrive, which included not only the 210th Prussian Regiment but also the Bavarian 7th Mineur Company. With this in mind, he told Kübler, "You will hold the position to which you have been assigned."[86]

As the time for the American attack approached, Vollmer's position was fairly secure, for the terrain favored the Germans. Furthermore, on his left was the 125th Württemberg Regiment, with the nearest company from that regiment under the command of Leutnant Paul Lipp, a friend with whom Vollmer served between 1914 and 1916.[87] Tied in with Lipp, and on Vollmer's battalion seam, was his most trusted leutnant in the battalion, Fritz Endriss. Endriss had an excellent reputation as a soldier and an eye for good terrain. In this case, Endriss used a French seventeenth-century border trench as the central point for his company's defensive line. This trench was on the southern face of Lipp's center hill and had excellent line of sight to Castle Hill, making it the center of gravity for Vollmer's entire defensive scheme. The valley here would be covered by German units on the hills to the north (125th Regiment), south (120th Regiment and Bavarian 7th Mineur Company), and west (120th and 125th Regiments), in addition to Vollmer's battalion in the meadow.[88] There was no way for the Americans to win.

The German plan for 8 October was that the remnants of Battalion Müller on Castle Hill would defend as long as their ammunition held out. Once they delayed the Americans in this fashion, Battalion Müller would withdraw from that hill and reinforce the 125th on Humserberg.[89] As the Americans chased these "retreating" Germans, they would fall into the trap. Once the Americans were halfway across the valley behind Châtel Chéhéry, the Germans would open fire on them from the ridges to the north, west, and south. This would destroy the attacking American battalion.[90]

After this, the 120th (reinforced by the 210th Prussian Regiment) and the 125th (reinforced by the 212th Prussian Regiment) would launch a counterattack at 10:30 A.M. on 8 October that would completely sweep the Americans from the valley and retake Castle Hill (Hill 223) and Beautiful View Hill (Hill 180). This would threaten the American main attack up the Meuse Valley and secure the German position in the Argonne, potentially throwing off the American scheme of maneuver for weeks. It was the perfect plan. It was into this death trap that Alvin York's 2nd Battalion, 328th Regiment, 82nd Division, would attack.[91]

7

One Day in October

I'm a-telling you that-there valley was a death trap. . . . The
Germans done got us. . . . I'm a-telling you they were shooting
straight, and our boys jes done went down like the long grass
before the mowing machine at home. Our attacks jes faded
out.

—Alvin York

The concept of American operations for 8 October 1918 was to
launch a three-prong attack into the Argonne, with York's battalion
advancing in the center while the 1st Battalion pushed from its position on Castle Hill to the right.[1] The 3rd battalion would serve in
reserve, and the nearby 28th Division would attack just south of the
82nd. The 328th Regiment's attack was part of a larger assault that
day, which included the 110th Infantry Regiment of the 28th U.S.
Division providing a supporting attack to seize the high ground
on the left, while another regiment of the 82nd Division, the 327th,
would attack on the right, toward the village of Cornay.[2] The time
of the attack that would propel Alvin York to renown was changed
from 5:00 A.M. to 6:00 A.M., to give artillery, as well as the men, a
chance to be in place. The attack would be preceded by a ten-minute
artillery barrage, with the men stepping off immediately after that
at 6:10 A.M. Understanding that its sister battalion had had a terrible battle there on 7 October fighting for Hill 223, York's unit was
reinforced with a machine gun company and a one-pounder mortar
platoon. A company of fifteen American-manned French light tanks
was also available to support the attack if needed. Unfortunately,
the terrain was not suitable for the tanks to operate.[3]

York and his battalion attempted to sleep on the drenched,
muddy ground near the Aire River, only getting wetter and dirtier
as heavy rain fell on them through the night. At 3:00 A.M., Captain
Danforth and Lieutenant Stewart organized the men to begin their

York passed through the village of Châtel Chéhéry early in the morning on 8 October 1918 just before participating in a bloody attack against German defensive lines. The village, nestled against the dense Argonne Forest, was untouched for most of the war and was used by German soldiers between 1914 and 1918 as a rest area. By the time that York's regiment arrived, the town had suffered damage from American artillery. (AHEC)

movement to Châtel Chéhéry.[4] According to the plan, York's battalion would pass through the remnant of the Americans holding Hill 223 and then wait for the moment to attack.[5] Most of the bridges of the Aire River had been destroyed by the Germans, so American engineers laid narrow boards for the crossing. Despite the darkness, this was accomplished without incident. Once across the river, the battalion reformed and began the steep half-mile hike up to the village of Châtel Chéhéry.[6]

Although there was a fog in the Meuse Valley the morning of 8 October, the day promised to be clear and sunny, giving the Germans excellent observation. As the Americans made the climb to the village, German lookouts on the edge of the Argonne saw them.[7] Within moments, enemy artillery harassed the 328th Regiment's movement to its jump-off line. This included poisonous gas, which further slowed the formation, as they had to stop to don their masks and then move through the darkness with them on. One of the German artillery rounds exploded in the midst of the column, killing an entire squad.[8] York reflected on this: "They done laid down the meanest kind of a barrage too, and the air was jes full of gas. But we put on our masks and kept plugging and slipping and sliding, or falling into holes and tripping over all sorts of things and getting up again and stumbling on for a few yards and then going down again, until we done reached the hill."[9]

York remembered this movement to Hill 223 as slow and chaotic. There was no quiet in the Meuse Valley. Rather, it was alive with the movement of tens of thousands of men, trucks, and horses, mingled with the terrific explosions of artillery and the splattering of machine gun fires. The men constantly slipped and fell onto the muddy ground and easily lost their way in the darkness despite the frequent bright flashes. Of this, York says, "We were marching, I might say floundering around, in column of squads. The noise were worse than ever, and everybody was shouting through the dark, and nobody seemed to be able to hear what anybody else said."[10]

Just as twilight was breaking, the men made it to Hill 223, much to the relief of the survivors who had held the hill against incredible odds since the previous day. One of the units that York's men relieved was "B" Company, which had lost sixty-three men.[11] As the men of the 2nd Battalion waited for the order to attack, they all knew that this would be a vicious fight. On the brink of entering the abyss of a violent battle, their thoughts were on everything from home to loved ones. For Private Mario Muzzi, it was his thirtieth birthday. His gift would be his life. He would be the sole survivor of his squad, with the rest being killed in only a few hours.[12]

In York's platoon was Corporal Cutting. York and Cutting had never overcome their antipathy. Cutting distrusted York and wondered if he would do his duty and kill Germans. As York led the squad on the left of the attack formation, Cutting wondered, "Would he run and leave us exposed?"[13] Yet, Cutting was troubled by even greater matters. Since he had lied about his name to join the army, he wondered how his mother would ever know of his death. His entire service record was a fabrication, with a false name, a fictitious hometown, and an invented career listed on it. There were no clues that Cutting was really Otis B. Merrithew.[14] Fearing that he would be kicked out of the army for perjury if he told the truth, he never uttered a word of this, not even to his friend Bernie Early.[15] As

"Cutting" was about to come clean about this to Early, it was time to "go over the top," and the secret went with him into battle and nearly into the grave.[16]

As the Americans waited for the order to attack, the Germans were making final preparations to repulse them from the Argonne entirely. The German battalion commander, Leutnant Paul Vollmer, only a mile across the valley from the Americans, had a mix of good and bad reports that morning. Organizing his defense from a small wooden hut in the meadow below Humserberg, he still had concerns about gaps on his right flank. Adding to this anxiety was that his adjutant, Leutnant Bayer, was being treated by medics as the result of being gassed near Apremont the previous day. Vollmer directed Leutnant Karl Glass to serve as the acting adjutant until Bayer returned, leaving one less officer in the line.[17]

But things started to look up after the Bavarian 7th Mineur (Sapper) Company, under Leutnant Max Thoma, arrived with a lead detachment of men from the 210th Prussian Reserve Regiment. Vollmer expertly placed the two units in the gaps on Hill 2 that Kübler and Endriss complained about previously. The Bavarian lieutenant, Max Thoma, was satisfied with his position and he colocated with the machine guns of Vollmer's 2nd Company, which had excellent fields of fire up the valley. All of the gaps in Vollmer's line were now sealed, and his men were ready to make this a bloody day for the Americans.[18]

As the hour struck, things started to go terribly wrong for the Americans. The American infantry units were ready to attack and waited for the explosions of supporting artillery to blast a way through the Germans. The barrage, however, never materialized. As the time ticked away toward the 6:10 A.M. assault, the officers had a quick meeting, with Captain Tillman deciding that the men would go over with or without the barrage. Tillman ordered the light mortar platoon and the machine gun company supporting his unit to open fire with everything they had.[19] Although making a lot of noise, these did nothing to the German defenders, who were safe in their positions.[20]

At precisely 6:10 A.M., the officers of 2nd Battalion, 328th Infantry Regiment, blew their whistles and ordered the men to attack. As there were few trenches on Hill 223, the men were largely crouching or sitting on the back slope of the hill jutting above Châtel Chéhéry. The large American battalion attacked into the valley in two waves,

York's nemesis was Leutnant Paul Vollmer. After four years of combat experience, Vollmer had demonstrated that he was a reliable and hard fighting officer. Vollmer set up his battalion headquarters in a small shack similar to the one in this photograph along the eastern edge of the Argonne Forest. York would capture Vollmer near his headquarters on the morning of 8 October 1918. (NARA)

with two companies in each wave moving parallel.[21] A hundred yards separated the waves. York's unit was in the second half of the lead attacking company, on the left. Immediately they crashed into the remnants of Battalion Müller hidden along the low western slope of Castle Hill.[22] York noted of these defenders, "And there were some snipers and German machine guns left there hidden in the brush and in fox holes. And they sniped at us a whole heap. I guess we must have run over the top of some of them, too, because a little later on we were getting fire from the rear."[23] Battalion Müller held on until its 1st Company, 47th MG Sharpshooters, ran out of ammunition. After this, the Germans here retreated across the valley to the lines of the 125th Regiment.

With Battalion Müller out of the way, the Americans cleared Hill 223 and plunged into the valley. The Americans could not but be disheartened by the terrain that was now before them. As they came out of the woods behind Hill 223, the battalion entered a clear and steep valley about a half-mile wide. This dead space was devoid of trees, with the ground sloped down to a narrow stream and from there jutting up sharply to the large, heavily forested hills of the ancient Argonne Forest. The soldiers knew that the ground favored the German defenders greatly, and this notion was made clear when the Germans opened fire on them from the north, south, and west.[24] York described the terrible situation that they faced:

> The Germans met our charge across the valley with a regular sleet storm of bullets. I'm a-telling you that-there valley was a death trap. It was a triangular-shaped valley with steep ridges covered with brush, and swarming with machine guns on all sides. I guess our two waves got about halfway across and then jes couldn't get no further nohow. The Germans done got us and they done got us right smart. They jes stopped us in our tracks. Their machine guns were up there on the heights overlooking us and well hidden, and we couldn't tell for certain where the terrible heavy fire was coming from. It 'most seemed as though it was coming from everywhere.[25]

Things were far worse than any of the Americans realized. Not only were the Germans well positioned to defend here, but Major Tillman's battalion was attacking alone, with no support on either its left or right flanks. The Pennsylvanians, who were to advance on the left flank, had hit tough German resistance and were unable to advance.[26]

Due to a last-minute change in the plan, Tillman's battalion was also attacking in the wrong direction. Corps headquarters had changed the unit's attack plan and objective early on the morning of 8 October. Instead of attacking in a northwesterly direction to sever the German supply road in the Argonne, York's unit was supposed to attack due west, so as to have the protection of the Pennsylvanians on the left flank. But the runner delivering the message to Major Tillman was killed just below Hill 223 and the order never arrived. The 82nd unit attacking on the right flank *did* receive the order, although only after it had attacked.[27] Having the new plan of attack, the supporting unit on the right flank of York's battalion swung away to the north, leaving York's battalion on its own, with both its right and left flanks "in the air."[28]

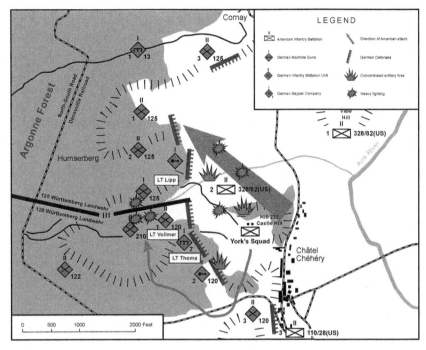

Map 6. York's unit attacks into the Argonne Forest, 8 October 1918.

Leading the attack in front of York was his platoon leader, Lieutenant Kirby Stewart, holding his Colt pistol high in the air as he waved them forward. As Lieutenant Stewart and his men reached the center of the open valley, a burst of machine gun fire from the center hill cut the lieutenant down, throwing him about like a rag doll. His legs were shattered by a blast of German machine gun bullets. With every attempt to get up, he crumpled into a heap. With incredible bravery Stewart continued forward, dragging himself on the ground and every few seconds waving his pistol in the air and yelling to encourage his men. Before the platoon could reach the lieutenant, another German bullet hit him in the head, killing him instantly.[29] Command of the platoon now went to Sergeant Parsons.[30]

By now, the attack was stopped in the middle of the valley, with the men facing in a northwesterly direction. Now began the impossible task of digging into indefensible ground. Sergeant Parsons tried to get orders from Captain Danforth, but could not. Captain Danforth was farther to the right, leading the preponderance of the company in trying to get around the northeastern portion of Hum-serberg, the hill in the center of the valley. The burden of command in the middle fell to Parsons. He moved about checking his men and surmised the situation.[31]

As the Americans had attacked to the northwest, the left flank was being racked by German machine guns from the large hill in the center of the valley. Seeing this, Parsons saw that the center hill that the Germans often referred to Humserberg was his biggest problem and that the machine guns on that specific hill had to be taken out. In this he was absolutely correct, as a large group of soldiers from the German 125th Landwehr Württemberg Regiment and a com-pany from the 5th Prussian Guards were positioned there and had excellent lines of sight into the American flank. One of the German company commanders stationed on this center hill was Leutnant Paul Lipp, who would play a key part in the York story.[32] Parsons ordered Early, Cutting, York, and Savage to lead their squads to take out the German machine guns on the center hill.[33]

Corporal Early was serving as acting sergeant and was in charge of these four squads, with Cutting, York, and Savage being his other noncommissioned officers.[34] Two men from this element had already fallen in combat, leaving seventeen soldiers to make the flank attack that would decide the outcome of the day's battle. The platoon included Bernard Early, Corporal York, Corporal Savage, Corpo-ral Cutting, and Privates Maryan Dymowsky, Carl Swansen, Fred Wareing, Ralph Wiler, Mario Muzzi, William Wine, Percy Beards-ley, Patrick Donohue, Thomas Johnson, Joseph Kornacki, Michael Sacina, Feodor Sok, and George Wills. Early surveyed the ground as the squad leaders gathered their men in the midst of German artil-lery that was now falling upon them.[35] Directly south, Early saw a deep, natural notch cut into the ridge and determined that this was the best place to attempt the flanking maneuver.[36]

However, moving the men in a parallel direction under German machine gunners across exposed ground would be difficult—if not impossible—to accomplish. As the group of seventeen began their sprint for the southern hill, suddenly a barrage of artillery erupted near them. It was the belated American artillery support, and at that moment it was actually rolling across the southern ridgeline where the seventeen Americans were attempting to move. This artillery fire was exploding upon the German 2nd Württemberg Machine Gun Company, which was deployed there. The timing of the barrage

A 75 mm gun of the 108th Field Artillery fires against German positions near Châtel Chéhéry to support the attack of York's 82nd Division in October 1918. (NARA)

caused the German gunners to seek cover just at the moment when the seventeen Americans were in their sights. Because of this, all seventeen of the Americans made it up the hill unseen and unhurt.[37]

Bernie Early led the group in good order up the hill and into the forest. For the men, it was a relief to be out of the death trap of a valley. Early next turned the men west so that they could move into the Argonne Forest. This would enable them to move behind and around the flank of the German machine guns on the center hill that were holding up the attack in the valley. An hour elapsed during this movement. The men advanced slowly to ensure that they would not be discovered by Germans.[38]

Early's platoon continued moving behind the German lines for some five hundred yards, then stopped so he could confer with York, Cutting, and Savage. Early thought they needed to go farther before turning the German flank, but he wanted to see what his leaders thought. Savage and Cutting thought they had gone far enough, while York suggested that they move a bit farther west

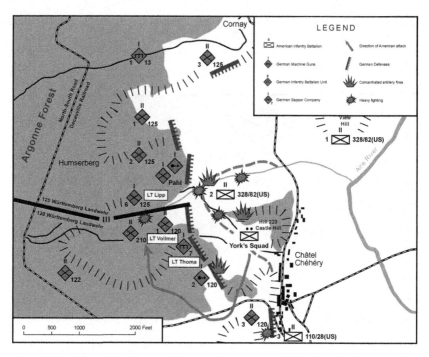

Map 7. York's unit is stopped in the Argonne, and York and sixteen other soldiers maneuver into the German flank.

before attacking into the German flank. Early went with York's recommendation and continued moving. After a few minutes the seventeen Americans came across a shallow trench cutting across the northern face of the ridge. Early held another leaders' conference and asked York, Savage, and Cutting what they thought—continue west into the forest or turn the German flank. This time the consensus was to turn the flank by moving down this trench. The trench was about three feet deep and was great a way to reduce their vulnerability to observation.[39]

The trench was actually not part of the German defenses. It was a border line between private and communal land, dug in the seventeenth century.[40] As it was not constructed for military purposes, it was a straight trench, carved into the northern face of the southern ridgeline that overlooked the valley from which these Americans had come.[41] The trench ended near the base of the hill, facing north, and just above a supply road that the Germans had carved into the Argonne Forest. The Americans followed the supply road for a short distance to the west, where they came upon a small stream. Bending over the stream were two German sanitation soldiers, with Red Cross armbands, filling canteens. Leutnant Vollmer had sent these men a few minutes earlier from his headquarters to retrieve water for the men.[42]

The Germans froze momentarily in disbelief. When they saw the Americans surge toward them, the two dropped their water bottles, which made a series of loud, hollow metallic clangs, and ran for their lives. The Germans ran northeast, across a dense meadow, headed straight back to Vollmer's headquarters to alert the commander to the presence of the Americans. The Germans ran as fast as they could, with the Americans hot on their trail.[43] York recollected:

> They jumped out of the brush in front of us and run like two scared rabbits. We called to them to surrender, and one of our boys done fired and missed. And they kept on a-going. And we kept on after them. We wanted to capture them before they gave the alarm. We now knowed by the sounds of the firing that we were somewhere behind the German trench and in the rear of the machine guns that were holding up our big advance [on the big center hill]. We still couldn't see the Germans and they couldn't see us. But we could hear them machine guns shooting something awful. Savage's squad was leading, then mine, and then Cutting's. Sergeant Early was out in front, leading the way.[44]

Meanwhile, Leutnant Vollmer had moved forward with his battalion to bolster the 2nd Machine Gun and 7th Bavarian Companies, which bore the brunt of the American attack. After weeks of setbacks, it looked like at last the Germans would take the initiative in the Argonne. Although the barrage caused considerable German casualties on Hill 2, Vollmer, acting on his own initiative, directed Leutnant Endriss to send a platoon to plug the gaps on Hill 2 so as to shore up the area from American penetration.[45]

Vollmer adjusted his battalion to block an American advance up the valley and retained control of the situation, with the Americans suffering heavy casualties. As the Germans reported, "Without any artillery preparation, the adversary launched a violent attack and there was heavy fighting, which lasted well into the evening. The enemy was repulsed almost everywhere. [The 120th Württemberg's]

1st battalion [led by Vollmer] absorbed the brunt of the enemy attack without wavering, due to its good defensive position."[46]

Vollmer was busy directing his battalion against the Americans when his adjutant, Lieutenant Glass, approached. Vollmer was relieved to hear that two companies of the Prussian 210th Reserve Infantry Regiment had just arrived at the battalion command post and were waiting for his orders.[47] The 210th was the force that Vollmer needed to launch the much-anticipated counterattack to push the Americans out of the eastern portion of the Argonne Forest. This would defeat the American attack, save the day for the Germans in the Argonne, and expose the flank of the main American attack in the Meuse Valley.[48]

Vollmer told Glass to join him in meeting the senior 210th Prussian soldier on-site. They needed to be ready for the counterattack no later than 10:30 A.M. There was no time to waste if the attack would be launched on time. The 210th was only a few hundred feet up the valley, near Vollmer's humble battalion command post. Vollmer's headquarters had its usual number of orderlies, stretcher bearers, and runners standing around the shabby wooden shack awaiting orders. However, it was the Prussians that concerned him.[49]

Vollmer was appalled at what he saw. About seventy soldiers of the 210th had laid down their arms and were eating breakfast. The Prussians had loaves of bread, marmalade, and canned meat out and were in no hurry to do anything.[50] Leutnants Vollmer and Glass rebuffed the 210th for their lack of preparedness and carelessness. Vollmer reminded them that there was a fight going on and that he needed them. The weary men of the 210th were unmoved by Vollmer's appeals and merely replied: "We hiked all night and first of all we need something to eat." Indeed, these soldiers had moved from the Meuse Valley, through the night, and frequently under artillery fire. They were tired and hungry. Frustrated by this lack of energy, Vollmer told Glass to go back to the front and then turned to order the Prussians to move quickly. Vollmer's responsibilities were divided between the ongoing battle and organizing his taskforce for the 10:30 A.M. counterattack. He was about to wheel around to make a report to his regimental commander, Major Ziegler, but something was moving across the meadow.[51]

Suddenly, bursting from the foliage of the meadow came the two soldiers that Vollmer had sent to fill canteens, yelling, "Die Amerikaner kommen!" Off to the right, Vollmer noticed a group of 210th soldiers dropping their weapons and belts, yelling "Kamerad" with their hands in the air. Not knowing what was going on, Vollmer threateningly drew his pistol and yelled to them to pick up their weapons and arm themselves.[52] Just out of Vollmer's vision, to his rear, the Prussians had reacted to what looked like a large group of Americans charging across the meadow.[53] Believing it was an American penetration of some one hundred troops, or perhaps American shock troops, the soldiers of the 210th were caught by surprise and surrendered. Before Vollmer realized what had happened, a "large and strong American man with a red-mustache, broad features and a freckle face" captured him. It was Corporal Alvin C. York.[54]

Meanwhile, Leutnant Glass, whom Vollmer had just moments before sent back to the front, returned to the command post to report that he had seen American troops moving near the meadow. Before he realized it, Glass too was a prisoner. Everything occurred so quickly that both Vollmer and the 210th Regiment's soldiers believed that this was a larger surprise attack launched by the Americans, not just a patrol of seventeen soldiers.[55]

Bernie Early ordered his men to quickly search the seventy prisoners, line them up, and get ready to move. It was a chaotic situation. Around the seventeen Americans there were the sounds of war—from the valley to the east and the hills in front and behind them—as German gunners fired upon their brothers at arms in the death trap less than half a mile away. While the Americans were busy getting the prisoners in order, the 4th and 6th Companies of the 125th Württemberg Landwehr Regiment on Humserberg, the hill just above the American patrol, realized that there was trouble below.[56]

A crew of German machine gunners under the command of Leutnant Paul Lipp were directly above Vollmer's headquarters and had been firing to the east, into the diminishing ranks of the besieged American battalion.[57] On seeing the capture of their countrymen below, the machine gun's crewmen yelled and signaled to the captured Germans to lie down. As soon as that happened, the Württembergers opened fire. The hail of bullets killed six of the seventeen Americans and wounded three more.[58] The situation was so chaotic that several Germans were also killed by the machine gun fire.[59] With that, the German POWs started waving their hands wildly in the air, yelling, "Don't shoot, there are Germans here!"[60] German leutnant Paul Adolf August Lipp, the

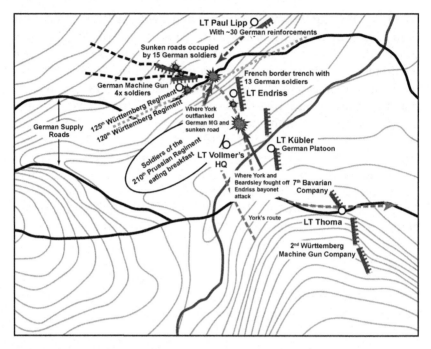

Map 8. York's 8 October 1918 battle.

commander of 6th Company, 125th Regiment, steadied his men and had them aim more carefully, looking for the distinctive British-style helmets worn by the Americans. Lipp then went off to bring up riflemen to join the machine gunners and help Vollmer out of his predicament.[61]

The situation for York and the other Americans was not promising. Six of the seventeen Americans were killed (Corporal Murray Savage and Privates Maryan Dymowsky, Carl Swansen, Fred Wareing, Ralph Wiler, and William Wine), while three others were wounded (Acting Sergeant Bernard Early, Corporal William Cutting, and Private Mario Muzzi). The remaining eight soldiers still able to fight included Corporal Alvin York (the only NCO left standing) and Privates Percy Beardsley, Patrick Donohue, Thomas Johnson, Joseph Kornacki, Michael Sacina, Feodor Sok, and George Wills.[62]

The survivors were scattered across the meadow floor, lying on or near their German prisoners, who were also sprawled on the ground trying not to get shot. The German machine gun above them fired at anything that moved. The Americans shouted to each other to ascertain who was injured. Bernie Early was severely injured by five bullets that had ripped into his body, while Cutting was incapacitated after being shot by three bullets that tore up his arm, and Mario Muzzi was shot in the shoulder.[63] The worst was Corporal Murray Savage, York's close friend, who was shot to pieces. His body and clothes were spread across the meadow in a heap of bloody shreds. York was shocked and dismayed to see the remains of the person he most cared about in the army.[64]

Whatever misgivings York had about fighting vanished upon seeing the death of Savage. Being the only noncommissioned officer not dead or wounded, and with the burden of command now upon him, York determined to stop the killing.[65] After taking a quick analysis of the situation, Alvin seized the initiative. According to the account on his Congressional Medal of Honor citation, "He charged with great daring a machine gun nest which was pouring deadly and incessant fire upon his platoon."[66] The seven other American survivors provided covering fires for Alvin anytime he moved, with Beardsley shooting his Chauchat in support.[67] Most of the American

One of York's men, Private Percy Beardsley, carried the notoriously unreliable Chauchat light machine gun into battle on 8 October 1918. This weapon had a propensity to jam in the midst of a fight. When this occurred, the gunner often had to resort to using his sidearm. Ballistic forensic analysis demonstrates that Beardsley did just that on the morning of 8 October. (NARA)

German soldiers man the MG 08/15, Germany's premier machine gun of World War I. The Germans had mastered the integration of the machine gun with deadly effect during the First World War, killing many of York's platoonmates. It was this type of machine gun that York charged, killing its crew, on 8 October 1918. (NARA)

survivors said that the positions that they ended up in after the German machine gun opened fire prevented them from doing much to aid Alvin's assault other than keeping watch over the prisoners.[68]

To eliminate the machine gun that was causing so much death, York charged partly up Humserberg and crossed a German supply road that was about 160 yards above the meadow.[69] He took a prone shooting position just above this road. What York saw about fifty yards to the west were groups of German soldiers occupying two sunken roads that ran above and parallel with the supply road he had just crossed. York's position was the tip of a "V" where the two ancient sunken roads converged. From here Alvin had clear lines of sight up both roads and opened fire,[70] killing the machine gun crew and its supporting riflemen, a total of nineteen Germans.[71] He had fired nearly all of the rifle bullets from his front belt pouches in this engagement, some forty-six rounds.[72] In an unusual coolness of mind, he frequently yelled to the Germans to surrender so that he would not kill more than he had to. His squadmates could hear him demanding their surrender in the meadow below. In spite of this, the Germans were oblivious to his presence and perished as a result.[73] As York contemplated what to do next, Leutnant Lipp was arriving from farther up the hill with more riflemen. Taking advantage of the lull, York wheeled about to make his way back to the meadow to his men and the prisoners.[74]

As York came down the hill, he passed behind the border trench occupied by Leutnant Fritz Endriss and part of his platoon. Endriss saw York running down the hill and ordered his men to prepare for a bayonet attack. With bayonets fixed and ready, Endriss led the attack and charged out of the trench toward York. Twelve soldiers followed dutifully, but they had no idea against whom they were charging.[75] As far as they were concerned, the battle was to the east, not the west. But they nonetheless followed Endriss.[76]

Seeing this, York slid on his side, dropped his rifle, and pulled out his M1911 Automatic Colt Pistol (ACP). Each magazine in this weapon held seven rounds. York stopped adjacent to Private Beardsley, who also had his own .45 ACP and fired in support of York against the bayonet attack. York used a hunting skill he had learned when faced with a flock of turkeys. He picked off the advancing foes from back to front. The logic behind this was that if the lead Germans fell, the trailing Germans would seek cover and be all the more difficult to kill. As Germans fell, several of the other attackers broke off and headed back to the trench. By now, half of the charging soldiers were dead. Right next to York, and unbeknownst to him, Private Beardsley was also firing into the German throng. Between the two, there was no way that this bayonet attack would succeed. During the fracas a nearby German threw a hand grenade at York and Beardsley, which exploded behind them in the meadow, wounding several German prisoners.[77]

With his platoon either dead or back in the trench, Endriss was now charging alone. The last attacking German now only a few feet away, York fired, throwing Endriss back as the .45 bullet slammed into his body. He was hit in the abdomen, writhing and screaming in agony less than ten feet from York. This event occurred in clear view of Leutnant Vollmer, who was still lying on the meadow as a prisoner. There were now twenty-five dead Germans across the side of the hill.[78]

Much as York mourned the loss of Savage, now Vollmer wanted to save his friend Endriss. In the midst of the fight, Vollmer stood up and walked over to Alvin and yelled above the din of battle in English (he had lived in Chicago before the war), "English?"

York replied: "No, not English."

Vollmer: "What?"

York: "American."

Vollmer: "Good Lord! If you won't shoot any more I will make them give up."[79]

York told him to do it, and pointed his pistol at him as a warning against any trickery. Vollmer blew a whistle and yelled an order. Leutnant Lipp was in charge of the 125th Regiment's troops on this part of the hill. He was not sure what was going on, but he had lost a lot of men and he knew and trusted Vollmer. Hearing Vollmer's order, Lipp told his men to drop their weapons and to make their way down the hill to join the other prisoners, who were under the charge of only eight Americans.[80]

York used Vollmer to translate orders to the one hundred or so prisoners.[81] As they were readying for the return trip to the American lines, York's men expressed concern about whether they could handle so many prisoners. Hearing this, Vollmer realized that there were not many Americans after all and asked how many men York had, to which York replied, "I have plenty." York ordered Vollmer to quickly line the Germans in a column of twos and tell them to carry out the wounded Americans and Germans, which included Vollmer's dying friend, Leutnant Endriss, and Corporal Cutting.[82] Alvin then checked on the wounded Americans, seeing first Bernie Early, who said, "York, I'm shot and shot bad. What'll I do?" Seeing he needed help moving, Alvin answered, "You can come out in rear of the column with the other boys." With that, fellow Irishman Private "Patty" Donohue and several of the German prisoners assisted Early, Cutting, and Muzzi to the back of the formation to get out of the Argonne.[83]

York took the German officers (Lipp and Vollmer) and placed them at the head of the formation, with Vollmer at the lead. Another officer, Leutnant Glass, had an overcoat on and was not observed as being an officer. York stood directly behind Vollmer, with a .45 Colt semiautomatic pistol pointed at his back, and had to decide which route to take back to the lines. Retracing their steps up into the hills would be suicide, as there would be no way that they could control this large group of prisoners in that difficult terrain. Vollmer suggested that York take the men down a gully in front of Humserberg off to the left, which was occupied by a large group of German soldiers. Sensing that this was a trap, York balked at the idea and took them instead down the road that skirted the ridgeline to the south. This was the same road Early had led the men across when they spotted the first two Germans with the canteens. It was a good choice, as it led back to Hill 223 and Châtel Chéhéry, and it was the only route by which he could have safely moved the prisoners.[84]

Meanwhile, slightly forward of York's position was another of Vollmer's officers, Leutnant Kübler, and his platoon. Kübler realized that it was too quiet behind the lines and to his left and told his second in command, Sergeant Major Haegele, "things just don't look right." Kübler ordered his men to grab their weapons and follow him to the battalion command post. As they approached, he and his men were immediately surrounded by several of York's men. Kübler and his platoon surrendered and joined the prisoners. Vollmer used the opportunity to alert nearby troops by loudly ordering Kübler's men to drop their weapons and equipment belts.[85]

Leutnant Thoma, the commander of the Bavarian 7th Mineur Company, heard Vollmer's order to Kübler. He turned and saw several of York's men moving up the road. Thoma ordered his men to follow him with their bayonets fixed and ran in the direction of York and the one hundred–plus German prisoners, yelling, "Don't take off your belts!" Thoma's men took a position near the road for a fight. York shoved his pistol in Vollmer's back and demanded that he order Thoma to surrender. The following exchange occurred:

Vollmer: "You must surrender!"
Thoma: "I will not let them capture me."
Vollmer: "It is useless, we are surrounded."
Thoma: "I will do so on your responsibility!"
Vollmer: "I take all responsibility."[86]

Thoma and his men, with elements of the 2nd Machine Gun Company, surrendered.[87] They dropped their weapons and belts and joined the large formation of prisoners.[88] As they crossed the valley, the battalion adjutant of York's unit, Lieutenant Joseph A. Woods, saw the formation from Hill 223 and believed that it was a German counterattack. Woods gathered as many scouts and runners as he could to fight off this potential threat. But after a closer look he realized that the Germans were unarmed and noticed Alvin

```
Garner        (325 524.)
Bn P.C.
8/10/18    9/25    Runner
Tomasello
            (325 524.)

These men came from our left flank (132 in all besides
wounded) Have not taken time to examine them for
papers etc.

        Garner

Recd 12.45
```

This is the original message sent to York's divisional headquarters announcing the capture of 132 German soldiers. Brigadier General Lindsey saw York moving the prisoners through Châtel and said to him, "Well, York, I hear you have captured the whole damned German army."

York at the head of the formation, just behind Vollmer. At Hill 223, York saluted and said, "Company G reports with prisoners sir."[89] Lieutenant Woods answered, "How many prisoners have you corporal?" York replied, "Honest lieutenant, I don't know." Woods answered, "Take them back to Châtel Chéhéry and I will count them as they go by."[90] He counted 132 German soldiers, with the battalion commander, Major Tillman, present as an eyewitness. Lieutenant Woods noted that Cutting and Early were at the back of the formation and "severely wounded, whereby they were taken to the aid station in Châtel Chéhéry with Mario Muzzi." Private Patrick Donohue was also wounded but remained with the men.[91]

Meanwhile, a German artillery forward observer on Humserberg saw the large formation of troops near Hill 223 and called for artillery fire. As the shells began to land, York ordered the Germans to double time out of the valley. After they made it safely back to Châtel Chéhéry an American officer saw Vollmer and cut off his rank and Iron Cross. Vollmer protested but was told to shut up. The battalion intelligence officer quickly asked Vollmer a few questions and found the German orders to counterattack and seize Castle Hill at 10:30 in Vollmer's pocket.[92] Near Châtel Chéhéry the column was stopped by the brigade commander, General Lindsey, who said to York, "Well, York, I hear you have captured the whole damned German army."[93]

The wounded Germans and Americans were helped off to the aid station in Châtel Chéhéry, with the Americans being told to walk the remaining German prisoners back to Varennes, some six miles south, as the regimental holding area could not keep so many. To keep control of the prisoners, various soldiers were solicited to help out, including a tank mechanic, Sergeant A. N. La Plante, of the 321st Company, 1st Tank Brigade, who was returning to his unit in Varennes. He testified that the Americans treated the prisoners kindly, stopping for rest breaks, and freely provided water to them. When the men at last made it to Varennes, the group stopped and was fed. After eating they headed for a larger prisoner cage near the village of Boureuilles.[94] On the way, a 35th Infantry Division photographer snapped a picture of York and his German captives, being clearly identified by the presence of Vollmer, Thoma, and Lipp at the head of the group.[95]

York and his platoon frustrated the German plan and bagged a portion of Vollmer's 1st Battalion, 120th Regiment, elements of

This photo was taken outside of Varennes-en-Argonne and is confirmed to be of York's group of prisoners. The three German officers in the front of the formation each played a central role in the 8 October battle. At left is Leutnant Paul Vollmer, the commander of 1st Battalion, 120th Württemberg Regiment, who personally surrendered his unit to York after losing many men and seeing his friend Fritz Endriss fall in combat. The German officer in the center is Leutnant Max Thoma, commander of the Bavarian 7th Mineur Company, the officer who refused to surrender unless Vollmer accepted responsibility, and to the right is Leutnant Paul Lipp, who commanded the 125th Württemberg machine gun that killed or wounded half of the Americans with York. The American in the center of the photo, just behind the German officers, is Alvin York. (AHEC)

the 210th Prussian Reserve Regiment, the Bavarian 7th Mineur Company, elements of the 2nd Machine Gun Company, and elements from the 4th and 6th Companies of the 125th Landwehr. This cleared the American front and left flank and caused the Germans to abandon more than thirty machine guns, which were recovered there after the battle. Because of this, the 2nd Battalion, 328th Infantry Regiment, was able to resume the attack.[96] They continued up the valley to reach their objective, the Decauville Railroad and the North–South Road. This placed the flanks of the 120th and 125 Landwehr Regiments at risk. The German line was broken, and the 120th Landwehr would never recover from the loss.[97] The report of the 120th Regiment said:

The flank of 6th Company reported an enemy surprise attack. Next, the remnant of 4th Company and personnel from the 210th Regiment were caught by this surprise attack, where Leutnant Endriss was killed. The company was shattered or was captured. Also First Leutnant Vollmer ended up in the enemy's hands. Now the situation was worse. Bad news followed more bad news from Chatel to the Schöne Aussicht a large enemy column moved towards the Schliesstal Mulda and the Boulassonbachs [up the valley into the Argonne]. By this, we knew that the enemy was moving against the North–South Road.

Several 7th Bavarian troops evaded capture and reported that the Americans had broken through and captured over a hundred Germans. The command had trouble believing that this could happen to Vollmer, who was known as a confident, reliable, and proven soldier. A patrol was sent out to ascertain what happened. When reports reached the 2nd Landwehr commander that the line was breached by an American surprise attack, General Franke took action and placed the 122nd Landwehr Infantry Regiment in the gap as a temporary remedy. They deployed on a reverse slope defense in the deep ravine about 600 yards south of the York site. This is where a delaying action was fought by the Germans around 2:00 P.M.[98]

Although there were fears of other American penetrations, there was no panic among the 2nd Landwehr. The unit adjusted its line back to resist further American advances. Portions of the 45th Prussian Reserve Division were unnerved when word reached them that the line was broken, which compelled General Franke to deploy his reserve cavalry squadron to restore order. Despite this, the Argonne was all but lost. The planned counterattack to take Castle and Beautiful View Hills was preempted by this American surprise attack. The 2nd Landwehr lacked the manpower now to conduct the operation or to even hold the line against the Americans. If the 82nd Infantry Division pressed the attack now, it would result in the capture of thousands of troops, supplies, and artillery.[99] Fortunately for the Germans, the 328th U.S. Infantry had taken a beating as well and did not take advantage of the opportunity. Shortly after this, the order to withdraw from the Argonne was given to the embattled German army:

We received the depressing order at 1030 to withdraw. In good order did the Company move. We did have some luck. . . . There was no fire on the North–South Road. But, we did see terrible things on the road. The results of the artillery; dead men, dead horses, destroyed vehicles blocking the way and destroyed trees were scattered to and fro. Somewhere along the road, between the middle of Hohenborn-höhe and Humserberg, the battalion moved east of the road near the Benzolbahn and east again to our new positions. And what about the enemy? The North–South Road was closed by Machine Gun fire. This happened around 1200 noon. It was amazing that the Americans did not press the attack. In the afternoon of 8 October, the headquarters of 3rd and 5th Army ordered a withdraw from the Argonne line.[100]

A temporary line was established slightly back in the Argonne to give the command time to evacuate its troops from the forest. A counterattack was made north of the valley against the village of Cornay. This German attack drove the Americans from Cornay, capturing about one hundred U.S. soldiers.[101] On 9 October 1918, the final order was issued to evacuate the Argonne and to withdraw into the fortified Siegfried Line for the final defense before the war ended.[102] "It was now that . . . the leader of 5th Army, gave the last word. We needed to occupy the secondary defensive positions further back. In the evening of 9/10 October, the regiment departed from the Argonne. The German soldiers gave so much after hard battles since 1914—more than 80,000 dead were left here. American artillery briefly hit the Humserberg line during the retreat and always there were the shrapnel. By Cheviers, the Regiment was in shelters. We were dead tired, too tired to contemplate, but able to hold onto hope."[103]

Yet, before the Germans retreated from the Argonne, York and his men would clash with the Germans one more time.

8

The War without End

And we were all shot to pieces. There were not many of them—
there Greeks and Italians left. But what was left were still
fighting like a sackful of wildcats. I shore did like those boys
now.

—Alvin York, 12 October 1918

Corporal York and his detail would not return to their unit until
10:00 A.M. the next day, 9 October, and throughout this time the 82nd
Division continued to face fierce German resistance.[1] What occurred
dispels notions that the German units in the Argonne were merely
waiting for a chance to quit the war. As already described, the 7
October capture of Hill 223 virtually crippled the 1st Battalion in
York's regiment, and the losses that York's battalion suffered on 8
October would be the bloodiest single day in the history of that unit,
even unmatched in World War II. Unfortunately, 9 October would
again prove to be costly, not only for the 328th Regiment, but for
the entire division.[2] This was a result of German commander General
Max von Gallwitz's deploying reinforcements to the Argonne
to safeguard his flanks.[3]

After York's detail marched off the battlefield with the 132 German
prisoners, his battalion continued to attack. By 5:00 P.M. they
reached the German supply road and rail network, but were prevented
from advancing farther by German gunners in the forest.
Meanwhile, two American companies under Captain Danforth
were ordered to attack north near Cornay to take the high ground
that had caused so many casualties for York's unit (Champrocher
Ridge), of which Danforth wrote: "Upon reaching about the centre
of this valley we were stopped by a withering fire of machine
guns from the front, from the unsalable heights of the Champrocher
Ridge on our right."[4] This ridgeline west of Cornay was defended
by the 125th Württemberg Regiment, reinforced by the Prussian

212th Reserve Regiment.[5] The Americans managed to make it to the high ground, but withdrew due to horrific losses in men.[6]

As the men endeavored to weather the German storm of steel, another unit from the 82nd Division captured the village of Cornay, some 1.25 miles north of Châtel Chéhéry. Here, the 125th Württemberg, the 212th Prussian Regiment, and the German 41st Infantry Division launched a counterattack against the Americans.[7] The Germans recaptured Cornay, killed scores of Americans, and captured more than one hundred in the town.[8] With Cornay back in German hands, Hill 223 and Châtel Chéhéry were at risk; however, this was the last German attack in the Argonne, as they were ordered to withdraw from the forest later that night.[9] Looking back on the conduct of his 120th and 125th Württemberg Regiments, the two primary units that York fought against, General Max von Gallwitz had nothing but praise, saying they "conducted themselves excellently."[10] Indeed, the combat record of the Württembergers proved steady and reliable throughout the final days of the war.

When York and his men returned from their hike to Varennes, they found their unit deployed along the German supply road, about a half-mile in the Argonne. Captain Danforth was there and was surprised to see them, asking where they had been. York explained what had transpired, much to the amazement of the captain.[11] Danforth then realized that it was because of York that he had been able to advance, as the fires from the German gunners on the center hill had slackened enough for him to attack.[12] Before going back into the line, York made an unusual request of Danforth. He asked permission to go to his battlefield to see if any of the men they left behind were still alive.[13] Danforth acquiesced and sent stretcher bearers with him.[14]

On arriving at his field of battle, York was astounded at how torn up the place was. The U.S. Army had already cleared the site of the dead and had removed major pieces of equipment, and there was an eerie stillness to the place which only twenty-four hours before had been a scene of death and destruction. Despite this, York and the men with him walked the terrain, calling out for any survivors. There were none. He had hoped that just perhaps his friend Murray Savage had come out of it.[15] This return visit had a profound effect on York:

> All was terribly quiet in the field. And I jes couldn't help thinking of the boys that only the day before was alive and

like me. Dymowski dead. Weiler dead. Waring dead. Wine dead. Swanson dead. Corporal Murray Savage, my best pal, dead. Oh, my, it seemed so unbelievable. I would never see them again. I would never share the same blanket with Corporal Savage. We'd never read the Bible together again. We would never talk about our faith and pray to our God. I was mussed up inside worser than I had ever been. I'm a-telling you when you lose your best buddie and you know you ain't never going to see him again, you sorter know how terrible cruel war is. There was nothing I could do now for Corporal Murray Savage or any of the other boys that done lost their lives.[16]

After reporting back to Captain Danforth, York was deployed near the German North–South Road. But he was consumed with thoughts on how he had survived: "Two men on both sides of me and two others right behind me were killed, and I hadn't been touched. I tried to figure it out how it come that everybody around me who was exposed done got picked off or wounded and that I alone come out unharmed."[17] Alvin was certain that he had only survived because of divine intervention: "I am a witness to the fact that God did help me out of that hard battle; for the bushes were shot off all around me and I never got a scratch. So you can see that God will be with you if you will only trust him and I say that He did save me. Now He will save you if you will only trust Him."[18]

York's unit attempted an advance up the right side of the German supply road but only made it about three hundred yards forward of their position before being stopped. Their nemesis from the day before, the Württembergers, put up a robust defense and would stand firm to cover the withdrawal of German forces from the Argonne.[19] With that, Major Tillman ordered his men to dig in for the night, preparing for an advance to clear the Argonne on the 10th.[20] During this time Private Patrick Donohue was ordered to the aid station in Châtel Chéhéry to treat a shoulder injury he had sustained on 8 October.[21]

On 10 October, the Germans completed their retreat from the Argonne. Simply put, the loss of the North–South Road made it impossible to hold the forest. During this time, York's men were given a few hours to rest before moving out. Burial details were sent out to move the dead to a cemetery hastily dug in Châtel Chéhéry while the unit sorted casualty numbers. York's regiment had suffered 718 casualties, including 28 of its officers.[22] Despite the losses, the men would remain in the line. Later on the 10th they moved out of the Argonne Forest and into the Meuse Valley under constant German artillery fires, which killed Chaplain Smart.[23] The men first served as the divisional reserve, being positioned near the village of Fleville.[24] A small French village in the Meuse Valley, it had been the scene of particularly terrible fighting only a week before and was in terrible condition.[25]

Over the next three weeks, York's unit would be involved in a series of life-and-death struggles that would contribute to bringing the war to it final conclusion. While waiting for orders to push forward on 12 October 1918, all three battalions of York's regiment were again together, spread out in positions recently vacated by the Germans near Fleville. The terrain in the Meuse Valley was different from the Argonne. Here, the land included open fields, rolling hills, and few wooded areas.[26] While waiting for orders to advance, the men were frequently attacked by German aircraft. They not only dropped bombs and strafed the Americans, but also directed artillery barrages onto them.[27]

On 13 October, York's unit moved to the eastern flank of the division, to support an attack against the German Siegfried Line (the Western powers called it the Hindenburg Line). The portion of this defensive network in the American zone was named the Kriemhilde Line. The name Kriemhilde was from German legend. Kriemhilde was the wife of the great hero Siegfried.[28] The line itself was only a solid defense system in theory. Although there were wire, bunkers, and trenches, these were not continuous, but rather a series of positions that used the terrain to channel the Americans into kill zones. The Germans would defend their strongpoints with machine guns and artillery, and use counterattacks to take back any ground lost. For York's unit, the bad news was that in its sector the Kriemhilde Stellung was a line of wire and obstacles.[29]

The 14–15 October American attack, in which York participated, was a three-division attack up the Meuse Valley.[30] This included the 82nd in the center, the 42nd Rainbow Division on the right, and the 77th Liberty Division on the left. These were some of the best divisions in the AEF, and there were hopes that the Kriemhilde Line would be penetrated by them. York's regiment covered the right flank of the attack, near the town of Sommerance.[31]

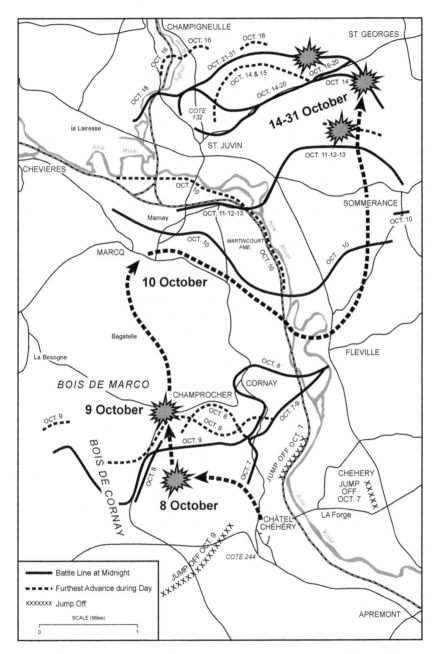

Map 9. York's unit advance from the Argonne to the Meuse Valley, 7 October–1 November 1918.

On 14 October, a barrage preceded the 8:30 A.M. attack. York's sister battalion led the assault, with York's unit following about 550 yards behind. As soon as the attack began, the Germans unleashed their own barrage, laced with poisonous gas.[32] York's men were ordered to dig in as the barrage crashed around them. It was here that York came close to being killed. He was digging near an apple tree outside of Sommerance, "and then bang! one of the big shells struck the ground right in front of us and we all went up in the air. But we all come down again. Nobody was hurt. But it sure was close."[33]

Forward of York's position, the 1st Battalion was in another battle for its life. After advancing across the rolling hills of the Meuse Valley northwest of Sommerance, the unit was in the midst of breaking through the forward zone of the Kriemhilde wire when the German barrage began. Scores of men fell due to the artillery and machine gun fires. The German strongpoints here were centered on a dozen forested patches, where concealed machine gun emplacements were backed by infantry from the 45th Prussian Reserve Division. York's men had encountered these Germans in the form of the 210th and 212th Prussian Regiments near Châtel Chéhéry. The German unit was recently reinforced and showed no signs of breaking.[34] Adding to the contest, German artillery fire was particularly accurate on 14 October. They had excellent observation thanks to their having command of the skies, with scores of aircraft up and a series of sausage-shaped observation balloons overhead as well.[35]

Despite the robust German resistance, the Americans pressed the attack and managed to outflank the Germans, thereby breaching the Kriemhilde wire obstacles.[36] Similar success was experienced on the left. However, there were problems on the right flank. The 42nd Rainbow Division did not advance on this portion of the front, being caught in a vicious battle further east. This meant that once again York's unit had an exposed flank, which the Germans would exploit.[37]

As the 1st Battalion withered under intense fire, York's unit was ordered to exploit the gap they had cut in the Kriemhilde Line. As he and his men advanced through exploding German artillery and the rat-a-tats of machine guns, they passed the scene of the battle. Lying scattered across the area were scores of dead and wounded men. Medics and stretcher bearers worked to save the injured, while pieces of flesh, clothing, and the accoutrements of war were spread across this French field. The sight was sickening, the moans and screams nightmarish.[38] It was a sober reminder of how real and costly this war was. Many of these men were killed the instant they stood up to attack, with most of the officers falling in the first five minutes of the fight.[39]

York's unit, led by Captain Danforth, pushed on and saw that they were to attack up the back slope of a hill that was about a half-mile across and devoid of trees. The Germans held the high portion of it. With the dominant terrain in their hands, the Germans had the Americans under constant artillery and machine gun fires. As York's unit advanced, they saw that the men of the 1st Battalion clung to the ground and were only advancing by crawling on their bellies.[40] Despite a wall of German fires, York's men pushed forward through their comrades with élan, advancing some two hundred yards beyond the regimental objective, the St. Georges–St. Juvin Road.[41] The advance by the Rainbow Division's 166th Infantry on the right again had not kept up with the All-Americans. Because of this, York's battalion found itself under terrible flanking fires, primarily by a company of German machine guns on the high ground northwest of them (just outside of St. Georges). Being fired upon from three sides was untenable, and as a result Captain Danforth and Major Tillman pulled the men back and ordered them to dig in along the road to prepare for a German counterattack. While here, they were under constant German artillery and machine gun fires.[42]

In the meantime, due to heavy losses, York's 2nd Battalion was merged with the survivors of the 1st Battalion. Major Boyle of the 1st Battalion, being more senior than Major Tillman, was given command. This was followed on 15 October by the merging of York's 328th Regiment with the 327th Regiment, also due to the casualties that both of these units had suffered over the past week.[43] Despite the mounting losses, later on 14 October the division issued orders for an attack across the front the next day. The plan called for artillery fires directed against the German positions throughout the night, with nonpersistent chemical attacks beginning at 4:00 A.M. The artillery fire intensified at 7:25 A.M., with the infantry being ordered to advance at 7:30 A.M. behind a creeping barrage. They were to advance more than a half-mile forward to seize the high ground above a steep ravine (Ravine aux Pierres) west of St. Georges village.[44]

Throughout the night, American artillery fired into the German lines as planned. As York and the rest of the division prepared for their broad frontal attack, suddenly, at 7:00 A.M., a heavy German artillery barrage crashed into the Americans. After fifteen minutes of this, the Germans attacked. Striking across the 82nd Division's front, Germans from the Prussian 45th Division, the 90th Division, and the 15th Bavarian slammed into the American front. The Germans intended to drive them out of the Kriemhilde Line.[45]

But just before the German infantry attacked, they deceived the Americans into coming out of their holes prematurely by briefly stopping their artillery barrage, only to then open up with machine guns, which inflicted more harm than the artillery. Driven back into their holes, and with visibility reduced by a low, thick fog, the Americans had no advance warning of the actual German infantry assault until suddenly, emerging out of the mist, were gray-clad figures. The Germans were upon them![46]

York's unit received the brunt of the attack, with vicious hand-to-hand battles breaking out across the line in a desperate struggle. In some areas the Americans were forced back several hundred yards. However, the German left flank was exposed. Tillman and Danforth rushed men into the exposed flank, raking their lines from the side with their rifles, Chauchat light machine gun (Beardsley still had his), and Colt pistols. The German attack began to waver, until another regiment of Germans attacked. But these German reinforcements never made it, thanks to the planned 7:25 A.M. barrage for the 82nd's own attack that erupted among them just as they emerged from their lines to attack. This compelled the German survivors to withdraw.[47]

The timing of the American barrage was perfect in stopping the exploitation of any German gains along the front. All the same, the German attack desynchronized the planned American offensive, which turned into a series of regimental assaults.[48] Several American units did seize the initiative and pursue the Germans, which resulted in the temporary capture of the Ravine aux Pierres. Even so, these gains failed to take the well-fortified heights, and under heavy German counterattacks and unremitting artillery the Americans returned to the lines roughly where they started the day.[49]

The weather turned miserable later on 15 October, with heavy rain, yet the Germans seemed particularly interested in reducing the salient that York's unit had created in the lines. This was in large part due to the inability of the neighboring 42nd Rainbow Division to advance in line with the 82nd, giving the enemy an opportunity to fire upon York's unit from the north and east. German machine gun teams continually sprayed the men from the high ground near

St. Georges, while German artillery was directed against them by aircraft. Several times German aircraft strafed York's men in their water-filled holes. Because of this, the regiment refused the line (bent back the right portion of the line) to prevent German infiltration.[50]

To reinforce York's regiment, two 75 mm field artillery guns were moved forward and placed in direct support, with a forward observer literally in the holes along the St. Georges Road with the men. This enabled the destruction of several German machine gun positions that had been particularly troublesome. Additionally, the 37 mm platoon was brought forward to provide additional support. German artillery ravaged the line throughout the day, but thanks to this support there were fewer harassing fires from German machine gunners on the surrounding high ground.[51]

By now the miserable weather had begun to take its toll on the men. Nearly everyone in York's unit was sick. The 328th history wrote of this situation, saying, "The Regiment had been actively engaged night and day since the night of October 6th. The mental and physical strain had been indeed great and the constant rain with resulting mud and shell holes filled with water added greatly to the hardship of the troops. The men and officers patiently and with good spirits stuck to their posts while the wearing-out process continued to take its toll."[52] The regimental surgeon added, "at least 90 per cent of men suffering from diarrhea and exhaustion. The great majority unable physically to endure an advance much less attack."[53] Even the equipment began to fail, with the division reporting that nearly all of the Chauchat light machine guns were inoperable.[54]

A rotation schedule was established to give each battalion time out of the front line, moving them into the trenches farther back in nearby Sommerance. The schedule was one day in the line, one day in reserve, and one day in support, then back into the line. In the reserve and support trenches, food was brought up and equipment maintained, with the men being able to dry out their clothes.[55] "Through the efforts of General Lindsey, bathing facilities as if by magic sprung up from the shell-wrecked ruins of Sommerance. Here was a place where the men could be and were dried out, warmed up, fed up, slept, reclothed and re-equipped."[56]

While in the line along the St. Juvin–St. Georges Road, York and his men were constantly fired upon by German artillery, snipped at by German machine guns, and engaged in aggressive patrols. On a rare sunny day, the Americans finally had planes in the skies, which resulted in impressive dogfights; on one day there were some three hundred planes fighting across the Meuse Valley. York and his men enjoyed these air combats and were gladdened to see several German planes shot down. One of these, a German Fokker D.VII biplane with a light gray fuselage and camouflage-pattern wings, came crashing down near them. The German pilot parachuted to safety and was captured by the machine gunners sent up to support York's unit.[57] The men cut pieces of his parachute for souvenirs.[58] Despite the occasional surge of American aircraft, the Germans maintained air superiority the majority of the time, which caused York's men to suffer all the more from air-to-ground attacks as well as from directed artillery fires.[59]

General Pershing intended to keep these units in the line until 1 November, when he would launch the knockout blow across the front. This would include an offensive by both a reinforced First U.S. Army and the new Second U.S. Army.[60] As the divisions that would participate in the offensive were moving into position, York's unit had to make do with what it had. From 21 October until being relieved from the line ten days later the men did not conduct any major attacks, but rather maintained the rotation schedule in and out of the lines.

Finally, after being in the line continuously since 7 October, the 82nd Infantry Division was relieved. York's unit was the last out. Through the last night they had to conduct aggressive patrols forward of the lines to prevent the Germans from gathering intelligence that the American 80th "Blue Ridge" Division was conducting a relief in place of the 82nd. At 1:00 A.M., 1 November, York and his men came out of the line and began a long and dark walk to a rest area in the Argonne. All of the men who came out of the Argonne with him on 8 October also came out alive with him on 1 November. This included Privates Percy Beardsley, Thomas Johnson, Joseph Kornacki, Michael Sacina, Feodor Sok, George Wills, and Patrick Donohue (who was back after having his 8 October injury treated).[61]

As the men made their way through the dark French morning, massive artillery fires shook the ground and lit up the sky in the distance as the final American offensive of the Great War commenced. Although facing 25 percent of Germany's entire strength on the Western Front, the AEF broke the German lines here on 1 November and burst forth into open warfare. Writing about this, the German commander opposite the Americans, General von Gallwitz, said,

"We were surprised by the vastness and vigor of America's military expansion. We admired the intensity with which a big army had been created, with a marvelous all-round equipment. The American Army had numerically strong, well set-up, substantial, human material endowed with great energy. . . . Wherever operations were developed systematically, . . . superior forces won. After all, it was the astonishing display of American strength which definitely decided the war against us."[62]

To get to this point, the units in the line paid a heavy price. York's regiment lost 30 percent of its men, 1,189 soldiers.[63] The unit moved to Champ Mahaut, the former headquarters for the German command in the Argonne, and Camp de Bouzon, near Varennes. While here, York was promoted to sergeant for his conduct in the face of the enemy.[64] Alvin wrote of this in a bittersweet manner: "I was made a sergeant just as quick as I got back out of the lines. But, oh, my! so many of my old buddies were missing and we scarcely seemed the same outfit."[65]

The men were fed hot food and given billets to rest in. The next day, the regiment marched south to Florent-en-Argonne, near Ste. Menehould, and loaded onto busses moving them into barracks at Martigney-les-Gerbonvaux on 5 November 1918. For the next several weeks the division received replacements and prepared to go back into the line. York and the other veterans were granted a seven-day leave.[66] He and his men were sent to the Roman bath resort town of Aix les Bains, near the Italian border. Although he did some sightseeing, York said, "We had been in the Argonne for several weeks without any relief and were tired and worn out and went down there to rest."[67]

While on leave, word reached the men that the Armistice was signed and that the war was to end on 11 November at 11:00 A.M. Aix les Bains erupted into rejoicing, with both the French and Americans joining in the celebration. York did not join the jubilant throngs, but instead went off by himself, as he was still mentally and physically exhausted from his experience in battle. He went to the town's church to pray, and after that he went to his hotel room to write a letter home. "I was glad the armistice was signed, glad it were all over. There had been enough fighting and killing. And my feelings were like most all of the American boys. It was all over. And we were ready to go home."[68] That was the question; just when would he go home?

Headquarters, 728th Infantry,
American E. F., France,
November 3, 1918.

SPECIAL ORDERS)
:*
XXXXXXX NO 134)

5. Upon the recommendation of Company Commanders, the following reductions, appointments, and promotions of non-commissioned officers
are hereby made, effective as of November 1, 1918:

TO BE PRIVATES:

	Co.		Co.
Cpl. Valente 1910231 Sabo,	G	Cpl. Clark 1910296 Wallace W.	G
Cpl. Griffin 1910216 George G.	G	Cpl. Reiblick 189777 John C.	H
Cpl. Chabanian 1910496 Ajcig,	H	Cpl. Lehmann 2230539 Frank,	H
Cpl. Straw 1910443 John B.	H	Cpl. Henderson 1908892 Frank H.	MG

TO BE SERGEANTS:

Cpl. Snyder 1909214 Albert,	A	Cpl. Schmader 1909183 Sylvester,	A
Cpl. Shank,1909200 Raymond I.	A	Cpl. Stucky 1825144 Sydney C.	C
Cpl. Gaio 1909601 Alfonso,	C	Cpl. Tripp 1908981 Henry A	D
Cpl. Rivard 1898282 Joseph	D	Pvt.qJoyce 2140492 William J.	D
Cpl. York 1910421 Alvin C.	G	Cpl. Bonsall 1910288 Joseph C.	G
Cpl. McDongal 1899727 Samuel C.	H	Cpl. Pitman 1899756 James F.	H
Pvt. Wylie 2229589 John T.	H	Cpl. Shaffer 2230841 Joseph,	H
Cpl. Putman 1910458 Artemus,	H	Cpl. Lange 2230700 Hugh,	H
Cpl. Eager -- Charles J.,	L	Cpl. Murphy 1910796 Frank H.	I
Cpl. Martineau 1911108 Leo T.,	L	Cpl. Bozes 1908851 Charles J. Jr.MG	
Cpl. Baker 1898397 Harry D.,	MGCo	Pvt. Matthews 1585767 W. A.	MGCo
Cook.Rodgers 1908847 Harry P.,	MGCo	Plcl.Schroppler 1908927 Erwin	MGCo

TO BE CORPORALS:

Plcl. Basile 1909241 Antonio,	A	Plcl. Budreau 1909250 Leo H.	A
Pvt. Dolan 1909669 William,	C	Pvt. Sanble 1909761 Harry P.,	C
Plcl. Roy 1909754 Le Roy,	C	Pvt. Stephens 1933154 Marvin R.,	C
Pvt. Whatley 1930099 Thomas J., Jr.C		Plcl. Barnes 1931683 John H.	D
Plcl. Brock 3502278 Roy T.	D	Plcl. Malloy 1909097 Adrian S.	D
Plcl. Frederickson 2143539 Nels,	D	Plcl. Stoner 2424420 William M.,	D
Plcl. McDaniel 1930899 Trivillis M,L		Pvt. Birkett 1911180 John H.	L
Pvt McDonough 1896898 John A.,	L	Plcl. Murray 1911259 Cornelius J, L	

York's company commander, Captain Danforth, recommended York for promotion to sergeant after watching his incredible performance in battle. The promotion came through just as the men were being moved to a rest camp after three weeks of continual combat. (NARA)

York and his platoon returned to the division in mid-November and moved with it to the Prauthoy training area, 125 miles south of the Argonne.[69] Although Germany had agreed to an armistice, the formal peace treaty had not yet been signed. While some Allied units prepared to march into Germany, the 82nd prepared for renewed fighting. York and his men were billeted in the surrounding villages and spent their time training and marching.[70] General Pershing's headquarters "directed that maneuvers of all kinds be commenced with great vigor."[71] Because of this, the division threw itself into a rig-orous training schedule in late November and early December. The

This photo is of York's regiment moving in French trucks from Florent-en-Argonne into barracks at Martigney-les-Gerbonvaux for a long-needed rest on 5 November 1918 after three weeks in combat. This was only one day after York's promotion to sergeant.

men were to apply the lessons learned during the Meuse-Argonne Offensive, refine combined arms operations, and improve tactical deployments. With so many veterans now in the ranks, the command was impressed by how rapidly the unit improved. It certainly was a more professional force than it had been one month before.

Yet challenges remained for the 82nd Division. There was a turnover in the unit's staff, in addition to numbers of men succumbing to sicknesses or gas-related injuries that they had suffered during the Meuse-Argonne Offensive. This was exacerbated by the arrival of replacements to bring the division back up to strength. Despite this, by December 1918 the 82nd was back up to pre-Meuse-Argonne strength levels. For York and the other survivors, however, the division just did not feel the same, as so many of their comrades were either dead or wounded.[72] York summed it up: "The boys were longing to get home. They felt they had done their jobs. The war was over. They were kinder restless. I was that way too."[73] Despite this, the training had to be done. Yet it was not as simple as just getting on with army training. The Prauthoy training area was not equipped as a winter cantonment, so the men were kept busy with weatherproofing their billets.

The frustration and monotony of this time was broken briefly by the Christmas visit of President Wilson and his wife, who were in France to attend the preliminary to the Paris Peace Conference.[74] York and his comrades were able to attend this event near Pershing's headquarters at Chaumont. Although York missed the unit's Christmas dinner, he wrote, "Mrs. Wilson was dressed very nice and she had a smile on her face all the time . . . and Mr. Wilson was wearing a large black silk hat with a light grey fur coat he also had a smile on his face. So that cheered the boys to see them."[75]

After Christmas, the unit had a rigorous training regimen and was soon able to conduct battalion-, regiment-, and brigade-level operations and maneuvers.[76] Some of the men commented that they should have had this sort of training *before* they went into action. One soldier in York's regiment correctly surmised, "In reality, we got some excellent training [here]. It is however, a matter of grave discussion, why, when at Camp Gordon, we were taught to sing, while after the armistice we were taught to fight."[77]

The corps commander, Major General Charles Summerall, watched the 82nd excel at unit-level operations and officially designated it an assault division.[78] At long last, *after* the war, the men in York's unit knew how to fight. "By this time we had learned that after all the infantryman's weapon is . . . the rifle. Bayonets are simply a clumsy can opener for bully beef and cracker cans. The 'Cho-Cho' [Chauchat light machine gun] was made by a plumber and not a very good plumber either. Grenades were originally designed for killing fish and gas masks are excellent for company punishment."[79]

Training was to end with a divisional exercise supervised by the corps commander, but it nearly turned into a catastrophe. The winter weather turned worse, causing large numbers of men to suffer cold-weather injuries. It was one of the stormiest, wettest, windiest periods that these men had experienced in France.[80] Because of this, the training was scaled back in January and no further division-level training events were planned.[81] One soldier in York's unit said, "Many a disposition, which was nearly completely spoiled, as evidenced by the unusual amount of profanity used, was just saved from complete destruction by the timely order to call off the maneuver."[82]

With the division's training scaled back, the men had a lot

more time on their hands. This made the wait for orders to return home seem unbearable. Idleness was not acceptable. The units were expected to conduct frequent inspections and training to maintain readiness and a soldierly appearance.[83] Major General Duncan made it a point to speak often with the troops. Also, services were held to honor the memory of the men who fell in action. To keep unit morale high, Duncan tasked division chaplain Reverend John Paul Tyler with the job of leading and organizing schools to prepare the men for civilian life. Tapping the expertise of the men in the ranks, the schools included instruction in writing, American history, reading, French, spelling, mathematics, and agriculture.[84] At one point, some eight thousand of the division's men were attending school.[85]

Yet, tensions in the unit were high, with the men wanting to go home sooner rather than later. The problem came to a head during a dance where there was almost a fight between the officers and drunk enlisted soldiers who crashed the party so as to secure the affections of the local French girls. York said, "I'm a-telling you that made them-there captains and lieutenants mad. They ordered me to call out the guard and get the boys off the floor. But that was a harder job than busting the Siegfried Line. The boys hung on to the girls and didn't want to give them up or stop dancing nohow."[86] York defused the conflict by roping off half of the floor for the officers and the other half for the enlisted men, all enforced with armed guards.

At long last orders arrived to sail home in January, which "spread a wave of happiness across the regiment." The men's enthusiasm faded soon thereafter when the shipping date was postponed or changed every few weeks.[87] After several weeks of these emotional highs and lows, Duncan took action. He ordered that the 82nd would stay the course with its training program and that he would enforce its high standards of conduct and discipline:

> Although the training of the Division at the present time is very different from the training required in anticipation of operations, it is no less important and fully as difficult. Within a short time all but a few members of the Division will return to civil life and they should be as well lifted to take up civil pursuits as the present conditions permit. The qualities acquired during the period of military training should make all members of this command more useful

citizens than they would otherwise be, and the knowledge of foreign countries and customs, submission to discipline, individual initiative, pride of organization and self-sacrifice for a cause, are just as necessary after discharge from the army as they have been in the A. E. F. No effort should be neglected to continue the development of these qualities.[88]

The division command also hoped to boost the men's morale with a generous leave program. Captain Danforth organized the AEF's only leave train to Italy, in which eleven hundred soldiers participated.[89] There were also trips to Paris, which York visited in March with several other men from his unit. On this visit he toured the wholesome side of the city alone, because the soldiers with him were interested in other diversions. Of this, York commented, "I could have gone out like a whole heap of the boys and fooled around with the mademoiselles and the vin rouge; and sorter tried to forget the war and them-there Germans I done killed in the Argonne. But I didn't drink and I had a girl of my own back home in the mountains."[90] A few days after returning from Paris, York was back on a train headed there again. He had been selected by Major General Duncan as one of the 82nd Division's representatives for the creation of the American Legion.[91] Incidentally, Alvin's mentor, G. Edward Buxton, was a founder of the American Legion, even writing its constitution.[92] York attended all of the Legion's sessions in the Hotel de Gabriel and predicted that it would grow into an influential organization.

While in Paris, York became hopelessly lost in the metropolis. Laughing at the situation afterward, he said, "That is the only time that I ever got bewildered as to direction. Right in the middle of that-thar old city the streets are all sorter mixed up. They seem to have no beginnings and no ends. And when they do have ends they sorter go plumb up against a blank wall. . . . I tried to get my direction by the sun, but I could not see it. Ho! Ho! And I'm telling you I couldn't make heads nor tails out of the names of the streets. I didn't know where I was."[93] In desperation, York asked an attractive French lady for help. The "mademoiselle" escorted York to a streetcar and put him on it. She spoke to another "right-smart girl," who was driving the streetcar, and she took York back to his hotel. Sensing the humor in this, York wrote, "So you see I never takened any girls home in France but one of them had to take me home, ho, ho."[94]

After returning from Paris, York planned on settling into his unit's routine; however, Chaplain Tyler had other plans for him. Chaplain Tyler knew of York's heroism and saw an opportunity to reach the unit's soldiers with the Gospel by having York share his faith with them. York's talks were such a hit that soon Chaplain Tyler was traveling across France with him to speak to thousands of other Doughboys over a period of some six weeks. These were simple revival services sanctioned and supported by the AEF command, where York would not only share his testimony but often would lead singing as well. York says some of the trips were more harrowing than fighting in the Argonne.[95] To get to one speaking engagement, the chaplain arranged for Alvin to ride in a motorcycle sidecar.[96] After breezing across rough French country roads at eighty miles per hour, York said, "It was asking too much of God, travelling like that. In front of the machine guns in the Argonne I couldn't protect myself. So I expected Him to look after me. And He done it and I come out unharmed. But there was no sense rushing like mad over those old roads on a motor cycle."[97]

The size of the groups that York addressed varied from small events in a YMCA hut to entire units. It seemed that no matter where he went, the crowds came to hear his story. This was a tremendous time for Alvin. His experience in teaching Sunday school and preaching sermons in Pall Mall helped him. Often when he finished sharing his testimony he would be given a standing ovation, of which Alvin always answered with a smile and "I thank yea."[98] One author wrote about this: "His simple faith impressed even the most skeptical, and there was not a man present who did not acknowledge that perhaps after all the mountaineer knew what he was talking about."[99]

As the weeks wore on, York found the groups growing larger. Chaplain Tyler would often top off York's testimony with a sermon of his own. York had a high regard for Chaplain Tyler's desire to reach the soldiers with the Good News, saying, "He was a nice man and a powerful preacher."[100] Major General Duncan supported these efforts to keep up the men's morale. He expected his unit chaplains to play a central role in such work.[101]

While in the Prauthoy training area, the division took time to recognize its soldiers for acts of heroism during the Meuse-Argonne Offensive. The command took affidavits on what York accomplished in the Argonne from the surviving soldiers. The first review of York's heroism had been led by Captain Danforth, on 23 October, when units were still fighting. Based on Danforth's request, General Lindsey authorized a deeper investigation into York's feat.[102]

To ensure the integrity of the inquiry, an officer from outside York's regiment was assigned as the investigation officer. Captain Frank M. Williams of the 82nd Division's 325th Infantry Regiment was selected as the lead. Captain Williams had no relationship with York and was viewed as an honest broker. The investigation included interviews and signed affidavits by all available eyewitnesses.

For starters, Captain Williams had Danforth's first investigation to review. This included the signed affidavits of Privates Beardsley and Kornacki.[103] Incidentally, this first investigation (before Williams was involved) was used to award York the Distinguished Service Cross. The background of this was that after Danforth completed his look, the award was approved by Colonel Wetherill and Brigadier General Lindsey. Major General Duncan approved the award on 30 October, with the statement to General Pershing (the approving authority), "This case has been investigated and the recommendation for the award of Distinguished Service Cross is concurred in."[104] The award was approved by the American commander in chief in early November, and York was awarded the Distinguished Service Cross (DSC) on 30 November 1918.[105] The DSC is second only to the Medal of Honor in recognizing acts of heroism and gallantry on the battlefield.

It was during the postwar period at Prauthoy that Captain Danforth reviewed the AEF policy on the Medal of Honor and submitted a request to have York's DSC rescinded and recommended that York be awarded the Medal of Honor instead. By January 1919, Danforth's request reached the division commander, Major General Duncan. Duncan not only gave his consent to conduct a thorough investigation into the matter, but also would personally be involved in the walk-over of the terrain where Alvin fought. This triggered a rigorous investigation into York's 8 October battle, and thus Captain Williams's doing an investigation on York's heroism.

Prior to the formal investigation, a chance meeting would forever change life for York. Had this not occurred, he most likely would have received the Medal of Honor and then faded into obscurity. When the United States entered World War I in 1917, one of America's greatest portrait artists, Joseph Cummings Chase, lived in Paris. The U.S. government sought his services to paint portraits of

A sketch of Sergeant York done in January 1919 by Samuel Cummings Chase on behalf of the U.S. Army. While doing this artwork, Chase was amazed by the York story and contacted his friend journalist George Pattullo, whose subsequent article on York would make him a national hero.

American DSC recipients during and after the war. Chase accepted this commission, for which he was given the rank of colonel, and then was let loose to capture portraits of American heroes. This assignment brought Chase into the trenches and everywhere else to paint the soldiers. By the time he completed this task in the spring of 1919, he had painted 142 portraits.[106]

In January 1919, Chase caught up with the 82nd All-American Division to complete portraits of its DSC awardees. Among the first he painted was Major General Duncan, who recently had been awarded that medal. During the sitting, Duncan and Chase discussed the division's other DSC recipients, including York. Duncan's description of York's transition from conscientious objector to warrior captivated Chase. Duncan told Chase, "The exploit of this tall, raw-boned Tennessee mountaineer, with a red face and red hair, is the most remarkable I have heard of in the whole war."[107] Once Chase completed his portrait of Duncan, he painted York. Chase found York humble and quiet about his feat and sensed that there was something different about this man.[108] On his own initiative, Chase contacted *Saturday Evening Post* war correspondent George Pattullo and suggested that he write a story about York. Pattullo at that moment was on assignment with the Third U.S. Army headquarters, in the occupied German city of Koblenz. Pattullo followed up on Chase's recommendation and contacted the 82nd.[109]

Pattullo's interest in York served another purpose, for he had hoped to do a piece on the Argonne battle via an interview with the 82nd Division's commander, Major General Duncan. There were criticisms in the United States about the tactics used by General Pershing in the Meuse-Argonne Offensive, which many believed cost the American Expeditionary Forces more casualties than it should have. It seems that Pattullo saw York as another public interest piece that would have little enduring value.[110] But doing a study on York would give Pattullo access to the 82nd's senior officers for a critical discourse on the tactics used in the Argonne. Furthermore, Pattullo had already encountered false heroes during his days covering the war. Of this, he said, there were many "alleged war heroes . . . so many are newspaper made; the soldiers over here could explode many a bubble reputation at home."[111] Because of this scepticism, Pattullo did considerable research into the York story—more than one would normally expect from a news reporter. Only after he checked its accuracy would he publish any story on York. What intrigued Pattullo about Alvin York was his personal struggle to reconcile Christian faith with patriotic duty.[112] Just in case he found York to be genuine, Pattullo arranged with the 82nd Division's chief of staff, Colonel Gordon Johnson, for an exclusive interview with Alvin. Although Pattullo had difficulty in finding transportation from Germany to France, he managed to join York and Major General Duncan on the battlefield near Châtel Chéhéry.[113]

The battlefield investigation occurred on a cold Argonne morning in early February. Several inches of snow covered the ground and there was a heavy wintry overcast. With Pattullo, Duncan, and York was an army photographer, who snapped a series of photos of the York site, the surrounding terrain, and the graves of the soldiers who fell that day.[114] Soldiers were on hand to go over the terrain on Hill 223 as well, so there was a large entourage in the area that morning. But York was the only Medal of Honor inquiry and had priority for Duncan. Joining them on the investigation was Alvin's regimental commander, Colonel Wetherill, and his brigade commander, Brigadier General Lindsey.

The group went over the ground, peppered York with questions, and had him retrace his steps. Throughout the walk the army photographer was busy documenting the terrain. Toward the end of the investigation Brigadier General Lindsey asked, "York, how did you do it?" To which Alvin answered, "It was not man-power but it was divine power that saved me." York told Lindsey that "before I went to war I prayed to God and He done gave me my assurance that so long as I believed in Him not one hair of my head would be harmed; and even in front of them-there machine guns He knowed I believed in Him." Lindsey, moved by York's comments, put his arms around York's shoulders and said in a low voice, "York, you are right."[115] York's regimental commander, Colonel Richard Wetherill, agreed with York's belief that this was an act of divine intervention, and not luck, or skill, when he said to Alvin during the tour of the battleground, "It is not human to do what you have done."[116]

Even George Pattullo was astounded by what he saw and heard. This seasoned reporter could not come up with a rational way to explain how York got out of the fight alive. Pattullo later wrote of their visit to the battlefield: "At last I said, 'I cannot understand, even now, how any of you came out alive.' York replied, simply but earnestly, 'We know there were miracles, don't we? Well, this was one. I was taken care of—it's the only way I can figure it.'"[117]

In February 1919, an investigation was conducted to see if York's action of 8 October 1918 merited the Medal of Honor. While walking the ground with York, Brigadier General Lindsey asked him, "York, how did you do it?" To which, Alvin answered, "It was not man-power but it was divine power that saved me." Lindsey, moved by York's comments, put his arms around York's shoulders and said in a low voice, "York, you are right." This photo would be an important piece of evidence used ninety years later to rediscover the location of the York battlefield. (AHEC)

The officers on the investigation team discussed various temporal explanations of how York accomplished the feat. Some suggested that it was luck, being the right man in the right place, while others commented that as mountain man York had the skills to accomplish such a deed.[118] Alvin patiently listened to their speculations, but flatly rejected each one, saying:

> There had to be something more than man power in that fight to save me. There can't no man in the world make me believe there weren't. And I'm a-telling you the hand of God must have been in that fight. It surely must have been divine power that brought me out. No other power under heaven could save a man in a place like that. Men were killed on

both sides of me and all around me and I was the biggest and the most exposed of all. I have got only one explanation to offer, and only one: without the help of God I jes couldn't have done it. . . . There can be no arguments about that. I am not going to believe different as long as I live.[119]

The investigation into the awarding of the Medal of Honor to York included several interviews. On 6 February, the eyewitnesses were also interviewed by Lieutenant Edwin Burkhalter and George Pattullo.[120] Those interviewed included every soldier present for duty: Privates Kornacki, Sok, Sacina, and Donohue. After being interviewed, their statements were typed, and each soldier swore an oath and signed an affidavit recognizing Alvin York as being responsible for the heroic deed of 8 October.[121]

More interviews were conducted over the next weeks. This included questioning the remaining members from York's platoon as well as the officers who witnessed any aspect of the event. For this portion of the inquiry, the 82nd Division's adjutant, Major R. L. Boyd, conducted the inquest. After completing the interviews, these eyewitness too swore an oath and signed affidavits that supported York as the chief player in the action. This set of testimonies was sworn and signed on 21 February, and included the supporting testimony of Privates Beardsley, Johnson, and Wills; Captain Cox (the only officer to traverse the York site on 8 October); and Lieutenant Woods, who was the first officer to see the men moving out of the Argonne with 132 German prisoners.[122]

Pattullo departed the division convinced that this feat was in fact accomplished by York, and he set about writing the article that would propel York to fame. Meanwhile, the division staff continued to work on York's Medal of Honor packet, finally submitting it on 1 March 1919. The packet was endorsed by Captain Danforth, Major Tillman, Colonel Wetherill, Brigadier General Lindsey, and Major General Duncan. General Pershing made the final endorsement before securing approval from President Wilson.[123] Pershing approved the recommendation and a cable was sent to President Wilson on 15 March supporting the Medal of Honor for York.[124] As the command waited for a decision on York's Medal of Honor, General Pershing directed that an investigation be conducted to ascertain if awards should be given to any of the other seven soldiers with York in the battle.[125]

The 82nd had already looked into granting awards to the other soldiers. Captain Cox, the primary investigation officer assigned to this review, concluded on 14 March after two weeks of looking into the matter that the "result of investigation does not justify recommendation for any of the seven men engaged with Sgt. Alvin C. York."[126] This was reviewed before going forward to General Pershing and was endorsed by Major Tillman, Colonel Wetherill, Brigadier General Lindsey, and Major General Duncan.

York's Medal of Honor was approved on 20 March 1919,[127] stating: "For conspicuous gallantry and intrepidity above and beyond the call of duty in action with the enemy near Chatel-Chéhéry, France, 8 Oct., 1918. After his platoon had suffered heavy casualties and three other noncommissioned officers had become casualties, Cpl. York assumed command. Fearlessly leading seven men, he charged with great daring a machine gun nest, which was pouring deadly and incessant fire upon his platoon. In this heroic feat, the machine gun nest was taken together with four officers and one hundred and twenty-eight men and several guns."[128]

Major General Duncan inquired whether General Pershing would be available to give the award, but unfortunately he was not. The honor then fell to Duncan, who ordered a division parade to officially present the Medal of Honor to Sergeant York on 18 April 1919.[129] As Duncan presented the medal to York, he said, "The commanding general takes particular pride in announcing to the command this fine example of courage and self-sacrifice. Such deeds are evidence of that spirit and heroism which is innate in the highest type of American soldier and responds unfailingly to the call of duty wherever or whenever it may come."[130]

This was followed by Marshal Foch's awarding the French Medaille Militaire and the French Croix de Guerre with Palm to York.[131] Ironically, in preparing for the French event, York was with his men on police call, picking up cigarette butts, just as he had been his first day in the army at Camp Gordon.[132] The ceremony led by Marshal Foch is worth recounting. The French call this event a Prise d'Arme. The ceremony for Sergeant York commenced with the command "Attention," followed by "Gardez-vous!" Gardez-vous triggered a trumpet call, and the words, "Sergeant York, Troix pas en Avance!" With that, York took his place at the front of the formation, adjacent to Marshal Foch. Once York was in position, the following citation was read in French, "All the non-commissioned officers of his platoon having been put out of battle, he took command and with 7 men succeeded in reducing to silence a nest of enemy machine-guns, capturing 132 prisoners, 4 of whom were officers, and several machine-guns."[133] With that, Marshal Foch pinned the award on York's chest, near his heart, and said to him, "Le plus grand exploit jamais realise par un simple soldat de toutes les armees en Europe!" (The greatest achievement accomplished by a common soldier in all the armies of Europe!)[134]

After word spread to several of the other Allied nations of York's heroism, they too recognized him with their own awards for heroism. The first of these to do so was the Balkan nation of Montenegro. Under direction of King Nikolas I, the Montenegrin Minister of War ordered that York be awarded that nation's Silver Medaille pour la Bravoure Militaire.[135] Italy followed by awarding York its highest award, the Croce di Guerra.[136]

Interestingly, despite receiving these high awards, York never wrote home about them or what he did on 8 October. Instead, his letters discussed the farm, planting season, discourses on the health of the animals, and the like. Such humility tends to say a lot about his character. In fact, his family would only get word of what Alvin did in France from an unusual source a month later.

In April, the division finally entrained for Bordeaux.[137] The men camped some twenty-five miles outside of the port city, at St. Selve.[138] They were kept busy with drilling, range firing, school, basketball games, and baseball tournaments, which York's regiment won.[139] There were even soldier talent shows, musical reviews, theatrical dramas, and vaudeville acts put together.[140] Helping the men's morale was the fact that the billeting at St. Selve was the most comfortable they had yet experienced in Europe.[141] Despite this, York said, "I jes sat around . . . waiting for that-thar old ship to come and take us home. Oh, my! The days went by slower and slower. It jes seemed as if we would never get away from France. I'm a-telling you them were the homesickest days I ever had in my life."[142]

When orders arrived to board a ship for home, the division marched with shouts and cheers to the Bordeaux embarkation camp for debugging, equipment cleaning, and filling out paperwork for the return journey.[143] The ship designated to take York's battalion home was the SS *Scranton*, which they would board at the American docks at Bassens.[144] York said: "I'm a-telling you I was tickled. So were the boys."[145] The mood at the docks was invigorating. The

Soldiers of the 82nd Division board the SS *Ohioan* at the American Docks in Bordeaux, France, on 9 May 1919. The preponderance of York's regiment had set sail for the United States the day before on the SS *Scranton*. However, there was not enough room on board that ship for York and sixty-six other men from his unit, who had to wait for the next troop transport. York would spend two seasick weeks on this ship before reaching New York City. (AHEC)

Red Cross was giving the men candy, gum, chocolate, coffee, and jam sandwiches, while a military band played stirring music as they stood in formation waiting for their names to be called.[146] The sunny weather matched the men's mood as, one by one, each was called to enter the ship. York and the last sixty-six men waiting to board the vessel were turned away, as the ship was too full to carry them. This was devastating as the men watched their battalion sail off without them.[147] Thankfully, their wait was of short duration, for the SS *Ohioan* arrived the next day. York and his sixty-six comrades boarded the ship, with the regiment machine gun company and the 3rd Battalion taking up the rest of the vessel. With great cheers and yelling, their journey home began at 2:26 P.M. on 10 May.[148]

York spent the twelve-day trip seasick, as the SS *Ohioan* was a small vessel and took rough seas hard. Although the weather proved not too bad for the North Atlantic, it was more than Alvin could stand, and he was so sick some days that he just wanted to be alone.[149] Things got worse for him on 15 May when the ship's captain received a wire that there would be a big welcoming ceremony for him when they arrived in New York. Alvin did not want any attention and just wanted to go home, saying, "And that hed me worried. I would hev got out and walked if I could hev."[150] York had no idea what was yet before him, but things were out of his hands.

9

Emergence of a National Hero

Here sits in the gallery the man who has been credited with the greatest individual feat of bravery of the war . . . Sergeant Alvin C. York, of Tennessee.

—Tennessee Congressman Cordell Hull, 24 May 1919, Introducing York to the U.S. Congress

The SS *Ohioan* arrived in New York at 2:00 A.M. on the 22nd of May, but a heavy fog prevented the ship from proceeding to the dock. With that, the ship dropped anchor, waited for the fog to clear, and did not get under way again until 10:00. The trip up the channel seemed particularly slow to the men, who were eager to be back on American soil. As the fog parted, York shared the thrill of his shipmates: "I can't tell you how I felt when our ship steamed up New York Harbor and I seed the skyscrapers sorter standing up against the sky. In the distance they looked jes a little like the mountains at home when you see them from a long way off. Oh, my, I was so homesick."[1] Finally, at 2:00 P.M., the ship, escorted by two tugboats, docked at pier number 2 in Hoboken, New Jersey.[2] Upon seeing the Statue of Liberty, York noted that a soldier said to her, "Take a look at me, Old Girl. Take a good look at me, because whenever you want to see me again you will have to turn around."[3]

What York did not know was that as he was waiting for his ship in France, George Pattullo's article hit the newsstands on 26 April 1919 in America's largest paper, the *Saturday Evening Post*. Titled "The Second Elder Gives Battle," the article was received in America with unexpected jubilation, making York an instant star. The story of Alvin York seemed to captivate the American imagination and in some way reflect the collective psyche of the populace that was reluctant to enter the war, but once in it, was committed to

145

winning it. He seemed to represent how Americans viewed themselves: pioneers, devout, patriots, slow to action but firm in resolve.[4]

Editorials soon appeared in American papers about the Pattullo article, extolling the virtues of the American Doughboy and patriotism as personified by Alvin York. One of these editorials published in New Jersey in May reflected the tone of these writings, saying, "From them, who did so much for America, comes the call to us to do our duty to our country."[5] A group of influential Tennesseans in New York City stepped in to arrange the greatest reception that any returning soldier would receive in the aftermath of the Great War.

This group called itself the "Tennessee Society of New York." The Tennessee Society was founded in 1899 by a group of elite sons of their native state who were living in the "strange and unfriendly city" of New York.[6] This group included powerful businessmen and influential political figures, and was well positioned to give York an unforgettable welcome-home ceremony.[7] As soon as they read about York in Pattullo's article, the chairman of the society, Dr. James J. King, immediately sent a letter to Alvin York, who was still in France. York wrote back to Dr. King informing him of his anticipated return and that he was in good health.[8]

With that, Dr. King tasked the chairman of the Society's Entertainment Committee, Captain E. A. Kellogg, with coordinating the reception for York. This proved to be no small endeavor. Using his "Bakers and Confectioners Manufacturing Company" letterhead, E. A. Kellogg wrote to the U.S. Army adjutant in Washington, D.C., and Major General David Shanks, the senior officer at the port of Hoboken, asking them to allow York to attend a banquet in New York City in his honor and to permit him to stay at the prestigious Waldorf Astoria Hotel.[9]

These letters caused the U.S. Army bureaucracy to slowly begin staff actions to determine where exactly York was and on what ship he would return. At the beginning of this process, the chair of the Tennessee Society, Dr. James King, actually had more current information on Alvin's situation than the army did. There was quite a bit of confusion in the army's Hoboken Troop Movement Office, as York was supposed to be on the *Scranton* and they had not been advised of his being bumped onto the *Ohioan*.[10]

Major General Shanks expressed reservations about granting York any leave, saying, "It is always a dangerous thing to give special favors to a man because they are quoted as precedents in other applications. . . . I have, however . . . arranged . . . to give him a forty-eight hour pass so that he may join you."[11] This was insufficient, and the War Department was contacted by a string of influential Tennesseans that compelled the army adjutant general to order Major General Shanks to grant York a five-day furlough. This would give time for York to attend the New York City events and visit Washington, D.C. This was accomplished in no small measure through the influence of York's congressman, Cordell Hull.[12] York was informed at sea that the Tennessee Society intended to welcome him home, but he had no idea how big the welcome would be.

After the ship docked, York saw a throng of people waiting to greet him on the deck below. He was "plumb scared to death" and hid on the ship until most of the passengers disembarked. Finally, the delegation came on board, and York was warmly greeted by a group of Tennessee Society leaders.[13] A photographer snapped photos of York, bedecked with medals, with the rigging of the *Ohioan* behind him. As he was led off the ship by the delegation, a throng of cameramen and reporters pressed into him. Only then did the 328th Regiment soldiers traveling with him realize that they had a hero in their midst and they cheered him on enthusiastically. Some of these men on the *Ohioan* were interviewed, and they were unanimous in saying, "Not once . . . has he shown any disposition to regard his exploit as important."[14]

As York and his hosts endeavored to make their way to the car, reporters peppered Alvin with questions about the war, being a conscientious objector, and his faith in God. York responded in his characteristic brief folksy manner, which seemed to endear him to them. In none of his answers did he take credit for the feat, and he actually rebuffed attempts to pin the deed on his personal heroism by saying, "It was the hand of God that guided us all and brought about the victory. . . . I feel it was through Him that I accomplished what I did." When asked about what was next, he said that he planned on entering the ministry.[15] York later wrote: "I knowed, of course, that a committee from the Tennessee Society was going to meet my boat. And they did. They tried to make a most awful fuss over me. They seemed to think I done done something wonderful. I couldn't see it that way no how. I done done my duty like most any other soldier would have done when he was up against the same thing."[16] It took the group thirty minutes to push through the throng to reach their touring car. Much of the excitement in New York was fueled by

York nervously poses for the camera on the deck of the SS *Ohioan* after docking in Hoboken, New Jersey, on 22 May 1919. York had no idea that the April 1919 piece in the *Saturday Evening Post* about his battle exploits had made him a national hero. He was officially welcomed by the Tennessee Society and whisked away to be feted in New York City and Washington, D.C. (AHEC)

the Tennessee Society. Neil Cullom was the lead planner for York's welcome to New York. He worked tirelessly with city officials to hold nothing back in welcoming Alvin. Cullom shrewdly named this project the "York must see New York Committee."[17]

After reaching the car, they begin their trip to New York City. After a short ferry ride across the Hudson River, York was driven in an open car across New York City and welcomed by throngs of cheering citizens, who lined the streets and filled windows of the skyscrapers above.[18] York said of this reception, "It seemed as most everybody knowed me. They throwed a most awful lot of paper and ticker tape and confetti out of the windows of those big skyscrapers. I wondered what it was at first. It looked like a blizzard. I didn't understand that it was for me until they told me. I thought that they did the same thing for 'most every soldier that came back."[19] When the Tennessee Society escorts in the car with York informed him that this welcome was solely for him, York was shocked.[20] Two complete strangers attended the ticker tape parade who would later play an important role in perpetuating the York story: movie mogul Jesse Lasky and Australian author Tom Skeyhill.

While working in his office on the eighth floor of the Famous Players–Lasky offices, at the corner of Forty-First and Fifth Avenue, Jesse Lasky heard the "hysteric demonstration that welcomed Sergeant Alvin C. York back from the . . . War." Lasky looked out the window and saw the sky full of confetti as the car carrying York passed. At that instant he had "a hot flash of inspiration" and set about to buy the rights to York's story.[21] Over lunch that afternoon, Lasky ran into Flo Ziegfeld, who said to him, "Did you see York's reception? I've got a great idea. I'm going to spot him in the Follies. If I can get him in just a little piece . . . opposite Will Rogers he'll be a sensation." Lasky had already sent his agent to see York and answered, "Well. Good luck. I expect to put him in a picture." Lasky ran into another famous entertainer, Lee Shubert, who said he wanted York in a revue. It seemed that the entire New York entertainment industry was abuzz with excitement.[22]

A few blocks from Lasky was Tom Skeyhill. A veteran of the Australian–New Zealand Army Corps (ANZAC), Skeyhill had landed at ANZAC Cove on the Gallipoli Peninsula on 25 April 1915 facing robust Turkish opposition.[23] His unit later was transferred to Cape Helles, where during the fighting it lost one-third of its men.[24] Skeyhill was one of the casualties, partially blinded by a Turkish shell exploding near his position. After being discharged from the army, Skeyhill arrived in the United States in 1917, where he earned national acclaim as an orator in garnering American support for the war effort. After the war, Skeyhill published his second book, *A Singing Soldier*,[25] had his vision restored by an American physician, and settled in New York as a playwright.[26]

Skeyhill later recalled the scene on that street in New York: "I was one of the thousands that stormed the streets of the city. . . . It seemed as if the floodgates of men's very souls had burst apart and all the pent-up passion of centuries had stormed forth in a mighty surge. Mobs everywhere, with banners, bands, bells, whistles, singing, screaming, clanging, whistling, and in every other way acclaiming the big hero of the day. Everybody's hero, everywhere. Ticker tape in endless waves streamed down from the tall buildings. . . . At first I was skeptical. . . . Yet it was done."[27] Skeyhill wanted to know more about the York story, and would tell it, if no one else would.[28]

After this York was escorted to the Waldorf Astoria Hotel, where he was treated like royalty. The hotel manager, Oscar Tschirkey, usually welcoming dignitaries and powerful political figures, personally escorted the mountain man to a luxurious suite. Once there, E. A. Kellogg showed York a framed photo of his mother that they thoughtfully put in his room. Alvin was excited to see this photograph.[29] Later an attempt was made to telephone his family, since Pastor Pile had recently had a phone installed in his general store. York said that after some minutes of trying the call failed to go through.[30]

Later, York was feted by the Tennessee Society at a dinner in the Waldorf Astoria. He was surrounded by dignitaries, generals, and admirals, including Representative Cordell Hull. Thankfully, there were people familiar to him, such as his division commander, Major General Duncan, and Joseph Cummings Chase, the artist who had painted York's portrait and propelled him to fame by passing word to George Pattullo that previous January.[31] Although glad to reacquaint himself with these men, York was preoccupied by the table setting before him: "I didn't know what all the plates and knives and forks and spoons were for. So, I kinder slowed up and jes kept a couple of moves be hin'd the others. So I knowed what to do."[32] The evening was full of speeches, all in praise of York—something he neither sought nor desired. As the night droned on, York's mind wandered back to the mountains of Pall Mall: "In the middle of that-there old banquet I got to kinder dreaming about home and the little log cabin and my mother and Gracie and them-there hound dogs of mine. I knowed I was to be with them soon, and I sorter couldn't think of anything else."[33]

After Major General Duncan gave a moving introduction to Alvin, the audience called for a speech, wanting York to tell his 8 October war story. York only hesitatingly stood up and said, "I guess you folks all understand that I'm just a soldier boy and not a speaker. I'd love to entertain you-all with a speech to-night, but I just can't do it. I do want to thank Major General Duncan for his courtesy in coming to this dinner-party you-all have given for me, and I want you-all to know that I thoroughly appreciate all your kindness and attention. I just never will forget it."[34] As York sat back down there were shouts from the dinner guests for York to tell his war story. General Duncan leaned over to him and said, "Sergeant, you are with friends, tell them about [the war] just as you would tell me." But Alvin politely refused, saying, "I will do anything the General orders me to do but it is one of the things I want to forget." With that, Duncan relented, telling him, "You don't have to say a word."[35] The Tennessee Society ended the dinner by giving York a $2,000 Victory Note.[36]

Although exhausted, York would not enjoy his presidential suite.[37] Later that evening Congressman Hull took York on a late train to Washington, D.C. They first visited the War Department to meet Secretary Newton D. Baker as well as the army adjutant general, Peter Harris, who had granted him the furlough. After that they visited the White House to meet the president. However, President Wilson was not available, and instead they met his secretary, Joe Tumulty.[38] Then there was a visit to the House of Representatives, where from the floor of the House Congressman Hull said: "Here sits in the gallery the man who has been credited with the greatest individual feat of bravery of the war . . . Sergeant Alvin C. York, of Tennessee." The House rose in a standing ovation, which York acknowledged by standing and saluting.[39] York had the honor of being escorted to the House floor, where "the members all come around me. And there was more questioning and a whole heap of cheers and applause. By this time I was sorter feeling like a red fox circling when the hounds are after it. I was beginning to wonder if I ever would get back to my own home again."[40] After this, York was whisked back to New York City, where he was given a tour of the

Stock Exchange at Wall Street and business was suspended to give him a rousing welcome.[41] Speaking about the Stock Exchange: "That didn't mean nothing to me nohow. A country boy like me jes couldn't understand what it was all about. Rifle-guns, hounds, foxes, coons, mountains, shootin' matches, I understand these things."[42]

When asked what he most wanted to see in New York City, York answered that he wanted to see the subway system. The people of New York obliged, with the president of the Interborough Rapid Transit Company, Theodore P. Shontz, arriving at Grand Central Station in his private subway car, the *Mineola,* and giving York the grand tour of the subway, with a host of experts joining the ride to explain the system to him. Coming out of the tour, Alvin was asked by a reporter if the subway was anything like the trenches, to which York replied in his taciturn and blunt way, "Not much."[43] After that, Alvin was taken to a musical revue at the Winter Garden, where he said, "Some of the women had on fewer clothes than in Paris."[44]

As Alvin's time in New York came to an end, entrepreneurs approached him with offers of vast sums of money if he would only lend his name to their products.[45] York was taken aback: "They offered so much money that it almost takened my breath away."[46] One of the first business propositions was from Jesse Lasky, who sent one of his aides to buy the film rights to the York story. The aide was instructed to "get York's name on a contract no matter what it cost." The aide went straight to the Waldorf Astoria, but despite offering hefty sums of money he could not convince York to sign. The other business propositions offered to York were from the Shuberts, Florenz Ziegfeld, and other producers and vaudeville acts.[47] This included a $20,000-a-week deal to appear in a revue.[48]

Other offers included magazine deals and a $10,000 book deal.[49] On being asked to perform on stage, York said, "wouldn't I look funny in tights, ho, ho."[50] The total offering exceeded $250,000, which would have made Alvin the richest man in Pall Mall.[51] Yet Alvin's rebuff was clear: "My life is not for sale and I don't allow Uncle Sam's uniform for sale."[52] This would not be the last time that Lasky would try to "bag Alvin York."[53] With such a man before them, York-mania seemed to infect everyone. Even one of York's Tennessee Society hosts, Malcolm Meacham, went to the press saying, "I would not be surprised if York would be the next Governor of Tennessee. He can have anything he wants down there."[54] York was unmoved: "I sorter felt that to take money like that would be commercializing my uniform and my soldiering. . . . So I didn't take their thirty pieces of silver and betray that-there old uniform of mine." He wanted to go home "to the mountains where I belonged."[55]

Despite the refusals of publicity and movies, Alvin did leave a vague opening for something to be written about or by him in the future if they would "show what the boys done done over there and also to show what faith will do for you if you believe right."[56] But this exception to his refusal to sign the rights of his life story to anyone was sealed in his diary and none knew that this was the only angle he would accept. It would take Jesse Lasky nearly twenty years to figure out this winning approach with Alvin York.[57]

Alvin departed New York without signing any contracts or deals and reported back to his unit. Ironically, this response by York endeared him even more to the American public. Here at last was a man willing to stand up for the ideals and values that made America great, even giving up the opportunity to become materialistically rich. York had indeed captured the American imagination.[58]

It seems inevitable, however, that fame also attracts its detractors. Even as Alvin stepped off of the ship, on 22 May, controversy was stirring. Unfortunately, some of the articles and news reports added hyperbole to the tale. This actually began with the Pattullo piece. Although there were several inconsistencies in the story, overall it was fairly accurate. But its chief weakness was downplaying the role of the other squad members by saying, "There were seven other Americans present at the fight, but it was York's battle and only York's."[59] The fact of the matter was that in both the personal interviews and the soldiers' affidavits provided to Pattullo it was manifest that they also played a role—albeit a lesser one—in the action.

As the story broke across the nation it stirred newspaper copycat versions of the battle, written by ambitious reporters eager to add some new aspect to the tale. Each of these early pieces borrowed extensively from Pattullo, but merely copying what was already in print was not enough. These new articles took the tale a step further, adding a new twist to it. The most problematic addition to the York story came from articles that stated York captured the 132 Germans single-handed. An example of this is from New Jersey's *South Amboy Citizen*, which published an article on the battle in early April. The piece went to great lengths to remind the readers that there were seventeen men in the attack, and York was just one of them. Listing them by name, the article gave the entire seventeen great credit, but added, "York did the fighting and killing single-handed."[60]

Neither York nor the U.S. Army made such bold assertions. When asked, York tended to mention the other men and downplay his own role ("I only did my duty the best I could"), and when he did speak of himself, he reminder the listeners that he did what he did only because of God.[61] This is demonstrated by a speech he delivered in July 1919: "I live and practice a full salvation and I believe in continual prayer. While I was in France, I prayed continually to God."[62] Furthermore, York's Medal of Honor citation states clearly that he was *not* alone, but had seven men with him during the action. Despite this, the press spun the tale, and their story seemed to grow the more it was retold.

And then there were the detractors, who doubted the York tale from the start. The first of these was a skeptical *New York Times* reporter, who questioned Major General Duncan as he stepped off of the transport *Sierra* at New York City. Duncan's answer was blunt: "The case was thoroughly investigated . . . and the result was the recommendation for the Congressional Medal of Honor. . . . He is one of the bravest men and entitled to all the honor that may be given to him."[63] This same reporter ambushed York a few days later as he also stepped off of the ship onto American soil. When the reporter told York that there were soldiers in his unit who doubted his courage, Alvin was taken aback, "Sure 'nough? Well the [soldiers] made affidavits . . . that I had done all the things claimed."[64]

It is worth noting that the reporter's assertion that soldiers of the 328th protested the award was unlikely. The ships bearing those men had been at sea, with no way for a reporter to have established contact with them. Furthermore, there are no reports or documentation of any protests against York's being awarded the Medal of Honor while the division was in France. This *New York Times* reporter's question, with the added assertion that 328th Regiment members opposed York's Medal of Honor, was a fabrication. He would be the first of many who would attack the York story over the next century.

One soldier's receiving so much attention, this *New York Times* reporter correctly surmised, eventually would lead someone to protest. For York, the bar was set high, arriving to a ticker-tape parade greater than any other given to a single, junior enlisted soldier in American history. Then there was also York's never-ending statement that his God made this deed possible. Such statements tended to make people uncomfortable, because if such were true it had ramifications for one's life. The idea that York survived the carnage because of divine intervention also speaks of a miracle.

Had York faded into obscurity, a controversy over his exploits would not exist. But this was not to be his lot. He would be thrust into the public eye and would suffer added scrutiny, which makes a good story. Thus, any controversy becomes a self-fulfilling prophesy. A reporter makes an unfounded assertion in the form of a question, knowing that it will be just a matter of time before someone steps forward with an axe to grind. When a disgruntled veteran comes forth, he finds a willing press interested in controversy, all in an effort to sell papers. Ironically, it was the press that exaggerated York's feat, and reporters would fuel the flames of jealousy between Alvin and his "buddies" by giving rivals a prominent platform to attack York. Indeed, jealousy is a powerful emotion, and it would turn men who once fought shoulder to shoulder against each other.

For York, however, controversy was far from his mind in May 1919. He had only one thing on his mind: home. With his furlough up, York reported to Camp Merritt, New Jersey, to begin the process of demobilization. He was offered a chance to forego army out-processing and go directly home, but he refused special treatment. "I want to see the thing through from start to finish." From Camp Merritt, York was sent to Fort Oglethorpe, near Atlanta.[65] After a long train ride, Alvin arrived there on 29 May 1919 and paid 20 cents for two pairs of lost army stockings from his military issue. After this he received his final pay through 30 May (his final authorized travel day) and began the last leg of his journey.[66]

York's final character evaluation in his Military Service Record was rated as "Excellent," thus ending his short but illustrious career in the U.S. Army. In his records there are no derogatory annotations, no infractions of military law, and no reports of being AWOL or of violating any orders. Every officer signing his records stated that he had either "Very Good" or "Excellent" character.[67] Alvin reflected on his experience in the army and wrote, "I'm a-saying right here that they treated me right smart all the time that I was in the Army. They done played the game with me and they played square. So far as I am concerned the officers and everybody connected with the Army done done the right thing by me. They were right-smart folk."[68]

Alvin arrived at Crossville, Tennessee, in the afternoon of 29 May. This was the closest the train could bring him to Pall Mall. Here, Alvin was surprised to see six cars from Jamestown (reputed to be the entire fleet of cars in Jamestown at the time) lined up to take him home. Jamestown would be the final stop before heading home to Pall Mall. After greeting the welcoming home committee and other well-wishers, York looked at the line of cars and said, "Which rig do you-all want me to get in?" To this, every driver waved for him to take a seat in his car.[69] Alvin was thrilled to see the two most important Christians in his life there. Pastor Pile and Sam Williams had driven their Model Ts up to Crossville to meet Alvin.[70]

Alvin arrived in Jamestown at 7:00 P.M., where, to his great delight, his mother and his brothers and sisters were eagerly waiting for him. The same Dr. Mullinix who had recommended his draft was on hand and recorded that there were no outward emotions. Mother York simply said, "Hello Alvin," with Alvin answering, "Hello Ma." The doctor observed that Mother York had tears in her eyes.[71] After being welcomed home, he climbed onto a mule-pulled wagon and began the thirteen-mile ride to Pall Mall with his family along a windy, hilly path. Pastor Pile drove ahead in his car. Along the way his neighbors and friends came down to the path to welcome their hero back.[72] Greetings, such as "How are you Al?" were answered by him with, "Oh, fair to middlin. How's the hogs and crops?"[73] This was a thrilling time for York, being back with his family and friends and in his valley. The closer he was to home, the happier he became.[74]

Alvin arrived at Pall Mall, where a group of well-wishers waited for him, all shooting their guns into the air in celebration.[75] He had a conversation with Pastor Pile, who was relieved to hear that Alvin still was strong in his faith.[76] Concerning what had happened to York, the pastor could only say, "The Hand of God was on you Alvin."[77] Pastor Pile admired York's ability to so easily turn down the opportunities to make money, laughingly saying that had he been offered $10,000 to write his life story, "I reckon I'd have been a getting busy writing if it had been me."[78]

As soon as Alvin's hunting dogs heard his voice near the cabin, they came running. "And, oh, my, what a joyful time I had with them-there hound dogs of mine. I done set down and looked at them and patted them and they wagged their tails and licked my hands, and then, ho, ho, they bayed and sorter circled round, and sorter lit out for the woods; jes to sorter remind me that they hadn't been foolin' round nohow while I was away, and they still knowed where the coons and possums and the foxes were."[79]

Although his dogs were ready to go hunting, Alvin "went a-hunting for Gracie."[80] Alvin met Gracie at her home near Butterfly Branch, where the two went off alone to speak. York had reason to be concerned. Although they technically had been engaged in 1917, Gracie was the one who wanted to wait for marriage until he was back from the war. With this on his mind, Alvin wanted to set a date for the wedding.[81] Although they never disclosed the details of their dialogue, it was here she consented to marriage. York could not be happier. The girl for whom he had stayed pure, despite ample opportunities in France to do otherwise, would be his wife.[82] For Alvin, things just seemed as if they could not get any better than this.[83] Alvin and Gracie would be married within the week.

There was much that York wanted to do on arrival back home. The first thing he did the next morning was climb up his mountain to where he had gone a year before to ascertain God's will for his life when struggling with the idea of serving in the army and where he felt God speak to him. York said, "He had given me my assurance that even if I didn't think it right I should go jes the same; and would be protected from harm; and would come back without a hair of my head injured." On this spot York raised his hands to heaven in thanksgiving for all God did to bring him through the storm in the Argonne, and so much more. After that, York wanted to get back to the way things were, saying, "In a few days I had the old uniform off and the overalls on. I done cleaned up the old muzzle-loader. It was all over. I was home."[84]

Meanwhile, the governor of Tennessee, Albert H. Roberts, had been trying to catch up with York at Fort Oglethorpe to convince him to come to Nashville for a state welcome home parade. When this did not materialize, the governor attempted to get York to commit to a 4th of July celebration in Nashville, something else York was not interested in. Finally, on hearing about York's impending marriage, Governor Roberts offered to conduct the wedding. Although Alvin preferred to have Pastor Pile conduct the ceremony, the governor's offer was too much to refuse, and they agreed as long as it was conducted in Pall Mall.[85] Governor Roberts relented, but insisted that immediately following the ceremony the entire wedding party should travel to Nashville with him.[86] Upon meeting York later that week, Governor Roberts was impressed by the man's character, saying later, "York is no faker. There is nothing about this whole York setup that is not absolutely genuine."[87]

Alvin and Gracie were married on 7 June in Pall Mall. Between three thousand and six thousand people came from around the region to attend the ceremony, jointly led by Governor Roberts and Pastor Pile.[88] The wedding was conducted outside, on a large rock on the York farm property. York's bride, Miss Gracie (as he would call her throughout his life), spoke often of how the Christian symbolism of being married on the "solid rock" was like the marriage being built on Christ.[89] The people of Pall Mall provided the food for the celebration, which was bigger than anything the town had experienced. The weather was perfect, and it truly was idyllic in its setting in the Valley of the Three Forks of the Wolf River. York said, "And the mountain people provided the vittles. They brought in goats and hogs and turkeys and slaughtered and dressed them right there on the hillside. They set up a table, the largest I ever seed, and they done piled it up with all the meats and eggs there was and with sweet potatoes and cornbread and milk and jams and cakes and a whole mess of other things. We were married on the mountainside above the spring and under the shady trees and with the blue mountains and green grass and the flowers all around."[90] After they exchanged their vows, Alvin and Gracie kissed for the first time to the cheers of the throng of spectators.[91]

After celebrating in Pall Mall, the wedding party, complete with Pastor Pile and Mother York, started its journey to Nashville to be entertained by the governor on 9 June.[92] There were rousing speeches, cheers, and applause by proud Tennesseans. At the largest of these events, twenty thousand people attempted to hear Alvin speak at the Ryman Auditorium in Nashville, with only six thousand of these being allowed into the theater.[93] As usual, Alvin kept his remarks few, and firmly set the pattern of how he would contend with his war talk, saying, "You have come here to honor me. I am willing to believe that this honor you are doing here is for me personally. Every American soldier that took the oath of allegiance to his country and the flag could have done exactly the same thing I did if it had been his to do it. You don't owe me any honor. Every reason you have now for honoring me you have for honoring each and all of these boys. God gave me the opportunity to do this great service as I believe for the cause of humanity. I want you to realize every soldier here would have done the same thing."[94]

But during this tour York refused to talk about anything he had done, and instead either gave the credit to God or to the American army generally. In the midst of the celebrations, the most important event for Alvin and Gracie was meeting with the Tennessee Rotary Club, which pledged to raise enough money to provide them with a farm, replete with good bottomland, in Pall Mall.[95]

After being feted, the couple was to travel to Salt Lake City, Utah, as a guest of the National Convention of Rotary Clubs being held there. The trip would include stops and speaking engagements along the way, but Alvin and Gracie were weary of the public exposure. They conferred with Pastor Pile, who said that this was "a vain glorious call of the world and the devil." Pile himself was remorseful in that he felt coerced into attending a vaudeville show, for which he later wrote a public apology of repentance to the newspaper expressing his regret at attending such a worldly event.[96] With that in mind, and wanting some peace, Gracie and Alvin canceled the trip and returned home on 11 June with the rest of the bridal party. The couple moved into the York cabin with his mother and a few of the younger siblings and settled down to a traditional life of running the York farm until the Rotary house was built.[97]

Alvin had hoped to escape the limelight and take up the quiet life of hunting and farming that he had known before the war. This had been the way of life of his forefathers for more than one hundred years, and it was what he intended to do as well. However, something inside York was stirring that would not allow him to accept things in Pall Mall as they were. Despite efforts to fade into obscurity, it seemed that the limelight always fell back onto him. This endeavor to return to a solitary life in Pall Mall was not helped by Alvin's new worldview. At first he desired to go back to the way things were, but it was not possible, as he had changed and the war had changed him. He had been exposed to progress, innovation, and other technological advances that were actually beneficial to people. This was the type of progress Pall Mall needed.

This divergence between Pall Mall and the rest of the world was evident during his journey across the United States and Europe. Life in Pall Mall seemed frozen in time. Additionally, it was quite an effort to actually travel in or out of Pall Mall, with the closest train being forty-seven miles away in Crossville. Even traveling to the county seat of Jamestown, less than twelve miles away on a battered mountain road, was an all-day endeavor. Alvin struggled with his dilemma: "The whole outside world seemed to have changed. But not our valley. Everything there was kinder the same. But I knowed, though, that I had done changed. I knowed I wasn't like I used to be. The big outside world I had been in and the things I had fought through had teched me up inside a most powerful lot."[98]

The tipping point for Alvin occurred at church, where he was appalled that nothing had changed for the children, with the same ones listening and the same ones sleeping in services. His thoughts raced across what he had witnessed, seeing entire towns razed, watching thousands of lives extinguished, yet the locals seemed unaware and unmoved by the cataclysm that had swept away so many. He was not sure what to do, but living in blissful isolation and ignorance from the rest of the world was no longer an option. "The war had come and gone. Millions of boys had been killed and wounded. Millions of dollars had been poured out jes like water. Homes all over the world had been desolated. Some of the old countries had been all mussed up and new ones had come up and sort of takened their places. The whole outside world seemed to have changed. But not our valley."[99] York was "sort of restless and full of dreams and wanting to be doing something." He wanted roads built into Pall Mall, modern schools, improved farming methods, libraries, and up-to-date homes. Alvin shared his dreams with Gracie, who supported this desire. But he was not sure what to do.

10

Back on the Farm
in Pall Mall

I ain't going to show any favoritism nohow. I fought with
Catholics and Protestants, with Jews, Greeks, Italians, Poles,
and Irish, as well as American borned boys in the World
War. They were buddies of mine and I learned to love them.
If there is any of them in these-here mountains we'll make
a place for them in these schools. I'm a-going to give all the
children in the mountains the chance that's a-coming to them.
I'm a-going to bring them a heap o' larnin.
> —Alvin York on improving life in Pall Mall

The war forever radically changed the world. Four Old World
empires vanished (the Ottoman, German, Austro-Hungarian, and
Russian), and four ancient dynasties ended (the Hohenzollerns of
Germany, the Hapsburgs of Austria, the Romanovs of Russia, and
the Ottomans of the Turks). Twelve million died directly from the
effects of the conflict, and up to 100 million more in the Spanish
influenza plague that swept the world after the war.[1] The map of
Africa was redrawn, and in the Middle East and Eastern Europe
new nations sprang forth, some out of the victor's imagination. Life
had changed, and it was York's desire for the folks of Pall Mall to
catch up with the world, or risk being consumed by it.

With Bible and rifle in hand, Alvin went to his prayer spot on
the mountain to contemplate his new dilemma.[2] His prayers were
answered quickly, and he believed that God had equipped him for
taking on the challenge of bringing changes to his valley. Reflecting
on this, Alvin said:

And the more I thought the more I kinder figured that all
of my trials and tribulations in the war had been to prepare

161

me for doing just this work in the mountains. All of my suffering in having to go and kill were to teach me to value
human lives. All the temptations I done went through were
to strengthen my character. All the associations with my
buddies were to help me understand and love my brother
man. All of the pains I done seed and went through were to
help and prepare me. And the fame and fortunes they done
offered me in the cities were to try me out and see if I was
fitted for the work He wanted me to do.[3]

And then there was Alvin's fame. He was willing to accept the
Rotary Club initiative to provide him with a farm.[4] It did not seem
right to take more.[5] Yet, he left the door open to accept an offer that
would glorify God and honor his fellow soldiers.[6] The key ingredi-
ent for York was that as long as he was not acting on selfish gain,
he could use his notoriety to help others. With this in mind, he saw
it morally right to use this fame for the improvement of life for his
people, especially that of the children.[7]

Alvin saw three things that were needed in his community:
roads, vocational schools, and the expansion of Christian teaching.
He wasted no time getting a good road built into Pall Mall. Using
his clout and the influence of the Tennessee governor, he visited the
State Highway Department in Nashville, who soon began work cutting a good road across the mountains into Pall Mall. This road is
now a ten-mile portion of U.S. Route 127 linking Pall Mall to Jamestown. Called the "York Highway," it gave the valley access to the
outside world.[8]

Next came the most difficult to achieve, building a school. Based
on the notion that he would use his fame to raise money, Alvin established the York Foundation. The foundation was a nonprofit association that would serve as the focal point for raising funds to build
schools in the region. His desire was that the foundation would not
only pay the construction costs, but also the teachers' salaries and
the maintenance of the facilities. York wanted to ensure that the next
generation had the education that he never received—and with it,
a greater chance of success.[9] Additionally, it was imperative that
the schools provide scholarships so that every child could attend
regardless of their parents' financial state.[10] He desired that the children be provided a high-quality education that would first teach the
basics, and then vocational skills. Alvin thought that the vocational

aspect should focus on skills needed in the region, such as animal husbandry, carpentry, dressmaking, farming, fruit tree growing, home economics, etc.[11]

With this vision, York took to the road to raise funds in the fall of 1919, which turned into a trip across the nation. He was assisted by his friends in the Nashville Rotary Club, who made arrangements with Rotarians around the country to plan and organize events to support Alvin's foundation. Traveling with Gracie for a portion of the journey, Alvin was received by large crowds and excited ovations. Naturally, they wanted to hear about his war experiences, which York continued to shy away from. His tour, although having a good start, was cut short. After a speaking engagement in Boston, Alvin suffered from acute appendicitis, forcing him to abruptly end that round of visits. This was the first in a string of health issues with which he would wrestle.[12] Despite this, his fund-raising was off to a good start, which he would continue through 1920 in New York, Pittsburgh, Chicago, and many other cities.[13]

Nevertheless, York's personal financial situation took a turn for the worse in 1921. The problem was that the Rotary Club failed to raise enough money to cover the cost of the farm, and Alvin simply did not have such money. E. J. Buren, a writer for *The World*, published a moving article in the *Washington Post* that was the first to help the public understand York's financial problems and the truth about the farm. Buren wrote that although the Nashville Rotary claimed to have purchased and given the farm to Alvin York, it had not done so as of December 1921. This had not happened as they still owed a considerable amount of money on the property because their donation solicitations had fallen well below what was needed. Because of this, Alvin, Gracie, and then eight-month-old Alvin Jr. were still living with York's mother.[14]

Upon hearing of York's financial dilemma, the federal government attempted to ameliorate his indebtedness. Congressman Cordell Hull and Senator Kenneth McKellar, both of Tennessee, lobbied to vote through Congress a bill, House Resolution 8599, granting York retired status as an army lieutenant (under the House version) or a captain (under the Senate version). If passed, this would have provided him a modest monthly pay allotment.[15] This included an appeal to Secretary of War Newton D. Baker, who answered the request with a hearty endorsement, noting that although it was an exception to policy, none deserved it more.[16]

As Congress discussed and debated the matter, the War Department's enthusiasm waned and faded, especially when a new secretary of war entered the fray. This process dragged on for nearly a decade. By 1928, the bureaucracy prevailed, with Secretary of War Dwight F. Davis paying lip service to Alvin York but laying down all the reasons why he should not receive such a benefit. Davis claimed that doing this for York put the national defense at risk by paying out annuities to inactive members, saying that the Congressional Medal of Honor was sufficient recognition of his heroism.[17]

The congressional effort to commission York as a retired officer with pay benefits would go on for sixteen years before the bill was passed.[18] By the time the bill reached the president for his signature it was 1942, and Franklin Delano Roosevelt was in the Oval Office. He signed it into law without question.[19] No doubt the outbreak of the Second World War was the only thing that made this possible. The bill promoted two Great War heroes to major: Alvin York and Sam Woodfill. Woodfill and York were two of the three greatest heroes of the First World War according to General Pershing.[20] The third, Major Whittlesey, the commander of the Lost Battalion, was given no benefit as he had died in 1921.[21]

The 1920 public did not know that these initiatives to help York had failed and assumed that he was taken care of by his nation. When asked by E. J. Buren when was the last time he received anything from the U.S. government, York replied that he received $60 on 30 May 1919 as his final pay from the army.[22] Since then, there was nothing.[23] In this he was treated no differently than any other AEF veteran. This was all the pay and benefits any soldier would receive coming back from the Great War. Alvin expected no more.

The misperception about Alvin's housing situation started on his return from France in May 1919. While being escorted around New York City, he was told that the Nashville Rotary Club had not only purchased the land and the farm, but that it was his without any debt or hitches.[24] However, this was not so. The massive 410-acre farm had been purchased for $23,000, with the Rotary raising $10,937.50 of the cost, leaving York with the burden of paying the remaining $12,062.50.[25] This did not include the extra $15,000 that it would cost to have a home built on the farm, with barns, etc.[26] Raising such money was nigh impossible for York even in a good farming season. The year 1921 proved particularly difficult, and even though York worked night and day, "His hay was practically burned up and other crops failed."[27] Although Alvin appreciated the Nashville Rotary Club's generous donation, this was more than he could handle financially, especially as he also had to purchase $3,000 worth of machinery and animals to start working the land. This placed him, for the first time in his life, in a debt that he could not pay no matter how hard he worked.[28]

To get out from under this crushing debt, York's friends urged him to sign a film or vaudeville deal to raise money. Alvin refused to compromise on the matter, saying that the same God that brought him safely through the war would likewise also safely see him through this trial.[29] Of this he said, "My conscience told me that both propositions were wrong and I refused to consider them at any price."[30] York added during a speaking engagement at Asbury College that "he would rather be 'a pauper and homeless knowing that he was serving God and would have a Home in heaven.'"[31] This moral stance earned him condemnation in some circles, by individuals who saw nothing wrong with taking the expedient way out of his financial crisis and selling his story to vaudeville. Some of the critics were so angered by his morality against signing stage deals that they not only withdrew their pledges to help pay off the farm, but also slandered his performance as a soldier. When asked to respond to the personal attacks, Alvin refused.[32]

The Nashville Rotary, with help from the local newspaper, attempted to raise the remaining money but could not, and members told E. J. Buren that it looked like they would fail in even making the next payment. Nevertheless, the matter gained national attention, garnering an outpouring of support for Alvin. The Tennessee Society of New York again rose to the occasion and solicited generous donations from its members. Additionally, the *Chicago Tribune*, Edgar Foster of the *Nashville Banner*, the New York Stock Exchange, and Marvin Campbell, an Indiana banker, used their influence and personal funds to raise money for the indebted and "homeless" sergeant.[33]

A fund-raising drive to provide York with the money he needed by Christmas was undertaken across the nation in 1921.[34] At last, the public had the truth on Alvin's financial need and rallied to pay off his land and house. With a heart of thanksgiving, York was given the deed to the land, and he thanked both America and God for providing for his needs. Several years after the land was pledged to him, work could begin on a house for Alvin, Gracie, and their grow-ing family.[35]

Although facing mounting debt, York refused to give up on his dream of building schools for the children of his area. By 1922 he had collected $12,000 in hard cash (in the York Foundation Fund) and had a further $20,000 in pledges. True to his morals, 100 percent of the money raised in this endeavor was strictly for the construc-tion of schools. A board of advisors was appointed to dutifully and faithfully monitor the use of all York Foundation funds, as well as to ensure the integrity of this undertaking.[36] Yet, he set aside none of this money to cover taxes, something the IRS would come after him for later.

In the midst of this, York received a boost in notoriety with the publication in 1922 of a book by Sam Cowan called *Sergeant York and His People*.[37] Cowan claimed to hail from York's region of Tennes-see and took an interesting approach to the story. Instead of making Alvin's military exploits the center of this work, he focused on life in Appalachia. As the *New York Times* review of the book said, "Mr. Cowan has utilized Sergeant York as the 'peg' upon which to hang a more or less intimate description of the people of the Cumber-land Mountains."[38] To develop this portrayal of the mountain life, Cowan spent two months living in Pall Mall and witnessed the now legendary turkey shoots, the logrollings, and the importance of the Christian faith to these people. Cowan was spellbound by the sim-ple yet difficult life that these Appalachian Tennesseans lived. It was because of this, Cowan suggested, that men such as Davy Crockett, Daniel Boone, and Alvin York exist.[39] Yet sales of the book were dis-appointing, as interest in the Great War had already faded in the United States.

In the meantime, York continued criss-crossing the country over the next several years to raise money for his schools. A major break-through occurred when the State of Tennessee and Fentress County each pledged $50,000 in support of York's vocational high school in 1926.[40] Meanwhile, the land for this facility was given by sev-eral generous donors. The county gave York 135 acres of prime land near Jamestown, while several lumbermen donated more than 1,235 acres for the endeavour. With these, in addition to the many finan-cial gifts that had been safely tucked away in the York Foundation account in Nashville, it was time to start construction.[41]

The decision to build the school in Jamestown instead of Pall

Mall was logical, as it offered the children from across the county an opportunity for an education in a central location. Because of this, York's school would have to add dorms for those coming from farther out. On 8 May 1926, Alvin broke ground for what would be called the "Alvin C. York Industrial Institute" before the applause of some two thousand supporters. This first building would be made of stone and brick and was to be ready for use in the fall. Despite this, much work remained. Constructing dormitories and barns, clearing a pasture, and erecting a woodworking shop were all yet to be accomplished. The plan was to have ten teachers and two hundred students. While the construction was ongoing, the York Institute would formally begin in an old building across the street. The eighth anniversary of York's 8 October 1918 battle (1926) was the appointed day to officially open the school, but this had to be postponed to 1927.[42] Although Alvin proudly graduated his first class in May 1927, he would soon discover that fighting the Germans was easier than fighting local politicians.

The selection of the site in Jamestown pitted York against the local power brokers, who had been growing in their opposition to him. Although York leveraged his popularity to push through his agenda, he would find that this tactic could only go so far. Alvin would soon discover that "a prophet is not without honor except in his own town and in his own home." There was a segment of influential officials and rich businessmen who resented York's celebrity and political power. They made up half of the board of the York Foundation.[43] Although Alvin had powerful political friends in Nashville and Washington, the local faction was scheming to push him aside as quickly as possible. Alvin soon found that it was easier to work with people outside the region, who did not have agendas or ambitions to sidetrack his vision for educating the area's youth. He also felt acutely betrayed by these former "friends" who had turned against him. The challenge he faced was daunting. "The Board they give me couldn't see things the way I did. So I have had a most awful hard fight, a much worser one than the one I had with the machine guns in the Argonne."[44]

The local power brokers included a list of influential Fentress County figures: W. L. Wright, the Bank of Jamestown president; Judge H. N. Wright; J. T. Wheeler; County Superintendent Ocie O. Frogge; Ward R. Case; George Stockton; and W. E. Porter.[45] They seemed to oppose his every move. Alvin was only able to break the impasse by holding public hearings, which won local support and state government intervention.[46] Yet, the local power brokers did all they could to stymie his school, with the aim of pushing York out of the way altogether. In their defense, they did have a different vision as to how the York Foundation and school should be run. York lacked formal education, lacked qualifications to run the institution, and was inclined to install similarly unqualified friends and family into key positions. Meanwhile, those opposed to him preferred to install qualified people with professional educational experience. As the driving force behind the effort, York wanted to keep control of his institution. With these polar opposite views, things were about to come to a head.[47]

The bickering forced York to initiate legal action against those whom he saw as standing in the way of the school, causing him much anguish. In one incident, York had the furniture and equipment removed from a temporary school building so that the court would have to decide who had the legal right of its use. In the midst of this, Alvin continued to raise money for the school while trying to take care of his family and farm.[48]

After losing the support of the local power brokers, it became difficult for Alvin to run the institute. He appealed to the state to intervene, and in response the Tennessee government took over the York Institute in 1936, much to Alvin's chagrin. This was the price of overcoming the local power brokers.[49] Understandably, not having a formal education put York at a distinct disadvantage with the state administrators, who forced him to resign. As a consolation, the Prohibition Party named Alvin as its 1936 vice presidential candidate the same week that he lost control of his school, an honor that he graciously declined.[50]

Despite the tribulations, York had accomplished the impossible, and the school is still vibrant and active today. He brought education to his region and thereby gave his people opportunities that he had lacked. Without his tireless leadership, this project never would have come to fruition.

Throughout the seventeen-year odyssey to raise the Alvin C. York Institute, Alvin poured his heart and soul into the work. His family and farm suffered for this, with him gone so much trying to raise funds to make the dream a reality. With every speech, Alvin was asked about the Great War, something he shied away from or downplayed.[51] All he wanted to discuss was his school and the kids in Fentress County. In exasperation to a war question, he answered: "I'm trying to forget the war. I occupied one space in a fifty-mile front. I saw so little—it hardly seems worth while discussing it. I'm trying to forget the war in the interest of the mountain boys and girls that I grew up among."[52] He only slowly grasped the idea in 1927 that it was the war that drew the crowds and provided the donations to build his school. It fell to someone whom York had never met to come into his life with an idea on how to address this. That person was Tom Skeyhill, who had witnessed York's arrival in New York in May 1919.

In 1927, Skeyhill made his way to Pall Mall to convince York to write a biography. At first York refused, but after "reminiscing of old days of the front," Skeyhill convinced him, saying that the money earned from this could be used to build and expand the school for mountain children that he so desired.[53] Skeyhill would help York by serving as the book's editor.[54] Tom Skeyhill proved the right choice. He convinced *Liberty Magazine* to invest $40,000 to buy the rights for a two-part serial release of portions of the book in the summer of 1928. He also secured an agreement with Doubleday for a nation-wide release of the completed book later in 1928, titled *Sergeant York: His Own Life Story and War Diary.*[55] In 1930 Skeyhill worked with York to publish a children's version of his story, which included Appalachian pioneer vignettes. That book was *Sergeant York: Last of the Long Hunters.*[56] To write these books, Skeyhill imitated Cowan's idea of spending time in the region watching everyday life, turkey shoots, and church services. But he also had a grasp of life as a soldier. Because of this, he surpassed Cowan's work.

Skeyhill helped York put together a well-presented biography. The book's strength was that it laid out a convincing case of the evidence supporting York's actions on 8 October 1918. This was to answer what Skeyhill suggested was a common reaction to the story. "At first I was skeptical. Who was not? It sounded too much like a fairy tale. It just could not be done. It was not human. Yet it was done," he wrote in the preface of his book.[57] To answer such questions, Skeyhill included affidavits as well as portions of the investigation that the AEF conducted in February 1919. The book was a resounding success and was quickly followed by the "boy's" version of the story, *Sergeant York: Last of the Long Hunters.* The latter book was dedicated to Alvin's sons, Alvin Jr., George Edward Buxton, Woodrow Wilson, Sam Houston, and Andrew Jackson.[58]

York on the 1929 cover of the U.S. Army War College Annual Exposition. The U.S. Army featured York as its guest of honor during its annual expo in Washington, D.C., in 1929, which included an exaggerated reenactment of his 8 October 1918 battle. (AHEC)

York continued to travel around the country raising money for his school. It seemed that America could not get enough of him, and with the story out at long last, perhaps the clamoring for war stories from him would end. However, between 3 and 5 October, the U.S. Army War College conducted its annual fair in Washington, D.C., with the highlight of the exposition being a twice-daily reenactment of the Sergeant York action.[59] The "Smashing through the Argonne with Sergeant York" show drew ten thousand spectators each day. The exposition included displays of the U.S. Army's and U.S. Air Corp's latest weapons.[60]

To reenact the York action accurately, the U.S. Army assigned several officers to go through the archives and to interview eyewitnesses. However, the officers could not find maps that accurately depicted the location in France. To fill this historical gap, the researchers contacted Buxton and Danforth. The problem was that neither of these officers was an eyewitness to the action and therefore both had to rely on second- and third-hand information to develop their own grossly inaccurate sketches.[61] Despite this, the army made the best of what it had to support the reenactment. These grossly inaccurate maps would later mislead future investigations in France trying to find the York site.

York and the surviving members of his platoon were invited as guests of the U.S. Army to participate in this event. The expo culminated with the presentation of the Distinguished Service Cross to Sergeant Early for leading the sixteen men into the German flank that morning in 1918. Among the others invited from York's outfit was Corporal William Cutting.[62] Having enlisted under the false name of William Cutting, Otis B. Merrithew had begun a campaign in the early 1920s against the U.S. Army to secure an award for himself, and claimed that it was he who took over when Sergeant Early fell, not York.[63] It will be remembered that Merrithew confessed to a personal dislike of Alvin York while they served together in the 328th Infantry Regiment. Ironically, the difference between the two remained stark. York wanted to forget the war and would rather talk about his school, while Merrithew continually talked about the war and wanted others to know his point of view on this matter.[64] To set the record straight, Merrithew began a letter-writing campaign to local newspapers in 1920. Having not achieved headway there, Merrithew found another way with his invitation to the 1929 Army War College Exposition, which put him in contact with Danforth, Harry Parsons, Buxton, and the other squad members.

Nevertheless, his endeavors to get a medal were not supported. Cutting's platoon sergeant, Harry Parsons, flatly rebuffed him. This was the same Parsons whom Cutting claimed he handed the prisoners to on Hill 223. Of this, Parsons said in his thick Brooklyn brogue, "It was York's party. . . . It was York's Battle."[65] To be sure that he was understood, Parsons added in another interview that he rejected Cutting's allegations, saying, "Alvin York deserves every bit of the credit given him."[66] Cutting also hit a dead end with his former company commander, Captain Danforth, who rejected the assertion that Cutting was the hero of the battle, saying, "Credit was given where credit was due."[67] Cutting's last avenue was Colonel Buxton. Buxton was not at all involved in the action, and instead was far from the battle and working on the division staff in October 1918. Buxton, ever judicious, offered to review any facts that Cutting could present.[68]

The Army Exposition not only put Cutting in contact with his squadmates, but with the press as well, who were attracted by the controversy regardless of its merits. As for Cutting's demand that he be awarded a Silver Star, Buxton refused to support him because the affidavits that Cutting produced were too vague to support his side of the story, but the colonel did tell him that he was authorized the Purple Heart. The only concession given was by Brigadier General Lindsey, who mentioned Privates Wills, Beardsley, and Kornacki in his brigade commendations report in 1919. Lindsey conceded that all the men in the attack should have been listed therein.[69]

Buxton was quick to point out that the facts were with York, saying: "All investigations by those in authority and the affidavits of the surviving enlisted men clearly indicate that York bore the chief burden of initiative and achievement in the fire fight and during the later stages of the engagement." Buxton was quick to reject the press-generated hyperbole about York's feat being "single-handed" or that he was a one-man army.[70] Neither York nor the U.S. Army ever made such a claim; it was the media that created that notion. Although willing to provide Cutting with advice, and a listening ear, Buxton could not throw his support behind a claim that lacked material evidence. Despite this, Merrithew would persist in his undertaking to receive a medal to the end of his days.[71]

11

Another War with Germany

We are standing at the crossroads of history. The important
capitals of the world in a few years will either be Berlin and
Moscow, or Washington and London. I, for one, prefer Congress
and Parliament to Hitler's Reichstag and Stalin's Kremlin.
                                                —Alvin York, May 1941

Alvin's odyssey in the Great War changed his life and his understanding of the world. Like most veterans, he desired that the
nation not be involved in another war. However, as the international situation darkened in the 1930s, York was not easily led
down the noninterventionist path. During this turbulent interval,
York would find himself a key public figure standing against the
popular view of isolationism. His most influential move would
be to agree to the making of the movie that would depict his life,
and serve as a device for Hollywood moguls to advance the idea
of intervening in Europe. This movie, combined with the attack on
Pearl Harbor, would help solidify the nation's role in the Second
World War, in addition to shaping America's remembrance of York
for future generations.

Between the Great Depression and the rise of belligerent powers in Germany, Japan, and Russia, the 1930s were uncertain for
the world. The failure of Wilson's push for American membership
in the League of Nations marked a return to American isolationism. Watching the rise of Hitler in Berlin in the early 1930s caused
many in the United States to wonder what was the value of American intervention in the Great War. From an American point of view,
most believed that the world should be left to sort out its own problems. As Hitler consolidated his grip over the Rhineland, Germany
rearmed in contravention to the Versailles Treaty. In Spain the fas-
cists seized Madrid, and in the Far East Imperial Japan invaded
and mercilessly occupied Manchuria, China. Meanwhile, American

church groups, peace societies, and veteran organizations rallied the masses "to a common resistance to the next war."[1]

The political discourse of the 1930s was driven by a new brand of conspiratorial isolationists, more properly called anti-interventionalists, led by North Dakota senator Gerald P. Nye.[2] Although tracing its roots to George Washington's 1796 farewell address, anti-interventionalists had been more active in American politics since the 1898 Spanish-American War, whereby the nation had acquired former Spanish possessions that stretched from the Caribbean Sea to the Philippines. The strength in the anti-interventionist movement was not just in its general appeal but also that its followers spanned the American political spectrum from the far left to the far right.[3]

The outcome of the First World War and the growth of the American arms industry seemingly empowered the anti-interventionalists' populist base, which found strong political advocates in the form of Senators Burton Wheeler (Montana) and Gerald Nye. In 1936, Senator Nye published a report suggesting that the powerful American arms industry, in collusion with American bankers, had manipulated international affairs to deceive the nation into entering the Great War.[4] Nye went on to say that the modern arms industry would draw the United States into another war.[5] Because of this belief, Senator Nye was a leading voice in Congress in pushing through a series of Neutrality Acts to prevent the United States from entering the next war.[6] As the last chances to reign in Hitler or to contain Imperial Japan faded, Senator Nye and Senator Wheeler ensured that the United States would do nothing as the world slipped into chaos.[7] Ironically, many leading anti-interventionalists went to great lengths to blame Hitler's invasions of Poland, Denmark, Norway, Belgium, the Netherlands, Luxembourg, France, Yugoslavia, and Greece on both British and American policies and not on the Nazis. This view was alluded to by Wendell Wilkie, the Republican nominee during the 1940 presidential election: "It is the duty of the President of the United States to recognize the determination of the people to stay out of war and to do nothing by word or deed to undermine that determination."[8]

Taking advantage of their popular movement, Nye and other proponents of the anti-interventionalists' brand drew together like-minded citizens under the organization of the America First Committee (AFC) in September 1940, quickly drawing 850,000 members into its ranks. Polls taken in 1941 suggested that some 80 percent of the nation agreed with the AFC's position of not becoming militarily involved in another European war.[9] Those stepping outside of the isolationist view were typically condemned as warmongers.[10] This shortcoming notwithstanding, those embracing the AFC worldview seemingly reached around the nation, with even the popular American aviator Charles Lindbergh becoming one of its spokesmen.[11] Having visited Germany in 1936, Lindbergh fell under the spell of Nazi goodwill. Claiming a warmongering tripartite conspiracy among British interests, Jewish influence, and the Roosevelt administration, Lindbergh spoke around the country in support of Senator Nye's passion to keep the nation out of any war at all costs.[12]

This popular inclination to avoid foreign wars should be no surprise, as Americans historically perceived themselves as isolationists. This perception of the nation as historically isolationist in its nature was not necessarily connected with reality. The United States conducted its first war after independence in 1801 against the North African Barbary pirates, to protect its commerce. This was followed by nearly continuous frontier wars against the native population, a war against Britain, a war against Mexico, and another against Spain, with that latter war giving the United States a string of possessions around the world. Certainly, in addition to this historical view, the Great Depression made Americans more inward looking than they naturally tended to be. Furthermore, many veterans viewed their 1917–1918 involvement in France to have had little enduring value, seeing the Germans once again spilling blood across Europe.[13] This caused many to reject York's calls for preparedness, saying, "You fought to make the world safe for democracy. What did it get you?"[14]

Despite the overwhelming popularity of the anti-interventionalist point of view, York boldly spoke against the prevailing political winds and advocated intervention in both Europe *and* the Pacific to stop the imperial advances of both Germany and Japan. In remarks given on Armistice Day 1937 he stated that he was "ready to fight again in the interest of . . . peace." Prophetically commenting on Japan's recent aggression in Asia, York added, "Japan is fighting an undeclared war in China and after it conquers that country it is going to come over here. . . . I'd just as soon we got into it now as later."[15] Here at long last was a prominent and respected spokesman for the interventionists. York's "warmongering" could not be ignored by his detractors, especially when, a few weeks after he said this, the Japanese Imperial Army stormed into Nanking, the capital of Chiang Kai-shek's Nationalist China. This Japanese victory was celebrated by Tokyo's unleashing a six-week-long demonic orgy of murder, rape, and atrocities that claimed three hundred thousand Chinese lives.[16]

York wasted no time giving his view of Nazi Germany as well. On the twentieth anniversary of his 8 October Argonne Forest battle, a reporter caught up with York in Pall Mall and asked him about the deal that British prime minister Neville Chamberlain made with Hitler, at the cost of Czechoslovakia. Displaying uncanny understanding, he answered, "I believe if we want to stop Hitler we must knock him off the block. He has been given what he wanted this time, but he'll ask for more."[17] When asked if he would be willing to go again and fight for his country, Alvin answered that he would be and that all men should be willing to defend their nation. York's sons came forward to say they were ready to fight Germany, starting with Alvin York Jr.[18] York's detractors could not ignore his bold statements, especially when, just a few weeks later, the Nazis unleashed their persecution of the Jews across Germany in what is now called Kristallnacht.

As the anti-interventionalists turned up their rhetoric, so did York. He was selected by President Roosevelt as the guest speaker at Arlington National Cemetery. Speaking at the Tomb of the Unknown Soldier in May 1941, York went to great lengths to delineate the error of the anti-interventionists: "We must fight again! The time is not now ripe, nor will it ever be, to compromise with Hitler, or the things he stands for." Alvin went on to directly assault the credibility of Senator Wheeler and Charles Lindbergh and pointed out that they had not served their country in time of war, saying, "Both . . . were denied that privilege, which . . . explains why they feel differently than the veterans do about this country's most pressing problems." Finally, he urged the nation's leaders to act now to help Great Britain, to include fighting by its side "to renew the lease on liberty."[19] The words were stirring, if not prophetic. The president was so moved that in later speeches he quoted York's works, especially the following portion:

> There are those in our country who ask me . . . "You fought to make the world safe for democracy. What did it get you?" Let me answer them now. It got me twenty-three years of

living in an America where humble citizens from the mountains of Tennessee can participate in the same ceremonies with the President of the United States. It got me twenty-three years of living in a country where . . . Liberty is stamped on men's hearts. . . . By our victory in the last war, we won a lease on liberty, not a deed to it. Now after 23 years, Adolf Hitler tells us that lease is expiring, and after the manner of all leases, we have the privilege of renewing it, or letting it go by default. . . . We are standing at the crossroads of history. The important capitals of the world in a few years will either be Berlin and Moscow, or Washington and London. I, for one, prefer Congress and Parliament to Hitler's Reichstag and Stalin's Kremlin. And because we were for a time, side by side, I know this Unknown Soldier does too. We owe it to him to renew that lease of liberty he helped us to get.[20]

By the time he spoke at Arlington in May 1941, York was already a committed advocate of American intervention. In fact, the changing international situation finally prompted him to let a feature film be made of his Great War exploits. Jesse Lasky, the Hollywood mogul who first approached Alvin in his hotel room in May 1919, never lost interest in the Alvin York story. It was he who peered out of his Fifth Avenue office building that afternoon to see the outpouring of excitement in welcoming Sergeant York back to the United States, only to have his movie idea rebuffed with "Uncle Sam's uniform ain't for sale."[21] When Lasky wrote a letter to Alvin York in late 1939, York "didn't even bother to answer." After that, Lasky sent a telegram suggesting that they meet in Jamestown, which they did.[22] Alvin brought Gracie, whom he did not even introduce to Lasky, and the three sat in his hotel room to converse.

By the time Lasky and York met, Europe was in turmoil again. The Germans had invaded Poland, occupied Austria, and seized all of Czechoslovakia. France and Great Britain had declared war on Hitler. For Lasky, the time was now for a movie on York's life. The discussion, or rather the lack thereof, between Lasky and York was quite fruitless. Lasky did not make headway in convincing York to sign a movie deal. Further frustrating him was that Alvin hardly said a word. Of this meeting, Lasky wrote, "[I kept] dribbling the conversational ball myself the whole time, with that huge hulk blocking the goal." Once Lasky ran out of "verbal ammunition" he asked York to meet with him again, to which Alvin answered, "I won't refuse that, but I don't want you to be hopeful."[23] On that note, Lasky returned to Hollywood trying to think of a way to get Alvin to relent on his stubborn refusal to a movie deal. The idea of having a movie made of his life was something that the Tennessean had refused since 1919, and it seemed to be a symbol to York of his refusal to profit personally from his war experiences. Lasky needed a more convincing approach if he were to maneuver York out of that position.

Finally, on his fourth visit to Tennessee, Lasky asked York to meet him in Nashville, and to bring a lawyer. Lasky was certain that he had found a way to help York get over his resistance to a movie deal. Meeting in the Andrew Jackson Hotel, Lasky began by asking him about agreeing to a movie, to which Alvin seemed even more resistant than before.[24] The conversation between them changed when Lasky launched into his prepared discourse: "Sergeant, you risked your life for your country in the World War and you'd do it again if your country needed you, wouldn't you? That need exists right now and I know that you're going to give your life to your country—through the powerful medium of the screen. This country is in danger again and the people don't realize it yet. It's your patriotic duty to let your life serve as an example and the greatest lesson to American youth that could be told."[25]

This was an honest and timely appeal, in that the United States was in the midst of debate about starting the Selective Service that would lead to the draft.[26] The country was warming to the urgent calls of York and others to intervene. How could Alvin refuse now? Lasky was hopeful when York answered, "Maybe we do have something to talk about."[27] Lasky went on to explain to York that his struggle of reconciling Christianity with fighting for freedom would help young American men reconcile their own struggles, as the nation was on the brink of another war.[28] Nevertheless, the lawyers spent the next few days wrangling over details of whether Tennessee law or California law should dictate the contract terms.[29] The important part for York, beyond embracing "his patriotic duty," was that he would use the proceeds of the film to complete the Bible school he was building in Pall Mall. During this struggle between the lawyers, Lasky noticed that Alvin would often leave the room for periods of time. Wondering what Alvin was doing, Lasky followed him and saw that York was in his room, on his knees, praying to God for guidance.[30]

Although Alvin was willing to sign a movie deal, his lawyer could not come to terms with Lasky. On 21 March 1940, Lasky was ready to give up until he thought of a trick that would include Tennessee governor Prentice Cooper. With this in mind, he slipped away, contacted the governor, and asked him to witness the signing of the movie contract, to which Governor Cooper eagerly agreed. To get York to the governor's office, Lasky tipped a bellboy to come into where he, York, and their lawyers were debating and announce that there was a call for Lasky from the Tennessee governor. Lasky pretended to get the call in the lobby and returned after a few minutes to say that Governor Cooper wanted the entire party at his office immediately to photograph the signing of the movie deal. York's lawyer was flabbergasted and demanded that they would not sign a real contract and would tear up the photo if no agreement was reached.[31]

Upon arrival, Governor Cooper was told that they were not quite ready to sign the real contract just yet, but were posing for the cameras. The governor played along. He pulled a bill that he could not get through the legislature out of his desk and had York and Lasky sign that official-looking document. On cue, the photographers snapped pictures of the signing. The group returned to the hotel to resume arguments over the contract. That afternoon, when breaking for a meal, York and his lawyer saw boys on the streets selling newspapers that proclaimed that he had signed a movie deal. When Alvin saw this, he said, "I guess we'll *have* to sign it now!"[32] The ruse worked!

The actual contract was signed on 23 May 1940 by Lasky and York in Nashville.[33] Having secured a movie deal with York, Lasky now needed a studio willing to do the project. First he contacted RKO, which turned the idea down flat. This was followed by a rejection from Paramount, the studio that Lasky founded. Their reason for the refusal was "that war pictures were dead, that nobody had made a war picture for ages because the public didn't want them."[34]

Finally, Lasky approached Harry Warner of Warner Brothers Studio. Lasky met with Harry at the Warner Brothers farm, where his friend Charles Einfeld spun the story with patriotic flare (based upon advice from a former employee working at Warner Brothers). As he talked through the York storyline, Harry picked up his phone, called his brother, and said, "Jack, I want you to make a deal with Jesse for a story he wants to do. I believe in it so do it for my sake."[35]

After more than twenty years of persistence, Lasky was about to make his most successful motion picture ever.[36] The working title was "The Amazing Story of Sergeant York."[37] A team of researchers was dispatched to Pall Mall, and all the facts and information available on Alvin York were compiled.[38] The Warner Brothers researchers were granted access to York's military records and the Congressional Record, and they interviewed anyone who had information about him.

York insisted that the movie not be a war picture, and that it should be a broad presentation of his life, focusing on God's role in his life and the community service he had provided to his region.[39] With that in mind, the writers Lasky assigned to the script included Abem Finkel, Harry Chandlee, John Huston, and Howard Koch. Howard Hawks would serve as the film's director.[40] To support their work, some eleven months of research went into the film. This included having the researchers spend several weeks in Pall Mall observing local culture and even a turkey shoot. Lasky had Gary Cooper pegged as the perfect "Alvin York," and with that in mind sent a telegram to Cooper on behalf of Alvin, saying, "I have just left the motion picture producer. Lasky to film the story of my life. I would be honored to see you on the screen as myself, Sergeant Alvin C. York."[41]

The problem was that in the golden age of American cinema, accomplished and popular actors like Gary Cooper were contract employees of individual studios, and Cooper belonged to Sam Goldwyn, another movie mogul, former business partner, and ex-brother-in-law of Jesse Lasky. Warner was livid that Lasky would make such a bold move, but Lasky would not be deterred, saying that Cooper was the only actor who would do for Sergeant York. As the wrangling for Cooper went on, Warner Brothers considered Ronald Reagan for the role if Goldwyn would not concede. Reagan was known for "playing the companion of the leading stars. . . . He hardly ever got the girl." Because of this, most believed that he would not be a good fit for Sergeant York.[42]

After several weeks of discussion, Goldwyn agreed to loan Cooper in exchange for Warner Brothers' biggest star, Bette Davis. The deal loaned Cooper for twelve weeks to Warner Brothers in exchange for Bette Davis's playing the lead in the hit movie *Little Foxes*.[43] Once the deal was set, Lasky brought York to Cooper's house in Los Angeles (Lasky and Cooper were neighbors) to get them acquainted. Lasky wrote that it was like being at a funeral wake, with neither saying much until they got onto the topic of guns, and then all bets were off.[44]

Putting the script together proved daunting, between the demands of various folks in Pall Mall and diverse threats of lawsuits by people trying to squeeze the studio for money. Additionally, York wanted a wholesome actress to portray Gracie, not "any cigarette smoking actress." The sixteen-year-old Joan Leslie seemed a good fit, as she had never smoked and was the same age as Gracie when York proposed to her. She was perfect for the role.[45]

Pastor Pile also had concerns that Hollywood would be tempted to take great liberties in the characterization of him and his Christianity. He feared that Hollywood would depict Christianity as a harsh, superstitious religion.[46] To provide just the right touch to the portrayal of Pile as a down-to-earth, kindred spirit sort of preacher, Walter Brennan was selected to play the part.[47] Brennan was another great pick, not only because he was a good fit for the role, but because he was a veteran of the Great War, having served in the 101st Field Artillery in four campaigns and been wounded in action by gas. Ironically, this veteran would be a conscientious objector in the film. Knowing of Pile's concerns for an accurate portrayal, Brennan "played the part with reverence and with deep respect for the sterling qualities of the mountain preacher."[48]

With that in mind, Pile only signed the movie release form when Warner Brothers agreed in writing that they would not misrepresent him, or portray anything in the movie contrary to his beliefs. Key to this agreement was the understanding that "Pile was not a 'hell and brimstone shouting preacher' so typical of the . . . revivalist. He would strongly object to any change that would make his religion appear dogmatic, or based on any belief in the superstitious."[49] Beyond this, Warner Brothers was dogged by a few minor challenges, such as Gracie's father refusing to be depicted in the movie. The resolution to this was replacing him with a fictitious uncle on the screen.

The biggest challenge was securing consent forms from the people depicted in the film. This was new territory for Hollywood, as most films portrayed fictitious or historical personalities. Apart from securing approval from the diverse folks in Pall Mall, Warner Brothers had the daunting task of contacting soldiers from York's unit. William Guthrie, the Warner Brothers studio location manager, was given the job of tracking down these people and having them sign releases to be portrayed in the movie.[50] Guthrie traveled some ten thousand miles across the United States to accomplish this mission. In the end, he secured thirty-four releases, including ones from all of the men still living that were involved in York's action of 8 October 1918.[51] Knowing this, York requested that "those men receive credit for their share of the engagement" in the movie.[52]

Despite this goodwill, there was a flaw in Guthrie's approach in having the affidavits signed. The intent was to secure these without payment, and if payment were necessary, to pay as little as possible. Most of York's ex-platoonmates signed their releases by October 1940, with some receiving as little as five dollars. However, Merrithew wrangled for and received $250, and then told the others what he received. Merrithew took advantage of this opportunity to stir up the soldiers, saying to Warner Brothers, "You will hear from all the other survivors looking for the balance of the $250.00 in addition to demanding that his version of the battle be portrayed in the film, and not York's."[53] After receiving several threats from him, the Warner Brothers legal department labeled Merrithew the "principal beefer."[54]

Merrithew began writing to Warner Brothers as soon as he read in a newspaper about the movie being made about Sergeant York. In his letters, Merrithew claimed that none of the soldiers in the unit signed affidavits to support York's feat and that the story was patently false. To explain away the affidavits in the War Department that supported York, Merrithew said that whatever the soldiers signed was a supply slip and not a legal document.[55] Merrithew went on to threaten William Guthrie if they did not go with his story, saying, "Warner Brothers will have a court case on their hands."[56]

These threats caused the Warner Brothers legal and story departments some discussion on how to calm Merrithew. They even contemplated using Ronald Reagan to depict him in the movie. They decided against that when Merrithew could not present convincing evidence in support of his allegations. With that, Warner Brothers ruled out working with Merrithew. However, they were concerned about the potential bad press he could generate. Although having no legal obligation, the studio decided to pay all the men in York's element the same amount given to Merrithew.[57] The studio also decided to go through the Veterans of Foreign Wars (VFW) to facilitate tracking down the men faster, and to shield themselves from criticism.[58]

For Warner Brothers, there was no drama in securing consent forms from the preponderance of the people depicted in the movie. Sergeant Parsons, Lieutenant Colonel Buxton, Brigadier General Lindsey, Major General Duncan, Major Tillman, General Pershing, Secretary of State Cordell Hull, and many others signed the release forms without financial compensation.[59] With these, the screenwriters determined that the battle scene "would follow as closely as possible the facts as stated in the Congressional Record." This was wise from a presentation standpoint as well as from a legal point of view, considering the threats from Merrithew. When all was said and done, the research by Warner Brothers was exhaustive.[60]

The movie was to be about a man, and not a soldier, who when called upon to defend his nation was able to reconcile his religious beliefs with his patriotic duty. The movie was divided into three parts, York's life before the war, his service in the army, and his return to the United States.[61] Although trying to stay close to reality, there were liberties taken in the story. The most dramatic was the depiction of York being struck by lightning, thus leading to his conversion.[62] Alvin approved this dramatization of his conversion, saying that when he heard and understood the Gospel presentation on 1 January 1915, it was indeed as if lightning struck his soul.[63] Another addition to the story was a fictitious character named Pusher Ross. "Pusher" was created by writer Harry Chandlee and portrayed as York's army companion. The point of having this New York subwayman was to make York's asking to see the subway seem less peculiar.[64]

Another adaptation to the movie was the portrayal of York's feat occurring in the context of the popular remembrance of the Great War. The attack into the Argonne Forest on 8 October 1918 depicts long lines of trenches, severed trees, and land scarred by four years of artillery bombardments. Actually, when York marched into the Argonne that October morning there were very few trenches and the land was virtually untouched. Instead of charging through bands of barbed wire and into heavily fortified networks of trenches, the American platoon actually faced a thick forest punctuated by pockets of German defenders.[65]

Another was the debate between Major Buxton, Captain Danforth, and Alvin York when they discussed his objection to fighting in war. The truth of the matter was that when the three discussed this in 1918, the conversation was focused solely on what the Bible said about the topic. However, one of the writers, Harry Chandlee, added the scene where Buxton gives York a lesson on American history and loans him a history book with which to contemplate his decision. This was to make the debate more palatable to the less religious and to more heavily appeal to patriotism.[66] By doing this, one can almost see York handing the torch to the next generation to finish the job.

Although there were more minor adaptations, the only other one worth pointing out is a scene of Gracie stealing a kiss from Alvin before they were married. All of the York children interviewed made it a point to mention that their mother was not pleased with that scene, as the first time they kissed was on their wedding day. They said that Gracie York expressed concern that people would think that she was morally loose.[67]

The studio went all out on the production of this movie, even hiring Donohue Hall to teach the actors the dialect of the Cumberland Valley.[68] The treatment included some ninety camera days, seventy production days, 123 studio sets, eight outdoor locations, and an eighty-acre battlefield. The largest set was the mountain depicted in the film where Alvin would pray. This stood forty feet high and included 121 trees.[69]

When the movie was completed, Jesse Lasky and Warner Brothers Studio pulled out all the stops to triumphantly open the picture. The release date was centered on 4 July 1941, and would include a rare double premier, one in New York City and the second in Washington, D.C. The grand premier in New York City was Wednesday night, 2 July.[70] Alvin and Gracie York were welcomed to New York City by scores of Boy Scouts, the American Legion Band, color guards, drum and bugle corps, Veterans of Foreign Wars Posts 516 and 599, and hundreds of well-wishers, with Colonel Buxton among them. Even the 1940 Republican presidential candidate, Wendell Wilkie, turned up to support what would be Hollywood's single most important interventionalist film.[71] The drive down Broadway was nearly a repeat of the reception York received in May 1919, with scores of fans lining the way.[72] The celebration culminated at the Astor Theater, where the film opened.

A few weeks later the entourage arrived in Washington, D.C., for a similar grand opening at the Earle Theater. York, Gracie, and their son Woodrow Wilson York were escorted to Washington, D.C., by Tennessee governor Prentice Cooper. Upon detraining in

Washington, York was welcomed by a similar group of Boy Scouts, veterans, and scores of congressmen. After giving a few remarks, the group was whisked to the White House for a meeting with President Roosevelt, who was thrilled by the movie (having had an advance screening). Joining York was Tennessee senator Kenneth McKellar, his division commander, Major General Duncan, and Jesse Lasky.[73]

The film was a smashing success, no doubt due to its timing. When the movie was released, Nazi Germany had recently invaded Russia and already had conquered most of Western Europe. Meanwhile, in the Pacific, tensions were on the rise as America imposed tough sanctions on Japan. The movie reviews endorsed the patriotic message.[74] It was to be the most successful movie that Lasky ever made, out of the hundreds that he generated over the course of his life.[75] By December 1941 it had grossed more than $4 million in theater rentals, and by March would take in more than $10 million.[76] Lasky truly had a keen sense of timing, as it is doubtful that the movie would have had such an impact on the American psyche had it not been released just five months before the Japanese attack on Pearl Harbor.[77] Cooper would walk away with an Academy Award for Best Actor, and was rated the "leading money-making star," while Joan Leslie would be thrust into fame and stardom due to her performance as Gracie York.[78] The movie may also be responsible for the 82nd All-American Division's being among the first divisions brought back to active service, with Major General Omar Bradley serving as its commander at Camp Claiborne, Louisiana. This was part of the army's initial expansion to 3.6 million men under arms.[79]

In the midst of the jubilation, Senators Nye and Wheeler and their anti-interventionist colleagues in Congress held hearings to indict the producers for making anti-German "war propaganda" films, which Nye described as "the most vicious propaganda that has ever been unloosed upon a civilized people."[80] Senator Nye attempted to use his platform to intimidate Hollywood from producing films he viewed as provocative.[81] In a speech before the America First Committee, Nye said Hollywood studios had "been operating as war propaganda machines almost as if they were directed from a . . . central bureau." He went on to list the offending pictures, "*Sergeant York, Man Hunt, I Married a Nazi,* and the *Great Dictator.*"[82] In trying to rally the masses, Nye's boosters in the America First Committee attempted a failed boycott of theaters showing these movies in New Jersey.[83]

Hollywood had long been a target of Senator Nye. In an earlier speech, Nye proclaimed at an America First meeting in St. Louis that Hollywood studios were "the most gigantic engines of propaganda . . . to rouse the war fever in America. . . . Are you ready to send your boys to bleed and die in Europe for [movie executives]?"[84] Later in his speech Nye made what would prove to be the fatal error of describing the ethnic background of Hollywood's producers as both foreign born and Jewish.

The Republican 1940 presidential candidate, Wendell Wilkie, rose to Hollywood's defense: "The motion picture industry and its executives are opposed to the Hitler regime in Germany; they have watched with horror the destruction of a free life within Germany and the ruthless invasions of other countries by Nazis. . . . We abhor everything which Hitler represents."[85] Wilkie went on to label Nye's hearings as being "a barefaced attempt at censorship and racial persecution." Nye's retort to Wilkie was just as pointed: "I detest race prejudice and I shall be found in the very front lines of those who give battle to it."[86] There is no evidence that Nye was anti-Semitic. Wilkie, however, had so pithily framed the argument that Nye would spend the remainder of his political career fending off charges of anti-Semitism.[87]

Harry Warner was among the producers and studio owners summoned to testify before a Senate committee investigation (a subcommittee of Senator Wheeler's Interstate Commerce Commission). Warner denied that *Sergeant York* was designed to incite war, or that he had attended any secret conspirator conferences to orchestrate propaganda. He demonstrated that the movie was an accurate portrayal of an American hero and the first screen biography of a living person.[88] Additionally, Warner laid out a convincing rebuke to Nye's allegation of a broad Hollywood conspiracy, saying that there was fierce rivalry among the studios.[89] His most powerful remark, however, against these hearings was, "You can correctly charge me with being anti-Nazi. But no one can charge me with being anti-American."[90] Despite this robust defense, the hearings dragged on, with the Senate investing scores of hours trying to contain, or at least curb, Hollywood's anti-Nazi position.[91]

Despite their efforts otherwise, the America First Committee, Nye, and Wheeler would be overtaken by events in December 1941,

Alvin York (center with civilian hat) is next to Major General Omar Bradley, then commander of the 82nd Division at Camp Claiborne, Louisiana, in 1942. York is about to give a patriotic/inspirational speech to the men of his former division before they ship off to the European Theater of Operations. York would make scores of such speeches, encouraging the men to trust in God, pray, and read their Bibles. (AHEC)

with the Japanese attack on Pearl Harbor on 7 December and Hitler's declaration of war against the United States the following day. With that, the debate over intervention became passé, with history remembering Nye and the like-minded in a negative light. In the end, the timing of York's movie could not have been better in that it helped to prepare America morally and mentally for the need to go to war. Twenty-three years after his 1918 battle, Sergeant York again rendered his country a great service.[92]

During the Second World War Alvin volunteered to serve as a soldier, but due to health issues his offer was declined. He was, however, put in charge of the local draft board. York also placed himself at the disposal of the War Department, which sent him to speak to troops around the country. He gave rousing speeches and admonished the men not to fall under the spell of alcohol. Alvin's most personal and recurrent topic, of course, was the importance of faith. He encouraged servicemen to read the Bible as he did in the Great War, to find hope and God's purpose for their lives. Alvin reminded them that it was this same faith that carried him through difficult and turbulent times, and that his God would do the same for them if they only trusted in Him. Perhaps the most moving visit he made was speaking to his old unit, the 82nd All-American Division, before it headed overseas.[93]

Alvin also supported war-related fund-raising initiatives, starting in early 1942 when he encouraged the nation to donate to the Red Cross.[94] He also used his fame to raise money for war bonds and loaned his name to the Citizens Committee to Display the Flag. This patriotic organization encouraged Americans to display the flag at all times as a symbol of their support for the men serving in harm's way.[95] At the same time, Alvin continued to expand his Bible school, pouring the money from the movie into it, and for a time he even toyed with the idea of running for Congress to fill Tennessee's Fourth District seat vacated by Albert Gore.[96]

York's mother died at seventy-seven years of age at his home in Pall Mall on 22 May 1943. Meanwhile, his sons Woodrow "Woody" Wilson and George E. "Edward" Buxton were heading off to the army.[97] After the war ended and both sons returned safely from military service, life in Pall Mall returned to normal, with Alvin now keeping a watchful eye on the Russians. Nevertheless, his remaining years would be dogged by financial and health troubles.

York suffered two strokes and colitis in 1949, with his doctor saying that "he was a pretty sick man."[98] The next year Alvin suffered from pneumonia and was admitted to the hospital for high blood pressure and heart disease.[99] In 1954 he suffered a cerebral hemorrhage and a stroke that caused him to be bedridden for the last ten years of his life.[100] The American Legion donated a special electric bed on 8 October 1960 to ease York's life a bit.[101] In 1962 he underwent prostate surgery and had an intestinal hemorrhage. His health continued to decline in 1963.[102]

Meanwhile, the Internal Revenue Service had been hounding York to pay taxes they had calculated he owed from the proceeds of the movie. In their zealotry, the IRS managed to drive Jesse Lasky nearly to the poorhouse because of the film's success, and it seemed they would do the same to America's most highly decorated Great War hero.[103] The IRS belligerently refused to consider any compromise for York, despite the facts that he built two schools for his region (the York Institute and a Bible college) and poured his soul into supporting the nation in World War II. The pressure and stress that the IRS pushed on him exacerbated his rapidly declining health. By 1959, the IRS declared that he still owned them $85,442. At seventy-two years of age and bedridden, there was nothing York could do to address the IRS's claims.[104]

Speaker of the House Sam Rayburn of Texas created the Sergeant York Fund in Washington, D.C., in 1961 to alleviate York's financial troubles.[105] Heavily supported by Tennessee congressional members, and the American public at large, the fund raised more than $50,000. Under heavy political pressure, the IRS finally relented and agreed to settle the matter for $25,000. The remaining $25,000 from the fund was put into a trust to be "given to him as he needs it."[106]

On 2 September 1964, Alvin York passed away at seventy-six years of age. President Johnson issued a statement of sympathy for the family and sent General Matthew Ridgway to the funeral as his representative. More than eight thousand people attended the ceremony, including Tennessee's governor, Frank Clement, and the former governor, Prentice Cooper, who had played such an important role in Alvin's life. The 82nd All-American Division sent an honor guard and its band to pay tribute to its most famous soldier. Presiding over the ceremony was the former pastor of the "York Chapel," which Alvin helped build in Pall Mall, Reverend R. D. Brown. He honored York's life by preaching a message of salvation to all in attendance. Alvin C. York was laid to rest where his odyssey began some fifty years before, at the same church where he went forward to accept the Lord on 1 January 1915. Who would have known that day in 1915 would be the single most important day of his life. What would have happened had he left that church without going forward? Alvin said that day turned out to be the "peg upon which the rest of his life swung." When he went forward that cold January morning in 1915, everything changed, although York did not know how significant this one decision would be for him.[107]

12

Honoring a Hero

In great deeds, something abides. On great fields, something
stays. Forms change and pass; bodies disappear; but spirits
linger, to consecrate ground for the vision-place of souls. And
reverent men and women from afar, and generations that
know us not and that we know not of, heart-drawn to see
where and by whom great things were suffered and done for
them, shall come to this deathless field, to ponder and dream;
and lo! the shadow of a mighty presence shall wrap them in
its bosom, and the power of the vision pass into their souls.
This is the great reward of service. To live, far out and on, in
the life of others; this is the mystery of the Christ,—to give
life's best for such high sake that it shall be found again unto
life eternal.

—Major General Joshua L. Chamberlain,
American Civil War hero

Although the battle near Châtel Chéhéry was not York's only fight
in the war, it was the one that defined him. With the exact location
of where York fought on 8 October 1918 seemingly lost to history, it
was imperative to locate it to ascertain the truth of what happened
that one day in October before writing this biography. Otherwise,
interpretation and opinion would guide my work. The research
paid off, with the York site being discovered in 2006. Because of this,
there is now carved into the Argonne Forest a three-mile historic
trail for visitors to this battlefield to "walk where York walked."
Named "Circuit du Sergeant York," the trail has nine interpretive
historic markers and two monuments that mark York's actual battle
location. These were dedicated on the ninetieth anniversary of the
battle, with the approval and endorsement of the York family and
French and American officials.

The 8 October 1918 battle for which York was awarded the

Medal of Honor was a turning point for him and left an indelible impression on American Great War literature. So notable were York's actions that they were written about extensively in the 82nd Division's history, and described in the biographies of Major General George Duncan (82nd Division commander), Major General Hunter Liggett (First Army commander), and General John Pershing (American Expeditionary Forces commander).[1] However, recently there has been a debate over the exact location of the 8 October 1918 site. This has caused some to question the authenticity of York's feat. They allege that since there is a lack of clarity on the site's location, how can we know for sure that it actually happened?[2] This begs the question, how did the York site come to be lost over time? Was it lost at all? Is the location where we dedicated the monuments and built a historic trail accurate? To all this, history has the answers—and the saga of the York site does have an interesting history.

Captain Bertrand Cox led his men across this ground just minutes after the battle. In fact, Cox was the only American officer known to have traversed the York site.[3] Then a lieutenant, Bertrand Cox was the support platoon leader for Company F, 2nd Battalion, 328th Infantry Regiment. He testified that during his unit's movement to the Decauville Railroad on 8 October 1918 they passed over the ground where York's fight occurred.[4] His sworn affidavit states: "On the morning of October 8th, I commanded a support platoon of 'F' Co., 2nd Bn of the 328th Inf. Shortly after Corporal York and his detachment of seven men succeeded in capturing the greater part of a German battalion, I advanced with my platoon and passed the scene of the fight which took place before this capture was accomplished. The ground was covered with German equipment and I should estimate that there were between 20 and 25 dead Germans on the scene of the fight."[5]

Captain Bertrand Cox's account is of great significance, as he was both the only American officer to traverse the York site and a key witness called to corroborate the York story in the 1919 investigation. Cox placed the location of the action approximately 1.5 kilometers northwest of Châtel Chéhéry, along the forward edge of the hill often referred to as Humserberg.[6]

The next recorded visit to the site of York's action was on 9 October 1918, the day after the battle. After returning from the overnight hike to drop his prisoners off at Varennes, York asked Captain Danforth for permission to go back to the site to see if any of the men they left behind were still alive. Danforth granted York permission to check and sent stretcher bearers with him. Upon arriving at the scene of the action, York wrote that the U.S. Army had already cleared the site of the dead and had removed abandoned equipment. This was the same location visited by Cox the day before.[7]

The next official visit to the battle site occurred in February 1919 during the investigation into York's feat. Attending the investigation were York, *Saturday Evening Post* journalist George Pattullo; York's regimental commander, Colonel Richard Wetherill; his brigade commander, Brigadier General Julian Lindsey; his division commander, Major General George Duncan; and an army photographer. There are no records of the group having used maps during this visit. However, the U.S. army photographer documented the event and took pictures of the terrain where York fought off the German bayonet attack. The caption on one of the photos is clear where this action happened, saying, "Vicinity of Sgt. York's raid, 1 1/2 kilo northwest of Châtel Chéhéry." This corresponds to the movement of Captain Cox's "F" Company and indicates that the York site was not actually lost.[8]

In 1929, the U.S. Army War College planned to perform a reenactment of Sergeant York's action at its annual exposition in Washington, D.C. To portray the York action accurately, the U.S. Army assigned several officers to go through the archives to reconstruct the event. However, the officers could not find maps that depicted the York location in France. To fill this information gap, the researchers contacted Buxton and Danforth.

The problem was that neither Buxton nor Danforth was an eyewitness to the action, nor was either of them present at the 1919 investigation. With this lack of firsthand knowledge, Buxton and Danforth could only guess where the action occurred.[9] The Buxton and Danforth sketch placed the action well outside of the 82nd's area of operations and in a deep gorge of no military value. Furthermore, their location is about 650 yards south of where Cox, the U.S. Army photographer, and the Germans say the fight occurred. Danforth warned the U.S. Army War College not to use the sketch, saying, "I am afraid that no one, not even York himself, can give you a very accurate lay-out of the fight." Because of this, the Buxton and Danforth map had no value to the Army War College researchers and was not used to support the exposition. However, this sketch would eventually find its way into the archives, which would be a pitfall for later American researchers.[10]

Meanwhile, German researchers gathered in Potsdam, Germany, to ascertain what happened on 8 October 1918. Many of the key players were interviewed: Leutnant Paul Vollmer,[11] Leutnant Paul Lipp, Leutnant Max Thoma, Leutnant Karl Kübler, and Sergeant Major Haegele. These soldiers represented the 120th and 125th Württemberg and the Bavarian 7th Mineur Company, the key units fighting against York. Unlike the postwar maps of Danforth and Buxton, who did not participate in the York action, the German officers were all present during the battle. Together, they annotated on the map where the battle occurred with an "X." This "X" location is within ten yards of Captain Cox's testimony and close to the 1919 AEF-annotated photograph.[12] This accurate depiction of where York's action occurred did not inform the 1929 U.S. Army War College investigation, because the Americans did not receive a copy of this study until 1936, seven years after their exposition and carnival.

The next attempt to document the location of the York scene of battle occurred in the 1990s and was undertaken by two American Special Forces soldiers, Lieutenant Colonel Taylor Beattie and Major Ronald Bowman. Ron Bowman described the challenge of narrowing down the search for the York site when he wrote, "The folks of the town and the American cemetery—only had vague ideas and knowledge of it, at least all the ones I talked to. They didn't know much more than where the big plaque was [in the village]. A little later I took Taylor with me and he took to the challenge with vigor. As I said, he developed a firestorm of a desire to retrace the tale and really know—how, what, where, and when, the reality of the Sgt York story occurred."[13]

Their methodology was to scrutinize the York historical records with an eye to combining what was published on the action with military terrain analysis. Terrain analysis is using geography to gain the best advantage militarily. How soldiers view terrain has changed little at the tactical level and remains a valuable tool both in combat situations and in trying to recreate a historical military action. The methodology encompassed the following considerations:

> We have approached the analysis of events in the ravine as soldiers would approach a tactical problem, through the application of the METT-T and OCOKA concepts. METT-T

stands for Mission. Enemy. Terrain and weather, Troops and Time available. OCOKA further breaks terrain consider-ations into Observation and fields of fire, Cover and con-cealment, Obstacles, Key terrain, and A venues of approach. While exploring Hill 223 and the ravine, we approached our question, "York, how did you do it?" as a tactical problem from both the American and German perspectives. Thus we analyzed how we would have attempted to accomplish Ser-geant Early's mission to "work around behind those guns" or, alternately, the mission of a German officer tasked with defending that terrain, applying the principles of METT-T and OCOKA.[14]

Using this approach of METT-T and terrain analysis, Beattie and Bowman placed the location of the action at the base of the large hill 1.5 kilometers northwest of Châtel Chéhéry. The Beattie and Bow-man site is close to the aforementioned Cox testimony and the 1919 photograph of the terrain. Interestingly, Beattie and Bowman did not have access to these two sources and did not use them to inform their assessment. Their primary source was the 1928 York autobiog-raphy edited by Tom Skeyhill.[15]

I began my research into the York story in the early 1990s. What was initially found on York lacked tactical clarity and depth. With-out knowledge of the Beattie and Bowman groundbreaking terrain study, I began gathering data on York's 8 October battle from various sources with a desire to reconstruct the battle as it really happened. What became clear was that much of the data readily available on the fight was disjointed and slanted from the American perspective. It also was apparent that no American had conducted research in the German archives to try to understand what happened from the other side. This was a shortfall that I desired to rectify.

I did my first field research trip to France in 2002. Using terrain analysis, the York biography, and the other sources I had uncovered, I found that the battle occurred close to where the Cox testimony, the German sources, and the AEF had placed it: 1.5 kilometers north-west of Châtel Chéhéry (although I did not yet have those sources to corroborate this analysis). Before long, I had assembled a large inter-national team to support this search. This group would be called the Sergeant York Discovery Expedition (SYDE). It would include some fifty members and affiliates, from eight nations, bringing a level of expertise and skill rarely gathered together for such work. It included historians, geospatial analysts, researchers, archeologists, museum curators, professional military members, family members, soldiers from several NATO nations, intelligence analysts, imagery analysts, and small arms weapons experts.

Over the next several years I scoured the archives for every piece of data I could find on the York battle. The research would eventually reach across North America and Europe. By 2006, I had uncovered a wealth of information from the German archives that brought a level of clarity to the 8 October 1918 battle hitherto unknown. Among the data collected were maps and overlays that would prove central to locating the battle site. These would later be found to correspond to Cox's testimony as well as AEF reporting.

As the U.S. and German archival data were analyzed, a clearer understanding of the York battle was discerned. I punctuated my archival research with trips to the Argonne, where I walked the actual battlefield and annotated on a map where the Americans and Germans wrote that events transpired, to see if this made sense from a military terrain analysis point of view. Additionally, I conducted a surface survey of the specific 300-foot-by-300-foot area in the Argonne that the sources all pointed to as being the scene of the York fight. This included walking the ground in the Argonne with an eye for any evidence of the battle. It would also include a gridding on a map and the ground to interpret the finds of the surface survey.[16] The initial surface survey showed the location of the German machine gun that York attacked, the 120th Landwehr garbage pit, the ancient border trench utilized by Leutnant Fritz Endriss and his platoon (the group which would bayonet attack York), several German fighting positions (at the base of Humserberg and visible in the AEF 1919 photography of the York fight), and the areas used by German riflemen to combat York's men.[17]

During these trips to the Argonne, I met a local historian, Dr. Lucien Houlemare. Dr. Houlemare resides in the village of Châtel Chéhéry, owns a portion of the land near the York action, and considers himself well informed on York. He took me to the location where he believed York fought, and it turned out to be very close to where I had determined the action to be, confirming that he was on the right course. Additionally, in 2005, I met with Taylor Beattie to discuss his analysis and findings and was pleased to find out that Beattie also was in the same area I had pinpointed.

As I prepared to conduct an in-depth archeological site survey, a group from Tennessee made a trip to France under the direction of Dr. Michael Birdwell of Tennessee Technical University. Birdwell was joined by Tom Nolan of Middle Tennessee State. They traveled to the Argonne in March 2006. The team used a metal detector to scan a very large area in four days.[18] However, their search was hampered by four inches of snow.[19] This group would eventually call itself the York Project. The problem with the York Project was that it based its assessment of the location of the York fight on the discredited 1929 Danforth and Buxton map. This is the same map that Danforth warned the army against using, saying, "I am afraid that no one, not even York himself, can give you a very accurate layout of the fight."[20] This placed them in a deep ravine about *650 yards south* of where the York site was declared to be by credible American and German sources.

This was compounded by premature claims of success. During their brief time in the Argonne they uncovered only 161 German 7.92x57mm casings, fifteen .30-06 live rounds, and three expended U.S. cartridges. This sort of evidence could be uncovered in nearly any ravine, hill, meadow, or valley in the Argonne.[21] The presence of the 7.92 casings does not confirm that a machine gun was in the spot. In fact, German rifles used the same caliber rounds as the German MG 08/15 machine gun. To verify that an MG 08/15 was located in a specific position, one either needs parts of the MG recovered from the area or fragments of the "patronengurt," the cloth belt used to feed the bullets into the gun. They found neither, and such a discovery would remain elusive to them in future trips.

Even more problematic, however, was the fact that there were no .45 cartridges recovered in their initial survey.[22] Birdwell speculated that these artifacts would never be found, as he presumed that after nearly ninety years they would have rotted away, saying, "the .45 casings may have deteriorated in the boggy ground."[23]

Lack of evidence notwithstanding, Birdwell and Nolan held a press conference after their return to the USA.[24] Their press conference was held in Tennessee on 22 March 2006.[25] They claimed, "We're 80 percent certain that we have found the right location."[26] But they had uncovered nothing to justify making such a statement. Nolan would admit some months later that "we don't have enough evidence to reach any definite conclusion."[27] They would make

These sets of unfired U.S. rifle bullets were found near the York site and perhaps came from one of the soldiers who fell in action on 8 October 1918. (Mastriano Collection)

several other trips to the Argonne over the next few years to continue their search.

Meanwhile, the SYDE would spend more than one hundred days conducting research in the Argonne. Working closely with a variety of American and French officials, and having the research evaluated by the U.S. Army Center of Military History, SYDE made considerable progress in the search for the York site. By October 2006, sufficient evidence was gathered to make a formal announcement describing the work and where the evidence pointed. In the end, the evidence supporting our claim would include forensically confirmed cartridge casings that came from the same type of pistol used by York (a Colt .45 ACP), .30-06 rifle casings that matched the type of rifle York used, the dog tags and personal effects of a German soldier involved in the York fight (a 125th Landwehr soldier), remnants of Vollmer's headquarters, hard evidence of the German MG 08/15 (both pieces of the machine gun and fragments of the patronengurt), and confirmed artifacts belonging to both the 120th Landwehr and the 210th Prussian Regiments. This, combined with several thousand other pieces of evidence, validated much of what we know of the York saga.

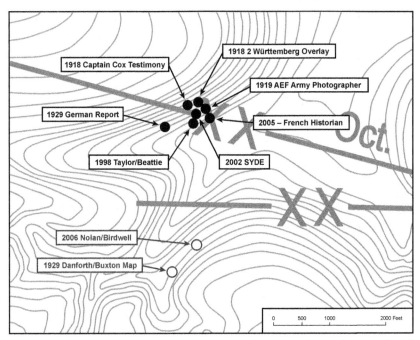

Map 10. Not lost to history. Reliable historical sources have always placed the York battle location on the south slope of the center hill 0.9 miles (1.5 kilometers) northwest of Châtel Chéhéry.

The history of the York site is intriguing. It seems that the location was never actually lost to history, as the historic records clearly placed it where the monuments now stand in the Argonne Forest.

How did we come to find the precise location where York fought? To do this required a well-rounded historical approach that integrated data from both the German and American sources, in addition to applying military terrain analysis, geospatial technology, battlefield archeology, and ballistic firearms forensics. This provided a process that both historically and scientifically gets to the bottom of the York story.

What Battlefield Archeology Says of This Battle

Having ascertained where the German and American sources say the York site is located geographically, we next conducted battlefield archeology. This enabled us to measure the eyewitness accounts and the terrain analysis to see if the story surrounding the events was supported by physical evidence. Finding the location of the German machine gun involved in the action was perhaps the easiest endeavor due to its specific description in the German sources. The site had to be slightly above the German supply road on Humserberg based upon York's testimony, as well as what the German reports say of it.[28] The leveled ground to support the machine gun position stood out quite plainly as being a location improved for such an end and was carved above the road overlooking both the meadow and the valley. Furthermore, just behind and above here are two sunken roads, which the infantry support platoon used as fighting positions.[29] The machine gun position yielded hundreds of cartridges and shell casings. These were buried between two to four inches in the Argonne and were in considerably good condition. The discovery encompassed approximately 800 spent cartridges and 150 live rounds.[30] The cartridges and live rounds recovered from this position had head stamp markings consistent with what the 2nd Landwehr Württemberg Division carried, with the markings around the primer being S67/P/2/18.[31] This meant that these rounds were manufactured in 1918 at the *Polte Werke, Zentrale* in Magdeburg, Germany.[32] The head stamps denote that these cartridge cases were composed of 67 percent copper and 33 percent zinc.[33]

As the German infantry M1898 rifle and the Maxim MG 08/15 machine gun fired the same caliber round (7.92x57mm), it was important to find actual evidence of the cloth belt or the metal brackets that the machine gun used to feed the rounds.[34] Unfortunately, the cloth material would have been exposed to the elements for ninety years, so the chances of finding pieces of it were not promising. Nonetheless, this concern was abated when a series of the metal separators from the MG 08/15 patronengurt were recovered. These separators were both loose in the ground and also fused to several of the live rounds. Fragments of the cloth patronengurt had also survived the effects of ninety years of exposure and were recovered with the rounds. These provided firm evidence that a MG 08/15 was indeed in action here. In addition, there were some one hundred other artifacts collected from the location, including German uniform buttons, metal equipment buttons, and scores of eyelets from German shelter halves. An interesting find was at the far eastern side of the machine gun position, where the rifle stripper clips were uncovered. It was an M1898 rifle butt plate.[35]

Fired cartridges from the German machine gun engaging York and his men. The location of the German machine gun in action against York was found overlooking a meadow in the precise location both German and American sources indicated. (Mastriano Collection)

Two heavily decayed American tunics were found near the York battle site from soldiers who fell in action on 8 October 1918. (Mastriano Collection)

The sources say that there was a group of riflemen firing in support of this machine gun.[36] This is where the two sunken roads above and behind this machine gun position play a part. The first was six feet above and behind (north of) the machine gun, and the second, rising slightly higher than the first, approximately eighteen feet behind the machine gun. The depth of each was more than six feet. From a tactical perspective, these two sunken roads provided excellent observation, fields of fire, and both cover and concealment to anyone using them. As to their location geographically, these were perfect for infantrymen to utilize in providing supporting fires to their machine gun team, especially shooting into the meadow below, where York and the other sixteen Americans would have been positioned.[37]

As nineteen soldiers died in action here, these two sunken road trenches were filled with thousands of artifacts.[38] There was an assortment of expended cartridges, stripper clips, and live rounds, as one would expect from a location where soldiers were killed in action. There were scores more buttons (uniform shirt and under-garment buttons), equipment latches, a German pocket watch, fragments of a Württemberg belt buckle, and dozens of eyelets from German shelter halves. Additionally, the bones of a horse, a bridle, a horse brush, and several horseshoes were recovered in this area. These were the remains of one of the nine horses that the 125th Württemberg Landwehr Infanterie Regiment reported being killed in action in a particularly lethal American artillery barrage that swept across Humserberg in support of the attack of the 82nd.

Spent American .30-caliber bullets were found here, suggesting that a soldier was engaging targets in these positions. The next question, then, related to the German machine gun and its supporting sunken road riflemen. Just how did an American contend with these well-emplaced soldiers? A clue to how this occurred is found in Alvin York's Medal of Honor citation: "The Argonne Forest, France, 8 October 1918. After his platoon suffered heavy casualties, Alvin York assumed command. Fearlessly leading 7 men, he charged with great daring a machine gun nest which was pouring deadly and incessant fire upon his platoon. In this heroic feat the machine gun nest was taken, together with 4 German officers and 128 men and several guns."[39]

York crossed the road on the southern perimeter of Humserberg during his charge against the machine gun. However, any attack against the front, right flank, or the rear of the machine gun would expose him to the fires of the infantry men in the sunken roads. There was only one place where York could outflank both the German machine gunners as well as their infantry support platoon, and York found it.

As to this area, the lower of the two sunken roads runs parallel with the supply road, which is just ten feet from it. The other, and higher sunken road runs at an angle against the other, and converges with it some fifty feet east of the machine gun position, pointing toward Châtel Chéhéry. It is here, where the two sunken roads converge, that they form a "V." From the tip of this "V" one has perfect lines of sight up both sunken roads, as well into the flank of the MG 08/15 machine gun position.

The archeology here yielded some of the most important finds of the York battle. Within an area five feet in diameter we recovered forty-six American Remington Arms .30-06-caliber cartridges. Of these, all except one were fired. Additionally, the nine associated American .30-06 stripper clips were also recovered at this site among the cartridges.

Douglas Mastriano (right) and his son, Josiah, at the location where the first U.S. .45-caliber pistol bullet was recovered. This discovery led to finding the spot where York used his Automatic Colt Pistol to fight off a German bayonet attack. (Kory O'Keefe)

The discovery of forty-six cartridges is consistent with what York fired during this engagement. The eyewitness accounts say that York fired all the ammo from the front of his belt pouches.[40] The basic combat load of American soldiers, which they carried on a cartridge belt, was one hundred rounds in ten pouches, fifty on the front half of the belt and fifty on the back half.[41] Based upon this, York fired a maximum of fifty rounds from his rifle during this engagement.[42]

In addition to the recovery of York's .30-06 Model 1917 Eddystone rifle cartridges, another momentous find was to occur on Humserberg. Here, the personal effects of a missing German soldier were recovered. This included both of his shoes, his undergarment and uniform buttons, his gas mask, and numerous assorted accoutrements. However, the single most important artifact was the recovery of this soldier's complete identification tag. The tag provided the following information:

SCHÜTZE WILH HAERER
[Gunner/Private Wilhelm Härer]
STEINBACH O/A BACHKNANG
[Hometown of Steinbach am Backnang]
2. M.G.K L.125 [2nd Machinegun Company,
Landwehr Regiment 125]
GEB 1. 11. 1882 [Birth date 1 November 1882]

The soldier, Wilhelm Härer, was assigned to the machine gun company of the 125th Landwehr Württemberg Regiment, the same unit that fired on York and the other Americans.[43]

The recovery of Härer's military identification tag was a major coup in the search for York. Härer was assigned to Leutnant Lipp's portion of Humserberg. Lipp commanded the machine gun which Alvin York assaulted, and Lipp was captured by York.[44]

Other discoveries from Humserberg encompassed a large collection of American-related artifacts that tell the story of the intense struggle that transpired for this hill on 8 October 1918. These included American aluminum combs, field mirrors, a pocket frame, a pocket watch, several mess kits with eating utensils, buttons, rifle cleaning kits, several U.S. Model Carlisle first aid kits (used and unused), canteens, and coins. The location and condition of these

Personal effects of German machine gunner Wilhelm Härer. Härer was involved in the 8 October fight and fell in action as the 125th Württemberg fell back after York broke its line. The discovery of Härer's personal effects was a major breakthrough in the search for the York site. (Mastriano Collection)

signify that they were from York's unit, the 2nd Battalion, 328th Infantry Regiment, 82nd U.S. Infantry Division.[45]

The battlefield archeology in the meadow at the base of Humserberg provided even more clues to what transpired during this battle. Here, the history tells us that Vollmer and his staff were captured at a small wooden shack that served as his battalion headquarters.[46] It was here that soldiers of the 120th Württemberg Landwehr Infantry and 210th Prussian Regiments were captured without a fight by the seventeen Americans. An important find was evidence of Vollmer's battalion headquarters building.[47]

The meadow yielded numerous artifacts related to the 210th Prussians and the 120th Württembergers.[48] In addition to scores of live rounds, hundreds of military accoutrements, latches, equipment brackets, and clasps were recovered. This encompassed the metal pieces one would find attached to German belts, web gear, cartridge belts, helmet chin strap mounts, pouches, and straps. A half-dozen harmonica reed plates were found as well among the items.

Military uniform buttons associated with both Württemberg and Prussian infantry regiments were also recovered from the meadow. These included several buttons with the Prussian Eagle emblazoned on them. The 210th Prussian Reserve Regiment would have had these on their uniforms. Additionally, a large Imperial Prussian Crown brass stickpin was recovered from this area. It is of some importance to note that the Württemberger regiments did not have these Prussian Eagle buttons, giving tangible evidence of the 210th Prussian Regiment being in this location.

Some of the most noteworthy discoveries were near the Endriss trench. As described, the trench was a seventeenth-century border trench, carved into a portion of Humserberg facing due east. It was used on 8 October by Leutnant Fritz Endriss's platoon during the American attack. It was also from here that Endriss led a forlorn bayonet attack against Alvin York. At the lower end of the trench was a trove of artifacts, and this was the most likely location where the preponderance of the charging Germans would have fallen in action. This included an assortment of items, clasps, buttons, ammunition, and a German officer's whistle, complete with cork and reed. As Endriss was the only German officer recorded to fall in action along the southern half of Humserberg, it is highly likely that this whistle was his.

However, it was a discovery behind the Endriss trench that would lead us to the place where York fired his pistol. Nearly in a line near the Endriss trench we recovered three American .45-caliber rounds lodged into the earth. Triangulating these, we were able to locate the position from which York fired his .45 Automatic Colt Pistol. Twenty-four spent .45-caliber cartridges were recovered from this location.

Three U.S. pistol cartridges identified as being from York's sidearm. (Mastriano Collection)

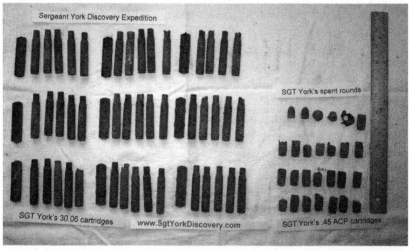

These cartridges were confirmed to have come from the same types of rifle and pistol used by Corporal York on 8 October 1918. A monument now marks the spot in France where they were recovered. (Mastriano Collection)

Five of forty-six U.S. rifle cartridges recovered from the location where York outflanked a German machine gun. (Mastriano Collection)

These American cartridges and bullets were uncovered near the trench used by Leutnant Fritz Endriss, who was killed by York while leading a bayonet charge against him. Using ballistic forensic analysis, Dr. Doug Scott confirmed that these matched the type of weapon used by York. (Kory O'Keefe)

Firearm Identification to Confirm or Deny the York Story

Firearms ballistics identification is a scientific discipline to apply in the evaluation of the York site. Each rifle and sidearm has a distinct "fingerprint" that it leaves upon both bullets and cartridges fired from it.[49] Although there is overwhelming historic evidence to support the supposition that the forty-six .30-06 cartridges, three .45-caliber bullets, and twenty-four .45-caliber cartridges are York's, forensic analysis was used to verify this.[50] Forensic-based firearms identification is a scientific approach and removes subjectivity from the process.

Dr. Douglas Scott offered his services to conduct this important task. There is none more qualified than Dr. Scott, as he is the expert in this field. Having conducted archeology work since the 1960s, Dr. Scott gained notoriety from his forensic-based battlefield assessment of the Battle of the Little Bighorn. Speaking of the importance that forensic analysis can provide to battlefield archeology, Dr. Doug Scott said, "The historical record is a truly astounding data set, but it is just one data set that should be used in studying the past. Oral tradition or historical documents are impressions of those who set them down. While they may be more or less accurate, I will reiterate that the archaeological record is often more precise about past events in space and time, as well as an independent line of evidence that can be compared and contrasted with the other lines of evidence to achieve a fuller picture and understanding of the past."[51] Dr. Scott was given the forty-six American .30-06 cartridges recovered from the position where York outflanked the 125th Württemberg machine gun nest.[52] Additionally, Dr. Scott was provided with the twenty-four .45-caliber cartridges from the edge of the Humserberg meadow and two of the fired .45-caliber bullets that were recovered near the Endriss trench.[53]

Alvin York was armed with an M1917 Eddystone rifle, and Dr. Scott sought to ascertain if the cartridges had been fired from the same make and model. He used an "American Optical Universal Comparison Microscope," with magnifications ranging from 10x to 40x.[54] During this evaluation, he scrutinized each cartridge to check and assess the condition of ejector marks, chamber marks, extractor marks, breech face marks, the firing pin impression, and other features that would identify the casing with a specific weapon.[55]

Dr. Scott determined that the "cases have strong extractor and ejector marks that are consistent with being fired and extracted from a Model 1917 Enfield rifle."[56] Using microscopic pattern analysis on the fired cartridge cases, he found that "each primer exhibited a series of unique breech face marks imprinted on the case when it was fired as well as the hemispherical firing pin imprint." From this, he determined that the "fired cartridge cases were consistent with being fired in the same M1917 Enfield Rifle."[57]

The arrow points to an extractor mark on the head of a .30-06-caliber cartridge case that is consistent with the M1917 Enfield rifle, the same type of rifle used by Alvin York. (Photograph courtesy of Dr. Doug Scott)

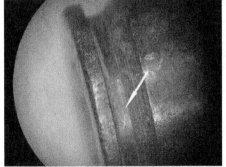

The arrow points to an extractor mark on the head of a .30-06-caliber cartridge case that is consistent with the M1917 Enfield rifle, the same type of rifle used by Alvin York. (Photograph courtesy of Dr. Doug Scott)

Comparison microphotograph of two .30-06-caliber cartridge cases. The firing pin and breech face marks on both cases match, indicating they were fired by the same M1917 Enfield rifle. (Photograph and caption courtesy of Dr. Doug Scott)

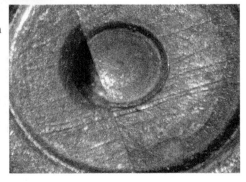

The next area of analysis was the .45-caliber bullets and cartridges. Dr. Scott studied two of the .45 bullets recovered adjacent
to the Endriss trench, conducting a thorough analysis of the artifacts, measuring not only the pitch and twist of the groves on each
bullet, but also the depth, width, and number.[58] From this analysis,
one can determine both the make and model of the firing weapon
and the specific rifle or pistol that it was shot from. In conducting
his microscopic analysis Dr. Scott identified "clear land and groove

Comparison microphotograph of
a land impression on the bullet
jackets of the two recovered bullets
indicating that they were fired from
the same M1911 Colt pistol.

A second comparison
microphotograph of a
land impression on the
bullet jackets of the two
recovered bullets. (Above
and right photographs
and captions courtesy of
Dr. Doug Scott)

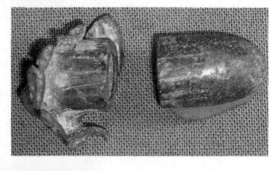

The heads of two of the
.45-caliber cartridge cases
illustrating the range of
preservation observed. All
.45-caliber cartridge cases
were made by Remington-
UMC and dated 1917. These
were fired from two different
weapons. (Photograph and
caption courtesy of Dr. Scott)

impressions" on the bullets. He determined that these bullets were fired from the same M1911 .45 ACP.[59]

The final forensic ballistic analysis conducted by Dr. Scott encompassed the twenty-four .45-caliber cartridge cases recovered southwest of the Endriss trench. Dr. Scott conducted comparative microphotographic analysis of the twenty-four .45 cartridges. Using 10x–40x magnification, he found an interesting twist to the York story.

Microscopic analysis of the firing pin impressions provides

The arrow points to an ejector mark on the head of the .45-caliber cartridge case, confirming that it was fired from the type of pistol used by York. (Photograph and caption courtesy of Dr. Doug Scott)

Comparison microphotograph of two .45-caliber cartridge cases and primer indicating they were fired in the same weapon. (Photograph and caption courtesy of Dr. Doug Scott)

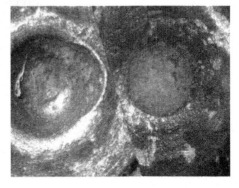

Comparison microphotograph of two .45-caliber primers with firing pin imprints. Note the drag mark on the left image. The mark shows the firing pin did not fully retract during case ejection from the pistol, indicating two different pistols. (Photograph and caption courtesy of Dr. Doug Scott)

abundant information related to the specific weapon that a cartridge was fired in. This includes the type, class, and condition of the firing weapon.[60] The first conclusion from these firing pin impressions was that all twenty-four cartridges had been fired from a .45 ACP. However, nine of the cartridges displayed a distinct drag to the firing pin impression, with the other remaining casings showing a clean firing pin impression in the primer. This means that there were two .45 ACPs in action here, one firing fifteen rounds and the other firing nine.[61]

This groundbreaking finding resolves a ninety-year-old controversy surrounding the battle. Several of the other squad members had claimed that they had played a more significant role in the battle. In this vein, two of these men were subsequently each awarded a medal for heroism. However, the only soldier who has clear evidence supporting his claim is Private Percy Beardsley.

Beardsley quietly maintained after the war that he also fired his .45-caliber pistol in support of York. Besides York, the others in the group of seventeen soldiers armed with .45 ACPs were Sergeant Early, Corporal Cutting, Corporal Savage, and Private Beardsley. Sergeant Early was shot by six bullets; and Corporal Cutting (Merrithew) was severely injured by five bullets; thus neither was able to play a pivotal role in the battle after being injured. Corporal Savage was killed outright when the German machine gun on the hill opened fire on the group. As the only other soldier in the group armed with a .45 ACP who was not critically injured, it is likely that these nine rounds were fired by Private Beardsley.[62]

Private Beardsley would have fired his sidearm when German Leutnant Fritz Endriss led the bayonet attack against York. This course of action is the most logical in that the Germans state that some dozen soldiers initially charged against York, with more than half of them falling in action. The intensity of the firing caused the surviving six Germans to return to their trench for cover, evidently due to the combined effects of York and Beardsley's firepower.[63] Sergeant Bernard Early and Corporal Cutting (Merrithew) were belatedly awarded medals for heroism due to their personal efforts to be thus publicly recognized.[64] Unfortunately, due to Beardsley's unassuming nature, he did not seek recognition for his role in the battle and therefore remained overlooked. The irony is that, based on battlefield archeology and firearm identification analysis, Beardsley is the only soldier other than Alvin York for whom there is physical evidence to support a claim of an active and important role in the battle. Dr. Scott concluded his analysis:

> The . . . examined cartridge cases represent two gun types, an M1917 Enfield rifle and a Colt M1911 pistol. The forty-five .30-06-caliber cartridge cases are each consistent in class and individual characteristics with being fired in a single M1917 30-06-caliber Enfield rifle. The 24 .45-caliber Colt M1911 cartridge cases appear to represent two separate M1911 Colt semi-automatic pistols. . . . The bullets examined represent a .45-caliber M1911 Colt pistol. . . . The .45-caliber bullet and bullet jacket are consistent in class and individual characteristics as being fired from the same gun.[65]

Such validation for this type of investigation into a battle is rare and has thereby greatly contributed to what we know of the battle of 8 October 1918 near Châtel Chéhéry in the French Argonne Forest. Dr. Scott's analysis confirms scientifically that we accurately located where York fought.

Conclusion

With this array of evidence, we know with certainty the location of the York action. The key is not to hinge such an assessment on a few artifacts. Only by holistically reviewing what was recovered and overlaying it with the military terrain analysis, forensic study, and history can we make such a determination. The important consideration is that these various aspects tell the York story in total. That is, the various pieces corroborate the events recorded in both the German and American archives.

It is of some importance to review the findings in the context of the battle. Starting in the meadow, the artifacts recovered illustrate that the Germans surrendered without resistance. In the midst of these various German items there were found American .30-06 shell casings, showing that among the German prisoners there were American soldiers firing in support of York's movements. Slightly further up the hill and near the trench is where the Colt .45 shell casings were discovered. Near these were a number of buttons and miscellaneous pieces of German equipment that likely came off those York and Beardsley shot during the German bayonet attack.

On the hill, the German machine gun and rifle positions contained not only firm evidence of a machine gun, but also numerous shell casings, some cartridges, and buttons and equipment pieces. The Germans here fought and then surrendered. Finally, York's rifle position was discovered—the site from which he eliminated the 125th's machine gun position in a location supported by both U.S. and German reports. Another vital link to the Sergeant York story was the complete recovery of the identification tag and personal effects of the aforementioned Wilhelm Härer, a machine gunner assigned to the 125th Landwehr Württemberg Regiment.

Taken together, the events of the 8 October 1918 battle seem to come to life. Everything was exactly where it should have been based on the numerous threads of information discernible from the German and American battle accounts.

The York site was located through the use of primary source research in German and American archives, military terrain analysis, geospatial mapping, doctrinal templating (using contemporary German 1917–1918 doctrine), battlefield artifact evidence, and ballistic forensic analysis. After an independent review of these findings was conducted, and having received the endorsement of numerous independent authorities in North America and Europe, the French government authorized the construction of the Sergeant York Historic Trail (Circuit du Sergeant York) and the installation of two battlefield monuments to commemorate and preserve what occurred on 8 October 1918. The trail and monuments were officially dedicated under the full authority and endorsement of American and French government officials in October 2008 in honor of the ninetieth anniversary of the battle. Three generations of the York family were present, with military and civilian representatives from the Republic of France, the United States of America, and NATO to dedicate the Circuit du Sergeant York and the monuments in one of the largest ceremonies held in the Meuse-Argonne region in recent times. Now, at long last, visitors can walk with assurance where York walked.

The Sergeant York Historic Trail and monuments are maintained by the Sergeant York Discovery Expedition (SYDE). For further information about SYDE, please visit www.sgtyorkdiscovery.com.

Acknowledgments

Alvin York: A New Biography of the Hero of the Argonne is the culmination of a decade of labor. I am blessed to have a family that actively participated in this adventure. Therefore, this work is dedicated to the two most important people in my life: my wife, Rebbie, and son, Josiah. Rebbie is the hero behind this endeavor. She never hesitated to share in the time-consuming undertaking of digging deeper into the York story, which included numerous journeys to the remote Argonne Forest. She was there from the start, and at the cost of a sprained ankle discovered the specific location where the German 125th Württemberg Regiment machine gun position was situated— the one that York fought against on 8 October 1918. Having a wife willing to share in the spartan adventures of traversing a century-old battlefield is commendable enough, but add to it her keen tactical sense and I am blessed beyond measure. Also with me on nearly every journey to the Argonne Forest was my son, Josiah, who literally grew up exploring the sacred soil where so many Americans fought in 1918. From the age of five, Josiah was with me climbing up and down the rugged Argonne hills, and he helped unearth the actual artifacts fired from York's weapons that put to rest any honest debate whether York was the hero the army claimed him to be. Since then, Josiah has poured his energy into preserving this piece of our American military heritage by undertaking the most ambitious Eagle Scout service project I have seen in some thirty years of Scouting. Josiah improved and expanded the Sergeant York Historic Trail (Circuit du Sergeant York). Looking back, I am humbled that this endeavor was one in which my family participated, sharing the ups and downs, the sorrows and joys that it entailed. What an incredible journey, what an incredible story!

My interest in Sergeant York began as a youth when I watched the movie of his life with my father. There was something striking about the story—namely, a hero that never set out to be one and who did not use his notoriety for personal gain. Later in my army career I began looking into heroes worthy of emulation, and of course York made my top three list, alongside George Washington and Joshua Lawrence Chamberlain. However, upon digging deeper into the York story I was troubled by the lack of precision in the record about York's military service as well as the assertions of revisionist historians who questioned York's actions without a historical reason to do so. Thus was launched a decade-long endeavor to get to the bottom of the York story. Arriving at this point would not have been possible without the generous help and support of scores of people, too many to name, but I will give it a go in the hopes that I do not miss someone who played an important role in bringing this story together. This will be long, for over the years many people have helped me not only to locate the York site, but also to help us place two monuments and build the Circuit du Sergeant York (Sergeant York Historic Trail), where visitors to the Argonne can actually walk where York walked.

Heartfelt thanks to Kory and Beth O'Keefe, who have not only been the best of friends and principal coworkers in the endeavor to discover the York site, but also were leaders in building and maintaining the Sergeant York Historic Trail in the Argonne Forest. Memories of the Argonne diet (turkey and cheese on white bread), waffles, and a sighting of the Jersey Devil in the Argonne (perhaps it was a cow) combine with thoughts of days of hard work. I am blessed to have such faithful and dedicated friends who have selflessly given so much of their time and energy to preserve the York legacy.

Sincere thanks to Major General David Zabecki, the U.S. Army's premier Great War historian, who has provided sage advice not only on how to proceed with the research but also on how to perpetuate the York story. He has been this project's mentor and the inspiration behind the historical approach to the research. Thanks also to Colonel Jerry Morelock (U.S. Army, ret.), who provided excellent support and the platform of his excellent history magazine, *Arm Chair General,* to get word out to the public on the latest Sergeant York discoveries and also provided wise counsel throughout my research.

Sincere appreciation to Eric Weider, president of Weider History Group. Eric's interest in protecting America's rich military heritage made the purchase, construction, and installation of the two Sergeant York monuments in the Argonne Forest possible. He is a historian that truly walks his talk. A salute to Ken Delfino of the California, Nevada, Hawaii Kiwanis, and a Vietnam veteran, for his tireless efforts to raise funds for the construction of the Sergeant York Historic Trail in France and for going above and beyond the call of duty to ensure we had everything necessary to conduct the ninetieth anniversary celebration of York's battle in 2008.

Sincere gratitude to the former director of U.S. Army Center of Military History, Dr. Jeff Clark, and his staff for providing support, advice, and oversight of the Sergeant York artifacts recovered from the Argonne.

A thank you to Lieutenant Colonel Jeff Parmer, who was the first to start the fieldwork in the Argonne Forest with me. Also, appreciation is due to Gary Martin (U.S. Army, ret.), a small arms expert whose skilled eye helped us to precisely locate the spot from which York fired his sidearm. We were also honored to have the support of Dr. Doug Scott, the nation's expert on historical ballistic analysis. His scientific analysis of the York bullets and cartridges confirmed our historical interpretation of these artifacts and at long last discredited the detractors.

Thank you to my brother, Sergeant Major Robert Mastriano (USMC), and his son, Ian, for their help in the archeological work for the search of the York site. Robert, an expert on battlefield excavation on Iwo Jima and Okinawa, applied his knowledge to our work in the Argonne. Thank you also to Bill and Karen Rudge (and BJ) of Bill Rudge Ministry of Living Truth. Bill and Karen threw their support behind our endeavors early on and have provided sound counsel, and support. Also, thanks to Steve Warren, Web Stone, Roger Cirillo, and Craig Smith for encouraging me to write this history.

A salute to our many valuable French friends who made the work in the Argonne Forest possible. As much of our work was done on communal land, we could only proceed with the approval of the mayor of Châtel Chéhéry and were honored to work with two fantastic mayors over the years, beginning with Mayor Roland Destenay, who supported our initial digs in the forest. After his election, we were thrilled to work with Mayor Alain Rickal, who not only took the bold step of endorsing our work, but also approved and supported the construction of the Circuit du Sergeant York. I also thank the people of Châtel Chéhéry, especially Dr. Lucien Houlemare and the Adjoints et Conseillers municipaux de la mairie de Châtel Chéhéry: Pascal Bechard, Anne-Marie Bousselet, Frederic Chopin (the "Sheriff"), Thierry Huet, Jean-Claude Lacreuse, Andre Philippe, Claude Vauche, Pierre Schmitt, Carole Renaut, and Ludovic Philippe.

Merci beaucoup to Richard Steffan of the Grandpre Development Department, who created the trail signs, information billboards, and charts that are along the Circuit du Sergeant York in France. Also, my appreciation goes out to forest manager Frederic Chopin, Mayor Damien Geroges of Fleville, and French senator Jean-Luc Warsmann, who stepped in to support our work when it became bogged down. Merci to Dominique Lacorde, the Arnould family of Montflix in Grandpre, and the Steele family.

The French Military Mission to NATO Land Headquarters in Heidelberg, Germany, provided excellent assistance throughout my research by translating scores of documents into French and overseeing our coordinating with local officials and law enforcement. Thanks to General Jean-Jacque Scellos, the military mission commander, and his staff, Adjoint au chef Lieutenant Colonel Patrick du Portal and Adjutants Laure Botreau, Patrick Delmotte, and Stephane Lucas, for not hesitating to help us. The prestige and professionalism of the French Military Mission gave us significant credibility in the Argonne and no doubt opened doors for our work. Merci also to Anne Brun and Sebastien Castet, great French service members with whom I had the pleasure to serve in Afghanistan, and who helped in my York research.

I owe a debt of gratitude to the Meuse-Argonne staff of the American Battle Monuments Commission (ABMC). Frankly, the monuments and trail construction would have been impossible without their support. In particular, the former director of the Meuse-Argonne American Cemetery, Mr. John Phil Rivers, deserves much acclamation. The United States was blessed to have Mr. Rivers serve in this region, as he had a level of clout and respect by the French that I have never seen achieved by any other American. Indeed, Mr. Rivers cared about historical commemorations and research of America's Great War Doughboys, and once he threw his support behind my work, everything fell into place. I am indebted to Mr. Rivers for all he did behind the scenes to make this possible. He opened doors that would have otherwise remained shut and was a pleasure to work with. Thanks also to his staff, Jeff Aarnio, Scott Desjardins, Denis Hebrand, Craig Rahanian, Alain Jerioek, Nicholas Raffa, Dominique Didiot, Frederic Francois, Philip Day, and G. Postal. Thanks to Jean-Paul and Brigit deVries of the Romagne 14–18 Museum for expert battlefield archeological advice and field assistance (based on his thirty-plus years of fieldwork and battlefield archeology). Their passion for the Great War is contagious.

Gratitude is also extended to my international friends in Allied Land Component Headquarters and other soldiers across NATO. Appreciation is owed to Lieutenant General Jack Gardner (U.S. Army) for his support and also to Lieutenant Colonels Mick Tingstrom and Paul Walter, who early on evaluated my research methodology. Thank you Oberst (Colonel) Hans Kling of the German Bundeswehr for your help in securing German archival support for this research and for translating several important documents in the endeavor to find where York earned the Medal of Honor. Danke also to German Oberstleutnant (Lieutenant Colonel) Steff Basener. Steff is like a brother to me. We served together for four years, including a tour in Afghanistan. Steff provided immeasurable research help, translation assistance, and advice on the German perspective of the York battle that I would have missed. Danke also to the following great German soldiers of the Bundeswehr: Hauptfeldwebel Julius Bonaccio, Oberstleutnant Frank Dietze, Major Max Katz, Hauptfeldwebel Bjoern Ehlenberger, and Dieter Schlottag. "Dank u" to my Dutch colleagues who assisted in this endeavor, namely Lieutenant Colonel Jelle De Jong and Captain Dennis de Waal. Heartfelt appreciation goes out to my dear Flemish brother, Gilbert Bosschaerts, and Danish brother, Anders Paavo Jenson, Major John Auranaune (Norway), Lieutenant Duval Link (Canada), Colonel Fulvio Poli (Italy), Major Enrico Tizzano (Italy), Lieutenant Colonel Geert Vanlingthout (Belgium), Sergeant Major Jose Salas of the 82nd Airborne Division, First Sergeant Gabriel Frank (U.S. Army), and Sergeant Brad Gilbert (U.S. Army). Also heartfelt thanks to SFC Mike Jenkins and especially SFC Nick Gallardo (as well as Jenna and Alayna), who went above the call of duty to make this possible.

Thanks to the many outstanding archivists across North America and Europe, especially to Mitch Yockelson of the U.S. National Archives (NARA) for incredible support. Also thanks to Lieutenant Colonel Gross and Major Peter Popp, German Bundeswehr, and their staff at the Militärgeschichtliches Forschungsamt, Potsdam, and the Militärarchiv, Freiburg im Breisgau, and thanks to Loretta Sylvia of the Joint Forces Staff College in Virginia. Thanks also to Sandra Lee and Jon Auxier of Warner Bros. Archives. Appreciation also is extended to Lieutenant Colonel Taylor Beattie and Major Ronald Bowman (U.S. Army) for their groundbreaking research on Alvin York and the "York Spot" in the Argonne Forest between 1999 and 2001.

Thanks to the many volunteers who gave their time and energy with the fieldwork in the Argonne. These included the Barber, Eggert, Perkins, and Brown families, Detlev Hohenstein, Chaplain David Druckenmiller, Brad Putenbaugh, Chaplain Bob Owen, and his sons Seth and John, and scores of others. Finally, this work would not have been possible without the excellent volunteer spirit of the Boy Scouts of America Transatlantic Council under the fantastic leadership of Vince Cozzone. Hundreds of Scouts and their families from France, Germany, and the Benelux contributed to making the Circuit du Sergeant York possible. Thanks to the Scouts who focused their Eagle Scout service projects on the Sergeant York Historic Trail over the past several years. Each of these Scouts took on a different portion of the trail, making it among the best in France. The Eagle Scouts are Nate Eggert (2007–2008), Jeffrey Perkins (2009), John Gerber (2010), Drew Burns (2011), Josiah Mastriano (2011), and Cameron Noble (2013).

Thank you also to the York family, especially Colonel Gerald York (U.S. Army, ret.), who has been a friend since 1995. I appreciate all he has done to support my effort to tell the York story. Thank you also to his children: Gerald Jr. and Deb. My gratitude also extends to Alvin's three surviving children, George Edward, Betsy Ross, and Andrew Jackson York. Thank you for sharing personal stories of your father. It has been an honor sharing this endeavor with you.

Sincere appreciation also to our dear friends at Oromocto Baptist Church, who embraced us during my resident studies in New Brunswick. We are grateful for the support of Pastor Perry Hanley and his family, Jeremy McWilliams, Chris and Marla Bruce, and the Howe, Sanford, Hone, and LaRocque families. Thank you for opening your arms and hearts to us. Also, deepest thanks to Bill Gibson and Mike Aube of Scouts Canada.

Finally, thanks to the University of New Brunswick (UNB), in Fredericton, Canada. It has been a pleasure to work with the professionals at UNB, who have given so much of their time to help me tell the York story. There probably is not a better history department anywhere in North America. I owe a great debt of gratitude to Dr. Marc Milner, who poured so much of his time and energy into making this book worth reading. Thanks also to Dr. Sean Kennedy, Dean of Graduate Studies, Dr. Lee Windsor, Brent Wilson, Dr. Craig Brown, Dr. Gail Campbell, Dr. David Charters, Dr. Susan Blair, Dr. Steve Turner, Elizabeth Arnold, Jackie Seely, Valerie Gallant, and UNB's Gregg Centre for their role in making this work possible.

Notes

1. A Life Well Lived

Epigraph: Mahoney, "Sergeant Alvin York," 45–46.

1. "Give Great Ovation to Sergeant York," *New York Times*, 23 May 1919, 15.

2. Lee, *Sergeant York*, 110–115.

3. Birdwell, *Celluloid Soldiers*, 87–101; Lee, *Sergeant York*, 110–115.

4. Olmsted, *Real Enemies*, 50–51.

5. "Canadian Private Seizes 160 Germans," *New York Times*, 22 August 1944; "Chinese Reds Come Up with Own Sergeant York," *New York Times*, 14 May 1949.

2. Without Prospect

Epigraph: York, *Sergeant York*, 133.

1. Cowan, *Sergeant York and His People*, 59, 100–106.

2. York, *Sergeant York*, 121–129.

3. Ibid., 124. York's diary often contains usages and spellings that are technically incorrect but will be replicated here as they were published, without corrections or editorial comments.

4. Cowan, *Sergeant York and His People*, 166.

5. Letter from Julien Josephson and Harry Chandlee to Jesse L. Lasky, 8 May 1940, document B00374, 2880, Warner Bros Archives, School of Cinematic Arts, University of Southern California, Los Angeles (hereafter cited as WBA), 2.

6. Cowan, *Sergeant York and His People*, 148–168.

7. Ibid., 163–166.

8. York, *Sergeant York*, 126.

9. Perry, *Sgt. York*, 30–37.

10. Cowan, *Sergeant York and His People*, 148.

11. York, *Sergeant York*, 45–50, 104–111.

12. Ibid., 137.

13. Ibid., 90–101; letter from Julien Josephson and Harry Chandlee to Jesse L. Lasky, 8 May 1940, document B00374, 2880, WBA, 2–4.

14. Cowan, *Sergeant York and His People*, 148–150; York, *Sergeant York*, 85–93.

15. York, *Sergeant York*, 43–49; Cowan, *Sergeant York and His People*, 109–111.

16. York, *Sergeant York,* 133–135.

17. Luther, *Smalcald Articles,* 453–477.

18. Letter from Julien Josephson and Harry Chandlee to Jesse L. Lasky, 8 May 1940, document B00374, 2880, WBA, 6.

19. York, *Sergeant York,* 74–79.

20. Lee, *Sergeant York,* 8–11.

21. Braodus, *A Treatise on the Preparation and Delivery of Sermons,* 2–17.

22. Cowan, *Sergeant York and His People,* 103–105.

23. Ibid., 203–204.

24. Ibid., 169.

25. Ibid., 169–173.

26. York, *Sergeant York,* 136.

27. Cowan, *Sergeant York and His People,* 144, 158.

28. Pattullo, "The Second Elder Gives Battle," 4.

29. Cowan, *Sergeant York and His People,* 210–212.

30. Pattullo, "The Second Elder Gives Battle," 3–4.

31. York, *Sergeant York,* 125–131; letter from Julien Josephson and Harry Chandlee to Jesse Lasky, 8 May 1940, Sergeant York notes, WBA.

32. Cowan, *Sergeant York and His People,* 210–211.

33. Ibid., 46–48.

34. York, *Sergeant York,* 5–9; Cowan, *Sergeant York and His People,* 210–212.

35. Wiley, *A Plot against the People,* 19–28.

36. Pattullo, "The Second Elder Gives Battle," 4; Skeyhill, *Sergeant York: Last of the Long Hunters,* 140.

37. Maurer, *Kentucky Moonshine,* 50–59.

38. Bassam Z. Shakhashiri, "Ethanol," University of Wisconsin, 9 February 2011, http://scifun.chem.wisc.edu/chemweek/pdf/ethanol.pdf (accessed 27 September 2011).

39. Skeyhill, *Sergeant York: Last of the Long Hunters,* 139–140; York, *Sergeant York,* 129.

40. Letter from Julien Josephson and Harry Chandlee to Jesse L. Lasky, 8 May 1940, document B00374, 2880, WBA, 4.

41. Memorandum from Harry Chandlee to Jesse L. Lasky, 15 October 1942, WBA, 5.

42. Robert S. Taplinger, "Sergeant York Production Notes," Director of Publicity, Warner Brothers Studio, 1941, WBA; Warner Brothers "Synopsis of Sergeant York," Warner Brothers Studio, 1941, WBA; Pattullo, "The Second Elder Gives Battle," 3–4, 71–74.

43. York, *Sergeant York,* 128–129.

44. Skeyhill, *Sergeant York: Last of the Long Hunters,* 143.

45. In his diary, Alvin York refers to this border area as "Ball Rock."

Its actual name is Bald Rock, off of Caney Creek Road, which leads south to Pall Mall. York, *Sergeant York,* 130. See also, Skeyhill, *Sergeant York: Last of the Long Hunters,* 140–141.

46. Skeyhill, *Sergeant York: Last of the Long Hunters,* 139–140; Perry, *Sgt. York,* 33–38.

47. York, *Sergeant York,* 129–133.

48. Lee, *Sergeant York,* 6.

49. Interview with Jim Crabtree by Robert S. Taplinger, "Sergeant York Production Notes," Director of Publicity, Warner Brothers Studio, 1941, WBA; Warner Brothers "Synopsis of Sergeant York," Warner Brothers Studio, 1941, WBA.

50. York, *Sergeant York,* 131–133; Skeyhill, *Sergeant York: Last of the Long Hunters,* 141–142.

51. York, *Sergeant York,* 132; Skeyhill, *Sergeant York: Last of the Long Hunters,* 141–142.

52. Skeyhill, *Sergeant York: Last of the Long Hunters,* 141.

53. Cowan, *Sergeant York and His People,* 210–212.

54. York, *Sergeant York,* 142.

55. Pattullo, "The Second Elder Gives Battle," 4.

56. York, *Sergeant York,* 141–142.

57. Ibid., 142–143.

58. Letter from Julien Josephson and Harry Chandlee to Jesse L. Lasky, 8 May 1940, document B00374, 2880, WBA, 7.

59. George Edward Buxton York was keen to point out to the author that his grandfather Francis Asbury Williams was named after Francis Asbury, a Christian evangelist during the American Revolution who laid the foundations of much of how Methodism operates today. See the following book for further details: Francis Asbury, *The Heart of Asbury's Journal* (New York: Eaton and Mains, 1906), x–xii.

60. Alvin's birthday was 13 December 1887, and Gracie's was 7 February 1900. Interview with Betsy Ross York, 29 May 2010, in Pall Mall, Tennessee.

61. Interview with George Edward Buxton York in Pall Mall, Tennessee, 28–29 May 2010.

62. Holy Bible, Joshua 24:15, King James Version; interview with George Edward Buxton York in Pall Mall, Tennessee, 28–29 May 2010.

63. Interview with George Edward Buxton York, 28–29 May 2010, in Pall Mall, Tennessee; verse quoted from King James Version of the Bible, which was the format used by Francis Asbury Williams and most Christians in the United States at that time.

64. York, *Sergeant York,* 149.

65. Pattullo, "The Second Elder Gives Battle," 3–4.

66. Cowan, *Sergeant York and His People,* 215–217.

67. Pattullo, "The Second Elder Gives Battle," 4.

68. York, *Sergeant York,* 148.

69. Some writers suggest that York's conversion was influenced by the death of his friend Everett Delk in a saloon fight. However, the sources are conflicted on this point. It seems that Everett did die, albeit more than a decade after York's conversion, as Tom Skeyhill interviewed him in 1928 to gather stories of Alvin's "wild days." See York, *Sergeant York,* 33, where Skeyhill says, "I had interviewed Everett Delk, his pal of hog-wild days."

70. Gracie Williams York, *The Reminisces of Mrs. Alvin "Sergeant" York*; York, *Sergeant York,* 146–151.

71. Cowan, *Sergeant York and His People,* 206.

72. Lee, *Sergeant York,* 39.

73. York, *Sergeant York,* 143.

74. A central theme of this type of preaching was 2 Corinthians 6:2, "For he saith, I have heard thee in a time accepted, and in the day of salvation have I succored thee: behold, now is the accepted time; behold, now is the day of salvation." Cowan, *Sergeant York and His People,* 206–208.

75. Perry, *Sgt. York,* 40–41.

76. York, *Sergeant York,* 144.

77. Interview with George Edward Buxton York, 28–29 May 2010, in Pall Mall, Tennessee; Romans 6:23, verse quoted from King James Version of the Bible.

78. Alvin York used this expression to describe his conversion experience to Hollywood screenwriters in 1940. Interview with Colonel Gerald York (U.S. Army) in Monterey, California, October 1996; interview with George Edward Buxton York in Montfaucon, France, 4 October 2008, during the ninetieth anniversary commemoration of his father's actions in the Great War.

79. Sam Williams's twelve-year-old son, Guy Williams, looked up to Alvin and often accompanied him on the hunting trips. Letter from Julien Josephson and Harry Chandlee to Jesse Lasky, 8 May 1940, Sergeant York notes, WBA; interview with Guy Williams by Robert S. Taplinger, "Sergeant York Production Notes," Director of Publicity, Warner Brothers Studio, 1941, WBA; Warner Brothers "Synopsis of Sergeant York," Warner Brothers Studio, 1941, WBA.

80. Interview with George Edward Buxton York in Montfaucon, France, 4 October 2008, during the ninetieth anniversary commemoration of his father's actions in the Great War; Gracie Williams York, *The Reminisces of Mrs. Alvin "Sergeant" York.*

3. At War with the Army

Epigraph: York, *Sergeant York*, 146.

1. York, *Sergeant York*, 144, 147.

2. Letter from Julien Josephson and Harry Chandlee to Jesse L. Lasky, 8 May 1940, document B00374, 2880, WBA, 6.

3. York, *Sergeant York*, 146.

4. O'Leary, *Brave Hearts under Red Skies*, 91–95.

5. York, *Sergeant York*, 145.

6. Bennett, *The Book of Man.*

7. O'Leary, *Brave Hearts under Red Skies*, 91–95.

8. Rogers, *Religious Bodies 1916*, 201–207.

9. Perry, *Sgt. York*, 42–45.

10. Pattullo, "The Second Elder Gives Battle," 3–4, 71–74.

11. York, *Sergeant York*, 147.

12. Cowan, *Sergeant York and His People*, 208–209.

13. Letter from Julien Josephson and Harry Chandlee to Jesse L. Lasky, 8 May 1940, document B00374, 2880, WBA, 5–7; Gracie Williams York, *The Reminisces of Mrs. Alvin "Sergeant" York.*

14. Gracie Williams York, *The Reminisces of Mrs. Alvin "Sergeant" York*, 1–2, 23–25; Perry, *Sgt. York*, 42–44.

15. York, *Sergeant York*, 148.

16. Gracie Williams York, *The Reminisces of Mrs. Alvin "Sergeant" York*; Cowan, *Sergeant York and His People*, 208–210.

17. York, *Sergeant York*, 148–152.

18. Interview with Virgil Pile by Robert S. Taplinger, "Sergeant York Production Notes," Director of Publicity, Warner Brothers Studio, 1941, WBA; Warner Brothers "Synopsis of Sergeant York," Warner Brothers Studio, 1941, WBA.

19. Letter from Julien Josephson and Harry Chandlee to Jesse L. Lasky, 8 May 1940, document B00374, 2880, WBA, 7–8.

20. Ibid., 8.

21. Gracie Williams York, *The Reminisces of Mrs. Alvin "Sergeant" York*; Cowan, *Sergeant York and His People*, 215–216.

22. Gracie Williams York, *The Reminisces of Mrs. Alvin "Sergeant" York*, 1–3; York, *Sergeant York: His Own Life Story and War Diary*, 150–152.

23. Cowan, *Sergeant York and His People*, 220.

24. Ibid., 218–219.

25. York, *Sergeant York*, 155.

26. Letter from Julien Josephson and Harry Chandlee to Jesse Lasky, 8 May 1940, Sergeant York notes, WBA.

27. Skeyhill, *Sergeant York: Last of the Long Hunters*, 150; Alvin C. York

Draft Registration Card, York File, National Archives—Southeast Region, Morrow, Georgia.

28. There are two Physical Examination Forms in York's Military Service Packet. The second, typed one states that he was 170 pounds. This second card was filed in after the Fentress County Board improperly filled in the first card. Alvin Cullum York Physical Examination Form Number 14, 28 August 1917, in pursuant to Selective Service Act of 18 May 1917, U.S. War Department.

29. Alvin Cullum York, Card Number 218, Serial Number 378, Docket of Local Board of Fentress County, Tennessee, Form 178, 28 August 1918, U.S. War Department.

30. Alvin C. York, "Claim of Appeal by Person Certified to District Board," filed by Alvin York to the Jamestown Draft Board, U.S. Army Service File, 1917; York, *Sergeant York: His Own Life Story and War Diary*, 156.

31. Alvin Cullum York appeal refused by Jamestown draft board, Order Number 218, U.S. Army Service File, Alvin Cullum York, Card Number 218, Serial Number 378, Docket of Local Board of Fentress County, Tennessee, Form 178, 28 August 1918, War Department; York, *Sergeant York*, 157.

32. Interview with Dr. Mullinix, recorded by Robert S. Taplinger, "Sergeant York Production Notes," Director of Publicity, Warner Brothers Studio, 1941, WBA; Warner Brothers "Synopsis of Sergeant York," Warner Brothers Studio, 1941, WBA.

33. York, *Sergeant York*, 156.

34. Letter from Roy A. Hill, U.S. Army Adjutant General's Office, to the Commanding General of the 82nd Infantry Division, April 1918, Alvin York Service File, Request for Conscientious Exemption from active military service.

35. Pattullo, "The Second Elder Gives Battle," 3.

36. Cowan, *Sergeant York and His People*, 222.

37. York, *Sergeant York*, 161.

38. Ibid., 156–165.

39. Alvin Cullum York, National Army Enlistment and Assignment Card, November 1917, U.S. Form 22-2, U.S. War Department; the discussed Scripture is in Isaiah 55, King James Version; Alvin York, *Sergeant York*, 164–167.

40. Cowan, *Sergeant York and His People*, 222–224.

41. Alvin Cullum York, National Army Military Personal File, 14 November 1917, U.S. Form 267, U.S. War Department.

42. Cowan, *Sergeant York and His People*, 227.

43. Ibid., 222–224.

44. York, *Sergeant York*, 166–167.

45. H. L. Scott, *Manual for Infantry*, 5–7.

46. Chandler, *History of the Three Hundred and Twenty-Eighth Regiment of Infantry*, 7.

47. Alvin Cullum York, National Army Military Personal File, 14 November 1917, U.S. Form 267, U.S. War Department.

48. American Battle Monuments Commission (hereafter referred to as ABMC), *82d Division: Summary of Operations in the World War*, 1.

49. Chandler, *History of the Three Hundred and Twenty-Eighth Regiment of Infantry*, 7–9; Cooke, *The All-Americans at War*, 1–6.

50. Holden, *War Memories*, 21–24.

51. ABMC, *82d Division: Summary of Operations in the World War*, 1–2; Buxton, *Official History of 82nd Division American Expeditionary Forces, 1917–1919*, 1–3.

52. Buxton, *Official History of 82nd Division American Expeditionary Forces, 1917–1919*, 2.

53. Ford, *Americans All!*, 80–88.

54. Cowan, *Sergeant York and His People*, 229–330.

55. Pershing, *My Experiences in the World War*, 1:380–381.

56. Chandler, *History of the Three Hundred and Twenty-Eighth Regiment of Infantry*, 7, 9.

57. Day, "The B That Stung," 2.

58. Marshall, *Memoirs of My Services in the World War*, 182–184.

59. Jones, *History of C. Company, 328th Infantry*, 6.

60. Day, "The B That Stung," 2.

61. Jones, *History of C. Company, 328th Infantry*, 7.

62. Chandler, *History of the Three Hundred and Twenty-Eighth Regiment of Infantry*, 9–10.

63. *Official Camp Gordon Songbook* (Camp Gordon, Ga.: 82nd Division, National Army, 1917); Buxton, *Official History of 82nd Division American Expeditionary Forces, 1917–1919*, 3.

64. Jones, *History of C. Company, 328th Infantry*, 6.

65. Day, "The B That Stung," 2.

66. Holden, *War Memories*, 22–24.

67. Terraine, *To Win a War*, 156; Grotelueschen, *The AEF Way of War*, 42.

68. Jones, *History of C. Company, 328th Infantry*, 7.

69. "How Polo Ponies Should Be Ridden," *New York Times*, 26 July 1914.

70. Gonzalo Edward "Ned" Buxton, Jr., May 13, 1880 to March 15, 1949, http://www.nogreatercalling.blogspot.com (accessed 15 October 2011).

71. York, *Sergeant York*, 169.

72. Ibid., 181.

73. Cowan, *Sergeant York and His People*, 241–243; York, *Sergeant York*, 31, 168–171.

74. Letter from Major J. M. Tillman to Jesse Lasky, 5 November 1940, B00374, Folder 2880, WBA.

75. York, *Sergeant York*, 186, 182.

76. Harry Parsons, affidavit in York, *Sergeant York*, 240.

77. York, *Sergeant York*, 180–182.

78. Ibid., 179–181.

79. York, *Sergeant York*, 157–158; Leatherman, *Diary*, 1–9.

80. Cowan, *Sergeant York and His People*, 229–333.

81. Pattullo, "The Second Elder Gives Battle," 3–4, 71–74.

82. York, *Sergeant York*, 157–160.

83. *Souvenir of Camp Gordon, Atlanta, Georgia.*

84. York, *Sergeant York*, 184.

85. Canfield, *U.S. Infantry Weapons of the First World War*, 76–80.

86. Buxton, *Official History of 82nd Division American Expeditionary Forces, 1917–1919*, 1–12; Cowan, *Sergeant York and His People*, 230.

87. Grotelueschen, *The AEF Way of War*, 30–43; Liddell Hart, *Reputations Ten Years After*, 145, 270–275, 278–284, 306–313; Pershing, *My Experiences in the World War*, 1:150–156.

88. York, *Sergeant York*, 159.

89. Chandler, *History of the Three Hundred and Twenty-Eighth Regiment of Infantry*, 11; Buxton, *Official History of 82nd Division American Expeditionary Forces, 1917–1919*, 1–12.

90. Lasky, *I Blow My Own Horn*, 258.

91. York, *Sergeant York*, 190; Cowan, *Sergeant York and His People*, 242–244.

92. York, *Sergeant York*, 168.

93. Lawrence, "Sergeant York—American Soldier," 9–12; York, *Sergeant York*, 168–169; Cowan, *Sergeant York and His People*, 240–242.

94. York, *Sergeant York*, 160–163, 169–170.

95. Gonzalo Edward "Ned" Buxton, Jr., May 13, 1880, to March 15, 1949, http://www.nogreatercalling.blogspot.com (accessed 15 October 2011). In modern leadership field manuals, the U.S. Army praises the approach that these officers applied to Private York. U.S. Army, *Military Leadership*, Field Manual 22-100, 26–27.

96. U.S. Army, *Military Leadership*, Field Manual 22-100, 26–27; U.S. Army, *Army Leadership*, Field Manual 6-22, 8-4, 8-5.

97. Lawrence, "Sergeant York—American Soldier," 9–12; York, *Sergeant York*, 168–169; Pattullo, "The Second Elder Gives Battle," 4; York, *Sergeant York*, 170–173.

98. York, *Sergeant York*, 171.

99. Gospel of Matthew 22:21, King James Version; Skeyhill, *Sergeant York: Last of the Long Hunters*, 160–163.

100. Pattullo, "The Second Elder Gives Battle," 4; Skeyhill, *Sergeant*

York: Last of the Long Hunters, 163–164. There is a conflict in the sources as to who read this to York. The 1928 York/Skeyhill book credits Buxton with this. As Danforth was interviewed for Pattullo's article, it is more likely that he read Ezekiel 33.

101. York, *Sergeant York,* 174.

102. Lawrence, "Sergeant York—American Soldier," 9–11, 32–34.

103. Skeyhill, *Sergeant York: Last of the Long Hunters,* 181–183.

104. Cahill, "America Needed a Hero," 30–38.

105. Mahoney, "Sergeant Alvin York," 22, 45–46.

106. York, *Sergeant York,* 173–174.

107. Ibid., 174–175.

108. Interview with George Edward Buxton York, 28–29 May 2010, in Pall Mall, Tennessee.

109. Cowan, *Sergeant York and His People,* 168.

110. Lawrence, "Sergeant York—American Soldier," 9–12.

4. Marching as to War

Epigraph: York, *Sergeant York,* 200.

1. Chandler, *History of the Three Hundred and Twenty-Eighth Regiment of Infantry,* 11–12.

2. Day, "The B That Stung," 3. The trigger for this late shuffling of personnel actually began with the division commander, who asked the War Department to reassign some two thousand of his authorized twenty-eight thousand men who had recently emigrated from the enemy nations of Turkey, Bulgaria, Germany, and Austria. The War Department rebuffed the division commander for this action, which was too late, and only permitted him to release German and Austrian immigrants from the ranks. See Cooke, *The All-Americans at War,* 21–25.

3. Chandler, *History of the Three Hundred and Twenty-Eighth Regiment of Infantry,* 13.

4. York, *Sergeant York,* 191.

5. Chandler, *History of the Three Hundred and Twenty-Eighth Regiment of Infantry,* 15.

6. Day, "The B That Stung," 3; Jones, *History of C. Company, 328th Infantry,* 7.

7. Barker, *History of the Machine Gun Company, 328 Infantry, 82nd Division,* 19.

8. Holden, *War Memories,* 31–35; Chandler, *History of the Three Hundred and Twenty-Eighth Regiment of Infantry,* 28–34.

9. Both of these ships were used throughout the war to transport Canadian soldiers to the Western Front as well. Canadian War Museum, "First World War (1914–1918): The Merchant Navy," http://www.

warmuseum.ca/cwm/exhibitions/navy/galery-e.aspx?section=2-C-5&id=0 (accessed 21 October 2011). See also the Allan Line/Montreal Ocean Steamship Company ship list, http://www.theshipslist.com/ships/lines/allan.shtml (accessed 21 October 2011). Chandler, *History of the Three Hundred and Twenty-Eighth Regiment of Infantry*, 15.

10. Holden, *War Memories*, 31–35; Chandler, *History of the Three Hundred and Twenty-Eighth Regiment of Infantry*, 36.

11. The USS *San Diego* was originally named *California*, but as a subsequent act by Congress mandated that only battleships could have state names, its name was changed to the *San Diego*. The USS *San Diego* was America's only major naval ship loss, sinking on 19 July 1918 off of New York by a suspected sea mine laid by German U-boat 156. George J. Albert, "The U.S.S. *San Diego* and the California Naval Militia," *California Naval History*, http://www.militarymuseum.org/USSSanDiego.html.

12. Jones, *History of C. Company, 328th Infantry*, 7.

13. York, *Sergeant York*, 192.

14. Ibid., 192.

15. Chandler, *History of the Three Hundred and Twenty-Eighth Regiment of Infantry*, 17.

16. Holden, *War Memories*, 31–35; Chandler, *History of the Three Hundred and Twenty-Eighth Regiment of Infantry*, 36–38.

17. Day, "The B That Stung," 4.

18. York, *Sergeant York*, 272.

19. Chandler, *History of the Three Hundred and Twenty-Eighth Regiment of Infantry*, 17.

20. Alvin York refers to this as Camp Knotteash on page 193 of his diary.

21. Jones, *History of C. Company, 328th Infantry*, 10.

22. Chandler, *History of the Three Hundred and Twenty-Eighth Regiment of Infantry*, 17.

23. Jones, *History of C. Company, 328th Infantry*, 10.

24. Chandler, *History of the Three Hundred and Twenty-Eighth Regiment of Infantry*, 16–18.

25. York, *Sergeant York*, 193–194.

26. Day, "The B That Stung," 5.

27. Holden, *War Memories*, 31–35; Chandler, *History of the Three Hundred and Twenty-Eighth Regiment of Infantry*, 42–43.

28. York, *Sergeant York*, 194.

29. Ibid., 193–195; Holden, *War Memories*, 31–35.

30. Chandler, *History of the Three Hundred and Twenty-Eighth Regiment of Infantry*, 21.

31. Ibid., 20–23; Holden, *War Memories*, 58–59.

32. York, *Sergeant York*, 195.

33. Buxton, *Official History of 82nd Division American Expeditionary Forces, 1917–1919*, 11–12

34. Herwig, *The First World War*, 394.

35. Trask, *The AEF and Coalition War Making*, 30, 43.

36. Ibid., 30, 75; Terraine, *To Win a War*, 69.

37. Pershing, *My Experiences in the World War*, 2:211.

38. Ibid., 2:391.

39. Trask, *The AEF and Coalition Warmaking*, 1–15.

40. Chandler, *History of the Three Hundred and Twenty-Eighth Regiment of Infantry*, 21.

41. Barker, *History of the Machine Gun Company, 328 Infantry, 82nd Division*, 19.

42. York, *Sergeant York*, 195.

43. Chandler, *History of the Three Hundred and Twenty-Eighth Regiment of Infantry*, 21.

44. York, *Sergeant York*, 172–173.

45. Ibid., 173.

46. Chandler, *History of the Three Hundred and Twenty-Eighth Regiment of Infantry*, 23.

47. Jones, *History of C. Company, 328th Infantry*, 10. "Gold fish" was canned salmon, a ration not generally liked in the army. "Corn Willie," also called "Sir William" and "Bill" by the soldiers, was a ration of canned corned beef.

48. Holden, *War Memories*, 58.

49. York, *Sergeant York*, 194–195; ABMC, *82d Division: Summary of Operations in the World War*, 4.

50. Buxton, *Official History of 82nd Division American Expeditionary Forces, 1917–1919*, 12.

51. York, *Sergeant York*, 195–196.

52. Buxton, *Official History of 82nd Division American Expeditionary Forces, 1917–1919*, 12; ABMC, *82d Division: Summary of Operations in the World War*, 4.

53. York, *Sergeant York*, 196.

54. "Back story information," letter from Harry Chandlee to Jesse Lasky, 8 May 1940, WBA, 12.

55. ABMC, *82d Division: Summary of Operations in the World War*, 4.

56. York, *Sergeant York*, 196.

57. Chandler, *History of the Three Hundred and Twenty-Eighth Regiment of Infantry*, 23; Day, "The B That Stung," 6.

58. York, *Sergeant York*, 198.

59. Cahill, "America Needed a Hero," 30–39; Mahoney, "Sergeant Alvin York," 22, 45–46.

60. York, *Sergeant York*, 198.

5. Into the Trenches!

Epigraph: York, *Sergeant York*, 199.

1. ABMC, *82d Division: Summary of Operations in the World War*, 4; NARA, 82d Division, entry 1241, RG 120; NARA, 328th Infantry Regiment Records, entry 2133, RG 391; NARA, ABMC Division files, 82nd Division, RG 117.

2. Chandler, *History of the Three Hundred and Twenty-Eighth Regiment of Infantry*, 25; Holden, *War Memories*, 66–68.

3. Holden, *War Memories*, 77.

4. Buxton, *Official History of 82nd Division American Expeditionary Forces, 1917–1919*, 12–13.

5. Holden, *War Memories*, 69–78; NARA, 82d Division, entry 1241, RG 120; NARA, 328th Infantry Regiment Records, entry 2133, RG 391; NARA, ABMC Division files, 82nd Division, RG 117.

6. Day, "The B That Stung," 7; Jones, *History of C. Company, 328th Infantry*, 14.

7. Barker, *History of the Machine Gun Company, 328 Infantry, 82nd Division*, 26.

8. Holden, *War Memories*, 27, 69–78; Chandler, *History of the Three Hundred and Twenty-Eighth Regiment of Infantry*, 25; Buxton, *Official History of 82nd Division American Expeditionary Forces, 1917–1919*, 14–16; Jones, *History of C. Company, 328th Infantry*, 13.

9. NARA, 82d Division, entry 1241, RG 120; NARA, 328th Infantry Regiment Records, entry 2133, RG 391; NARA, ABMC Division files, 82nd Division, RG 117; Alvin C. York, U.S. Army Service Record, Military Record, Army Service File, 1917–1919 under current enlistment, 4, National Personnel Records Center, St. Louis, Missouri. The War Department's Adjutant General's Office did a review of the file on 14 January 1927 and missed the file promoting York to corporal. Because of this lapse, the War Department added a note to the York file saying that he was promoted directly from private 1st class to sergeant on 1 November 1918. This poor staff work is incorrect based on the promotion remark annotated on page 4 of his service packet officially granting him corporal on 8 July 1918. This deficient service record review explains why the American Battle Monuments Commission described York as a private in October 1918.

10. York, *Sergeant York*, 201.

11. The division's zone was reduced in size on 18 July and thereafter referred to as the Lucey Sector; ABMC, *82d Division: Summary of Operations in the World War*, 4; NARA, 82d Division, entry 1241, RG 120; NARA, 328th Infantry Regiment Records, entry 2133, RG 391; NARA, ABMC Division files, 82nd Division, RG 117.

12. Booth, *The War Romance of the Salvation Army,* 207–234.

13. Day, "The B That Stung," 7; Holden, *War Memories,* 88; Chandler, *History of the Three Hundred and Twenty-Eighth Regiment of Infantry,* 27; NARA, 82d Division, entry 1241, RG 120; NARA, 328th Infantry Regiment Records, entry 2133, RG 391; NARA, ABMC Division files, 82nd Division, RG 117.

14. Jones, *History of C. Company, 328th Infantry,* 14.

15. Buxton, *Official History of 82nd Division American Expeditionary Forces, 1917–1919,* 16.

16. Chandler, *History of the Three Hundred and Twenty-Eighth Regiment of Infantry,* 25; Holden, *War Memories,* 31.

17. Holden, *War Memories,* 98

18. York, *Sergeant York,* 205.

19. Pershing, *My Experiences in the World War,* 2:249–259.

20. Holden, *War Memories,* 113–114.

21. Buxton, *Official History of 82nd Division American Expeditionary Forces, 1917–1919,* 16–18.

22. von Ledebur, "Rushing the St. Mihiel Salient," 172–179.

23. Ludendorff, *Meine Kriegserinnerungen,* 572–573; Hindenburg, *Aus Meinem Leben,* 364–366.

24. von Gallwitz, "Retreat to the Rhein," 230–235.

25. von Tschischwitz, *General von der Marwitz: Weltkriegsbriefe,* 319.

26. Harris, *The War as I Saw It,* 84–88.

27. Meilinger, "Mitchell Biography." Also see Michael Hanlon, *The St. Mihiel Battle,* http://www.worldwar1.com/dbc/stmihiel.htm (accessed 15 March 2011). Michael Hanlon is perhaps the expert on the St. Mihiel fight and is both well published on this subject and a frequent battlefield tour guide of the area.

28. Barker, *History of the Machine Gun Company, 328 Infantry, 82nd Division,* 37.

29. Chandler, *History of the Three Hundred and Twenty-Eighth Regiment of Infantry,* 25; Holden, *War Memories,* 33.

30. Buxton, *Official History of 82nd Division American Expeditionary Forces, 1917–1919,* 18–25; NARA, 82d Division, entry 1241, RG 120; NARA, 328th Infantry Regiment Records, entry 2133, RG 391; NARA, ABMC Division files, 82nd Division, RG 117.

31. Holden, *War Memories,* 113–114.

32. York, *Sergeant York,* 208–210.

33. Ibid., 208.

34. Buxton, *Official History of 82nd Division American Expeditionary Forces, 1917–1919,* 24.

35. Chandler, *History of the Three Hundred and Twenty-Eighth Regiment of Infantry,* 25; Holden, *War Memories,* 33.

36. York, *Sergeant York*, 208–209; Chandler, *History of the Three Hundred and Twenty-Eighth Regiment of Infantry*, 124–126.

37. York, *Sergeant York*, 209.

38. Buxton, *Official History of 82nd Division American Expeditionary Forces, 1917–1919*, 20–28.

39. Holden, *War Memories*, 128–133.

40. York, *Sergeant York*, 209.

41. Ibid., 209–210.

42. Pershing, *My Experiences in the World War*, 2:269–273.

43. NARA, 82d Division, entry 1241, RG 120; NARA, 328th Infantry Regiment Records, entry 2133, RG 391; NARA, ABMC Division files, 82nd Division, RG 117; Pershing, *My Experiences in the World War*, 2:266–2673.

44. ABMC, *82d Division: Summary of Operations in the World War*, 12–13; Buxton, *Official History of 82nd Division American Expeditionary Forces, 1917–1919*, 28–30; NARA, 82d Division, entry 1241, RG 120; NARA, 328th Infantry Regiment Records, entry 2133, RG 391; NARA, ABMC Division files, 82nd Division, RG 117.

45. Chandler, *History of the Three Hundred and Twenty-Eighth Regiment of Infantry*, 36.

46. NARA, 82d Division, entry 1241, RG 120; NARA, 328th Infantry Regiment Records, entry 2133, RG 391; NARA, ABMC Division files, 82nd Division, RG 117; ABMC, *82d Division: Summary of Operations in the World War*, 12–13; Cooke, *The All-Americans at War*, 77.

47. York, *Sergeant York*, 210.

6. Prelude to Battle

Epigraph: Brittain, *Testament of Youth*, 420–422.

1. Credit for perfecting the en echelon attack must be given to Napoleon, to whom France owes its tradition. However, the en echelon was the eighteenth-century trademark of Prussian king Frederick the Great.

2. Sheffield, *Forgotten Victory*, 207–210.

3. Hindenburg, *Aus Meinem Leben*, 366.

4. Sheffield, *Forgotten Victory*, 218–219.

5. Liggett, *A.E.F.*, 172–174.

6. Grotelueschen, *The AEF Way of War*, 125–128.

7. American divisions were 2–2.5 times larger than their European counterparts in men, translating to about fifty-five French, British, or German divisions.

8. Horne, ed., *Source Records of the Great War*, 6:401–402. These figures are taken from a joint report published by Field Marshal Foch and General John J. Pershing.

9. Terraine, *To Win a War*, 153.

10. Coffman, *The War to End All Wars*, 355.

11. Pershing, *My Experiences in the World War*, 2:390.

12. Ferrell, *America's Deadliest Battle*, preface.

13. Grotelueschen, *The AEF Way of War*, 30–43.

14. Ibid., 42.

15. Terraine, *To Win a War*, 156.

16. NARA, 82d Division, entry 1241, RG 120; NARA, 328th Infantry Regiment Records, entry 2133, RG 391; NARA, ABMC Division files, 82nd Division, RG 117; Pershing, *My Experiences in the World War*, 2:320.

17. Pershing, *My Experiences in the World War*, 2:320–333.

18. See the Congressional Medal of Honor website for details on this exploit, available at http://www.cmohs.org/recipient-detail/2612/woodfill-samuel.php (accessed 2 September 2011).

19. Pershing, *My Experiences in the World War*, 2:392.

20. York, *Sergeant York*, 210–211.

21. John J. Pershing, "In the Matter of MG William P. Burnham, 82nd Division," Pershing Papers, on Relief of Officers, August–October 1918, Box 8, NARA; Duncan, "Reminiscences, 1886–1919," 117–118.

22. Holden, *War Memories*, 137–140.

23. Jones, *History of C. Company, 328th Infantry*, 19; NARA, 82d Division, entry 1241, RG 120; NARA, 328th Infantry Regiment Records, entry 2133, RG 391; NARA, ABMC Division files, 82nd Division, RG 117.

24. Ayers, *The War with Germany*, 101–118.

25. Buxton, *Official History of 82nd Division American Expeditionary Forces, 1917–1919*, 30–32; Barker, *History of the Machine Gun Company, 328 Infantry, 82nd Division*, 42; NARA, 82d Division, entry 1241, RG 120; NARA, 328th Infantry Regiment Records, entry 2133, RG 391; NARA, ABMC Division files, 82nd Division, RG 117.

26. Jones, *History of C. Company, 328th Infantry*, 19.

27. Holden, *War Memories*, 140–141.

28. Buxton, *Official History of 82nd Division American Expeditionary Forces, 1917–1919*, 36.

29. Holden, *War Memories*, 142–144; Buxton, *Official History of 82nd Division American Expeditionary Forces, 1917–1919*, 35–37; Chandler, *History of the Three Hundred and Twenty-Eighth Regiment of Infantry*, 37–39; Barker, *History of the Machine Gun Company, 328 Infantry, 82nd Division*, 42; Day, "The B That Stung," 10; NARA, 82d Division, entry 1241, RG 120; NARA, 328th Infantry Regiment Records, entry 2133, RG 391; NARA, ABMC Division files, 82nd Division, RG 117.

30. NARA, 82d Division, entry 1241, RG 120; NARA, 328th Infantry Regiment Records, entry 2133, RG 391; NARA, ABMC Division files, 82nd Division, RG 117; York, *Sergeant York*, 215.

31. Buxton, *Official History of 82nd Division American Expeditionary Forces, 1917–1919*, 36–37.

32. ABMC, *82d Division: Summary of Operations in the World War*, 16–20; NARA, 82d Division, entry 1241, RG 120; NARA, 328th Infantry Regiment Records, entry 2133, RG 391; NARA, ABMC Division files, 82nd Division, RG 117.

33. Day, "The B That Stung," 10.

34. Holy Bible, 2 Timothy 4:1–8, King James Version.

35. Holden, *War Memories*, 143–145.

36. NARA, 82d Division, entry 1241, RG 120; NARA, 328th Infantry Regiment Records, entry 2133, RG 391; NARA, ABMC Division files, 82nd Division, RG 117; Buxton, *Official History of 82nd Division American Expeditionary Forces, 1917–1919*, 41.

37. Holden, *War Memories*, 145–148.

38. Ibid.

39. NARA, 82d Division, entry 1241, RG 120; NARA, 328th Infantry Regiment Records, entry 2133, RG 391; NARA, ABMC Division files, 82nd Division, RG 117; Buxton, *Official History of 82nd Division American Expeditionary Forces, 1917–1919*, 44–47.

40. Day, "The B That Stung," 10.

41. York, *Sergeant York*, 215.

42. NARA, 82d Division, entry 1241, RG 120; NARA, 328th Infantry Regiment Records, entry 2133, RG 391; NARA, ABMC Division files, 82nd Division, RG 117; Buxton, *Official History of 82nd Division American Expeditionary Forces, 1917–1919*, 41–49.

43. H.A. Drum, Field Order number 44, 6 October, 1918, in U.S. Army, *United States Army in the World War, 1917–1919*, vol. 16, *General Orders, GHQ, AEF*, CMH Pub 23-22, page 215.

44. ABMC, *82d Division: Summary of Operations in the World War*, 16–20; NARA, 82d Division, entry 1241, RG 120; NARA, 328th Infantry Regiment Records, entry 2133, RG 391; NARA, ABMC Division files, 82nd Division, RG 117.

45. Duncan, "Reminiscences, 1886–1919," 145–146.

46. Ibid., 148.

47. Day, "The B That Stung," 11–13.

48. Franke, *Die 2. Württemberg Landwehr Division Im Weltkrieg 1914–1918*, 48–58.

49. NARA, 82d Division, entry 1241, RG 120; NARA, 328th Infantry Regiment Records, entry 2133, RG 391; NARA, ABMC Division files, 82nd Division, RG 117; ABMC, *82d Division: Summary of Operations in the World War*, 16–20.

50. Buxton, *Official History of 82nd Division American Expeditionary Forces, 1917–1919*, 41.

51. Ibid.

52. Ibid., 50–51; NARA, 82d Division, entry 1241, RG 120; NARA, 328th Infantry Regiment Records, entry 2133, RG 391; NARA, ABMC Division files, 82nd Division, RG 117.

53. 120 Württemberg Landwehr Regimental Kriegstagebuch Rep M 384 and 385, Landesarchiv Baden-Württemberg—Hauptstaatsarchiv Stuttgart; I Battalion, 120 Württemberg Landwehr Regiment Kriegstagebuch, REP M 411, 381, 383, Landesarchiv Baden-Württemberg—Hauptstaatsarchiv Stuttgart, Germany; II Battalion, 120 Württemberg Landwehr Regiment Kriegstagebuch, Rep M 386 and 387 Landwehr Regiment Kriegstagebuch, Landesarchiv Baden-Württemberg—Hauptstaatsarchiv Stuttgart; III Battalion, 120 Württemberg Landwehr Regiment Kriegstagebuch, Rep M 388 Landwehr Regiment Kriegstagebuch, Landesarchiv Baden-Württemberg—Hauptstaatsarchiv Stuttgart; Franke, *Die 2. Württemberg Landwehr Division Im Weltkrieg 1914–1918*, 48–58.

54. Gustav Strohm, *Die Württembergishchen Regimenter im Weltkrieg 1914–1918*, Band 25, *Das Württembergishche Landwehr Infanterie Regiment nr. 120* (Stuttgart: Belser Verlasbuchhandklung, 1922), 151–177.

55. Day, "The B That Stung," 11–13.

56. Franke, *Die 2. Württemberg Landwehr Division Im Weltkrieg 1914–1918*, 48–58.

57. 125 Landwehr Regiment Kriegstagebuch, REP M 420 and 421, Landesarchiv Baden-Württemberg—Hauptstaatsarchiv Stuttgart; I Battalion, 125 Landwehr Regiment Kriegstagebuch, REP M 422, Landesarchiv Baden-Württemberg—Hauptstaatsarchiv Stuttgart; II Battalion, 125 Landwehr Regiment Kriegstagebuch, REP M 423, Landesarchiv Baden-Württemberg—Hauptstaatsarchiv Stuttgart; NARA, 82d Division, entry 1241, RG 120; NARA, 328th Infantry Regiment Records, entry 2133, RG 391; NARA, ABMC Division files, 82nd Division, RG 117.

58. Franke, *Die 2. Württemberg Landwehr Division Im Weltkrieg 1914–1918*, 48–58.

59. NARA, 82d Division, entry 1241, RG 120; NARA, 328th Infantry Regiment Records, entry 2133, RG 391; NARA, ABMC Division files, 82nd Division, RG 117; Buxton, *Official History of 82nd Division American Expeditionary Forces, 1917–1919*, 54–58.

60. Day, "The B That Stung," 10–13.

61. Lapple, *Das Württembergische Landwehr Infanterie Regiment Nr. 125 Im Weltkrieg 1914–1918*, Band 38, 169–173.

62. 5th Prussian Guards Division Kriegstagebuch, 5 October 1918–9 October 1918, Bundesarchiv, Freiburg, Germany.

63. NARA, 82d Division, entry 1241, RG 120; NARA, 328th Infantry Regiment Records, entry 2133, RG 391; NARA, ABMC Division files, 82nd Division, RG 117; Buxton, *Official History of 82nd Division Ameri-*

can Expeditionary Forces, 1917–1919, 54–58; Chandler, *History of the Three Hundred and Twenty-Eighth Regiment of Infantry,* 41–45.

64. Strohm, *Die Württembergishchen Regimenter im Weltkrieg 1914–1918,* Band 25, *Das Württembergishche Landwehr Infanterie Regiment nr. 120,* 161–173; Hauptmann Heinrich Müller, Kriegsrangeliste u. Personal Bogan, M430/3, 7891, Landesarchiv Baden-Württemberg—Hauptstaatsarchiv Stuttgart.

65. NARA, 82d Division, entry 1241, RG 120; NARA, 328th Infantry Regiment Records, entry 2133, RG 391; NARA, ABMC Division files, 82nd Division, RG 117; York, *Sergeant York,* 215–218; Chandler, *History of the Three Hundred and Twenty-Eighth Regiment of Infantry,* 41–45; Buxton, *Official History of 82nd Division American Expeditionary Forces, 1917–1919,* 54–58.

66. Jones, *History of C. Company, 328th Infantry,* 19; Buxton, *Official History of 82nd Division American Expeditionary Forces, 1917–1919,* 41; Holden, *War Memories,* 148–152.

67. York, *Sergeant York,* 215–218.

68. NARA, 82d Division, entry 1241, RG 120; NARA, 328th Infantry Regiment Records, entry 2133, RG 391; NARA, ABMC Division files, 82nd Division, RG 117; Chandler, *History of the Three Hundred and Twenty-Eighth Regiment of Infantry,* 45; Buxton, *Official History of 82nd Division American Expeditionary Forces, 1917–1919,* 58–59.

69. Day, "The B That Stung," 10–13; Franke, *Die 2. Württemberg Landwehr Division Im Weltkrieg 1914–1918,* 48–58.

70. NARA, 82d Division, entry 1241, RG 120; NARA, 328th Infantry Regiment Records, entry 2133, RG 391; NARA, ABMC Division files, 82nd Division, RG 117; Lapple, *Das Württembergische Landwehr Infanterie Regiment Nr. 125 Im Weltkrieg 1914–1918,* Band 38, 169–173; Buxton, *Official History of 82nd Division American Expeditionary Forces, 1917–1919,* 54–58; Chandler, *History of the Three Hundred and Twenty-Eighth Regiment of Infantry,* 41–45.

71. Lapple, *Das Württembergische Landwehr Infanterie Regiment Nr. 125 Im Weltkrieg 1914–1918,* Band 38, 169–173; Franke, *Die 2. Württemberg Landwehr Division Im Weltkrieg 1914–1918,* 48–58.

72. Strohm, *Die Württembergishchen Regimenter im Weltkrieg 1914–1918,* Band 25, *Das Württembergishche Landwehr Infanterie Regiment nr. 120,* 161–173.

73. Ibid.

74. Franke, *Die 2. Württemberg Landwehr Division Im Weltkrieg 1914–1918,* 48–58; 120 Württemberg Landwehr Regimental Kriegstagebuch Rep M 384 and 385, Landesarchiv Baden-Württemberg—Hauptstaatsarchiv Stuttgart; I Battalion, 120 Württemberg Landwehr Regiment Kriegstagebuch, REP M 411, 381, 383, Landesarchiv Baden-Württem-

berg—Hauptstaatsarchiv Stuttgart; II Battalion, 120 Württemberg Landwehr Regiment Kriegstagebuch, Rep M 386 and 387 Landwehr Regiment Kriegstagebuch, Landesarchiv Baden-Württemberg—Hauptstaatsarchiv Stuttgart; III Battalion, 120 Württemberg Landwehr Regiment Kriegstagebuch, Rep M 388 Landwehr Regiment Kriegstagebuch, Landesarchiv Baden-Württemberg—Hauptstaatsarchiv Stuttgart.

75. Group of Armies-Gallwitz order 6 October 1918, in U.S. Army, *United States Army in the World War, 1917–1919,* vol. 11, *American Occupation of Germany,* CMH Pub 23-17, page 539.

76. Landwehr-Infanterie-Regiment Nr. 120; File M 115, regimental structures and all operations 1914–1918; File M 411, Kriegstagebuch; File M433/2, Personnel Lists 1914–1921; File M 484, Kriegsstammrollen incl. Ersatzbataillon 1914–1918, all in Landesarchiv Baden-Württemberg—Hauptstaatsarchiv Stuttgart.

77. Paul Jürgen "Kuno" Vollmer, Kriegsrangeliste, M430/3, 11828, Landesarchiv Baden-Württemberg—Hauptstaatsarchiv Stuttgart.

78. Ibid.

79. Landwehr-Infanterie-Regiment Nr. 120, File M 115, regimental structures and all operations 1914–1918; File M 411, Kriegstagebuch; File M433/2, Personnel Lists 1914–1921; File M 484, Kriegsstammrollen incl. Ersatzbataillon 1914–1918, all in Landesarchiv Baden-Württemberg—Hauptstaatsarchiv Stuttgart.

80. Strohm, *Die Württembergishchen Regimenter im Weltkrieg 1914–1918,* Band 25, *Das Württembergishche Landwehr Infanterie Regiment nr. 120,* 161–173.

81. "Testimony of German Officers and Men about Sergeant York," translated by the U.S. Army War College, Carlisle, Pennsylvania, June 1936.

82. Strohm, *Die Württembergishchen Regimenter im Weltkrieg 1914–1918,* Band 25, *Das Württembergishche Landwehr Infanterie Regiment nr. 120,* 161–173; Württembergische Landwehr-Infanterie-Regiment Nr. 120, File M 115, regimental structures and all operations 1914–1918; File M 411, Kriegstagebuch; File M433/2, Personnel Lists 1914–1921; File M 484, Kriegsstammrollen incl. Ersatzbataillon 1914–1918, all in Landesarchiv Baden-Württemberg—Hauptstaatsarchiv Stuttgart.

83. Strohm, *Die Württembergishchen Regimenter im Weltkrieg 1914–1918,* Band 25, *Das Württembergishche Landwehr Infanterie Regiment nr. 120,* 161–173; "Testimony of German Officers and Men about Sergeant York," translated by the U.S. Army War College, Carlisle, Pennsylvania, June 1936.

84. "Testimony of German Officers and Men about Sergeant York," translated by the U.S. Army War College, Carlisle, Pennsylvania, June 1936; Württembergische Landwehr-Infanterie-Regiment Nr. 120, File

M 115, regimental structures and all operations 1914–1918; File M 411, Kriegstagebuch; File M433/2, Personnel Lists 1914–1921; File M 484, Kriegsstammrollen incl. Ersatzbataillon 1914–1918, all in Landesarchiv Baden-Württemberg—Hauptstaatsarchiv Stuttgart.

85. Karl Kübler, Kriegsrangeliste, M430/3, 6369, Landesarchiv Baden-Württemberg—Hauptstaatsarchiv Stuttgart.

86. Württembergische Landwehr-Infanterie-Regiment Nr. 120, File M 115, regimental structures and all operations 1914–1918; File M 411, Kriegstagebuch; File M433/2, Personnel Lists 1914–1921; File M 484, Kriegsstammrollen incl. Ersatzbataillon 1914–1918, all in Landesarchiv Baden-Württemberg—Hauptstaatsarchiv Stuttgart.

87. Lapple, *Das Württembergische Landwehr Infanterie Regiment Nr. 125 Im Weltkrieg 1914–1918*, Band 38, 5–31, 55–62, 169–173; Paul Adolf August, Kriegsrangeliste, M430/3, 6907 Lipp, Landesarchiv Baden-Württemberg—Hauptstaatsarchiv Stuttgart; Paul Jurgen "Kuno" Vollmer, Kriegsrangeliste, M430/3, 11828, Landesarchiv Baden-Württemberg—Hauptstaatsarchiv Stuttgart.

88. Lapple, *Das Württembergische Landwehr Infanterie Regiment Nr. 125 Im Weltkrieg 1914–1918*, Band 38, 169–173; 125 Landwehr Regiment Kriegstagebuch, REP M 420 and 421, Landesarchiv Baden-Württemberg—Hauptstaatsarchiv Stuttgart; I Battalion, 125 Landwehr Regiment Kriegstagebuch, REP M 422, Landesarchiv Baden-Württemberg—Hauptstaatsarchiv Stuttgart; II Battalion, 125 Landwehr Regiment Kriegstagebuch, REP M 423, Landesarchiv Baden-Württemberg—Hauptstaatsarchiv Stuttgart; II Battalion, 125 Landwehr Regiment Kriegstagebuch, REP M 425, Landesarchiv Baden-Württemberg—Hauptstaatsarchiv Stuttgart.

89. Chandler, *History of the Three Hundred and Twenty-Eighth Regiment of Infantry,* 45.

90. Lapple, *Das Württembergische Landwehr Infanterie Regiment Nr. 125 Im Weltkrieg 1914–1918*, Band 38, 169–173; 125 Landwehr Regiment Kriegstagebuch, REP M 420 and 421, Landesarchiv Baden-Württemberg—Hauptstaatsarchiv Stuttgart; I Battalion, 125 Landwehr Regiment Kriegstagebuch, REP M 422, Landesarchiv Baden-Württemberg—Hauptstaatsarchiv Stuttgart; II Battalion, 125 Landwehr Regiment Kriegstagebuch, REP M 423, Landesarchiv Baden-Württemberg—Hauptstaatsarchiv Stuttgart; II Battalion, 125 Landwehr Regiment Kriegstagebuch, REP M 425, Landesarchiv Baden-Württemberg—Hauptstaatsarchiv Stuttgart.

91. Lapple, *Das Württembergische Landwehr Infanterie Regiment Nr. 125 Im Weltkrieg 1914–1918*, Band 38, 169–173; 125 Landwehr Regiment Kriegstagebuch, REP M 420 and 421, Landesarchiv Baden-Württemberg—Hauptstaatsarchiv Stuttgart; I Battalion, 125 Landwehr

Regiment Kriegstagebuch, REP M 422, Landesarchiv Baden-Württemberg—Hauptstaatsarchiv Stuttgart; II Battalion, 125 Landwehr Regiment Kriegstagebuch, REP M 423, Landesarchiv Baden-Württemberg—Hauptstaatsarchiv Stuttgart; II Battalion, 125 Landwehr Regiment Kriegstagebuch, REP M 425, Landesarchiv Baden-Württemberg—Hauptstaatsarchiv Stuttgart.

7. One Day in October

Epigraph: York, *Sergeant York,* 220.

1. NARA, 82d Division, entry 1241, RG 120; NARA, 328th Infantry Regiment Records, entry 2133, RG 391; NARA, ABMC Division files, 82nd Division, RG 117; ABMC, *82d Division: Summary of Operations in the World War,* 23.

2. ABMC, *28th Division: Summary of Operations in the World War,* 67–69.

3. Chandler, *History of the Three Hundred and Twenty-Eighth Regiment of Infantry,* 57–59; ABMC, *82d Division: Summary of Operations in the World War,* 23.

4. York, *Sergeant York,* 217–218.

5. NARA, 82d Division, entry 1241, RG 120; NARA, 328th Infantry Regiment Records, entry 2133, RG 391; NARA, ABMC Division files, 82nd Division, RG 117; ABMC, *82d Division: Summary of Operations in the World War,* 22–24.

6. Chandler, *History of the Three Hundred and Twenty-Eighth Regiment of Infantry,* 45; Buxton, *Official History of 82nd Division American Expeditionary Forces, 1917–1919,* 58–59.

7. Pattullo, "The Second Elder Gives Battle," 3–4, 71–74.

8. NARA, 82d Division, entry 1241, RG 120; NARA, 328th Infantry Regiment Records, entry 2133, RG 391; NARA, ABMC Division files, 82nd Division, RG 117; Chandler, *History of the Three Hundred and Twenty-Eighth Regiment of Infantry,* 45; Buxton, *Official History of 82nd Division American Expeditionary Forces, 1917–1919,* 57–59; York, *Sergeant York,* 217–218.

9. York, *Sergeant York,* 219.

10. Ibid., 218.

11. Day, "The B That Stung," 11–13.

12. NARA, 82d Division, entry 1241, RG 120; NARA, 328th Infantry Regiment Records, entry 2133, RG 391; NARA, ABMC Division files, 82nd Division, RG 117; Chandler, *History of the Three Hundred and Twenty-Eighth Regiment of Infantry,* 45–46; Buxton, *Official History of 82nd Division American Expeditionary Forces, 1917–1919,* 58–59; York, *Sergeant York,* 219–230; Pattullo, "The Second Elder Gives Battle," 3–4.

13. This is based on a personal interview between Cutting and Tom Mahoney. Mahoney, "Sergeant Alvin York," 22, 45–47; George Larrabee, "Sharpshooter from the Hills," *Military History*, June 1987, 10, 56–57.

14. "Sgt York's Buddy to Get Late Medal," *Tuscaloosa News*, 29 September 1965, 7; "York's Buddy to Get Medal 47 Years Late," *Portsmouth Times*, 21 September 1965, 7; "Merrithew Gets Sendoff," *Boston Globe*, 2 October 1929, 6; Roland Corneau, "Brookline Veteran Recalls Argonne," *Boston Globe*, 8 October 1968, 37.

15. Otis B. Merrithew, "Statement Regarding Argonne Engagement," 11 December 1929, B00374, Folder 2880, WBA.

16. Cahill, "America Needed a Hero," 30–38.

17. "Testimony of German Officers and Men about Sergeant York," translated by the U.S. Army War College, Carlisle, Pennsylvania, June 1936; Franke, *Die 2. Württemberg Landwehr Division Im Weltkrieg 1914–1918*, 48–58; I Battalion, 120 Württemberg Landwehr Regiment Kriegstagebuch, REP M 411, 381, 383, Landesarchiv Baden-Württemberg—Hauptstaatsarchiv Stuttgart.

18. 120 Württemberg Landwehr Regimental Kriegstagebuch Rep M411 381, 383, Landesarchiv Baden-Württemberg—Hauptstaatsarchiv Stuttgart; I Battalion, 120 Württemberg Landwehr Regiment Kriegstagebuch, REP M 411, 381, 383, Landesarchiv Baden-Württemberg—Hauptstaatsarchiv Stuttgart; II Battalion, 120 Württemberg Landwehr Regiment Kriegstagebuch, Rep M 386 and 387 Landwehr Regiment Kriegstagebuch, Landesarchiv Baden-Württemberg—Hauptstaatsarchiv Stuttgart; III Battalion, 120 Württemberg Landwehr Regiment Kriegstagebuch, Rep M 388 Landwehr Regiment Kriegstagebuch, Landesarchiv Baden-Württemberg—Hauptstaatsarchiv Stuttgart; "Testimony of German Officers and Men about Sergeant York," translated by the U.S. Army War College, Carlisle, Pennsylvania, June 1936; Franke, *Die 2. Württemberg Landwehr Division Im Weltkrieg 1914–1918*, 48–58.

19. NARA, 82d Division, entry 1241, RG 120; NARA, 328th Infantry Regiment Records, entry 2133, RG 391; NARA, ABMC Division files, 82nd Division, RG 117; Chandler, *History of the Three Hundred and Twenty-Eighth Regiment of Infantry*, 45–46.

20. Buxton, *Official History of 82nd Division American Expeditionary Forces, 1917–1919*, 58–59; York, *Sergeant York*, 218–220; Pattullo, "The Second Elder Gives Battle," 3–4.

21. Strohm, *Die Württembergishchen Regimenter im Weltkrieg 1914–1918*, Band 25, *Das Württembergishche Landwehr Infanterie Regiment nr. 120*, 161–173; York, *Sergeant York*, 218–220.

22. Chandler, *History of the Three Hundred and Twenty-Eighth Regiment of Infantry*, 45–46.

23. NARA, 82d Division, entry 1241, RG 120; NARA, 328th Infantry

Regiment Records, entry 2133, RG 391; NARA, ABMC Division files, 82nd Division, RG 117; York, *Sergeant York,* 219.

24. NARA, 82d Division, entry 1241, RG 120; NARA, 328th Infantry Regiment Records, entry 2133, RG 391; NARA, ABMC Division files, 82nd Division, RG 117; Lapple, *Das Württembergische Landwehr Infanterie Regiment Nr. 125 Im Weltkrieg 1914–1918,* Band 38, 169–173; 125 Landwehr Regiment Kriegstagebuch, REP M 420 and 421, Landesarchiv Baden-Württemberg—Hauptstaatsarchiv Stuttgart; I Battalion, 125 Landwehr Regiment Kriegstagebuch, REP M 422, Landesarchiv Baden-Württemberg—Hauptstaatsarchiv Stuttgart; II Battalion, 125 Landwehr Regiment Kriegstagebuch, REP M 423, Landesarchiv Baden-Württemberg—Hauptstaatsarchiv Stuttgart; III Battalion, 125 Landwehr Regiment Kriegstagebuch, REP M 425, Landesarchiv Baden-Württemberg—Hauptstaatsarchiv Stuttgart. Württembergische Landwehr-Infanterie-Regiment Nr. 120, File M 115, regimental structures and all operations 1914–1918; File M 411, Kriegstagebuch; File M433/2, Personnel Lists 1914–1921; File M 484, Kriegsstammrollen incl. Ersatzbataillon 1914–1918, all in Landesarchiv Baden-Württemberg—Hauptstaatsarchiv Stuttgart. "Testimony of German Officers and Men about Sergeant York," translated by the U.S. Army War College, Carlisle, Pennsylvania, June 1936.

25. York, *Sergeant York,* 220.

26. Buxton, *Official History of 82nd Division American Expeditionary Forces, 1917–1919,* 54–58; NARA, 82d Division, entry 1241, RG 120; NARA, 328th Infantry Regiment Records, entry 2133, RG 391; NARA, ABMC Division files, 82nd Division, RG 117; ABMC, *82d Division: Summary of Operations in the World War,* 22.

27. Chandler, *History of the Three Hundred and Twenty-Eighth Regiment of Infantry,* 45.

28. Buxton, *Official History of 82nd Division American Expeditionary Forces, 1917–1919,* 57–59; ABMC, *82d Division: Summary of Operations in the World War,* 22–25.

29. NARA, 82d Division, entry 1241, RG 120; NARA, 328th Infantry Regiment Records, entry 2133, RG 391; NARA, ABMC Division files, 82nd Division, RG 117; Buxton, *Official History of 82nd Division American Expeditionary Forces, 1917–1919,* 59; York, *Sergeant York,* 220–222.

30. Lawrence, "Sergeant York—American Soldier," 9–11; NARA, 82d Division, entry 1241, RG 120; NARA, 328th Infantry Regiment Records, entry 2133, RG 391; NARA, ABMC Division files, 82nd Division, RG 117.

31. Pattullo, "The Second Elder Gives Battle," 3–4, 71–74; York, *Sergeant York,* 221–222.

32. Lapple, *Das Württembergische Landwehr Infanterie Regiment Nr.*

125 Im Weltkrieg 1914–1918, Band 38, 169–173; 125 Landwehr Regiment Kriegstagebuch, REP M 420 and 421, Landesarchiv Baden-Württemberg—Hauptstaatsarchiv Stuttgart; I Battalion, 125 Landwehr Regiment Kriegstagebuch, REP M 422, Landesarchiv Baden-Württemberg—Hauptstaatsarchiv Stuttgart; II Battalion, 125 Landwehr Regiment Kriegstagebuch, REP M 423, Landesarchiv Baden-Württemberg—Hauptstaatsarchiv Stuttgart; II Battalion, 125 Landwehr Regiment Kriegstagebuch, REP M 425, Landesarchiv Baden-Württemberg—Hauptstaatsarchiv Stuttgart. Württembergische Landwehr-Infanterie-Regiment Nr. 120, File M 115, regimental structures and all operations 1914–1918; File M 411, Kriegstagebuch; both in Landesarchiv Baden-Württemberg—Hauptstaatsarchiv Stuttgart.

33. York, *Sergeant York,* 221–222; Lawrence, "Sergeant York—American Soldier," 9–11, 32–34.

34. Duncan, "Reminiscences, 1886–1919," 151.

35. Mahoney, "Sergeant Alvin York," 22, 45–47.

36. Cahill, "America Needed a Hero," 30–39.

37. "Testimony of German Officers and Men about Sergeant York," translated by the U.S. Army War College, Carlisle, Pennsylvania, June 1936; Strohm, *Die Württembergishchen Regimenter im Weltkrieg 1914–1918,* Band 25, *Das Württembergishche Landwehr Infanterie Regiment nr. 120,* 161–173; York, *Sergeant York,* 220–223; Franke, *Die 2. Württemberg Landwehr Division Im Weltkrieg 1914–1918,* 48–58; I Battalion, 120 Württemberg Landwehr Regiment Kriegstagebuch, REP M 411, 381, 383, Landesarchiv Baden-Württemberg—Hauptstaatsarchiv Stuttgart; 120 Württemberg Landwehr Regimental Kriegstagebuch Rep M 384 and 385, Landesarchiv Baden-Württemberg—Hauptstaatsarchiv Stuttgart.

38. Pattullo, "The Second Elder Gives Battle," 3–4, 71–74.

39. NARA, 82d Division, entry 1241, RG 120; NARA, 328th Infantry Regiment Records, entry 2133, RG 391; NARA, ABMC Division files, 82nd Division, RG 117; "Americans in the Meuse-Argonne Region," in U.S. Army, *United States Army in the World War, 1917–1919,* vol. 9, *Military Operations of the American Expeditionary Forces,* CMH Pub 23-14, page 229; York, *Sergeant York,* 223–224; Pattullo, "The Second Elder Gives Battle," 3–4, 71–74.

40. Interview with Mayor Roland Destenay of Châtel Chéhéry, October 2006.

41. Pattullo, "The Second Elder Gives Battle," 3–4.

42. Otis B. Merrithew, "Statement Regarding Argonne Engagement," 11 December 1929, B00374, Folder 2880, WBA; York, *Sergeant York,* 223–224; Cahill, "America Needed a Hero," 30–39.

43. Percy Beardsley, affidavit of 8 October 1918 battle near Châtel Chéhéry, given at Frettes, France, 21 February 1919; Alvin C. York, ex-

tract from York's Medal of Honor Citation, U.S. Army Service Record, Military Record, Army Service File, 1917–1919, under Awards, 1919, National Personnel Records Center, St. Louis, Missouri; York, *Sergeant York,* 223–224; Pattullo, "The Second Elder Gives Battle," 4; Cahill, "America Needed a Hero," 30–39.

44. York, *Sergeant York,* 224; Cahill, "America Needed a Hero," 31.

45. Strohm, *Die Württembergishchen Regimenter im Weltkrieg 1914– 1918,* Band 25, *Das Württembergishche Landwehr Infanterie Regiment nr. 120,* 161–173. Württembergische Landwehr-Infanterie-Regiment Nr. 120, File M 115, regimental structures and all operations 1914–1918; File M 411, Kriegstagebuch; File M433/2, Personnel Lists 1914–1921; File M 484, Kriegsstammrollen incl. Ersatzbataillon 1914–1918, all in Landesarchiv Baden-Württemberg—Hauptstaatsarchiv Stuttgart. "Testimony of German Officers and Men about Sergeant York," translated by the U.S. Army War College, Carlisle, Pennsylvania, June 1936.

46. Strohm, *Die Württembergishchen Regimenter im Weltkrieg 1914– 1918,* Band 25, *Das Württembergishche Landwehr Infanterie Regiment nr. 120,* 161–173.

47. Ibid.

48. "Testimony of German Officers and Men about Sergeant York," translated by the U.S. Army War College, Carlisle, Pennsylvania, June 1936; Franke, *Die 2. Württemberg Landwehr Division Im Weltkrieg 1914– 1918,* 48–58; 120 Württemberg Landwehr Regimental Kriegstagebuch Rep M411 381, 383, Landesarchiv Baden-Württemberg—Hauptstaatsarchiv Stuttgart.

49. Württembergische Landwehr-Infanterie-Regiment Nr. 120, File M 115, regimental operations 1914–1918; File M 411, Kriegstagebuch; File M433/2, Personnel Lists 1914–1921; File M 484, Kriegsstammrollen 1914–1918, all in Landesarchiv Baden-Württemberg—Hauptstaatsarchiv Stuttgart. "Testimony of German Officers and Men about Sergeant York," translated by the U.S. Army War College, Carlisle, Pennsylvania, June 1936.

50. George Wills, affidavit of 8 October 1918 battle near Châtel Chéhéry, given at Frettes, France, 21 February 1919; Percy Beardsley, affidavit of 8 October 1918 battle near Châtel Chéhéry, given at Frettes, France, 6 February 1919; Feodore "Sak" [Sok], affidavit of 8 October 1918 battle near Châtel Chéhéry, given at Frettes, France, 6 February 1919; York, *Sergeant York,* 225.

51. "Testimony of German Officers and Men about Sergeant York," translated by the U.S. Army War College, Carlisle, Pennsylvania, June 1936.

52. Strohm, *Die Württembergishchen Regimenter im Weltkrieg 1914– 1918,* Band 25, *Das Württembergishche Landwehr Infanterie Regiment nr. 120,* 161–173.

53. Pattullo, "The Second Elder Gives Battle," 3–4, 71–74.

54. NARA, 82d Division, entry 1241, RG 120; NARA, 328th Infantry Regiment Records, entry 2133, RG 391; NARA, ABMC Division files, 82nd Division, RG 117; Michael Sacina, affidavit of 8 October 1918 battle near Châtel Chéhéry, given at Frettes, France, 6 February 1919; Buxton, *Official History of 82nd Division American Expeditionary Forces, 1917–1919,* 60–61; "Testimony of German Officers and Men about Sergeant York," translated by the U.S. Army War College, Carlisle, Pennsylvania, June 1936.

55. "Testimony of German Officers and Men about Sergeant York," translated by the U.S. Army War College, Carlisle, Pennsylvania, June 1936.

56. Lapple, *Das Württembergische Landwehr Infanterie Regiment Nr. 125 Im Weltkrieg 1914–1918,* Band 38, 169–173; 125 Landwehr Regiment Kriegstagebuch, REP M 420 and 421, Landesarchiv Baden-Württemberg—Hauptstaatsarchiv Stuttgart; I Battalion, 125 Landwehr Regiment Kriegstagebuch, REP M 422, Landesarchiv Baden-Württemberg—Hauptstaatsarchiv Stuttgart; II Battalion, 125 Landwehr Regiment Kriegstagebuch, REP M 423, Landesarchiv Baden-Württemberg—Hauptstaatsarchiv Stuttgart.

57. York, *Sergeant York,* 265.

58. Feodor "Sak" [Sok], affidavit of 8 October 1918 battle near Châtel Chéhéry, given at Frettes, France, 6 February 1919; George Wills, affidavit of 8 October 1918 battle near Châtel Chéhéry, given at Frettes, France, 21 February 1919; Percy Beardsley, affidavit of 8 October 1918 battle near Châtel Chéhéry, given at Frettes, France, 6 February 1919; Buxton, *Official History of 82nd Division American Expeditionary Forces, 1917–1919,* 60–61.

59. "Americans in the Meuse-Argonne Region," in U.S. Army, *United States Army in the World War, 1917–1919,* vol. 9, *Military Operations of the American Expeditionary Forces,* CMH Pub 23-14, page 229.

60. "Testimony of German Officers and Men about Sergeant York," translated by the U.S. Army War College, Carlisle, Pennsylvania, June 1936.

61. "Testimony of German Officers and Men about Sergeant York," translated by the U.S. Army War College, Carlisle, Pennsylvania, June 1936; Paul Adolf August Lipp, Kriegsrangeliste, M430/3, 6907, Landesarchiv Baden-Württemberg—Hauptstaatsarchiv Stuttgart; Lapple, *Das Württembergische Landwehr Infanterie Regiment Nr. 125 Im Weltkrieg 1914–1918,* Band 38, 169–173; 125 Landwehr Regiment Kriegstagebuch, REP M 420 and 421, Landesarchiv Baden-Württemberg—Hauptstaatsarchiv Stuttgart; I Battalion, 125 Landwehr Regiment Kriegstagebuch, REP M 422, Landesarchiv Baden-Württemberg—Hauptstaatsarchiv

Stuttgart; II Battalion, 125 Landwehr Regiment Kriegstagebuch, REP M 423, Landesarchiv Baden-Württemberg—Hauptstaatsarchiv Stuttgart; Paul Adolf August Lipp, Kriegsrangeliste, M430/3, 6907, Landesarchiv Baden-Württemberg—Hauptstaatsarchiv Stuttgart; Buxton, *Official History of 82nd Division American Expeditionary Forces, 1917–1919*, 60–61.

62. Patrick Donohue, affidavit of 8 October 1918 battle near Châtel Chéhéry, given at Frettes, France, 6 February 1919; approval of Medal of Honor, letter from General John Pershing to Major General Duncan, 1 April 1919, Alvin C. York, U.S. Army Service Record, Military Record, Army Service File, 1917–1919, under Awards, 1919, National Personnel Records Center, St. Louis, Missouri; Lawrence, "Sergeant York—American Soldier," 9–11, 32–34.

63. The fact that all of the other noncommissioned officers were incapacitated, leaving Alvin York in command, is attested by the affidavits of Joseph Kornacki, Feodor Sok, and Percy Beardsley, each signed and sworn on 23 October 1918, in the Argonne, to Captain W. F. Enneking, 328th Regimental Adjutant.

64. Buxton, *Official History of 82nd Division American Expeditionary Forces, 1917–1919*, 60–61; Pattullo, "The Second Elder Gives Battle," 3–4, 71–74.

65. NARA, 82d Division, entry 1241, RG 120; NARA, 328th Infantry Regiment Records, entry 2133, RG 391; NARA, ABMC Division files, 82nd Division, RG 117; "Americans in the Meuse-Argonne Region," in U.S. Army, *United States Army in the World War, 1917–1919*, vol. 9, *Military Operations of the American Expeditionary Forces*, CMH Pub 23-14, pages 229–230.

66. Award of the Croix de Guerre to Corporal Alvin C York, Order Number 16046, General Headquarters the French Armies of the East, Personnel Bureau, 13 April 1919, Approved by Marshal Petain, in Alvin C. York, U.S. Army Service Record, Military Record, Army Service File, 1917–1919, under Awards, 1919, National Personnel Records Center, St. Louis, Missouri; extract from York's Medal of Honor Citation, in Alvin C. York, U.S. Army Service Record, Military Record, Army Service File, 1917–1919, under Awards, 1919, National Personnel Records Center, St. Louis, Missouri. Also see the affidavits of Joseph Kornacki, Feodor Sok, and Percy Beardsley, each signed and sworn on 23 October 1918, in the Argonne, to Captain W. F. Enneking, 328th Regimental Adjutant.

67. The Sergeant York Discovery Expedition recovered rounds in 2006 they believed were fired by Beardsley within ten yards of where York is believed to have been positioned. For further information, see http://www.sgtyorkdiscovery.com (accessed on 7 November 2011).

68. Pattullo, "The Second Elder Gives Battle," 3–4, 71–74.

69. NARA, 82d Division, entry 1241, RG 120; NARA, 328th Infantry

Regiment Records, entry 2133, RG 391; NARA, ABMC Division files, 82nd Division, RG 117; Major General Frank McIntyre, Acting Chief of Staff, Award of Medal of Honor to Alvin C. York, U.S. War Department General Orders Number 59, 3 May 1919, in Alvin C. York, U.S. Army Service Record, Military Record, Army Service File, 1917–1919, under Awards, 1919, National Personnel Records Center, St. Louis, Missouri.

70. Swindler, "Turkey Match," 349–350; Captain Bertrand Cox, affidavit given on 21 February 1919 in Frettes, France, and filed by the 328th Infantry Regiment Advocate General, with swearing of the affidavit on 26 February 1919; Strohm, *Die Württembergishchen Regimenter im Weltkrieg 1914–1918*, Band 25, *Das Württembergishche Landwehr Infanterie Regiment nr. 120*; Lapple, *Das Württembergische Landwehr Infanterie Regiment Nr. 125 Im Weltkrieg 1914–1918*, Band 38. Also see the following unit reports: 1st Battalion, 125 Landwehr Regiment Kriegstagebuch; 2nd Battalion, 125 Landwehr Regiment Kriegstagebuch; 3rd Battalion, 125 Landwehr Regiment Kriegstagebuch, all in Landesarchiv Baden-Württemberg—Hauptstaatsarchiv Stuttgart.

71. Patrick Donohue, affidavit of 8 October 1918 battle near Châtel Chéhéry, given at Frettes, France, 6 February 1919; Captain Bertrand Cox, affidavit given on 21 February 1919, filed by the 328th Infantry Regiment Advocate General, with swearing of the affidavit on 26 February 1919; Pattullo, "The Second Elder Gives Battle," 3–4, 71–74.

72. Report of the Sergeant York Discovery Expedition (SYDE), published in November 2011, as well as special report published by Dr. Doug Scott, "Sgt York's .45 ACPs and 30.06s," Department of Anthropology, University of Nebraska–Lincoln; Buxton, *Official History of 82nd Division American Expeditionary Forces, 1917–1919*, 61.

73. Pattullo, "The Second Elder Gives Battle," 3–4, 71–74.

74. Swindler, "Turkey Match," 349–350; Captain Bertrand Cox, affidavit given on 21 February 1919 in Frettes, France, filed by the 328th Infantry Regiment Advocate General, with swearing of the affidavit on 26 February 1919; Strohm, *Die Württembergishchen Regimenter im Weltkrieg 1914–1918*, Band 25, *Das Württembergishche Landwehr Infanterie Regiment nr. 120*; "Testimony of German Officers and Men about Sergeant York," translated by the U.S. Army War College, Carlisle, Pennsylvania, June 1936; Lapple, *Das Württembergische Landwehr Infanterie Regiment Nr. 125 Im Weltkrieg 1914–1918*, Band 38. Also see the following unit reports: I Battalion, 125 Landwehr Regiment Kriegstagebuch; II Battalion, 125 Landwehr Regiment Kriegstagebuch, both in Landesarchiv Baden-Württemberg—Hauptstaatsarchiv Stuttgart.

75. Lawrence, "Sergeant York—American Soldier," 32–33.

76. Patrick Donohue, affidavit of 8 October 1918 battle near Châtel Chéhéry, given at Frettes, France, 6 February 1919; Michael Sacina, af-

fidavit of 8 October 1918 battle near Châtel Chéhéry, given at Frettes, France, 6 February 1919; York, *Sergeant York*, 228–338.

77. Percy Beardsley, affidavit of 8 October 1918 battle near Châtel Chéhéry, given at Frettes, France, 6 February 1919; Pattullo, "The Second Elder Gives Battle," 3–4, 71–74; George Wills, affidavit of 8 October 1918 battle near Châtel Chéhéry, given at Frettes, France, 21 February 1919; Feodor "Sak" [Sok], affidavit of 8 October 1918 battle near Châtel Chéhéry, given at Frettes, France, 6 February 1919.

78. Captain Bertrand Cox, affidavit given on 21 February 1919, filed by the 328th Infantry Regiment Advocate General, with actual swearing of the affidavit on 26 February 1919; Pattullo, "The Second Elder Gives Battle," 3–4, 71–74.

79. York, *Sergeant York*, 229.

80. Percy Beardsley, affidavit of 8 October 1918 battle near Châtel Chéhéry, given at Frettes, France, 21 February 1919; Lapple, *Das Württembergische Landwehr Infanterie Regiment Nr. 125 Im Weltkrieg 1914–1918*, Band 38, 169–173; 125 Landwehr Regiment Kriegstagebuch, REP M 420 and 421, Landesarchiv Baden-Württemberg—Hauptstaatsarchiv Stuttgart; I Battalion, 125 Landwehr Regiment Kriegstagebuch, REP M 422, Landesarchiv Baden-Württemberg—Hauptstaatsarchiv Stuttgart; II Battalion, 125 Landwehr Regiment Kriegstagebuch, REP M 423, Landesarchiv Baden-Württemberg—Hauptstaatsarchiv Stuttgart; III Battalion, 125 Landwehr Kriegstagebuch, REP M 425, Landesarchiv Baden-Württemberg—Hauptstaatsarchiv Stuttgart.

81. Bachman, "Alvin C. York," 5.

82. Letter from Otis B. Merrithew to Warner Brothers agent Mr. Guthrie, 11 March 1941, Sergeant York document B00374, March 1941, WBA.

83. Letter from Major J. M. Tillman to Jesse Lasky, 5 November 1940, B00374, Folder 2880, WBA; Pattullo, "The Second Elder Gives Battle," 3–4, 71–74.

84. Percy Beardsley, affidavit of 8 October 1918 battle near Châtel Chéhéry, given at Frettes, France, 21 February 1919.

85. Karl Kübler, Kriegsrangeliste, M430/3, 6369, Landesarchiv Baden-Württemberg—Hauptstaatsarchiv Stuttgart.

86. "Testimony of German Officers and Men about Sergeant York," translated by the U.S. Army War College, Carlisle, Pennsylvania, June 1936.

87. "Americans in the Meuse-Argonne Region," in U.S. Army, *United States Army in the World War, 1917–1919*, vol. 9, *Military Operations of the American Expeditionary Forces*, CMH Pub 23-14, page 230.

88. Michael Sacina, affidavit of 8 October 1918 battle near Châtel Chéhéry, given at Frettes, France, 6 February 1919; "Testimony of Ger-

man Officers and Men about Sergeant York," translated by the U.S. Army War College, Carlisle, Pennsylvania, June 1936.

89. "Back story information," letter from Harry Chandlee to Jesse Lasky, 8 May 1940, WBA, 12.

90. Liggett, *A.E.F.*, 191–197.

91. Joseph A. Woods, affidavit of 8 October 1918 battle near Châtel Chéhéry, given at Frettes, France, 21 February 1919; letter from Major J. M. Tillman to Jesse Lasky, 5 November 1940, B00374, Folder 2880, WBA; also see affidavits of Joseph Kornacki, Feodor Sok, and Percy Beardsley, signed and sworn on 23 October 1918, in the Argonne, to Captain Enneking, 328th Regimental Adjutant; General John Pershing Recommendation for the Awarding of the Medal of Honor to Corporal York, cable, sent to the U.S. Army Adjutant General, 14 March 1919, in Alvin C. York, U.S. Army Service Record, Military Record, Army Service File, 1917–1919, under Awards, 1919, National Personnel Records Center, St. Louis, Missouri.

92. Buxton, *Official History of 82nd Division American Expeditionary Forces, 1917–1919*, 60–62; York, *Sergeant York*, 228–338.

93. York, *Sergeant York*, 235.

94. Letter from A. N. La Plante to William Guthrie, Warner Brothers Set Manager, 18 January 1941, WBA; Otis B. Merrithew, "Statement Regarding Argonne Engagement," 11 December 1929, B00374, Folder 2880, WBA.

95. Schiller, "An Einem Tag im Oktober," 134–146; Mastriano, "Sergeant York Fought Here!," 87.

96. The Germans had trouble believing that so few Americans could capture so many of their soldiers. After a history of Sergeant York's actions appeared in a Swedish paper in 1929, the German Archives in Potsdam launched an effort to script a rebuttal. The premise was that it was impossible for this to happen to German soldiers. Interviews were conducted with the survivors. During the process, it was evident that Kuno Vollmer did not want to make a statement. When he finally appeared for the interview he was quite uneasy. Before submitting his report, Vollmer asked to read the other statements. After that, he made changes to his and submitted it. The German report is very interesting, but is flawed at its base. This so-called storm tactic did not only happen on 8 October, but across the Western Front. In fact, the concept of storm tactics was perfected by the Germans and used effectively during their 1918 spring offensive. As with Sergeant York, the German shock troops would drive small groups deep into the British and French lines and capture hundreds of Allied soldiers. The speed, shock, and surprise caught both sides off guard.

97. NARA, 82d Division, entry 1241, RG 120; NARA, 328th Infantry

Regiment Records, entry 2133, RG 391; NARA, ABMC Division files, 82nd Division, RG 117. The German 120th Regiment reported the following strength late on 8 October. The regiment was greatly reduced by the fighting around Châtel Chéhéry.

Unit	Officers	NCOs	Enlisted Men
1st Battalion	7	20	180
2nd Battalion	4	18	93
3rd Battalion	4	4	40

98. Rektor Kling, *Das Württembergishche Landwehr Infanterie Regiment nr. 122 im Weltkrieg 1914–1918*, Band 27 (Stuttgart: Belser, 1923), 152–196; Das Württembergishche Landwehr Infanterie Regiment nr. 122 Kriegstagebuch, REP M 396, Landesarchiv Baden-Württemberg—Hauptstaatsarchiv Stuttgart.

99. Württemberg Landwehr Regiment Nr. 120, File M 115, regimental structures and all operations 1914–1918; File M 411, Kriegstagebuch; File M 433/2, Personnel Lists 1914–1921; File M 484, Kriegsstammrollen incl. Ersatzbataillon 1914–1918, all in Landesarchiv Baden-Württemberg—Hauptstaatsarchiv Stuttgart.

100. Strohm, *Die Württembergishchen Regimenter im Weltkrieg 1914–1918*, Band 25, *Das Württembergishche Landwehr Infanterie Regiment nr. 120*, 163–172.

101. Franke, *Die 2. Württemberg Landwehr Division Im Weltkrieg 1914–1918*, 55–56.

102. Württemberg Landwehr-Infanterie-Regiment Nr. 120, File M 115, regimental structures and all operations 1914–1918; File M 411, Kriegstagebuch; File M 433/2, Personnel Lists 1914–1921; File M 484, all in Landesarchiv Baden-Württemberg—Hauptstaatsarchiv Stuttgart. Strohm, *Die Württembergishchen Regimenter im Weltkrieg 1914–1918*, Band 25, *Das Württembergishche Landwehr Infanterie Regiment nr. 120*, 161–173.

103. Strohm, *Die Württembergishchen Regimenter im Weltkrieg 1914–1918*, Band 25, *Das Württembergishche Landwehr Infanterie Regiment nr. 120*, 161–173.

8. The War without End

Epigraph: York, *Sergeant York*, 281.

1. Ibid., 270.

2. NARA, 82d Division, entry 1241, RG 120; NARA, 328th Infantry Regiment Records, entry 2133, RG 391; NARA, ABMC Division files, 82nd Division, RG 117; ABMC, *82d Division: Summary of Operations in*

the World War, 25–29; Buxton, *Official History of 82nd Division American Expeditionary Forces, 1917–1919,* 70–77; Chandler, *History of the Three Hundred and Twenty-Eighth Regiment of Infantry,* 45–49.

3. von Gallwitz, "Retreat to the Rhein," 253–258; von Tschischwitz, *General von der Marwitz: Weltkriegsbriefe,* 327–331.

4. E.C.B. Danforth, affidavit on the events of 8 October 1918, in York, *Sergeant York,* 238.

5. Lapple, *Das Württembergische Landwehr Infanterie Regiment Nr. 125 Im Weltkrieg 1914–1918,* Band 38, 169–173; 125 Landwehr Regiment Kriegstagebuch, REP M 420 and 421, Landesarchiv Baden-Württemberg—Hauptstaatsarchiv Stuttgart; I Battalion, 125 Landwehr Regiment Kriegstagebuch, REP M 422, Landesarchiv Baden-Württemberg—Hauptstaatsarchiv Stuttgart; II Battalion, 125 Landwehr Regiment Kriegstagebuch, REP M 423, Landesarchiv Baden-Württemberg—Hauptstaatsarchiv Stuttgart.

6. Chandler, *History of the Three Hundred and Twenty-Eighth Regiment of Infantry,* 47.

7. Lapple, *Das Württembergische Landwehr Infanterie Regiment Nr. 125 Im Weltkrieg 1914–1918,* Band 38, 173–177; 125 Landwehr Regiment Kriegstagebuch, REP M 420 and 421, Landesarchiv Baden-Württemberg—Hauptstaatsarchiv Stuttgart; I Battalion, 125 Landwehr Regiment Kriegstagebuch, REP M 422, Landesarchiv Baden-Württemberg—Hauptstaatsarchiv Stuttgart; II Battalion, 125 Landwehr Regiment Kriegstagebuch, REP M 423, Landesarchiv Baden-Württemberg—Hauptstaatsarchiv Stuttgart; III Battalion, 125 Landwehr Regiment Kriegstagebuch, REP M 425, Landesarchiv Baden-Württemberg—Hauptstaatsarchiv Stuttgart.

8. Franke, *Die 2. Württemberg Landwehr Division Im Weltkrieg 1914–1918,* 55–56.

9. 82d Division, entry 1241, RG 120; NARA, 328th Infantry Regiment Records, entry 2133, RG 391; NARA, ABMC Division files, 82nd Division, RG 117; Strohm, *Die Württembergishchen Regimenter im Weltkrieg 1914–1918,* Band 25, *Das Württembergishche Landwehr Infanterie Regiment nr. 120,* 171–173; Buxton, *Official History of 82nd Division American Expeditionary Forces, 1917–1919,* 66–77; Chandler, *History of the Three Hundred and Twenty-Eighth Regiment of Infantry,* 47–49.

10. von Gallwitz, "Retreat to the Rhein," 253.

11. York, *Sergeant York,* 270.

12. E.C.B. Danforth, affidavit on the events of 8 October 1918, in York, *Sergeant York,* 238.

13. Swindler, "Turkey Match," 349–350; York, *Sergeant York,* 177–182.

14. York, *Sergeant York,* 271.

15. Ibid., 271–273.

16. Ibid., 272.

17. Ibid., 273.

18. Ibid., 276.

19. Group of Armies-Gallwitz Report, 10 October 1918, in U.S. Army, *United States Army in the World War, 1917–1919*, vol. 11, *American Occupation of Germany*, CMH Pub 23-17, page 549.

20. NARA, 82d Division, entry 1241, RG 120; NARA, 328th Infantry Regiment Records, entry 2133, RG 391; NARA, ABMC Division files, 82nd Division, RG 117; ABMC, *82d Division: Summary of Operations in the World War*, 25–29.

21. Patrick Donohue, affidavit on the events of 8 October 1918, in York, *Sergeant York*, 256–257.

22. NARA, 82d Division, entry 1241, RG 120; NARA, 328th Infantry Regiment Records, entry 2133, RG 391; NARA, ABMC Division files, 82nd Division, RG 117; Buxton, *Official History of 82nd Division American Expeditionary Forces, 1917–1919*, 87, 122.

23. Holden, *War Memories*, 143–145.

24. Chandler, *History of the Three Hundred and Twenty-Eighth Regiment of Infantry*, 49.

25. Buxton, *Official History of 82nd Division American Expeditionary Forces, 1917–1919*, 121–123.

26. NARA, 82d Division, entry 1241, RG 120; NARA, 328th Infantry Regiment Records, entry 2133, RG 391; NARA, ABMC Division files, 82nd Division, RG 117; Chandler, *History of the Three Hundred and Twenty-Eighth Regiment of Infantry*, 48–53.

27. Buxton, *Official History of 82nd Division American Expeditionary Forces, 1917–1919*, 120–126; Chandler, *History of the Three Hundred and Twenty-Eighth Regiment of Infantry*, 51.

28. Strohm, *Die Württembergishchen Regimenter im Weltkrieg 1914–1918*, Band 25, *Das Württembergishche Landwehr Infanterie Regiment nr. 120*, 161–173. The Hindenburg Line was an Allied name for the German Siegfried Stellung. The Kriemhilde Stellung was a southern sector of the overall Siegfried Stellung. Ironically, what the Allies called the Siegfried Line in World War II was never called that by the Germans. Then, the Germans called it the West Wall.

29. NARA, 82d Division, entry 1241, RG 120; NARA, 328th Infantry Regiment Records, entry 2133, RG 391; NARA, ABMC Division files, 82nd Division, RG 117; "82d Division: Record of Events," in U.S. Army, *Order of Battle of the United States Land Forces in the World War*, vol. 2, *American Expeditionary Forces: Divisions*, CMH Pub 23-2, page 355.

30. NARA, 82d Division, entry 1241, RG 120; NARA, 328th Infantry Regiment Records, entry 2133, RG 391; NARA, ABMC Division files, "82d Division: Record of Events," in U.S. Army, *Order of Battle of the*

United States Land Forces in the World War, vol. 2, *American Expeditionary Forces: Divisions*, CMH Pub 23-2, 355.

31. Duncan, "Reminiscences, 1886–1919," 155–157.

32. Buxton, *Official History of 82nd Division American Expeditionary Forces, 1917–1919*, 141–143.

33. York, *Sergeant York*, 281.

34. Jones, *History of C. Company, 328th Infantry*, 23.

35. Buxton, *Official History of 82nd Division American Expeditionary Forces, 1917–1919*, 134–136.

36. Ibid., 142.

37. NARA, 82d Division, entry 1241, RG 120; NARA, 328th Infantry Regiment Records, entry 2133, RG 391; NARA, ABMC Division files, 82nd Division, RG 117; Chandler, *History of the Three Hundred and Twenty-Eighth Regiment of Infantry*, 52–55.

38. Jones, *History of C. Company, 328th Infantry*, 22–25.

39. Buxton, *Official History of 82nd Division American Expeditionary Forces, 1917–1919*, 140–145.

40. Day, "The B That Stung," 13–15; Barker, *History of the Machine Gun Company, 328 Infantry, 82nd Division*, 44–48, Jones, *History of C. Company, 328th Infantry*, 23–25.

41. Group of Armies-Gallwitz Report, 15 October 1918, in U.S. Army, *United States Army in the World War, 1917–1919*, vol. 11, *American Occupation of Germany*, CMH Pub 23-17, page 557; Buxton, *Official History of 82nd Division American Expeditionary Forces, 1917–1919*, 144–159.

42. NARA, 82d Division, entry 1241, RG 120; NARA, 328th Infantry Regiment Records, entry 2133, RG 391; NARA, ABMC Division files, 82nd Division, RG 117; ABMC, *82d Division: Summary of Operations in the World War*, 23, 39–41; Buxton, *Official History of 82nd Division American Expeditionary Forces, 1917–1919*, 144.

43. Chandler, *History of the Three Hundred and Twenty-Eighth Regiment of Infantry*, 55–57.

44. NARA, 82d Division, entry 1241, RG 120; NARA, 328th Infantry Regiment Records, entry 2133, RG 391; NARA, ABMC Division files, 82nd Division, RG 117; Buxton, *Official History of 82nd Division American Expeditionary Forces, 1917–1919*, 158–160; Chandler, *History of the Three Hundred and Twenty-Eighth Regiment of Infantry*, 55.

45. ABMC, *82d Division: Summary of Operations in the World War*, 42–44; Buxton, *Official History of 82nd Division American Expeditionary Forces, 1917–1919*, 159; Chandler, *History of the Three Hundred and Twenty-Eighth Regiment of Infantry*, 55.

46. Buxton, *Official History of 82nd Division American Expeditionary Forces, 1917–1919*, 159–166.

47. NARA, 82d Division, entry 1241, RG 120; NARA, 328th Infantry

Regiment Records, entry 2133, RG 391; NARA, ABMC Division files, 82nd Division, RG 117; ABMC, *82d Division: Summary of Operations in the World War*, 42–44; Buxton, *Official History of 82nd Division American Expeditionary Forces, 1917–1919*, 161–166.

48. Day, "The B That Stung," 13–15; Jones, *History of C. Company, 328th Infantry*, 22–24; Buxton, *Official History of 82nd Division American Expeditionary Forces, 1917–1919*, 165–166.

49. NARA, 82d Division, entry 1241, RG 120; NARA, 328th Infantry Regiment Records, entry 2133, RG 391; NARA, ABMC Division files, 82nd Division, RG 117; ABMC, *82d Division: Summary of Operations in the World War*, 46–48; Chandler, *History of the Three Hundred and Twenty-Eighth Regiment of Infantry*, 55; Buxton, *Official History of 82nd Division American Expeditionary Forces, 1917–1919*, 166–173.

50. Buxton, *Official History of 82nd Division American Expeditionary Forces, 1917–1919*, 160–161; Day, "The B That Stung," 14–15.

51. NARA, 82d Division, entry 1241, RG 120; NARA, 328th Infantry Regiment Records, entry 2133, RG 391; NARA, ABMC Division files, 82nd Division, RG 117; Chandler, *History of the Three Hundred and Twenty-Eighth Regiment of Infantry*, 55, Buxton, *Official History of 82nd Division American Expeditionary Forces, 1917–1919*, 160–161, Day, "The B That Stung," 14–15; ABMC, *82d Division: Summary of Operations in the World War*, 46–48.

52. Chandler, *History of the Three Hundred and Twenty-Eighth Regiment of Infantry*, 59.

53. Jones, *History of C. Company, 328th Infantry*, 24.

54. NARA, 82d Division, entry 1241, RG 120; NARA, 328th Infantry Regiment Records, entry 2133, RG 391; NARA, ABMC Division files, 82nd Division, RG 117; Buxton, *Official History of 82nd Division American Expeditionary Forces, 1917–1919*, 204.

55. Buxton, *Official History of 82nd Division American Expeditionary Forces, 1917–1919*, 171–199.

56. Chandler, *History of the Three Hundred and Twenty-Eighth Regiment of Infantry*, 59.

57. Duncan, "Reminiscences, 1886–1919," 157.

58. Buxton, *Official History of 82nd Division American Expeditionary Forces, 1917–1919*, 196–199; Chandler, *History of the Three Hundred and Twenty-Eighth Regiment of Infantry*, 57; Day, "The B That Stung," 15–16; Jones, *History of C. Company, 328th Infantry*, 24.

59. Chandler, *History of the Three Hundred and Twenty-Eighth Regiment of Infantry*, 57–59.

60. NARA, 82d Division, entry 1241, RG 120; NARA, 328th Infantry Regiment Records, entry 2133, RG 391; NARA, ABMC Division files, 82nd Division, RG 117; "Americans in the Meuse-Argonne Region,"

in U.S. Army, *United States Army in the World War, 1917–1919,* vol. 9, *Military Operations of the American Expeditionary Forces,* CMH Pub 23-14, page 252.

61. Patrick Donohue, affidavit of 8 October 1918 battle near Châtel Chéhéry, given at Frettes, France, 6 February 1919; approval of Medal of Honor, Letter from General John Pershing to Major General Duncan, 1 April 1919, in Alvin C. York, U.S. Army Service Record, Military Record, Army Service File, 1917–1919, under Awards, 1919, National Personnel Records Center, St. Louis, Missouri.

62. Viereck, ed., *As They Saw Us,* 286–287. This portion of the book is a chapter written by German Army Group commander General Max von Gallwitz. Further related discussion of this is found in von Tschischwitz, *General von der Marwitz: Weltkriegsbriefe.*

63. ABMC, *82d Division: Summary of Operations in the World War,* 54.

64. NARA, 82d Division, entry 1241, RG 120; NARA, 328th Infantry Regiment Records, entry 2133, RG 391; NARA, ABMC Division files, 82nd Division, RG 117; Alvin C. York, U.S. Army Service Record, Military Record, Army Service File, 1917–1919, current enlistment, 4, National Personnel Records Center, St. Louis, Missouri.

65. York, *Sergeant York,* 282.

66. Chandler, *History of the Three Hundred and Twenty-Eighth Regiment of Infantry,* 63.

67. York, *Sergeant York,* 283.

68. Ibid., 284–285.

69. NARA, 82d Division, entry 1241, RG 120; NARA, 328th Infantry Regiment Records, entry 2133, RG 391; NARA, ABMC Division files, 82nd Division, RG 117; ABMC, *82d Division: Summary of Operations in the World War,* 53.

70. Chandler, *History of the Three Hundred and Twenty-Eighth Regiment of Infantry,* 63.

71. Buxton, *Official History of 82nd Division American Expeditionary Forces, 1917–1919,* 214–215.

72. Ibid., 210–215.

73. York, *Sergeant York,* 286–287.

74. "Visits of U.S. Presidents to France since 1918," U.S. Department of State, http://france.usembassy.gov/visitsfrance.html (accessed 12 November 2011).

75. York, *Sergeant York,* 284–285.

76. Day, "The B That Stung," 15.

77. Ibid., 16.

78. Major General Charles P. Summerall, Fifth Army Corps Commander, General Orders Number 8, February 1919, reproduced in Day, "The B That Stung," 32.

79. Day, "The B That Stung," 16.

80. Barker, *History of the Machine Gun Company, 328 Infantry, 82nd Division,* 56.

81. Buxton, *Official History of 82nd Division American Expeditionary Forces, 1917–1919,* 216–217.

82. NARA, 82d Division, entry 1241, RG 120; NARA, 328th Infantry Regiment Records, entry 2133, RG 391; NARA, ABMC Division files, 82nd Division, RG 117; Barker, *History of the Machine Gun Company, 328 Infantry, 82nd Division,* 55–56.

83. Buxton, *Official History of 82nd Division American Expeditionary Forces, 1917–1919,* 220.

84. Barker, *History of the Machine Gun Company, 328 Infantry, 82nd Division,* 58.

85. Buxton, *Official History of 82nd Division American Expeditionary Forces, 1917–1919,* 220.

86. York, *Sergeant York,* 289.

87. Chandler, *History of the Three Hundred and Twenty-Eighth Regiment of Infantry,* 63.

88. Buxton, *Official History of 82nd Division American Expeditionary Forces, 1917–1919,* 221.

89. Jones, *History of C. Company, 328th Infantry,* 28; Buxton, *Official History of 82nd Division American Expeditionary Forces, 1917–1919,* 220.

90. York, *Sergeant York,* 290.

91. Telegram by Major General Duncan to issue Sergeant Alvin C. York travel orders to represent the 82nd Division at the Executive Committee of the American Legion, 3 April 1919; divisional telegram granting authorization of special leave for Sergeant York in conjunction with travel to Paris for American Legion, 4 April 1919, in Alvin C. York, U.S. Army Service Record, National Personnel Records Center, St. Louis, Missouri.

92. American Legion History, http://www.legion.org/history (accessed on 12 November 2011).

93. York, *Sergeant York,* 291.

94. Ibid., 290–291.

95. Duncan, "Reminiscences, 1886–1919," 153.

96. York, *Sergeant York,* 224.

97. Ibid., 286.

98. Cowan, *Sergeant York and His People,* 266.

99. York, *Sergeant York,* 224.

100. Ibid., 286.

101. Buxton, *Official History of 82nd Division American Expeditionary Forces, 1917–1919,* 220–221; York, *Sergeant York,* 285–287.

102. Memorandum from 164th Brigade Commander to 82nd Division

requesting investigations officer, 23 October 1918; memorandum from Captain Williams to Major General Duncan, recommending the DSC for Alvin York, 14 November 1918.

103. Memorandum from Captain Williams to Major General Duncan, recommending the DSC for Alvin York, 14 November 1918; Alvin York, Affidavits, in Alvin C. York, U.S. Army Service Record, 23 October 1918, National Personnel Records Center, St. Louis, Missouri.

104. Recommendation for Distinguished Service Cross for Corporal Alvin C. York, memorandum from the 328th Commanding Officer to the 82nd Division Commanding Officer, in Alvin C. York, U.S. Army Service Record, Military Record, Military Awards, War Department, 1918–1919, 30 October 1918 and 2 November 1918, pages 23, 25, National Personnel Records Center, St. Louis, Missouri.

105. Alvin C. York, U.S. Army Service Record, Military Record, Military Awards, War Department, 1918–1919, 30 November 1918, National Personnel Records Center, St. Louis, Missouri.

106. Joseph Cummings Chase, *Script Magazine,* 11 April 1942, 11.

107. Chase, *Soldiers All,* 105–115.

108. See Secretary of War Newton D. Baker's comments in York, *Sergeant York,* ix; Chase, *Soldiers All,* 105–115.

109. Telegram from George Pattullo at Third Army Headquarters (Koblenz, Germany) to Colonel Gordon Johnson at 82nd Division Headquarters (Prauthoy, France), 30 January 1919, in Alvin C. York, U.S. Army Service Record, Press File, National Personnel Records Center, St. Louis, Missouri.

110. Ibid.

111. Pattullo, "The Second Elder Gives Battle," 4.

112. Telegram from George Pattullo at Third Army Headquarters (Koblenz, Germany) to Colonel Gordon Johnson at 82nd Division Headquarters (Prauthoy, France), 30 January 1919, in Alvin C. York, U.S. Army Service Record, Press File, National Personnel Records Center, St. Louis, Missouri.

113. Ibid.

114. Telegram from George Pattullo at Third Army Headquarters (Koblenz, Germany) to Colonel Gordon Johnson at 82nd Division Headquarters (Prauthoy, France), 29 January 1919, in Alvin C. York, U.S. Army Service Record, Press File, National Personnel Records Center, St. Louis, Missouri.

115. York, *Sergeant York,* 278.

116. Ibid., 222–223.

117. Pattullo, "The Second Elder Gives Battle," 74.

118. York, *Sergeant York,* 222–224, 272–274.

119. Ibid., 275–276.

120. Pattullo, "The Second Elder Gives Battle," 4; Medal of Honor Award Packet, prepared by Lieutenant Burkhalter, February 1919, Alvin C. York Military Service Packet, U.S. War Department, 1917–1919.

121. Joseph Konotski (Kornacki), affidavit of 8 October 1918 battle near Châtel Chéhéry, given at Frettes, France, 6 February 1919; Feodor "Sak" [Sok], affidavit of 8 October 1918 battle near Châtel Chéhéry, given at Frettes, France, 6 February 1919; Michael Sacina, affidavit of 8 October 1918 battle near Châtel Chéhéry, given at Frettes, France, 6 February 1919; Patrick Donohue, affidavit of 8 October 1918 battle near Châtel Chéhéry, given at Frettes, France, 6 February 1919.

122. Captain Bertrand Cox, affidavit given on 21 February 1919, filed by the 328th Infantry Regiment Advocate General, with actual swearing of the affidavit on 26 February 1919; Lieutenant Joseph Woods, affidavit of 8 October 1918 battle near Châtel Chéhéry, given at Frettes, France, 21 February 1919; Private Percy Beardsley, affidavit of 8 October 1918 battle near Châtel Chéhéry, given at Frettes, France, 21 February 1919; Private George Wills, affidavit of 8 October 1918 battle near Châtel Chéhéry, given at Frettes, France, 21 February 1919; Duncan, "Reminiscences, 1886–1919," 153.

123. Medal of Honor Award Memorandums, February–April 1919, Alvin York Military Service Packet, U.S. War Department, 1919.

124. General John Pershing, "Recommendation for the Medal of Honor," to the War Department, Washington, D.C., 15 March 1919, Alvin York Military Service Packet, U.S. War Department, 1919.

125. Adjutant Franklin L. Whitley, "Recommendation for Decorations," Personnel Division, Decorations Section, GHQ, AEF, 1 March 1919.

126. Investigation Memorandum, 14 March 1919, signed by Captain Cox, forwarded to the 328th Regimental Commander, Alvin York Military Service Packet, U.S. War Department, 1919.

127. Approval of Alvin C. York Medal of Honor, War Department Cablegram, to General Pershing, 20 March 1919.

128. General John Pershing, "Recommendation for the Medal of Honor," to the War Department, Washington, D.C., 15 March 1919, Alvin York Military Service Packet, U.S. War Department, 1919; Approval of Alvin C. York Medal of Honor, extract from War Department Cablegram to General Pershing, 20 March 1919; Alvin C. York Medal of Honor Citation, GHQ Personnel Division, 22 March 1919; Major General Frank McIntyre, Award of Medal of Honor to Alvin C. York, as directed by the Acting Army Chief of Staff, General Orders Number 59, U.S. War Department, Washington, D.C., 3 May 1919.

129. "Medal of Honor Presentation Guidance Request," message from Major General Duncan to General Pershing, U.S. Army Telegram,

8 April 1919; letter from Julien Josephson and Harry Chandlee to Jesse Lasky, 8 May 1940, WBA, 17.

130. Perry, *Sgt. York,* 96–97.

131. Alvin York Award Packet, from U.S. Army Adjutant General, to Representative Joseph W. Byrnes, 17 February 1922, Alvin York Service Packet, U.S. War Department; Individual Record of Decorations and Citations of Alvin C. York, corrected copy as of 5 April 1923, Alvin York Service Packet, U.S. War Department.

132. Perry, *Sgt. York,* 97.

133. Alvin York French Award, General Headquarters of the French Armies of the East, Order Number 16,046, Approved by Marshal Petain, 13 April 1919, Alvin York Service Packet, U.S. War Department.

134. York, *Sergeant York,* ix; Cowan, *Sergeant York and His People,* 256; Captain Carlysle, Warner Brothers Research Department, interoffice communication to Herman Lissauer, 23 April 1941, WBA.

135. Certificate from the Montenegrin Minister of War to Alvin C. York, May 1919, Alvin York Military Service Packet, U.S. War Department.

136. Order of Awarding the Cross of Military Valor to Alvin York, 9 December 1921, Alvin York Military Service Packet, U.S. War Department.

137. ABMC, *82d Division: Summary of Operations in the World War,* 53; Buxton, *Official History of 82nd Division American Expeditionary Forces, 1917–1919,* 222.

138. Captain T. B. Fay, Report of Changes, Alvin York signing in off of leave, 12 April 1919, to report to St. Selve, Alvin C. York, U.S. Army Service Record, 1919, National Personnel Records Center, St. Louis, Missouri.

139. Jones, *History of C. Company, 328th Infantry,* 28; Barker, *History of the Machine Gun Company, 328 Infantry, 82nd Division,* 63.

140. Jones, *History of C. Company, 328th Infantry,* 28; Barker, *History of the Machine Gun Company, 328 Infantry, 82nd Division,* 54–56.

141. Chandler, *History of the Three Hundred and Twenty-Eighth Regiment of Infantry,* 63.

142. York, *Sergeant York,* 292.

143. Jones, *History of C. Company, 328th Infantry,* 27; Chandler, *History of the Three Hundred and Twenty-Eighth Regiment of Infantry,* 63.

144. Barker, *History of the Machine Gun Company, 328 Infantry, 82nd Division,* 64.

145. York, *Sergeant York,* 292.

146. Barker, *History of the Machine Gun Company, 328 Infantry, 82nd Division,* 64–65.

147. Chandler, *History of the Three Hundred and Twenty-Eighth Regiment of Infantry,* 65.

148. The battalion cleared the embarkation camp that day; all of its soldiers were supposed to be on the SS *Scranton.* York's Military Ser-

vice Record states that he returned on that ship. The Tennessee Society of New York wanted to throw York a welcoming home ceremony, and cables were sent to the *Scranton* while at sea to confirm that York was on board. Finding that he was not, the War Department notified the Tennessee Society that he would arrive on 22 May, a day after his battalion, on the SS *Ohioan* at the Port of Hoboken, New Jersey.

149. Barker, *History of the Machine Gun Company, 328 Infantry, 82nd Division*, 64–65.

150. York, *Sergeant York*, 293–294.

9. Emergence of a National Hero

Epigraph: "Conscience Plus Red Hair Are Bad for Germans," *Literary Digest*, 14 June 1919, 44.

1. York, *Sergeant York*, 295.

2. Barker, *History of the Machine Gun Company, 328 Infantry, 82nd Division*, 65.

3. York, *Sergeant York*, 295–296.

4. Pattullo, "The Second Elder Gives Battle," 3–4, 71–74.

5. "Americans All!" *South Amboy Citizen*, 10 May 1919, 16.

6. Originally named the New York Tennessee Club, it expanded after five years of incredible success to a statewide organization and renamed itself the Tennessee Society of New York.

7. Dixie Dittfurth, "The Tennessee Society of New York," Tennessee State Library and Archives, Nashville, Tennessee; "Honor Sergt. York, Hero of Argonne," *Washington Post*, 23 May 1919, 2.

8. Record of telephone conversation between Dr. James J. King and the U.S. Army Troop Movement Office, 6 May 1919, Alvin C. York, U.S. Army Service Record, 1919, National Personnel Records Center, St. Louis, Missouri.

9. Letter from E. A. Kellogg to the U.S. Army Adjutant General, 2 May 1919; letter from E. A. Kellogg to Major General Shanks, 3 May 1919; telegram from E. A. Kellogg to the U.S. Army Adjutant, 3 May 1919, both in Alvin C. York, U.S. Army Service Record, National Personnel Records Center, St. Louis, Missouri.

10. U.S. War Department telegram to E. A. Kellogg that York was on the steamship *Scranton*, 21 May 1919; memorandum explaining why York was on the SS *Ohioan*, 22 May 1919, both in Alvin C. York, U.S. Army Service Record, 1919, National Personnel Records Center, St. Louis, Missouri.

11. Letter from Major General Shanks to A. Kellogg granting York a forty-eight-hour pass, 5 May 1919, in Alvin C. York, U.S. Army Service Record, National Personnel Records Center, St. Louis, Missouri.

12. Letter from the Army Adjutant General to Major General Shanks granting York a five-day furlough, 15 May 1919; official furlough form granting York five days' leave, with permission to visit Washington, D.C., by the command of Major General Shanks, 22 May 1919, both in Alvin C. York, U.S. Army Service Record, National Personnel Records Center, St. Louis, Missouri.

13. "Give Great Ovation to Sergeant York," *New York Times*, 23 May 1919, 15.

14. "Sergeant York: Argonne Hero Given Big Ovation," *Nevada State Journal*, 23 May 1919, 1; "Give Great Ovation to Sergeant York," *New York Times*, 23 May 1919, 15.

15. "Give Great Ovation to Sergeant York," *New York Times*, 23 May 1919, 15.

16. "Sergeant York: Argonne Hero Given Big Ovation," *Nevada State Journal*, 23 May 1919, 1.

17. "Give Great Ovation to Sergeant York," *New York Times*, 23 May 1919, 15.

18. "Conscience Plus Red Hair Are Bad for Germans," *Literary Digest*, 14 June 1919, 42–48.

19. York, *Sergeant York*, 296.

20. Ibid., 225–226; "Sergeant York: Argonne Hero Given Big Ovation," *Nevada State Journal*, 23 May 1919, 1; "Give Great Ovation to Sergeant York," *New York Times*, 23 May 1919, 15.

21. Lasky, *I Blow My Own Horn*, 252–253.

22. Bill Rice, "Sergeant York Movie," via Robert Taplinger, Director of Warner Brothers Publicity, Warner Brothers Studio, 1941,WBA; Theodore Strauss, "Out of the Incubator," *New York Times*, 29 June 1941.

23. Charles Bean, ed., *Official History of Australia in the War of 1914–1918*, vol. 1, *The Story of ANZAC from the Outbreak of War to the End of the First Phase of the Gallipoli Campaign, May 4, 1915*, 253–280.

24. Charles Bean, ed., *Official History of Australia in the War of 1914–1918*, vol. 2, *The Story of ANZAC from 4 May, 1915, to the Evacuation of the Gallipoli Peninsula*, 20–42.

25. Skeyhill, *A Singing Soldier*.

26. "Veteran's Sight Restored: Operation Relieves Skeyhill, Blinded at Gallipoli," *New York Times*, 4 May 1918.

27. York, *Sergeant York*, 1–3.

28. Ibid., 5.

29. "Conscience Plus Red Hair Are Bad for Germans," *Literary Digest*, 14 June 1919, 42–48.

30. York, *Sergeant York*, 298.

31. "Conscience Plus Red Hair Are Bad for Germans," *Literary Digest*, 14 June 1919, 42–48.

32. York, *Sergeant York,* 297.

33. Ibid.

34. "Conscience Plus Red Hair Are Bad for Germans," *Literary Digest,* 14 June 1919, 42–48.

35. Duncan, "Reminiscences, 1886–1919," 154.

36. "Sergeant York: Argonne Hero Given Big Ovation," *Nevada State Journal,* 23 May 1919, 1; "Give Great Ovation to Sergeant York," *New York Times,* 23 May 1919, 15.

37. "Sergeant York Is Feted," *New York Times,* 26 May 1919, 10.

38. "Conscience Plus Red Hair Are Bad for Germans," *Literary Digest,* 14 June 1919, 42–48.

39. "Sergt. York Visitor in City," *Washington Evening Post,* 24 May 1919, 1–3.

40. York, *Sergeant York,* 299, 227; "Washington Hails Brave Sergeant York," *New York Times,* 25 May 1919, 14.

41. Cowan, *Sergeant York and His People,* 50, 271.

42. York, *Sergeant York,* 299.

43. "York Sees Subway from Private Car," *New York Times,* 27 May 1919, 7; "Details on IRT Subway: 1919," letter from Irving Deakin to Herman Lissauer, Warner Brothers Research Department, 6 September 1940, WBA.

44. "Back story information," letter from Harry Chandlee to Jesse Lasky, 8 May 1940, WBA, 12.

45. Cowan, *Sergeant York and His People,* 50–51.

46. York, *Sergeant York,* 299.

47. Bill Rice, "The Private Life of a Motion Picture," a short story on how the Sergeant York movie came into existence, Warner Brothers Studio, Burbank, California, 1941, WBA, 1–3.

48. York, *Sergeant York,* 112–113.

49. "Sergeant York Home," *New York Times,* 1 June 1919, 1.

50. York, *Sergeant York,* 300.

51. Bill Rice, "The Private Life of a Motion Picture," a short story on how the Sergeant York movie came into existence, Warner Brothers Studio, 1941, WBA, 2–3.

52. Memorandum from Julien Josephson and Harry Chandlee to Jesse L. Lasky, Warner Brothers Studio, 8 May 1940, WBA, 18.

53. Lasky, *I Blow My Own Horn,* 253; memorandum from Julien Josephson and Harry Chandlee to Jesse L. Lasky, Warner Brothers Studio, 8 May 1940, WBA, 18.

54. "Sergeant York Is Feted," *New York Times,* 26 May 1919, 10; Cowan, *Sergeant York and His People,* 50–51.

55. York, *Sergeant York,* 300.

56. Ibid.

57. Lasky, *I Blow My Own Horn*, 253–255; memorandum from Julien Josephson and Harry Chandlee to Jesse L. Lasky, Warner Brothers Studio, 8 May 1940, WBA, 18–20; Bill Rice, "The Private Life of a Motion Picture," a short story on how the Sergeant York movie came into existence, Warner Brothers Studio, 1941, WBA, 2–5.

58. "Sergeant York Home," *New York Times*, 1 June 1919, 1.

59. Pattullo, "The Second Elder Gives Battle," 3.

60. "Americans All!" *South Amboy Citizen*, 10 May 1919, 16.

61. "Capital Hails York," *Washington Post*, 25 May 1919, 3.

62. "Honor York and Read," *Washington Post*, 13 July 1919, 7.

63. "Calls Sergt. York 'Bravest of Men,'" *New York Times*, 22 May 1919, 9.

64. "Give Great Ovation to Sergeant York," *New York Times*, 23 May 1919, 15.

65. Alvin C. York travel agreement, for final movement to Pall Mall, Tennessee, signed at Camp Merritt, 27 May 1919.

66. Alvin York, final endorsement on military clearing papers, signed by York and First Lieutenant Edward Harman, 29 May 1919; Alvin C. York final pay form, and final out clearing papers (page 9), May 1919, both in Alvin C. York, U.S. Army Service Record, 1919, National Personnel Records Center, St. Louis, Missouri.

67. Alvin C. York, U.S. Army Service Record, between 1917–1918, National Personnel Records Center, St. Louis, Missouri.

68. York, *Sergeant York*, 301.

69. "Sergeant York Home," *New York Times*, 1 June 1919, 1.

70. Interview with Guy Williams by Robert S. Taplinger, "Sergeant York Production Notes," Director of Publicity, Warner Brothers Studio, 1941, WBA; Warner Brothers "Synopsis of Sergeant York," Warner Brothers Studio, 1941, WBA.

71. "Back story information," letter from Harry Chandlee to Jesse Lasky, 8 May 1940, WBA, 12.

72. York, *Sergeant York*, 301.

73. "Sergeant York Home," *New York Times*, 1 June 1919, 1.

74. Cowan, *Sergeant York and His People*, 51.

75. Interview with Guy Williams by Robert S. Taplinger, "Sergeant York Production Notes," Director of Publicity, Warner Brothers Studio, 1941, WBA; Warner Brothers "Synopsis of Sergeant York," Warner Brothers Studio, 1941, WBA.

76. "Church Upholds Sergt. York," *Washington Post*, 3 June 1919, 6.

77. York, *Sergeant York*, 301.

78. "Sergeant York Home," *New York Times*, 1 June 1919, 1.

79. York, *Sergeant York*, 301.

80. Ibid.

81. Gracie Williams York, *The Reminisces of Mrs. Alvin "Sergeant" York,* 22–25.

82. "York to Wed Girl of 17," *Washington Post,* 5 June 1919, 4.

83. "Sergeant York Home," *New York Times,* 1 June 1919, 1.

84. York, *Sergeant York,* 301–303.

85. Gracie Williams York, *The Reminisces of Mrs. Alvin "Sergeant" York,* 22–25.

86. Phillips, *The Governors of Tennessee,* 154–155; Cowan, *Sergeant York and His People,* 75–79.

87. Interview with Guy Williams by Robert S. Taplinger, "Sergeant York Production Notes," Director of Publicity, Warner Brothers Studio, 1941, WBA; Warner Brothers "Synopsis of Sergeant York," Warner Brothers Studio, 1941, WBA.

88. "Sergt. York Marries Boyhood Sweetheart," *New York Times,* 8 June 1919, 14.

89. Gracie Williams York, *The Reminisces of Mrs. Alvin "Sergeant" York,* 3–4, 22–27.

90. York, *Sergeant York,* 305–306.

91. Interview with Betsy Ross York and George Edward Buxton York in Jamestown and Pall Mall, Tennessee, 30 May 2010.

92. "York Going to Nashville," *Washington Post,* 9 June 1919, 1.

93. "Back story information," letter from Harry Chandlee to Jesse Lasky, 8 May 1940, WBA, 12.

94. Interview with Guy Williams by Robert S. Taplinger, "Sergeant York Production Notes," Director of Publicity, Warner Brothers Studio, 1941, WBA; Warner Brothers "Synopsis of Sergeant York," Warner Brothers Studio, 1941, WBA.

95. "York Gives Up Honeymoon," *New York Times,* 12 June 1919, 5; "Alvin C. York Memorial Fund," Rotary Club of Nashville, 1919–1924, Metropolitan Archives, Nashville, Tennessee.

96. "York's Pastor Repents," *New York Times,* 18 June 1919, 22.

97. "York Gives Up Honeymoon," *New York Times,* 12 June 1919, 5; "Alvin C. York Memorial Fund," Rotary Club of Nashville, 1919–1924, Metropolitan Archives, Nashville, Tennessee.

98. York, *Sergeant York,* 303–304.

99. Ibid., 303–305.

10. Back on the Farm in Pall Mall

Epigraph: York, *Sergeant York,* 309.

1. Crosby, *America's Forgotten Pandemic,* 209–219; Pettit, *A Cruel Wind,* 1–9; Johnson and Mueller, "Updating the Accounts," 105–115.

2. York, *Sergeant York,* 231–233, 304.

3. Ibid., 304–305.

4. "Alvin C. York Memorial Fund," Rotary Club of Nashville, 1919–1924, Metropolitan Archives, Nashville, Tennessee.

5. Skeyhill, *Sergeant York: Last of the Long Hunters,* 233.

6. Lasky, *I Blow My Own Horn,* 253–255; memorandum from Julien Josephson and Harry Chandlee to Jesse L. Lasky, Warner Brothers Studio, 8 May 1940, WBA, 18–20; Bill Rice, "The Private Life of a Motion Picture," a short story on how the Sergeant York movie came into existence, Warner Brothers Studio, 1941, WBA, 2–5.

7. Cowan, *Sergeant York and His People,* 288–290.

8. York, *Sergeant York,* 232–235, 306.

9. Cowan, *Sergeant York and His People,* 288–289.

10. Ibid., 289.

11. York, *Sergeant York,* 307; Perry, *Sgt. York,* 136–137; Cowan, *Sergeant York and His People,* 288–289.

12. "Sergeant York Stricken," *New York Times,* 31 January 1920.

13. "Sergt. York Gets $215 for Schools," *New York Times,* 19 April 1920; William S. Howland, "War Hero's Dream Now Coming True," *New York Times,* 6 June 1926.

14. E. J. Buren, "Sergeant York, Homeless Hero of War Got $60: Awaits Farm," *Washington Post,* 4 December 1921, 34. Their first son was ill and died only four days after he was born.

15. U.S. Congress, House of Representatives, Bill H.R. 8599, sponsored by Representative Cordell Hull, 66th Cong., 1st Sess., 20 August 1919; U.S. Congress, Senate, Bill S. 2368, sponsored by Senator Kenneth McKellar, 5 August 1921.

16. Letter to Secretary of War Newton D. Baker from Representative Cordell Hull, requesting promotion and retired status for Alvin C. York, 22 May 1919; letter of support from the Secretary of War, Newton D. Baker, to Honorable Julius Kahn, Chairman of the House Committee on Military Affairs, 26 August 1919, both in Alvin C. York, U.S. Army Service Record, National Personnel Records Center, St. Louis, Missouri..

17. Letter from Secretary of War Dwight F. Davis to Honorable John M. Morin, Chairman of the House Committee on Military Affairs, opposed to commissioning of Alvin York, 31 January 1928, in Alvin C. York, U.S. Army Service Record, National Personnel Records Center, St. Louis, Missouri.

18. "Oppose Award to Sergeant York," *New York Times,* 20 August 1921.

19. "SGT. York Is Made Major in Infantry," *New York Times,* 8 May 1942; "Sergeant York, Woodfill Are Majors Now," *Washington Post,* 8 May 1942, 1.

20. Pershing, *My Experiences in the World War,* 2:392; "Passes Bill Rewarding York," *New York Times,* 13 February 1935.

21. John J. Pershing, "My Experiences in the World War," *New York Times*, 29 March 1931.

22. E. J. Buren, "Sergeant York, Homeless Hero of War Got $60: Awaits Farm," *Washington Post*, 4 December 1921, 34.

23. Alvin C. York pay voucher, Alvin York Military Service Packet, U.S. War Department, May 1919.

24. "Alvin C. York Memorial Fund," Rotary Club of Nashville, 1919–1924, Metropolitan Archives, Nashville, Tennessee.

25. E. J. Buren, "Sergeant York, Homeless Hero of War Got $60: Awaits Farm," *Washington Post*, 4 December 1921, 34.

26. Ibid.

27. "Hero York Harassed, Can't Make Farm Pay," *New York Times*, 21 July 1921.

28. E. J. Buren, "Sergeant York, Homeless Hero of War Got $60: Awaits Farm," *Washington Post*, 4 December 1921, 34.

29. "Hero York Harassed, Can't Make Farm Pay," *New York Times*, 21 July 1921.

30. E. J. Buren, "Sergeant York, Homeless Hero of War Got $60: Awaits Farm," *Washington Post*, 4 December 1921, 34.

31. "Refused $1,000 a Night," *New York Times*, 31 May 1922.

32. E. J. Buren, "Sergeant York, Homeless Hero of War Got $60: Awaits Farm," *Washington Post*, 4 December 1921, 34.

33. Ibid.

34. Lee, *Sergeant York*, 74–75.

35. "Tennessee Society to Help Sergeant York," *New York Times*, 5 October 1921.

36. E. J. Buren, "Sergeant York, Homeless Hero of War Got $60: Awaits Farm," *Washington Post*, 4 December 1921, 34.

37. Cowan, *Sergeant York and His People*, 1–6.

38. "Tennessee's War Hero," *New York Times*, 16 July 1922.

39. Cowan, *Sergeant York and His People*, 110–111.

40. York, *Sergeant York*, 306.

41. William S. Howland, "War Hero's Dream Now Coming True," *New York Times*, 6 June 1926.

42. Ibid.

43. Interview with Betsy Ross York and George Edward Buxton York in Jamestown and Pall Mall, Tennessee, 30 May 2010. Verse reference is Matthew 13:57b, King James Version.

44. York, *Sergeant York*, 174.

45. "Alvin C. York Presses Aim," *New York Times*, 18 September 1927, E6.

46. "York Sues Over School," *Washington Post*, 17 September 1927, 16.

47. Perry, *Sgt. York*, 165–175.

48. "Sergt. York's Troubles," *Washington Post,* 26 July 1927, 6.

49. "Sergt. York Quits School: Hero Leaves Institution He Founded in Row with State," *New York Times,* 9 May 1936.

50. "Dry's Draft York; He Refuses to Run," *New York Times,* 8 May 1936; "York Will Seek No Office," *New York Times,* 8 May 1936.

51. "Sergeant York Here in School Fund Drive," *New York Times,* 4 February 1928, 2.

52. "Sergeant York Winces," *New York Times,* 19 January 1927.

53. "War Hero Writes for School: Sergt. York Publishes Book to Get Funds for His Students," *Washington Post,* 28 October 1928, R12; York, *Sergeant York,* 24–28.

54. S. T. Williamson, "Sergeant York Tells His Own Story," *New York Times,* 23 December 1928.

55. York, *Sergeant York.*

56. Skeyhill, *Sergeant York: Last of the Long Hunters.*

57. Ibid., 2.

58. Ibid., 2–9.

59. Major R. B. Lawrence, "The Army Puts on Its Show," *Washington Post,* 29 September 1929, 6; "Sergeant York's Feat Exhibition Feature," *Washington Post,* 22 September 1929, 5.

60. "Daily 'War' at Capital: Sergeant York Captures 132 Foes amid Bombs at Army Show," *New York Times,* 5 October 1929; "Army Again Fights Battle of Argonne," *Washington Post,* 4 October 1929, 22; Major R. B. Lawrence, "Smashing through the Argonne," *Military Exposition and Carnival: War College 3–5 October, 1929* (Washington, D.C.: Government Printing Office, 1929), 38.

61. Major Danforth letter to Captain Swindler, 5 August 1929, RG 165, NARA; Lieutenant Colonel Buxton letter to Captain Swindler, 23 July 1929, RG 165, NARA.

62. "Plane Ride Refused by Sergeant York," *New York Times,* 22 September 1929.

63. Ibid.

64. Cahill, "America Needed a Hero," 30–38; "Sergeant York Winces," *New York Times,* 19 January 1927; "Sergeant York Here in School Fund Drive," *New York Times,* 4 February 1928, 2; Otis B. Merrithew, "Statement Regarding Argonne Engagement," 11 December 1929, B00374, Folder 2880, WBA; Cahill, "America Needed a Hero," 30–38; Mahoney, "Alvin York and Frank Luke," 22, 45–46.

65. "Sergeant York's Exploit," *New York Times,* 7 October 1929.

66. Robert Talley, "Eleven Years after War Finds Members in Different Jobs," *Niagara Falls Gazette,* 11 November 1929, 4.

67. "Upholds Sergeant York," *New York Times,* 13 August 1935.

68. Otis B. Merrithew, "Statement Regarding Argonne Engagement," 11 December 1929, B00374, Folder 2880, WBA; Cahill, "America Needed a Hero," 30–38; Mahoney, "Alvin York and Frank Luke," 22, 45–46.

69. "Sergeant York Story Is Denied," *Providence Journal,* September 1930.

70. Ibid.

71. Otis B. Merrithew, "Statement Regarding Argonne Engagement," 11 December 1929, B00374, Folder 2880, WBA; Cahill, "America Needed a Hero," 30–38; Mahoney, "Alvin York and Frank Luke," 22, 45–46.

11. Another War with Germany

Epigraph: "Must Fight to Keep Liberty, Says York," *New York Times,* 31 May 1941.

1. "Peace to Be Theme on Armistice Day," *New York Times,* 9 November 1936.

2. According to Bill Kauffman, "isolationists" was a pejorative term at the time. Kauffman states that it is an acceptable term for modern historians to use when defining anti-interventionalists as those who are (1) anti-imperialistic, (2) opposed to war for principle, such as keeping the world safe for democracy (Wilson's mantra in the First World War), and (3) opposed to international treaties and/or organizations that diminish American sovereignty, such as the League of Nations. This describes the policies of Senators Nye and Wheeler, as well as the platform of the America First Committee (AFC). See Kauffman, *America First!,* 16–17; Doenecke, *Storm on the Horizon,* x.

3. Doenecke, *Storm on the Horizon,* 2–9.

4. Bill Kauffman resists the notion that the AFC was at its core anti-Semitic and suggests that this allegation is based upon Lindbergh's oft-quoted 11 September 1941 speech in Des Moines, Iowa. To be sure, Senator Nye was careful not to directly attack those of Jewish roots. Reviewing the literature analytically, moreover, both Nye and the AFC leadership did repeatedly condemn areas of American society believed to be dominated by Jews. This included the usual suspects, such as Hollywood, banks, and agents of international commerce. These attacks did not necessarily make Nye anti-Semitic. It must be added that Nye was an unabashed Anglophobe. Nye, "Report of the Special Committee on Investigation of the Munitions Industry," 1–13; Kauffman, *America First!,* 16–25, 82–92.

5. Nye, "Report of the Special Committee on Investigation of the Munitions Industry," 1–13.

6. U.S. Department of State, Office of the Historian, "The Neutrality Acts, 1930s," http://history.state.gov/milestones/1921-1936/Neutrality_acts (accessed 21 November 2011).

7. Larsen, "Gerald Nye and the Isolationist Argument," 25–28.

8. Doenecke, *Storm on the Horizon,* 10–15, 21–22, 83–84, 159–160. Wilkie was, unlike his Republican rivals, an interventionist and would be among the first to defend Hollywood's interventionist movie productions.

9. Kauffman, *America First!,* 21–22.

10. Cole, *Senator Gerald P. Nye and American Foreign Relations,* 65–69.

11. Doenecke, *Storm on the Horizon,* 2–5.

12. The Charles Lindbergh website provides both audio and pdf files of speeches given by this influential American figure that are indicative of his isolationist proclivities. http://www.charleslindbergh.com/americanfirst/index.asp (accessed 21 November 2011).

13. Trout, *On the Battlefield of Memory,* 66–69.

14. George Bookman, "Sergt. York Urges Convoys for All-Out Aid," *Washington Post,* 31 May 1941, 4; "Must Fight to Keep Liberty, Says York," *New York Times,* 31 May 1941; "Text of the President's Armistice Day Speech," *New York Times,* 12 November 1941.

15. "Sergeant York Ready to Join War on Japan," *New York Times,* 12 November 1937.

16. Chang, *The Rape of Nanking,* ix–x, 4–7.

17. "Sergt. York Offers Plan to Stop Hitler; Must Knock Him off Block Says Hero of 20 Years Ago," *New York Times,* 9 October 1938.

18. "Sergeant York's Son 'Ready,'" *New York Times,* 14 September 1939.

19. George Bookman, "Sergt. York Urges Convoys for All-Out Aid," *Washington Post,* 31 May 1941, 4.

20. Ibid.; "Must Fight to Keep Liberty, Says York," *New York Times,* 31 May 1941; "Text of the President's Armistice Day Speech," *New York Times,* 12 November 1941.

21. Bill Rice, "The Private Life of a Motion Picture," a short story on how the Sergeant York movie came into existence, Warner Brothers Studio, Burbank, California, 1941, WBA, 1–2.

22. Lasky, *I Blow My Own Horn,* 252–253.

23. Ibid., 253–254.

24. Robert S. Taplinger, Director of Publicity, "Sergeant York Production Notes," Warner Brothers Studio, 1941, WBA, 1–2.

25. Bill Rice, "The Private Life of a Motion Picture," Warner Brothers Studio, Burbank, California, 1941, WBA, 2–4.

26. Bill Rice, "Sergeant York Movie Information," Warner Brothers Studio, 1942, WBA, 1–3; Lasky, *I Blow My Own Horn,* 254.

27. Lasky, *I Blow My Own Horn*, 254.

28. Bill Rice, "Sergeant York Movie Information," Warner Brothers Studio, 1942, WBA, 1–3.

29. "Sergeant York Balks at Lasky Film Offer; Like Trading for a Mule, Says War Hero," *New York Times*, 16 March 1940.

30. Lasky, *I Blow My Own Horn*, 254–255.

31. Robert S. Taplinger, Director of Publicity, "Sergeant York Production Notes," Warner Brothers Studio, 1941, 1941, WBA, 1–3; Lasky, *I Blow My Own Horn*, 255–256.

32. "Sergeant York in Film; To Be Lasky Technical Advisor in Picture Based on His Life," *New York Times*, 24 March 1940; Lasky, *I Blow My Own Horn*, 255–256.

33. Contract between Alvin York and Jesse Lasky signing movie rights to the latter, 23 March 1940, WBA.

34. Lasky, *I Blow My Own Horn*, 257.

35. Einfeld was Lasky's studio manager at Paramount and was at Warner Brothers as head of publicity. Lasky, *I Blow My Own Horn*, 255–256.

36. Lasky Jr., *Whatever Happened to Hollywood?*, 223–225.

37. "Screen News Here and in Hollywood; Jesse L. Lasky to Make 'The Amazing Story of Sergeant York' for Warner,'" *New York Times*, 5 April 1940.

38. Request from Tennessee governor Prentice Cooper to the U.S. War Department to cooperate with Warner Brothers on the movie, 10 April 1940, in Alvin C. York, U.S. Army Service Record, National Personnel Records Center, St. Louis, Missouri. It was preceded by a 10 January 1941 request from Warner Brothers Studio for access to York's Military Service Record.

39. "Sergeant York Balks at Lasky Film Offer; Like Trading for a Mule, Says War Hero," *New York Times*, 16 March 1940.

40. Lasky, *I Blow My Own Horn*, 252–261.

41. In his book, *I Blow My Own Horn*, Lasky claims sole credit for this decision on Cooper (255). However, Bill Rice's twenty-page discourse on the movie indicates that Lasky and Alvin York first discussed Cooper as the right choice. However, Jesse Lasky's son, Jesse Jr., also then in show business, wrote that his dad indeed resorted to "subterfuge" to secure Cooper in the role of York. This subterfuge, he says, included the forged telegram. See Bill Rice, "The Private Life of a Motion Picture," Warner Brothers Studio, Burbank, California, 1941, WBA, 4; Lasky Jr., *Whatever Happened to Hollywood?*, 224–225.

42. Much of this story is based on what Lasky Jr. records in his book. When Jack Warner heard that Ronald Reagan was running for governor of California in the 1966 election, he answered, "Governor, no.

Bad casting. The *friend* of the governor." Lasky Jr., *Whatever Happened to Hollywood?*, 224–225, 336–337. Jesse Lasky Jr. was an accomplished screenwriter and served as an assistant director for the Sergeant York movie. See Interview with Guy Williams by Robert S. Taplinger, "Sergeant York Production Notes," Director of Publicity, Warner Brothers Studio, 1941, WBA; Warner Brothers "Synopsis of Sergeant York," Warner Brothers Studio, 1941, WBA.

43. Interoffice communication between Sam Goldwyn and J. L. Warner, agreement on Cooper and Davis actor exchange, 30 August 1940, WBA; "Gary Cooper Expected to Play in Warner's 'The Amazing Story of Sergeant York,'" *New York Times*, 23 July 1940.

44. Koch, *As Time Goes By*, 74–75; Lasky, *I Blow My Own Horn*, 259.

45. Bill Rice, "The Private Life of a Motion Picture," a short story on how the Sergeant York movie came into existence, Warner Brothers Studio, Burbank, California, 1941, WBA, 4–5.

46. Interview with George Edward Buxton York, in Pall Mall, Tennessee, 29 May 2009, and in Châtel Chéhéry, France, 4 October 2008.

47. Interoffice communication from Abem Finkel to Hal Wallis, 9 January 1941, WBA.

48. Bill Rice, "The Private Life of A Motion Picture; for Veteran's Publications," Warner Brothers Studio, Burbank, California, 1941, WBA, 1–3, 7–8.

49. Interoffice communication from Abem Finkel to Hal Wallis, "The Sad Story of Sergeant York," 9 January 1941, WBA.

50. Bill Rice, "The Private Life of a Motion Picture," a short story on how the Sergeant York movie came into existence, Warner Brothers Studio, Burbank, California, 1941, WBA, 4–5.

51. Interoffice communication from Jesse Lasky to the Warner Brothers Research Department on "real" personalities to be portrayed in the movie, 20 September 1940, WBA.

52. Bill Rice, "The Private Life of a Motion Picture," a short story on how the Sergeant York movie came into existence, Warner Brothers Studio, Burbank, California, 1941, WBA, 6.

53. Letter to William Guthrie from Otis Merrithew, 13 January 1941, WBA; letter from Mary Kornacki to William Guthrie, 3 April 1941, WBA; letter from Joseph Kornacki to William Guthrie, 16 January 1941, WBA.

54. Interoffice communication from R. J. Obringer to Mr. Einfeld, "Sergeant York Billing," 16 April 1941, WBA.

55. Letter from Otis B. Merrithew (also signed William Cutting) to Jesse Lasky, 12 June 1940, WBA; letter from Otis B. Merrithew to William Guthrie, 11 March 1941, WBA.

56. Letter to William Guthrie from Otis B. Merrithew, 13 January

1941, WBA; letter from Otis B. Merrithew to William Guthrie, 11 March 1941, WBA.

57. Memorandum from R. J. Obringer to Mr. R. W. Budd, Warner Brothers Director of Personnel, 3 September 1941; interoffice communication from Abem Finkel to Hal Wallis, "The Sad Story of Sergeant York," 9 January 1941, WBA.

58. Letter from Bill Perkins (Warner Brothers general counsel) to R. J. Obringer on utilizing the headquarters of the VFW to eradicate any perceived ill-will and to make it less expensive finding the soldiers to be paid, 12 May 1941, WBA.

59. Interoffice communication from Jesse Lasky to R. J. Obringer, "Sergeant York Release Forms," 25 October 1940, WBA.

60. Interoffice communication from Abem Finkel to Hal Wallis, "The Sad Story of Sergeant York," 9 January 1941, WBA.

61. Bill Rice, "Movie Synopsis," Warner Brothers Studio, 1942, WBA.

62. Koch, *As Time Goes By*, 74–75.

63. Although the screenwriters took credit for this, Alvin York used this expression to describe his conversion experience to Hollywood screenwriters in 1940. (Interview with Colonel Gerald York [U.S. Army] in Monterey, California, October 1996; interview with George Edward Buxton York in Montfaucon, France, 4 October 2008, during the ninetieth anniversary commemoration of his father's actions in the Great War.)

64. Letter from Harry Chandlee to Jesse L. Lasky, "Conception Ideas Added to Sergeant York," 15 October 1942, WBA; Bill Rice, "Movie Synopsis," Warner Brothers Studio, 1942, WBA, 8–11; "Back story information," letter from Harry Chandlee to Jesse Lasky, 8 May 1940, WBA, 22–23; interoffice communication from Abem Finkel to Hal Willis, 9 January 1941, WBA.

65. Trout, *On the Battlefield of Memory*, 240–248.

66. Letter from Harry Chandlee to Jesse L. Lasky, "Conception Ideas Added to Sergeant York," 15 October 1942, WBA.

67. Interview with Colonel Gerald York (U.S. Army) in Monterey, California, October 1996; interview with George Edward Buxton York in Montfaucon, France, 4 October 2008, during the ninetieth anniversary commemoration of his father's actions in the Great War; interview with Betsy Ross York and George Edward Buxton York in Jamestown and Pall Mall, Tennessee, 30 May 2010.

68. Bill Rice, "Movie Synopsis," Warner Brothers Studio, 1942, WBA.

69. Interview with Guy Williams by Robert S. Taplinger, "Sergeant York Production Notes," Director of Publicity, Warner Brothers Studio, 1941, WBA; Warner Brothers "Synopsis of Sergeant York," Warner Brothers Studio, 1941, WBA.

70. "Of Local Origin," *New York Times*, 30 June 1941.

71. Sherry, *In the Shadow of War*, 53–55. Wilkie favored intervention and would soon find himself defending Hollywood's interventionalist movies in front of Senator Nye's committee.

72. "Sergeant of Screen, Sergeant in Person," *New York Times*, 2 July 1941; "Of Local Origin," *New York Times*, 2 July 1941; Bosley Crowther, "The Screen in Review," *New York Times*, 3 July 1941.

73. "Sergt. York Here for Film Premier," *Washington Post*, 3 July 1941; Gerald G. Gross, "President Greets Sergt. York," *Washington Post*, 31 July 1941, 1; "Sergeant Alvin C. York Coming to His Premier," *Washington Post*, 27 July 1941, L3.

74. Nelson B. Bell, "Twenty Years of Effort Results in Mighty Film," *Washington Post*, 27 July 1941, L3.

75. Zierold, *The Moguls*, 166.

76. "Film Money-Makers Selected by Variety," *New York Times*, 31 December 1941.

77. Lasky, *I Blow My Own Horn*, 252–262; Lasky Jr., *Whatever Happened to Hollywood?*, 224–225.

78. "Academy Award to Joan Fontaine: Gary Cooper Takes Honor for Sergeant York," *New York Times*, 27 February 1942; Frank S. Nugent, "The All-American Man," *New York Times*, 5 July 1942; "War Films Shoot the Girls to Stardom," *New York Times*, 15 January 1950; "Gary Cooper, Dead of Cancer," *New York Times*, 14 May 1961.

79. "Army Rebuilds 3 Divisions of 1918 Fame," *Washington Post*, 26 March 1942, 8.

80. U.S. Congress, Senate, *Propaganda in Motion Pictures*, 6–7.

81. Kauffman, *America First!*, 16–25, 85–88.

82. "Nye Says Films Spread War Wave," *New York Times*, 2 August 1941. Nye would ask Harry Warner why there were no anti-British movies, and instead just anti-Germany ones. Interestingly, the 1939 movie *Drums along the Mohawk*, despite fulfilling this desire, was not mentioned by Nye or Warner as being a balance to *Sergeant York.*

83. "War Films Face Boycott Threat," *New York Times*, 20 September 1941; Trumpbour, *Selling Hollywood to the World*, 77–81; Ceplair and Englund, *The Inquisition in Hollywood*, 160.

84. Cole, *Senator Gerald P. Nye and American Foreign Relations*, 186–188; Stenehjem, *An American First*, 148–149.

85. U.S. Congress, Senate, *Propaganda in Motion Pictures*, 18–19.

86. Ibid., 11.

87. Stenehjem, *An American First*, 148–149; Cole, *Senator Gerald P. Nye and American Foreign Relations*, 188–190.

88. U.S. Congress, Senate, *Propaganda in Motion Pictures*, 318–320.

89. Ibid., 338–339.

90. Trumpbour, *Selling Hollywood to the World*, 79. At the same hearing, Darryl Zanuck, another Hollywood mogul, gave a fiery statement that disproved Nye's conspiratorial contention in addition to informing the committee that he was a Methodist, illustrating that not all the producers were Jewish, as had been alleged.

91. Sherry, *In the Shadow of War*, 53–55; Gabler, *An Empire of Their Own*, 344–347.

92. U.S. Congress, Senate, *Propaganda in Motion Pictures*, 338–340.

93. S. J. Woolf, "Sergeant York—Then and Now," *New York Times Magazine*, 15 August 1948.

94. "SGT. York Urges Aid for Red Cross," *New York Times*, 19 February 1942, 11.

95. "McArthur Aids Flag Body," *New York Times*, 7 April 1942.

96. "Sergeant York May Seek Seat of Rep. Gore," *Washington Post*, 13 May 1942, 12.

97. "Sergeant York's Mother Dies at Home of Hero," *Washington Post*, 23 May 1943, 14.

98. "Sergeant York in Serious Condition after Stroke," *Washington Post*, 8 May 1949, M2; "Sergeant York Stricken," *New York Times*, 8 May 1949.

99. "Sergt. York Must Spend Week in Hospital," *Washington Post*, 5 July 1950, 5.

100. "Sergeant York Feeling Better," *New York Times*, 10 March 1954.

101. "Sergeant York Gets Tribute," *New York Times*, 9 October 1960.

102. "Sgt. York, 74, Acutely Ill," *New York Times*, 28 May 1962.

103. Lasky Jr., *Whatever Happened to Hollywood?*, 378–379.

104. "Go Easy on Sgt. York, Tennessee Asks," *Washington Post and Times Herald*, 18 February 1959, A1.

105. "$21,200 Given to York Fund," *New York Times*, 3 April 1961.

106. "Rayburn Starts Drive to Aid Alvin C. York," *New York Times*, 19 March 1961, 82; "10,000 Give to End Hero's Tax Debt," *New York Times*, 9 April 1961.

107. "Sergeant York, War Hero, Dies," *New York Times*, 3 September 1964, 1; "Sergeant York Buried Near His Home," *Washington Post and Times Herald*, 6 September 1964; "Sgt. York's Rites Attended by 8,000," *New York Times*, 6 September 1964.

12. Honoring a Hero

Epigraph: Major General Joshua L. Chamberlain at Bowdoin College in 1889, quoted in Smith, *Fanny and Joshua*, 278.

1. Buxton, *Official History of 82nd Division American Expeditionary Forces, 1917–1919*, 58–63; Duncan, "Reminiscences, 1886–1919," 145–

155; Liggett, *A.E.F.*, 172–174; Pershing, *My Experiences in the World War*, 2:390–392.

2. Marie Huret, "Il faut sauver le sergent York," *L'Express*, 9 November 2006, 60–61; Craig S. Smith, "Revisiting the Legend of an American War Hero," *New York Times*, 20 June 2006, A3.

3. Duncan, "Reminiscences, 1886–1919," 153.

4. Swindler, "Turkey Match," 349–350.

5. Captain Bertrand Cox, affidavit given on 21 February 1919 in Frettes, France, filed by the 328th Infantry Regiment Advocate General, with actual swearing of the affidavit on 26 February 1919.

6. Ibid.; Duncan, "Reminiscences, 1886–1919," 153.

7. Swindler, "Turkey Match," 349–350; York, *Sergeant York*, 271–273; Captain Bertrand Cox, affidavit given on 21 February 1919 in Frettes, France, filed by the 328th Infantry Regiment Advocate General, with actual swearing of the affidavit on 26 February 1919.

8. York photographs, Army Historical Education Center, Carlisle, Pennsylvania; York, *Sergeant York*, 222–223, 271–278.

9. Major Danforth letter to Captain Swindler, 5 August 1929, and Lieutenant Colonel Buxton letter to Captain Swindler, 23 July 1929, both in RG 165, NARA.

10. Major Danforth letter to Captain Swindler, 5 August 1929, and Lieutenant Colonel Buxton letter to Captain Swindler, 23 July 1929, both in RG 165, NARA.

11. Paul Vollmer would be haunted throughout his life for his decision to surrender on 8 October 1918.

12. "Testimony of German Officers and Men about Sergeant York," translated by the U.S. Army War College, Carlisle, Pennsylvania, June 1936, 2–21; York site photographs, Army Historical Education Center, Carlisle, Pennsylvania; York, *Sergeant York*, 222–223, 271–278; Swindler, "Turkey Match," 349–350; York, *Sergeant York*, 271–273; Captain Bertrand Cox, affidavit given on 21 February 1919 in Frettes, France, filed by the 328th Infantry Regiment Advocate General, with actual swearing of the affidavit on 26 February 1919.

13. Email from Ronald Bowman to Douglas Mastriano, 1 March 2013.

14. Beattie and Bowman, "In Search of York: Man, Myth, and Legend," 5.

15. Ibid., 1–14.

16. Interview with Dr. Susan Blair, Department of Archeology, University of New Brunswick, 8 May 2012.

17. King, *The Archeological Survey*, 1–15; Burke and Smith, *The Archeologist's Field Handbook*, 64–88.

18. Leon Alligood, "Scholars put Sgt York WW I Heroics on the

Map," Tennessean.com, available at http://www.freerepublic.com/focus/f-news/1600919/posts (accessed 4 March 2013).

19. Nolan, "Battlefield Landscapes," 69–73.

20. Ibid., 50–53; Major Danforth letter to Captain Swindler, 5 August 1929, and Lieutenant Colonel Buxton letter to Captain Swindler, 23 July 1929, RG 165, NARA.

21. Nolan, "Battlefield Landscapes," 69–71.

22. Ibid., 50–53.

23. Craig S. Smith, "Revisiting the Legend of an American War Hero," *New York Times*, 20 June 2006, A3; Jenny Barchfield, Associated Press, "France 'York Spot' May Have Been Located," 26 October 2006, http://www.washingtonpost.com/wp-dyn/content/article/2006/10/26/AR2006102601314.html (accessed 4 March 2013); Leon Alligood, "Scholars Put Sgt York WW I Heroics on the Map," Tennessean.com, available at http://www.freerepublic.com/focus/f-news/1600919/posts (accessed 4 March 2013). During their next trip to the Argonne, Nolan would find a large cache of American .45 cartridges. However, analysis determined that none of these came from an Automatic Colt Pistol (York's weapon). What he found came from a revolver. See Gina Fann, "In the Footsteps of Sgt York," *Murfreesboro Post*, 23 December 2012, http://www.murfreesboropost.com/in-the-footsteps-of-sgt-york-cms-33812 (accessed 5 March 2013).

24. Lisa Rollins, "Texas State Doctoral Student Tom Nolan Leads Discovery Team," Middle Tennessee State, 20 March 2006, http://www.txstate.edu/news/news_releases/external_news/2006/03/wwIhero-found032006.html (accessed 5 March 2013).

25. Ibid.

26. Associated Press, "Location of Sgt. York's WWI Heroics Found?," 22 March 2006, http://www.nbcnews.com/id/11965337/#.UTUMBKVJOAg (accessed 4 March 2013).

27. Jenny Barchfield, Associated Press, "France 'York Spot' May Have Been Located," 26 October 2006, http://www.washingtonpost.com/wp-dyn/content/article/2006/10/26/AR2006102601314.html (accessed 4 March 2013); Craig S. Smith, "Revisiting the Legend of an American War Hero," *New York Times*, 20 June 2006, A3.

28. Swindler, "Turkey Match," 349–350.

29. "Testimony of German Officers and Men about Sergeant York," translated by the U.S. Army War College, Carlisle, Pennsylvania, June 1936.

30. Merkatz, *Unterrictsbuch fur die Maschinengewehr=Koampagnien*, 153–187.

31. Eisnecker, "Kammer Diener: Vor 120 Jahren begann die Karriere der Patrone 8 x 57," 6–18.

32. Nathusius, "Vor 50 Jahren wurde Polte gegründet. Jubiläum der

angesehenen Magdeburger Maschinenfabrik," 7; Nathusius, *Polte Armaturen- und Maschinenfabrik.*

33. Brant Hamann and Dr. Windisch, *Die Militärpatronen Kaliber 7,9 mm.*

34. Ball, *Mauser Military Rifles of the World*, 160–167; Merkatz, *Unterrictsbuch fur die Maschinengewehr=Koampagnien*, 153–187.

35. Ball, *Mauser Military Rifles of the World*, 160–167. Also see Kent, *German 7.9 mm Military Ammunition, 1888–1945.*

36. Swindler, "Turkey Match," 349–350.

37. Kriegsministerium, *Schiessvorschrift für die Infanterie* (Berlin: Ernst Siegfried Mittler und Sohn, 1909), 2–11.

38. Captain Bertrand Cox, affidavit given on 21 February 1919 in Frettes, France, filed by the 328th Infantry Regiment Advocate General, with actual swearing of the affidavit on 26 February 1919.

39. Alvin C. York, extract from York's Medal of Honor Citation, in Alvin C. York, U.S. Army Service Record, Army Service File, 1917–1919, under Awards, 1919, National Personnel Records Center, St. Louis, Missouri.

40. Swindler, "Turkey Match," 58–63.

41. Biddle, *Soldier's Handbook of the Rifle*, 13; Major General H. L. Scott, *Manual for Noncommissioned Officers and Privates of Infantry of the Army of the United States 1917* (Menasha, Wisc.: George Banta Publishing, 1917), 148–161; Werner, *Uniforms, Equipment and Weapons of the American Expeditionary Forces in World War I*, 68–75.

42. Buxton, *Official History of 82nd Division American Expeditionary Forces, 1917–1919*, 58–63.

43. Idler, "Heimkehr nach 90 Jahren—Das Schicksal des im Ersten Weltkrieg vermissten Steinbachers Wilhelm Härer (1882 bis 1918)," 182–199.

44. Matthias Nothstein, "Ein einzigartiger Akt der Versoehung," *Backnang Kreiszeitung*, 30 April 2009, 19.

45. J. M. Tillman, 82nd Division Field Orders, History of Operations, Great War, 82nd Division Archives and Museum, Fort Bragg, North Carolina, 1929; Buxton, *Official History of 82nd Division American Expeditionary Forces, 1917–1919*, 59–62; "Testimony of German Officers and Men about Sergeant York," translated by the U.S. Army War College, Carlisle, Pennsylvania, June 1936.

46. Buxton, *Official History of 82nd Division American Expeditionary Forces, 1917–1919*, 59–62.

47. Gruppe Argonne unit deployment locations/unit situations/front line trace of German forces, 6 October 1918 (Nr. 46) (Generalkommando z.b.v. 58, Fifth German Army, German Imperial Army). Also see the following reports and unit histories: 125 Landwehr Regiment Kriegstagebuch of the Regimental Staff, October 1918; 125 Landwehr

Regiment Kriegstagebuch, July–November 1918, I Battalion, 125 Landwehr Regiment Kriegstagebuch; II Battalion 125 Landwehr Regiment Kriegstagebuch, all in Landesarchiv Baden-Württemberg—Hauptstaatsarchiv Stuttgart.

48. Cooke, *The All-Americans at War*; Buxton, *Official History of 82nd Division American Expeditionary Forces, 1917–1919*, 58–63; Gruppe Argonne unit deployment locations, 7 October 1918 (Nr. 47) (Generalkommando z.b.v. 58, Fifth German Army, German Imperial Army), in Landesarchiv Baden-Württemberg—Hauptstaatsarchiv Stuttgart; Gruppe Argonne Attack plan/objectives between Fleville and Gesnes, Ia 6512, 7 October 1918 (Nr. 47a), in Landesarchiv Baden-Württemberg—Hauptstaatsarchiv Stuttgart.

49. Physical Evidence Program Manager, *Firearm/Toolmark Procedures Manual DFS Document 240-D100*, 42–117.

50. Buxton, *Official History of 82nd Division American Expeditionary Forces, 1917–1919*, 58–63.

51. Dr. Douglas Scott, "The Archeology of Battlefields," interview conducted by the Archeology Institute of America, 11 October 2005, http://www.archaeology.org/online/interviews/scott.html (accessed 8 August 2011).

52. Swindler, "Turkey Match," 349; Buxton, *Official History of 82nd Division American Expeditionary Forces, 1917–1919*, 58–63.

53. Buxton, *Official History of 82nd Division American Expeditionary Forces, 1917–1919*, 58–63; Strohm, *Die Württembergishchen Regimenter im Weltkrieg 1914–1918*, Band 25, *Das Württembergishche Landwehr Infanterie Regiment nr. 120*, 160–166; Franke, *Die 2. Württemberg Landwehr Division Im Weltkrieg 1914–1918*, 52–60.

54. Dr. Douglas Scott, "An Examination of Cartridges Cases and Bullets from the World War I Châtel Chéhéry Area, Argonne Forest, France," 5–11.

55. Heard, *Handbook of Firearms and Ballistics*, 164–178.

56. Dr. Douglas Scott, "An Examination of Cartridges Cases and Bullets from the World War I Châtel Chéhéry Area, Argonne Forest, France," 7–9.

57. Ibid., 10.

58. Ibid., 11–13.

59. Ibid., 11–12.

60. Physical Evidence Program Manager, *Firearm/Toolmark Procedures Manual DFS Document 240-D100*, 30–35, 75–77, 110–113.

61. Dr. Douglas Scott, "An Examination of Cartridges Cases and Bullets from the World War I Châtel Chéhéry Area, Argonne Forest, France," 13–17.

62. Mahoney, "Sergeant Alvin York," 22, 45–47.

63. "Testimony of German Officers and Men about Sergeant York," translated by the U.S. Army War College, Carlisle, Pennsylvania, June 1936.

64. Mahoney, "Sergeant Alvin York," 22, 45–47.

65. Dr. Douglas Scott, "An Examination of Cartridges Cases and Bullets from the World War I Châtel Chéhéry Area, Argonne Forest, France," 17.

Bibliography

Archives

Army Historical and Education Center, Carlisle Barracks, Pennsylvania

82nd Division photos of the Meuse-Argonne battle terrain (including photos from where York fought on 8 October 1918 that were taken during the February 1919 investigation) and the original photo of York escorting the prisoners through Varennes-en-Argonne, a diverse photographic collection of the AEF in the Great War, Alvin C. York document collection, Meuse-Argonne document collection, 82nd Division documents and sources, 328th Regiment source data, list and citation of AEF Medal of Honor and Distinguished Service Cross recipients, U.S. War Department General Orders. Also:

Frasier, Lyman S. "Operations of the Third Battalion, 26th Infantry, First Division, Second and Third Phases of the Meuse-Argonne Offensive." Typescript, 1926.

"History of Company 'B,' 328th Infantry, 82nd Division." U.S. Army twenty-four-page typescript history containing an honor roll and a roster of all soldiers serving in the company.

U.S. Army. A.E.F. GHQ. American Official Communiqués. Bulletin no. 4, April 1920. Issued daily, 15 May–13 Dec 1918.

U.S. Army. Final Report of Gen. John J. Pershing. Washington, D.C.: Government Printing Office, 1920.

Bayerisches Hauptstaatarchiv, München, Federal Republic of Germany

History of the Bayerisches Mineur Battalion 3, Bayerisches Mineurkompanie 7, personal file and military service record of Leutnant Thoma.

Bundesarchiv-Militärarchiv, Freiburg, Federal Republic of Germany

Armee Gruppe Gallwitz, Armee Gruppe Argonnen, unit reports, daily records, orders, and directives.

Joint Forces Staff College Library, Norfolk, Virginia

Complete collection of American Battle Monuments Commission Great War battlefield guides/studies.

Landesarchiv Baden-Württemberg—Hauptstaatsarchiv Stuttgart,
Baden-Württemberg, Federal Republic of Germany

2. Landwehr Infanterie Division im Weltkrieg (1914–1918), officer roster, war service, battles, maps, overlays, deployment sheets, unit
log books, orders, guidance of division commander General Anton
Franke; 120. Württemberg Landwehr Infanterie Regiment im Weltkrieg (1914–1918), officer roster, war service, battles, maps, overlays, deployment sheets, unit log books, orders, personal files and
military service records of Leutnant Paul Vollmer, Leutnant Fritz
Endriss, Leutnant Karl Kübler; 122. Württemberg Landwehr Infanterie Regiment im Weltkrieg (1914–1918), officer roster, war service, battles, maps, overlays, deployment sheets, unit log books,
orders; 125. Württemberg Landwehr Infanterie Regiment im Weltkrieg (1914–1918), officer roster, war service, battles, maps, overlays, deployment sheets, unit log books, orders, personal files and
military service records of Hauptmann Müller, Leutnant Paul Lipp,
photographic collection of Württembergers im Weltkrieg. Also:

2. Württemberg Landwehr Division, Argonne Defensive Line, Ia 5608,
31 August 1918.

2nd Machine Company, 2nd Landwehr Division, Kriegstagebuch,
October 1918, Baden-Württemberg Hauptstaatsarchiv, Stuttgart,
Germany.

2nd Württemberg Landwehr Division, Divisional Situation Map, 4
October 1918, 1:25,000.

2nd Württemberg Landwehr Division, Divisional Situation Map, 5
October 1918, 1:25,000.

2nd Württemberg Landwehr Division, Divisional Situation Map/Over-
lay, 6 October 1918, 1:25,000 (Generalkommando z.b.v. 58, Fifth German Army, German Imperial Army).

2nd Württemberg Landwehr Division, Divisional Situation Map/Over-
lay, Ia6503, 7 October 1918, 1:25,000 (Generalkommando z.b.v. 58,
Fifth German Army, German Imperial Army).

2nd Württemberg Landwehr Division, Divisional Situation Map/Over-
lay, 9 October 1918, 1:25,000 (Generalkommando z.b.v. 58, Fifth German Army, German Imperial Army).

2nd Württemberg Landwehr Division, Divisional Situation Map/Over-
lay, 10 October 1918, 1:25,000 (Generalkommando z.b.v. 58, Fifth
German Army, German Imperial Army).

Gruppe Argonne and Gruppe Aisne unit deployment locations, 8 October 1918, 1:25,000 (Nr. 50, Nr. 51) (Generalkommando z.b.v. 58, Fifth
German Army, German Imperial Army).

Gruppe Argonne attack plan/objectives between Fleville and Gesnes,

Ia 6512, 7 October 1918 (Nr. 47a) (Generalkommando z.b.v. 58, Fifth German Army, German Imperial Army).

Gruppe Argonne Battle Log Book (Generalkommando z.b.v. 58, Fifth German Army).

Gruppe Argonne unit deployment locations, 7 October 1918 (Nr. 47) (Generalkommando z.b.v. 58, Fifth German Army, German Imperial Army).

Gruppe Argonne unit deployment locations/unit situations/front line trace of German forces, 6 October 1918 (Nr. 46) (Generalkommando z.b.v. 58, Fifth German Army, German Imperial Army).

Gruppe Argonne unit order of battle, 7 October 1918 (Generalkommando z.b.v. 58, Fifth German Army, German Imperial Army).

Landwehr-Infanterie-Regiment Nr. 120, Regimental structures and all operations, 1914– 1918, 120 Landwehr Regiment Kriegstagebuch.

Ludwigsburg Stadtsarchive, Baden-Württemberg, Federal Republic of Germany

History of and files associated with the Württembergers and Prussian army unit in the Great War.

Militärgeschichtliches Forschungsamt, Potsdam, Federal Republic of Germany

Regimental histories of the 120th, 122nd, and 125th Württemberg Landwehr Infanterie Regiments im Weltkrieg, 1914–1918.

National Archives and Records Administration, College Park, Maryland

Military records from the American Expeditionary Force, I Corps, V Corps, 82nd Infantry Division, 164th Infantry Brigade, 327th Infantry Regiment, 328th Infantry Regiment, unit dispatches, and courier messages between the 82nd Division, the 328th Regiment and its 1st, 2nd, and 3rd Battalions, several captured German documents on Armee Gruppe Argonne, Army Gruppe Gallwitz, and 2nd Landwehr Division, as well as German and American period photographs taken between 1914–1919, related Henry Swindler documents, York papers and documents to support 1929 Army War College York Exposition, American Battle Monuments Commission reports, and files related to battle. Also:

1st Foot Guard Regiment, written by Major General Eitel Friedrich, Prince of Prussia. Defense of the Tiefland Sector of Group Argonne, September–October 1918.

1st Guard Field Artillery Regiment, written by Herrmann Kohn. Defense of the Tiefland Sector of Group Argonne, September–October 1918.

2nd Foot Guard Regiment, written by Major General von Brauchtisch. Defense of the Tiefland Sector of Group Argonne, September–October 1918.

2nd Landwehr Division, Divisional Situation Report (Generalkommando z.b.v. 58, Fifth German Army, German Imperial Army notebooks 4, 5), 6–9 October 1918.

3rd Foot Guard Regiment, vol. 2, written by Lieutenant Michaelis. Defense of the Tiefland Sector of Group Argonne, September–October 1918.

4th Foot Guard Artillery Regiment, written by Lieutenant Colonel Freiherr von Braun. Defense of the Tiefland Sector of Group Argonne, September–October 1918.

4th Foot Guard Regiment, written by Colonel Wilhelm Reinhard. Defense of the Tiefland Sector of Group Argonne, September–October 1918.

270th Field Artillery Regiment, written by Dr. (Lieutenant) Hans Wiglow. Defense of the Tiefland Sector of Group Argonne, September–October 1918.

Artillery Kdr. No. 148, ktb., Kriegstagebuch, 1 September 1918 through 18 October 1918.

Burtt, Wilson B. "Explanation and Execution of Plans of Operation—5th Army Corps— Argonne-Meuse Operation." AEF, 1919.

Generalkommando z.b.v. 58, Fifth German Army, Battle Logs, 25 September 1918 through 4 October 1918.

Kohn, Herrmann. "Notes and Translations of Texts of the Histories of the Following German Regiment, which took part in the Defense of Teifland Sector of Group Argonne: Meuse-Argonne Offensive, September–October, 1918." Typescript, 1930.

Michaelis. "Notes and Translations of Part of Texts of the Histories of the German Regiment, which took part in the Defense of Tiefland Sector of Group Argonne: Meuse-Argonne Offensive, Sep–Oct 1918." Typescript, 1930.

U.S. American Battle Monuments Commission. *Terrain Photographs, American World War.* 69 vols. Photo Archives.

National Archives (Southeast Region), Morrow, Georgia

Alvin C. York conscientious objector records, exemption requests, and draft card, complete draft records.

National Personnel Records Center, Military Personnel Records (NPRC-MPR), St. Louis, Missouri

Alvin C. York Military Service Record, including the following primary source materials: Alvin C. York military records, medical records, conscientious objection requests/reports, discharge papers, congressional efforts to promote to officer and retirement, orders and rescinded request to recover the York .45 ACP, military award file, public disclosure requests, official correspondences, pension requests, American Legion requests, and requests to support making of the *Sergeant York* movie.

New York Times *Archive*

A wide range of hundreds of articles, stories, and press reports on Alvin C. York, commencing in April 1919 with the report of his exploits and ending in October 2006 with the discovery of the site where his battlefield exploit occurred.

Rottweil Stadtsarchive, Baden-Württemberg, Federal Republic of Germany

History of and files associated with the Württembergers im Weltkrieg.

Tennessee State Library and Archives, Nashville, Tennessee

Dittfurth, Dixie. "The Tennessee Society of New York."

Ulm Stadtsarchive, Baden-Württemberg, Federal Republic of Germany

History of and files associated with the Württembergers im Weltkrieg.

University of Kentucky, Special Collections, Lexington, Kentucky

Duncan, George Brand. "Reminiscences, 1886–1919." Typescript. 2 vols.

U.S. Library of Congress, Washington, D.C.

Congressional Record, Report of Alvin C. York, U.S. Senate, 75th Cong., 1st Sess., Report 120, 24 February 1937; Cordell Hull Papers, Hearing before Congress in Committee on Military Affairs related to House Resolution 8599 (1919), Propaganda Hearings in Motion Pictures, 77th Congress (1941).

Warner Bros. Archives, School of Cinematic Arts, University of Southern California, Los Angeles, California

Sergeant York movie archival information; *Sergeant York* still photo archive; Jesse Lasky movie, contractual, and other significant legal files; Jack Warner files, correspondences; Harry Warner correspondences, inter-office communication; screenplay and correspondences related to the story development between Joseph Josephson, Harry Chandlee, Abem Finkel; movie set sketches/drawings; interview sheets from York's neighbors; backstory history; research department commentary; payment sheets accounting for funds to pay living individuals and actors; signed affidavits of Cordell Hull, General Duncan, Colonel Buxton, Captain Danforth, Sergeant Parsons, Sergeant Early, Corporal Merrithew (Cutting), Privates Muzzi, Sacina, Beardsley, Sok, Wills, Johnson, Donohue, and Sok.

Published Sources

Alder, Major J. O. *History of the Seventy-Seventh Division.* New York: Hynkoop, Hallenbeck and Crawford, 1919.

Allen, H. Warner. "The American Achievement." *National Review,* June 1919.

American Battle Monuments Commission. *1st Division: Summary of Operations in the World War.* Washington, D.C.: Government Printing Office, 1944.

———. *28th Division: Summary of Operations in the World War.* Washington, D.C.: Government Printing Office, 1944.

———. *42d Division: Summary of Operations in the World War.* Washington, D.C.: Government Printing Office, 1944.

———. *77th Division: Summary of Operations in the World War.* Washington, D.C.: Government Printing Office, 1944.

———. *82d Division: Summary of Operations in the World War.* Washington, D.C.: Government Printing Office, 1944.

———. *American Armies and Battlefields in Europe: A History, Guide, and Reference Book.* Washington, D.C.: Government Printing Office, 1938.

Andrews, Peter. *Sergeant York: Reluctant Hero.* New York: Putnam, 1969.

Andriessen, J. H. J. *World War I.* Lisse, Netherlands: Rebo Publishers, 2006.

Arce, Hector. *Gary Cooper: An Intimate Biography.* New York: Morrow, 1979.

Asprey, Robert B. *The German High Command at War.* New York: Morrow, 1959.

Audoin-Rouzeau, Stephane, and Annette Becker. *14–18: Understanding the Great War.* New York: Hill and Wang, 2002.

Ayres, Leonard P. *The War with Germany: A Statistical Summary,* 2nd ed. Washington, D.C.: Government Printing Office, 1919.

Bachman, Senator Nathan L. "Alvin C. York." U.S. Congress, Senate Committee on Military Affairs. Report No. 120, 24 February 1937. Washington, D.C.: Government Printing Office, 1937.

Baker, Chester. *Doughboy's Diary.* Shippensburg, Pa.: Burd Street Press, 1998.

Baker, Newton. *America at War.* New York: Dodd and Mead, 1931.

Ball, Robert W. *Mauser Military Rifles of the World.* Iola, Wisc.: Krause, 2006.

Barker, Bryon W. *History of the Machine Gun Company, 328 Infantry, 82nd*

Division. Worcester, Mass.: Belisle Printing and Publishing Company, 1919.

Barnard, Ellsworth. *Wendell Willkie: Fighter for Freedom.* Marquette, Mich.: Northern Michigan Univ. Press, 1966.

Bean, Charles, ed. *Official History of Australia in the War of 1914–1918,* vol. 1, *The Story of ANZAC from the Outbreak of War to the End of the First Phase of the Gallipoli Campaign, May 4, 1915.* Brisbane, Australia: Univ. of Queensland Press, 1980.

———. *Official History of Australia in the War of 1914–1918,* vol. 2, *The Story of ANZAC from 4 May, 1915, to the Evacuation of the Gallipoli Peninsula.* Brisbane, Australia: Univ. of Queensland Press, 1980.

Beattie, Taylor V. "Continuing the Search for York." *Army History* (winter 2008): 20–28.

Beattie, Taylor V., and Ronald Bowman. "In Search of York: Man, Myth, and Legend." *Army History* (summer/fall 2000): 1–14.

Beery, Henry. *Make the Kaiser Dance.* New York: Arbor House, 1978.

Behlmer, Rudy. *Inside Warner Bros., 1935–1951.* New York: Simon and Schuster, 1985.

Behr, Edward. *Prohibition: Thirteen Years that Changed America.* New York: Arcade, 1996.

Belloc, Hilaire. "America in the Argonne." *American Legion* (November 1928): 44–46.

Bennett, William J. *The Book of Man: Who Are Men, Who Should Men Be, What Should Men Do?* Nashville, Tenn.: Nelson, 2011.

Bentley, Eric. *Thirty Years of Treason: Excerpts from Hearings before the House Committee on Un-American Activities, 1938–1968.* New York: Viking, 1971.

Biddle, John. *Soldier's Handbook of the Rifle: United States Rifle Model of 1917.* Washington, D.C.: Government Printing Office, November 1917.

Birdwell, Michael. *Celluloid Soldiers.* New York: New York Univ. Press, 2000.

Bloch, Marc. *Memoirs of War.* New York: Cambridge Univ. Press, 1988.

Booth, Evangeline. *The War Romance of the Salvation Army.* Philadelphia, Pa.: J. B. Lippincott, 1919.

Borchard, Edwin M., and William P. Lange. *Neutrality for the United States,* 2d ed. New Haven, Conn.: Yale Univ. Press, 1940.

Bowers, John. "The Mythical Morning of Sergeant York." *Military History Quarterly* 8 (winter 1996): 38–47.

Braim, Paul F. *The Test of Battle.* Shippensburg, Pa.: White Mane Books, 1998.

Braodus, John Albert. *A Treatise on the Preparation and Delivery of Sermons.* New York: A. C. Armstrong and Son, 1894.

Brinkley, Alan. *Voices of Protest: Huey Long, Father Coughlin and the Great Depression.* New York: Vintage, 1982.

Brisbane, Arthur. *U.S. Official Pictures of the World War.* Washington, D.C.: Pictorial Bureau, 1920.

Britt, George. *The Fifth Column.* New York: Cornwall Press, 1940.

Brittain, Vera. *Testament of Youth.* New York: Penguin Books, 1993.

Buchner, Adolf, and Hermann Hoppe. *In Stellung nach Vauquois.* Nördlingen: F. Steinmeier, 1986.

Budreau, Lisa M. *Bodies of War: World War One and the Politics of Commemoration in America, 1919–1933.* New York: New York Univ. Press, 2010.

Bull, Stephen. *World War I Trench Warfare.* 2 vols. Oxford, UK: Osprey, 2002.

Burg, Maclyn, ed. *The Great War at Home and Abroad: WW I Diaries and Letters of W. Stull Holt.* Manhattan, Kans.: Sunflower Univ. Press, 1999.

Burke, Heather, and Claire Smith. *The Archeologist's Field Handbook.* Crow's Nest, New South Wales, Australia: Allen and Unwin, 2004.

Butler, Alan B. *Happy Days!* New York: Osprey, 2011.

Buxton, G. Edward, Jr., et al. *Official History of 82nd Division American Expeditionary Forces, 1917–1919.* Indianapolis, Ind.: Bobbs-Merrill, 1920.

Byerly, Betty. *Dad's Diary—1918.* Bloomington, Ind.: 1st Books Library, 2002.

Cahill, Robert Ellis. "America Needed a Hero." In *War Wonders.* Peabody, Mass.: Chandler-Smith Publishing, 1984.

Canfield, Bruce. *U.S. Infantry Weapons of the First World War.* Lincoln, R.I.: Mowbray, 2000.

Carpozi, George. *The Gary Cooper Story.* New Rochelle, N.Y.: Arlington House, 1970.

Ceplair, Larry, and Steven Englund. *The Inquisition in Hollywood: Politics and the Film Community, 1930–1960.* Garden City, N.Y.: Anchor Press/Doubleday, 1980.

Chadwin, Mark Lincoln. *The Hawks of World War II.* Chapel Hill: Univ. of North Carolina Press, 1968.

Chaliand, Gerard. "Peter the Great." In *The Art of War in World History: From Antiquity to the Nuclear Age.* Los Angeles: Univ. of California Press, 1994.

Chambers, John Whiteclay. *To Raise an Army: The Draft Comes to Modern America.* New York: Free Press, 1987.

Chandler, Scott. *History of the Three Hundred and Twenty-Eighth Regiment of Infantry, Eighty-Second Division. American Expeditionary Forces, United States Army.* Atlanta: Foote and Davies, 1920.

Chang, Iris. *The Rape of Nanking: The Forgotten Holocaust of World War II.* New York: Basic Books, 1997.

Chase, Joseph Cummings. *Soldiers All: Portraits and Sketches of the Men of the A.E.F.* New York: Doran, 1920.

Churchill, Winston S. *Memoirs of the Second World War.* New York: Houghton-Mifflin, 1991.

Clausewitz, Carl von. *On War.* Princeton, N.J.: Princeton Univ. Press, 1984.

Clemenceau, Georges. *Grandeur and Misery of Victory.* New York: Harcourt, Brace, 1930.

Coffmann, Edward. *The War to End All Wars.* Lexington: Univ. of Kentucky Press, 1998.

Cole, Wayne S. *America First: The Battle against Intervention, 1940–1941.* Madison: Univ. of Wisconsin Press, 1953.

————. *Charles A. Lindbergh and the Battle against Intervention in World War II.* New York: Harcourt Brace Jovanovich, 1974.

————. *Senator Gerald P. Nye and American Foreign Relations.* Minneapolis: Univ. of Minnesota Press, 1962.

Colman, Juliet Cox. *John Gordon: Invictus.* New York: Vantage Press, 1981.

"Conscience Plus Red Hair Are Bad for Germans." *Literary Digest,* 14 June 1919.

Cooke, James J. *The All-Americans at War: The 82nd Division in the Great War, 1917–1918.* Westport, Conn.: Praeger, 1999.

Cowan, Sam K. *Sergeant York and His People.* New York: Funk and Wagnalls, 1922.

Crosby, Alfred W. *America's Forgotten Pandemic: The Influenza of 1918.* New York: Cambridge Univ. Press, 2003.

Culbert, David, ed. *Film and Propaganda in America: A Documented History.* New York: Greenwood Press, 1990.

Day, Charles M. "The B That Stung: B Company, 328th Regiment, on the War Path." Pamphlet. St. Paul: Minnesota Historical Society, War Records Commission, 1919.

Delbrück, Hans, *Modern Military History.* London: Univ. of Nebraska Press, 1997.

Dem Gedächtnis Unserer Gefallen Kameraden Das Offizierkorps des Infanterie Regiments Kaiser Wilhelm König von Preussen (2. Württ) Nr. 120. Bearb. Von Herbert Maisch, Ulm 1923.

Devlin, Patrick. *Too Proud to Fight: Woodrow Wilson's Neutrality.* New York: Oxford Univ. Press, 1975.

Divine, Robert A. *The Illusion of Neutrality.* Chicago: Univ. of Chicago Press, 1962.

Divisionstab. Die 26, Infanterie Division (1 Kgl.Württ) im Krieg 1914–1918. Stuttgart: Stable and Friedel, 1920.

Doenecke, Justus D. *In Danger Undaunted: The Anti-Interventionist*

Movement of 1940–1941 as Revealed in the Papers of the America First Committee. Stanford, Calif: Hoover Institute Press, 1990.

———. *Storm on the Horizon.* New York: Rowman and Littlefield, 2000.

Doherty, Thomas. *Projections of War: Hollywood, American Culture, and World War II.* New York: Columbia Univ. Press, 1993.

Duffy, Christopher. *The Military Life of Frederick the Great.* New York: Atheneum, 1986.

Durlewanger, A. *Das Drama des Lingenkopfes.* Ingersheim, Colmar, France: S.A.E.P., 1988.

Ebel, Jonathan H. *Faith in the Fight: Religion and the American Soldier in the Great War.* Princeton, N.J.: Princeton Univ. Press, 2010.

Edwards, Jerome E. *The Foreign Policy of Col. McCormick's Tribune, 1929–1941.* Reno: Univ. of Nevada Press, 1971.

Eisenhower, John S. D. *Yanks.* New York: Simon and Schuster, 2001.

Eisnecker, A. "Kammer Diener: Vor 120 Jahren begann die Karriere der Patrone 8 x 57." *Visier,* 12 December 2008.

Engelbrecht, H. C., and F. C. Hanighen. *Merchants of Death: A Study of the International Armament Industry.* New York: Harper and Brothers, 1934.

"Fentress Feud." *Time,* 25 May 1936, 26.

Ferrell, Robert H. *America's Deadliest Battle.* Lawrence: Univ. Press of Kansas, 2007.

Fogel, Robert. *The Fourth Great Awakening and the Future of Egalitarianism.* Chicago: Univ. of Chicago Press, 2000.

Fogel, Robert William, and G. R. Elton. *Which Road to the Past?* New Haven, Conn.: Yale Univ. Press, 1984.

Fogel, Robert William, and Stanley L. Engerman. *Time on the Cross: Evidence and Methods.* Boston: Little, Brown, 1974.

Ford, Nancy. *Americans All! Foreign Born Soldiers in World War I.* College Station: Texas A&M Univ. Press, 2001.

Fosten, Donald. *The German Army 1914–1918.* Oxford, UK: Osprey, 1978.

Franke, Anton. *Die 2. Württemberg Landwehr Division Im Weltkrieg 1914–1918.* Stuttgart: Verlag Bergers Literarchives, 1921.

Freedland, Michael. *The Warner Brothers.* New York: St. Martin's, 1983.

Gabler, Neal. *An Empire of Their Own.* New York: Crown Publishers, 1988.

Gawne, Jonathon. *Over There! The American Soldier in World War I.* Mechanicsburg, Pa.: Stackpole, 1997.

Gehman, Richard. *The Tall American.* New York: Hawthorne Books, 1963.

German General Staff. *The German Forces in the Field.* London: Imperial War Museum, 1995.

German Military History. Fort Leavenworth, Kans.: Combat Studies Institute, 1994.

Giehrl, Herman von. "Battle of the Meuse-Argonne." *Infantry Journal* (August 1921): 131–138.

Gillette, Ward, A. *The Meuse-Argonne Offensive, First Phase.* Fort Benning, Ga.: Infantry School, 1937.

Görlitz, Walter. *The Kaiser and His Court.* London: Macdonald and Company, 1961.

Graevenitz, Fritz von. *Die deutsche Oberste Fuhrung im Weltkrieg in ihnen Bedeutung fur die Württembergishchen Steitkrafte.* Stuttgart: Bergers, 1921.

———. *Die Entwicklung des Württembergishche Heerwesens im Rahmen des deutschen Reichheerews.* Stuttgart: Bergers, 1921.

Gregory, Barry. *Argonne.* New York: Ballantine, 1972.

Grieves, Keith. *The Politics of Manpower, 1914–1918.* Manchester, England: Manchester Univ. Press, 1988.

Grotelueschen, Mark Ethan. *The AEF Way of War: The American Army and Combat in World War One.* Cambridge, England: Cambridge Univ. Press, 2007.

Gruppo, Giunti. *Der Erste Weltkrieg.* Florenz: Gruppo Editoriale, 1999.

Gudmundsson, Bruce I. *Stormtroop Tactics: Innovation in the German Army, 1914–1918.* New York: Praeger, 1989.

Guerard, von. *Von Reims bis zu den Argonnen.* Leipzig: Grethlein, 1918.

Guthrie, Paul. "Tracking Sgt. York in the Argonne Forest." *Camraderie,* Western Front Association (August 2007): 11–12.

Hamann, Brant, and Dr. Windisch. *Die Militärpatronen Kaliber 7,9 mm: ihre Vorläufer und Abarten.* Schwabish Hall, Germany: Journal-Verlag Schwend, 1981.

Hanlon, Michael. *The St. Mihiel Battle.* http://www.worldwar1.com/dbc/stmihiel.htm. Accessed 15 March 2011.

Harder, Hans-Joachim. *Militäreschichtliches Handbuch Baden-Württemberg.* Stuttgart: Kohlhammer, 1987.

Harris, Harvey. *The War as I Saw It: 1918 Letters of a Tank Corps Lieutenant.* Saint Paul, Minn.: Pogo Press, 1998.

Hay, Donald. "Machine Guns, 35th Division, Meuse-Argonne, 26 Sep–1 Oct 1918." *Infantry Journal* (May/June 1933).

Heard, Brian J. *Handbook of Firearms and Ballistics: Examining and Interpreting Forensic Evidence.* The Atrium, Southern Gate, Chichester, West Sussex, England: Wiley-Blackwell, 2008.

Henry, Mark. *U.S. Army of World War I.* Oxford, UK: Osprey, 2003.

Herwig, Holger H. *The First World War: Germany and Austria-Hungary 1914–1918.* London: Arnold Publishing, 1997.

Higham, Charles. *Warner Bros.* New York: Charles Scribner's Sons, 1975.

Hiller, Marlene, chief ed. "Kaiser Wilhelm II 1859–1941." *DAMALS* (August 2004): 84.

Hinderburg, Generalfeldmarshall Paul von. *Aus Meinem Leben*. Leipzig: Hirzel, 1920.

Hirschorn, Clive. *The Warner Bros. Story*. New York: Crown, 1979.

Hoff, Thomas. *U.S. Doughboys 1916–1919*. Oxford, UK: Osprey, 2005.

Holden, Frank A. *War Memories*. Athens, Ga.: Athens Book Company, 1922.

Holt, Toni, and Valmai Holt. *Major and Mrs. Holt's Battlefield Guide to the Western Front—South*. South Yorkshire, UK: Pen and Sword, 2005.

Hoobler, James A. "Sergeant York Historic Area." *Tennessee Historical Quarterly* 38 (spring 1979): 3–8.

Horne, Charles F., ed. *Source Records of the Great War*, vol. 6. 1918. Reprint, New York: National Alumni, 1923.

Howard, Michael. *War in European History*. Oxford, UK: Oxford Univ. Press, 1976.

Hull, Cordell. "Hearing before the Committee on Military Affairs— House Resolution 8599 to Appoint Alvin C. York to Second Lieutenant, with Pay and Benefits of a Retired Officer." 66th Cong., 1st Sess. Washington, D.C.: Government Printing Office, 1919.

———. *The Memoirs of Cordell Hull*. New York: Macmillan, 1948.

Humble, R. G. *A Christian Patriot*. Circleville, Ohio: Churches of Christ in Christian Union, 1966.

Huston, John. *An Open Book*. New York: Knopf, 1980.

Ickes, Harold. *The Lowering Clouds, 1939–1941*. New York: Simon and Schuster, 1954.

Idler, Roland. "Die Geschichte des Wilhelm Härer." *Der Bezirksverbank Nord Württemberg*. Baden-Württemberg: Gerhard Fritz, 2009.

———. "Heimkehr nach 90 Jahren—Das Schicksal des im Ersten Weltkrieg vermissten Steinbachers Wilhelm Härer (1882 bis 1918)." *Backnanger Jahrbuch 2009*, Band 17. Backnang: Stroh, 2009.

Innes, T. A. *Covenants with Death*. London: Daily Express, 1934.

James, Garry. "Sgt. York American Rifleman American Hero." *American Rifleman*, March 2005, 46.

Johnson, Niall, and Jürgen Mueller. "Updating the Accounts: Global Mortality of the 1918–1920 Spanish Influenza Pandemic." *Bulletin of the History of Medicine* (spring 2002): 105–115.

Johnson, Thomas M. *The Lost Battalion*. Lincoln: Univ. of Nebraska Press, 2000.

Jomini, Henri. *The Art of War*. Westport, Conn.: Greenwood, 1971.

Jones, Herbert D. N. *History of C. Company, 328th Infantry*. Brooklyn, N.Y.: Hunter Collins, 1919.

Jünger, Ernst. *The Storm of Steel*. New York: Howard Fertig, 1996.

Katcher, Philip. *The American Soldier*. New York: Military Press, 1990.

Kauffman, Bill. *America First!: Its History, Culture and Politics*. New York: Prometheus, 1995.

Keegan, John. *The Face of Battle*. London: Penguin, 1976.

———. *The First World War*. New York: Knopf, 2001.

Keith, Jeanette. *Country People of the New South: Tennessee's Upper Cumberland Valley*. Chapel Hill: Univ. of North Carolina Press, 1995.

Kellermann, Bernhard. *Der Krieg im Argonnerwald*. Berlin, Germany: Julius Bard, 1916.

Kelly, C. Brian. Editorial on other WWI American heroes besides Alvin York. *Military History*, 6 December 1989, 6.

Kent, Daniel W. *German 7.9 mm Military Ammunition, 1888–1945*. Ann Arbor, Mich.: Edwards Brothers, 1973.

King, Thomas F., U.S. Department of Interior. *The Archeological Survey: Methods and Uses*. Washington, D.C.: Government Printing Office, 1978.

Kirchbach, Arndt. *Kampfe Im Champagne*. Oldenburg: Gerhard Stalling, 1919.

Kitchen, Martin. *The German Offensives of 1918*. Gloucestershire, England: Tempus Printing, 2005.

Kling, Rektor. *Das Württembergishche Landwehr Infanterie Regiment nr. 122 im Weltkrieg 1914–1918*, Band 27. Stuttgart: Belser, 1923.

Kniptash, Vernon E. *On the Western Front with the Rainbow Division: A World War I Diary*. Norman: Univ. of Oklahoma Press, 2009.

Koch, Howard. *As Time Goes By: Memoirs of a Writer*. New York: Harcourt Brace Jovanovich, 1979.

Koppes, Clayton R., and Gregory D. Black. *Hollywood Goes to War: How Politics, Profits and Propaganda Shaped World War II Movies*. Berkeley: Univ. of California Press, 1990.

Kriegsministerium. *Schiessvorschrift für die Infanterie*. Berlin: Ernst Siegfried Mittler und Sohn, 1909.

Kuhnhausen, Jerry. *The Colt .45 Automatic, A Shop Manual*. McCall, Idaho: Heritage—VSP Shop Manual, 1990.

Lacorde, Dominique. *Gesnes en-Argonne*. Fort Moselle, France: L'Imprierie, 2005.

LaFeber, Walter. *The American Age: United States Foreign Policy at Home and Abroad*. New York: Norton, 1994.

Langille, Leslie. *42: Men of the Rainbow*. Chicago: O'Sullivan Publishing House, 1933.

Laparra, Hean-Claude. *The German Infantryman 1914–1918*. Paris: Histories and Collections, 2008.

Lapple, Viktor-Karl. *Das Württembergische Landwehr Infanterie Regiment Nr. 125 Im Weltkrieg 1914–1918*, Band 38. Stuttgart: Belser, 1926.

Larrabee, George. "Sharpshooter from the Hills: The Amazing Sergeant

Alvin York Was the Ultimate Infantryman." *Military History,* June 1987, 10, 56–57.

Larsen, Lawrence H. "Gerald Nye and the Isolationist Argument." *North Dakota History* 47 (winter 1980): 25–27.

Lasky, Jesse L., with Don Weldon. *I Blow My Own Horn.* Garden City, N.Y.: Doubleday, 1957.

Lasky, Jesse L., Jr. *Whatever Happened to Hollywood?* New York: Funk and Wagnalls, 1975.

Lavine, Harold. *War Propaganda and the United States.* New Haven, Conn.: Yale Univ. Press, 1940.

Lawrence, Major R. B. *Military Exposition and Carnival: War College 3–5 October, 1929.* Washington, D.C.: Government Printing Office, 1929.

———. "Sergeant York—American Soldier." *Military Exposition and Carnival: War College 3–5 October, 1929.* Washington, D.C.: Government Printing Office, 1929.

Leatherman, Noah H. *Diary.* Rosenort, Manitoba, Canada: Prairie View Press, 1973.

Lee, David D. *Sergeant York: An American Hero.* Lexington: Univ. Press of Kentucky, 1985.

Legge, Barnwell R. *The First Division in the Meuse-Argonne September 26–October 12, 1918.* Fort Benning, Ga.: Infantry School, Dept. of General Studies, Military History Section, 1923.

Lengel, Edward G. *To Conquer Hell.* New York: Henry Holt and Company, 2008.

Liddell Hart, B. H. *Reputations Ten Years After.* Boston: Little, Brown, 1928.

Liggett, Major General Hunter. *A.E.F.: Ten Years Ago in France.* New York: Dodd, Mead, 1928.

———. *Commanding an American Army: Recollections of the World War.* Boston: Houghton Mifflin, 1925.

Lindbergh, Anne Morrow. *The Flower and the Nettle: Diaries and Letters, 1936–1939.* New York: Harcourt Brace Jovanovitch, 1976.

Lindbergh, Charles. *The Wartime Journals of Charles A. Lindbergh.* New York: Harcourt, 1970.

Lockridge, Kenneth A. "Historic Demography." In *The Future of History: Essays in the Vanderbilt University Centennial Symposium,* edited by Charles Delzell. Nashville, Tenn.: Vanderbilt Univ. Press, 1977.

Ludendorff, Erich. *Meine Kriegserinnerungen.* Berlin: Ernst Siegfried Mittler und Sohn, 1919.

———. *My War Memories 1914–1918.* London: Hutchinson, 1919.

Lupfer, Timothy. *The Dynamics of Doctrine: Changes in Tactical Doctrine during the First World War.* Fort Leavenworth, Kans.: Combat Studies Institute, 1981.

Luther, Dr. Rev. Martin. *Smalcald Articles*. 1537. Translated by F. Bente. St. Louis, Mo.: Concordia Publishing House, 1921.

Lynn, John. *Battle: A History of Combat and Culture*. Cambridge, Mass.: Westview Press, 2003.

MacDonald, S. C. "Machine Gun Operations during the Attack of the 28th Division, Meuse-Argonne Offensive, 26 September to 8 October, 1918." Fort Leavenworth, Kans.: Command and General Staff College, 1936.

Mahoney, Tom. "Alvin York and Frank Luke." *American Legion Magazine*, 20 November 1968, 22–23.

———. "Sergeant Alvin York." *American Legion Magazine*, 20 November 1968, 45–46.

Marshall, George. *Memoirs of My Services in the World War, 1917–1918*. Boston: Houghton Mifflin, 1976.

Mast, Gerald. *Howard Hawks: Storyteller*. New York: Oxford Univ. Press, 1982.

Mastriano, Douglas. "Sergeant York Fought Here!" *Armchair General*, July 2007, 84–89.

Mattox, John Mark. *Saint Augustine and the Theory of Just War*. New York: Continuum, 2006.

Maurer, David W. *Kentucky Moonshine*. Lexington: Univ. Press of Kentucky, 1974.

McCollum, Lee Charles. *History and Rymes of the Lost Battalion*. Chicago: Foley, 1919.

McPhail, Helen. *The Long Silence*. London: Tauris, 2001.

Meilinger, Phillip S. "Mitchell Biography." In *American Airpower Biography: A Survey of the Field*. Montgomery, Ala.: Maxwell Air Force Base, 1997.

Merkatz, Freidrich von. *Unterrictsbuch fur die Maschinengewehr= Koampagnien*. Berlin: Eisenschmidt, 1917.

Michelin Tire Company. *The Americans in the Great War*. 3 vols. Milltown, N.J.: Michelin Tire Company, 1920.

Mitchell, William. *Memoirs of World War I: "From Start to Finish of Our Greatest War."* New York: Random House, 1928.

Montell, Lynwood. *Don't Go Up Kettle Creek: Verbal Legacy of the Upper Cumberland*. Knoxville: Univ. of Tennessee Press, 1985.

Moser, Otto von. *Die Württemberger im Weltkrieg*. Stuttgart: Christian-Belser, 1928.

Murray, Williams, ed. *The Making of Strategy: Rulers, States, and War*. Cambridge, UK: Cambridge Univ. Press, 1997.

Nash, David. *German Army Handbook April 1918*. London: Arms and Armour Press, 1977.

Nathusius, Martin. *Polte Armaturen- und Maschinenfabrik: 1885–1935, 50 Jahre Armaturen*. Magdeburg, Germany: Polte, 1935.

————. "Vor 50 Jahren wurde Polte gegründet. Jubiläum der angesehenen Magdeburger Maschinenfabrik." *Magdeburgische Zeitung*, 6–7 April 1925.

Neal, Steve. *Dark Horse: A Biography of Wendell Willkie*. New York: Doubleday, 1984.

Neiburg, Michael, ed. *Finding Common Ground*. Boston: Leiden, 2011.

New York Times. *The European War*, vol. 17, *October–November–December 1918*. New York: New York Times Company, 1919.

Niethammer, Herman. *Erinnerungsblätter aus der Geschichte des Regiments Kaiser Friedrich König von Preussen (7. Württ) Nr. 125*. Stuttgart: Christian Belser, 1934.

Nolan, Thomas. "Battlefield Landscapes." Ph.D. diss., Texas State University, May 2007.

Nye, Gerald. "Report of the Special Committee on Investigation of the Munitions Industry" (also called "The Nye Report"). U.S. Congress, Senate, 74th Congress, 2nd Sess., February 24, 1936. Washington, D.C.: Government Printing Office, 1936.

Oertel, Walter. *Die Waffentaten Württemberger im Bewegungskrieg*. Stuttgart: Stuttgarter Neues Tagblatt, 1934.

Official Camp Gordon Songbook. Camp Gordon, Ga.: 82nd Division, National Army, 1917.

Ogden, August Raymond. *The Dies Committee: A Study of the Special House Committee for Investigation of Un-American Activities, 1938–1944*. Washington, D.C.: Catholic Univ. Press, 1945.

O'Grady, Joseph P., ed. *The Immigrants' Influence on Wilson's Peace Policies*. Lexington: Univ. of Kentucky Press, 1967.

O'Leary, Jeff. *Brave Hearts under Red Skies*. Colorado Springs, Colo.: Cook Publishers, 2003.

Olmsted, Kathryn S. *Real Enemies*. New York: Oxford Univ. Press, 2009.

Palmer, Frederick. *Newton D. Baker*. New York: Dodd, Mead, 1931.

————. *Our Greatest Battle: The Meuse-Argonne*. New York: Dodd, Mead, 1919.

Parsons, Lynn H. *John Quincy Adams*. Madison, Wisc.: Madison House Book, 1998.

Passingham, Ian. *All the Kaiser's Men*. Gloucestershire, England: Sutton Mill, 2003.

Pattullo, George. "The Second Elder Gives Battle." *Saturday Evening Post*, April 1919.

Peek, E. D. "Army Engineer Operations in the St. Mihiel and Meuse-Argonne Offensive." *Military Engineer* (November/December 1922).

Pencak, William. *For God and Country: The American Legion, 1919–1941*. Boston, Mass.: Northeastern Univ. Press, 1989.

Perry, John. *Sgt. York: His Life, Legend and Legacy*. Nashville, Tenn.: Boardman and Holman, 1997.

Pershing, John J. *My Experiences in the World War*. 2 vols. New York: Stokes, 1931.

Pershing, John J., and Major General Hunter Liggett. *Report of the First Army, American Expeditionary Forces*. Fort Leavenworth, Kans.: General Service School Press, 1923.

Peters, Charles. *Five Days in Philadelphia: The Amazing "We Want Willkie" Convention of 1940 and How It Freed FDR to Save the Western World*. New York: Public Affairs, 2005.

Pettit, Dorothy Ann. *A Cruel Wind: Pandemic Flu in American 1918–1920*. Murfreesboro, Tenn.: Timberlane Books, 2008.

Phillips, Margaret. *The Governors of Tennessee*. Gretna, La.: Pelican, 2001.

Physical Evidence Program Manager. *Firearm/Toolmark Procedures Manual DFS Document 240-D100*. Richmond, Va.: Virginia Department of Forensic Science, 2007.

Pistorius, Theodor. *Die Letzen Tage des Königreichs Württemberg*. Stuttgart: Kohlhammer, 1935.

Ralphson, George. *Over There with the Yanks in the Argonne Forest*. Chicago: Donohue, 1920.

Rarey, George H. "American Tank Units in the Foret d'Argonne Attack." *Infantry Journal* (April 1928): 389–395.

Reilly, Henry J. *Americans All: The Rainbow at War: Official History of the 42d US Infantry Division*. Columbus, Ohio: Heer Publishing, 1936.

———. *America's Part*. New York: Cosmopolitan Books, 1938.

Remarque, Erich Marie. *All Quiet on the Western Front*. New York: Little, Brown, 1929.

Ridout, G. W. *The Greatest Soldier of the War*. Louisville, Ky.: Pentecostal Publishing Company, 1929.

Rogers, Sam L. *Religious Bodies 1916: Part II, Separate Denominations History, Description and Statistics*. Washington, D.C.: Department of Commerce, Bureau of the Census, 1919.

Roosevelt, Elliott (editor of Franklin Roosevelt's Papers). *His Personal Letters, 1928–1945*. New York: Duell, Sloan, and Pierce, 1950.

Roosevelt, Theodore, II. *Rank and File: True Stories of the Great War*. New York: Charles Scribner and Sons, 1928.

Rumer, Thomas A. *The American Legion: An Official History, 1919–1989*. New York: Evans, 1990.

Scammell, J. M. "The Argonne, 1914 and 1918." *Infantry Journal* (October 1929): 354–361.

Schaper, Michael, ed. "Der Erste Weltkrieg." *Geo Epoche* 14 (2007).

Schiller, David. "An Einem Tag im Oktober." *Visier: Internationale Waffen-Magazine*, December 2008, 134–146.

Schmidt, Ernst. *Argonnen: Schlacten des Weltkrieges,* Band 28. Berlin: Gerhard Stalling, 1927.

Schreiber, Shane B. *Shock Army of the British Empire.* St. Catharines, Ontario: Vanwell, 2004.

Schwartz, Nancy. *The Hollywood Writers' War.* New York: Knopf, 1982.

Scott, Dr. Douglas. "An Examination of Cartridges Cases and Bullets from the World War I Châtel Chéhéry Area, Argonne Forest, France." Department of Anthropology, University of Nebraska–Lincoln, Lincoln, Nebraska, 10 May 2010.

Scott, H. L. Major General, Army Chief of Staff. *Manual for Infantry.* Menasha, Wisc.: George Banta Publishing, 1917.

———. *Manual for Noncommissioned Officers and Privates of Infantry of the Army of the United States 1917.* Menasha, Wisc.: George Banta Publishing, 1917.

Seldte, Franz. *M.G.K.: Maschinen Gewehr Kompanie.* Leipzig: Köhler, 1929.

Seymore, Charles. *The Intimate Papers of Colonel House,* vols. 1–3. New York: Houghton Mifflin, 1926.

Sheffield, Gary. *Forgotten Victory.* London: Headline Book Publishing, 2001.

Sherry, Michael S. *In the Shadow of War.* New Haven, Conn.: Yale Univ. Press, 1995.

Shipley, Thomas. *The History of the A.E.F.* New York: Doran, 1920.

Silberreisen, Leutnant der Reserve. *Schwäbische Kunde aus dem Großen Krieg.* Stuttgart: Deutschen Verlags Anstalt, 1918.

Simon, A. D. *Das Infanterie Regiment "Kaiser Wilhelm, König von Preussen" (2. Württ) Nr. 120. im Weltkrieg 1914–1918.* Berlin: Christian Belshersche, 1922.

Skeyhill, Thomas J. *Sergeant York: Last of the Long Hunters.* Philadelphia: Winston, 1930.

———. *A Singing Soldier.* New York: Knickerbocker Press, 1919.

Smith, Diane Monroe. *Fanny and Joshua.* Lebanon, N.H.: Univ. Press of New England, 1999.

Smythe, Donald. "St.-Mihiel: The Birth of an American Army." In *In Defense of the Republic: Readings in American Military History,* edited by David Curtis Skaggs and Robert S. Browning III. Belmont, Calif.: Wadsworth, 1991.

Sotheby, Lionel. *Great War: Diaries and Letters from the Western Front.* Athens: Ohio Univ. Press, 1997.

Souvenir of Camp Gordon, Atlanta, Georgia. Atlanta, Ga.: Byrd Printing, 1918.

Stein, Kurt. *Das Württembergishche Landwehr Infanterie Regiment nr. 121 im Weltkrieg 1914–1918.* Band 4. Stuttgart: Belser, 1925.

Stenehjem, Michelle Flynn. *An American First: John T. Flynn and the America First Committee.* New York: Arlington House, 1976.

Stone, Lawrence. "History and the Social Sciences in the 20th Century." In *The Future of History: Essays in the Vanderbilt University Centennial Symposium,* edited by Charles Delzell. Nashville, Tenn.: Vanderbilt Univ. Press, 1977.

Storms, Roger C. *Partisan Prophets: A History of the Prohibition Party.* Denver: National Prohibition Foundation, 1972.

Strachan, Hew. *The First World War.* New York: Penguin, 2003.

Straub, Elmer Frank. *A Sergeant's Diary in the World War: The Diary of an Enlisted Member of the 150th Field Artillery, Rainbow Division.* Indianapolis: Indiana Historical Commission, 1923.

Strohm, Gustav. *Das Württembergishche Landwehr Infanterie Regiment nr. 120 im Weltkrieg 1914–1918.* Band 4. Stuttgart: Belser, 1920.

———. *Die Württembergishchen Regimenter im Weltkrieg 1914–1918,* Band 25, *Das Württembergishche Landwehr Infanterie Regiment nr. 120.* Stuttgart: Belser Verlasbuchhandklung, 1922.

Swindell, Larry. *The Last Hero: A Biography of Gary Cooper.* Garden City, N.Y.: Doubleday, 1980.

Swindler, Henry O. "Turkey Match." *Infantry Journal* 37, no. 4 (October 1930): 343–351.

Synan, Vinson. *The Holiness–Pentecostal Tradition: Charismatic Movements in the Twentieth Century.* Grand Rapids, Mich.: Eerdmans, 1997.

Terraine, John. *General Jack's Diary, 1914–1918: The Trench Diary of BG J. L. Jack.* London: Eyre and Spottiswoode, 1964.

———. *To Win a War: 1918, The Year of Victory.* London: Papermac, 1978.

Thomas, Bob. *Clown Prince of Hollywood: The Antic Life and Times of Jack Warner.* New York: McGraw-Hill, 1990.

Thomas, Nigel. *The German Army in World War I.* 3 vols. Oxford, UK: Osprey, 2003.

Thompson, Leroy. *The Colt 1911 Pistol.* Long Island City, N.Y.: Osprey, 2011.

Trask, David. *The AEF and Coalition Warmaking, 1917–1918.* Lawrence: Univ. Press of Kansas, 1993.

Triplet, William S. *A Youth in the Meuse-Argonne.* Columbia: Univ. of Missouri Press, 2000.

Trout, Steven. *On the Battlefield of Memory: The First World War and American Remembrance, 1919–1941.* Tuscaloosa: Univ. of Alabama Press, 2010.

Trumpbour, John. *Selling Hollywood to the World.* New York: Cambridge Univ. Press, 2002.

Turlock, Alice. *In the Hands of Providence.* Chapel Hill: Univ. of North Carolina Press, 1992.

Uncle Sam's Boys. Chicago: J. P. Black Publishing, 1918.

U.S. Army. *Army Leadership.* Field Manual 6-22. Washington, D.C.: Department of the Army, October 2006.

———. *History of Three Hundred and Twenty Eighth Regiment of Infantry.* Atlanta, Ga.: Foote and Davis, 1922.

———. *Intelligence Analysis.* Field Manual 34-3. Washington, D.C.: Department of the Army, 1990.

———. *Intelligence Preparation of the Battlefield.* Field Manual 34-130. Washington, D.C.: Department of the Army, July 1994.

———. *Military Leadership.* Field Manual 22-100. Washington, D.C.: Department of the Army, July 1990

———. *United States Army in the World War, 1917–1919,* vol. 1, *Organization of the American Expeditionary Forces.* 1948. Reprint, Washington, D.C.: U.S. Army Center of Military History, 1988. CMH Pub 23-6, GPO S/N 008-029-00176-4.

———. *United States Army in the World War, 1917–1919,* vol. 2, *Policy-Forming Documents of the American Expeditionary Forces.* 1948. Reprint, Washington, D.C.: U.S. Army Center of Military History, 1989. CMH Pub 23-7.

———. *United States Army in the World War, 1917–1919,* vol. 3, *Training and Use of American Units with the British and French.* 1948. Reprint, Washington, D.C.: U.S. Army Center of Military History, 1989. CMH Pub 23-8.

———. *United States Army in the World War, 1917–1919,* vol. 4, *Early Military Operations of the American Expeditionary Forces.* 1948. Reprint, Washington, D.C.: U.S. Army Center of Military History, 1989. CMH Pub 23-9.

———. *United States Army in the World War, 1917–1919,* vol. 5, *Military Operations of the American Expeditionary Forces.* 1948. Reprint, Washington, D.C.: U.S. Army Center of Military History, 1989. CMH Pub 23-10.

———. *United States Army in the World War, 1917–1919,* vol. 6, *Military Operations of the American Expeditionary Forces.* 1948. Reprint, Washington, D.C.: U.S. Army Center of Military History, 1990. CMH Pub 23-11.

———. *United States Army in the World War, 1917–1919,* vol. 7, *Military Operations of the American Expeditionary Forces.* 1948. Reprint, Washington, D.C.: U.S. Army Center of Military History, 1990. CMH Pub 23-12.

———. *United States Army in the World War, 1917–1919,* vol. 8, *Military Operations of the American Expeditionary Forces.* 1948. Reprint, Washington, D.C.: U.S. Army Center of Military History, 1990. CMH Pub 23-13.

———. *United States Army in the World War, 1917–1919*, vol. 9, *Military Operations of the American Expeditionary Forces.* 1948. Reprint, Washington, D.C.: U.S. Army Center of Military History, 1990. CMH Pub 23-14.

———. *United States Army in the World War, 1917–1919*, vol. 10-1, *The Armistice Agreement and Related Documents.* 1948. Reprint, Washington, D.C.: U.S. Army Center of Military History, 1991. CMH Pub 23-15.

———. *United States Army in the World War, 1917–1919*, vol. 10-2, *The Armistice Agreement and Related Documents.* 1948. Reprint, Washington, D.C.: U.S. Army Center of Military History, 1991. CMH Pub 23-16.

———. *United States Army in the World War, 1917–1919*, vol. 11, *American Occupation of Germany.* 1948. Reprint, Washington, D.C.: U.S. Army Center of Military History, 1991. CMH Pub 23-17.

———. *United States Army in the World War, 1917–1919*, vol. 12, *Reports of the Commander-in-Chief, AEF, Staff Sections and Services.* 1948. Reprint, Washington, D.C.: U.S. Army Center of Military History, 1991. CMH Pub 23-18.

———. *United States Army in the World War, 1917–1919*, vol. 13, *Reports of the Commander-in-Chief, AEF, Staff Sections and Services.* 1948. Reprint, Washington, D.C.: U.S. Army Center of Military History, 1991. CMH Pub 23-19.

———. *United States Army in the World War, 1917–1919*, vol. 14, *Reports of the Commander-in-Chief, AEF, Staff Sections and Services.* 1948. Reprint, Washington, D.C.: U.S. Army Center of Military History, 1991. CMH Pub 23-20.

———. *United States Army in the World War, 1917–1919*, vol. 15, *Reports of the Commander-in-Chief, AEF, Staff Sections and Services.* 1948. Reprint, Washington, D.C.: U.S. Army Center of Military History, 1991. CMH Pub 23-21.

———. *United States Army in the World War, 1917–1919*, vol. 16, *General Orders, GHQ, AEF.* 1948. Reprint, Washington, D.C.: U.S. Army Center of Military History, 1992. CMH Pub 23-22.

———. *United States Army in the World War, 1917–1919*, vol. 17, *Bulletins, GHQ, AEF.* 1948. Reprint, Washington, D.C.: U.S. Army Center of Military History, 1992. CMH Pub 23-23.

U.S. Army, American Expeditionary Forces, General Staff College. *Staff Ride: Meuse-Argonne Operations.* Chaumont, France: AEF, January 1919.

U.S. Army, AEF, G2. *The German and American Combined Daily Order of Battle, 25 Sep to 11 Nov 1918.* Chaumont, France: AEF, 1919.

U.S. Army, Center of Military History. *Order of Battle of the United States*

Land Forces in the World War, vol. 1, *American Expeditionary Forces: General Headquarters, Armies, Army Corps, Services of Supply, and Separate Forces* (CMH Pub 23-1). 1988. Reprint, Washington, D.C.: Government Printing Office, 1937.

—————. *Order of Battle of the United States Land Forces in the World War,* vol. 2, *American Expeditionary Forces: Divisions* (CMH Pub 23-2). 1988. Reprint, Washington, D.C.: Government Printing Office, 1937.

—————. *Order of Battle of the United States Land Forces in the World War,* vol. 3, part 1, *Zone of the Interior: Organizations and Activities of the War Department* (CMH Pub 23-3). 1988. Reprint, Washington, D.C.: Government Printing Office, 1937.

—————. *Order of Battle of the United States Land Forces in the World War,* vol. 3, part 2, *Zone of the Interior: Territorial Departments, Tactical Divisions Organized in 1918, and Posts, Camps, and Stations* (CMH Pub 23-4). 1988. Reprint, Washington, D.C.: Government Printing Office, 1937.

—————. *Order of Battle of the United States Land Forces in the World War,* vol. 3, part 3, *Zone of the Interior: Directory of Troops* (CMH Pub 23-5). 1988. Reprint, Washington, D.C.: Government Printing Office, 1937.

U.S. Army, First Army. *First Army Lecture Courses: St. Mihiel and Argonne-Meuse.* Chaumont, France: AEF, 1919.

U.S. Congress. *Committee on Un-American Activities: 1938–1954.* Washington, D.C.: Government Printing Office, 1955.

—————. *Medal of Honor Recipients, 1863–1978.* 96th Cong, 1st Sess. Washington, D.C.: Government Printing Office, 1979.

U.S. Congress. House of Representatives. "Hearings Before the Committee on Military Affairs." 74th Cong., 1st Sess. Washington, D.C.: Government Printing Office, 1935.

U.S. Congress. Senate. *Propaganda in Motion Pictures: Hearings before a Subcommittee of the Committee on Interstate Commerce.* Washington, D.C.: Government Printing Office, 1942.

U.S. Congress. Senate. Committee on Military Affairs. *Alvin C. York.* Report No 120. 75th Cong., 1st Sess. Washington, D.C.: Government Printing Office, 1937.

—————. "Sergeant Alvin C. York." Washington, D.C.: Government Printing Office, 1924.

U.S. War Department. *AEF Field Intelligence Reports, 26 September–11 November 1918.* Chaumont: First U.S. Army, 1918.

U.S. War Department, Office, Chief of Engrs. *Report of the Engineer, First Army: American Expeditionary Forces on the Engineer Operations in the St. Mihiel and Meuse-Argonne Offensives, 1918.* Washington, D.C.: Government Printing Office, 1929.

Viereck, George Sylvester, ed. *As They Saw Us: Foch, Ludendorff, and Other Leaders Write Our War History.* Cranbury, N.J.: Scholar's Bookshelf, 2005.

von Gallwitz, Max. "Retreat to the Rhein." In *As They Saw Us,* edited by George Sylvester Viereck, 230–235. New York: Doubleday-Doran, 1929.

von Ledebur, Otto. "Rushing the St. Mihiel Salient." In *As They Saw Us,* edited by George Sylvester Viereck, 172–179. New York: Doubleday-Doran, 1929.

von Tschischwitz, General der Infanterie Erich. *General von der Marwitz: Weltkriegsbriefe.* Berlin: Ernst Steiniger, 1940.

Waggoner, Kim, ed. *Handbook of Forensic Services.* Quantico, Va.: U.S. Department of Justice, Federal Bureau of Investigation, FBI Laboratory Publication, 2007.

Walsh, Milly. *We're Not Dead Yet: First World War Diary of Private Bert Cooke.* St. Catharine's, Ontario: Vanwell Publishing, 2004.

Walter, John. *Allied Small Arms of World War One.* Sevenoaks, Kent, UK: Crowood Press, 2000.

———. *Military Handguns of the Two World Wars.* London: Greenhill, 2003.

———. *Military Rifles of the Two World Wars.* London: Greenhill, 2003.

Wanamaker, John. *The Wanamaker Diary: 1918.* Philadelphia, Pa.: Self-published, 1917.

Warner, Jack. *Hollywood Be Thy Name: The Warner Brothers Story.* Rocklin, Calif.: Prima Publishing, 1994.

Warner, Jack, with Dean Jennings. *My First Hundred Years in Hollywood.* New York: Random House, 1965.

Washington, George. "Farewell Address." Senate Document number 106-21. Washington, D.C.: Government Printing Office, 2000.

Weddle, Ethel H. *Alvin C. York, Young Marksman.* Indianapolis, Ind.: Bobbs-Merrill, 1967.

Werner, Bret. *Uniforms, Equipment and Weapons of the American Expeditionary Forces in World War I.* Atglen, Pa.: Schiffer Military History, 2006.

Wiley, Harvey W. *A Plot against the People.* Ontario, Canada: Hiram Walker and Sons, 1911.

Wilhelm, Crown Prince of Prussia [Frederick William Victor Augustus Ernest]. *Memoires of the Crown Prince of Germany.* Uckfield, East Sussex, England: Naval and Military Press, 2005.

Wilhelm, Kronprinzen. *Erinnerungen des Kronprinzen Wilhelm.* Stuttgart: Gotta'sche Buchhandlung Nachfolger, 1923.

Wiltz, John. *In Search of Peace: The Senate Munitions Inquiry of 1934–1936.* Baton Rouge: Louisiana State Univ. Press, 1963.

York, Alvin C. "The Diary of Sergeant York: A Famous Hero's Own Story of His Great Adventure." *Liberty Magazine,* 14 July 1928, 21 July 1928, 28 July 1928, and 4 August 1928.

———. *Sergeant York: His Own Life Story and War Diary.* Edited by Thomas J. Skeyhill. Garden City, N.Y.: Doubleday, Doran, 1928.

York, Gracie Williams. *The Reminisces of Mrs. Alvin "Sergeant" York.* Tennessee Regional Oral History Collection, Part 1, Number 8. Nashville, Tenn., 1976.

Zabecki, David. *Chief of Staff, Volume I.* Annapolis, Md.: Naval Institute Press, 2008.

———. *Steel Wind.* London: Praeger, 1998.

Zierold, Norman. *The Moguls.* New York: Coward-McCann, 1969.

Index

Page numbers in *italics* refer to photographs. The names of military units appear in alphabetical rather than numerical order; for example, "166th Infantry Regiment" appears before "110th Infantry Regiment."